# China & the World

# China & the World

EDITED BY DAVID SHAMBAUGH

OXFORD
UNIVERSITY PRESS

Oxford University Press is a department of the University of Oxford. It furthers
the University's objective of excellence in research, scholarship, and education
by publishing worldwide. Oxford is a registered trade mark of Oxford University
Press in the UK and certain other countries.

Published in the United States of America by Oxford University Press
198 Madison Avenue, New York, NY 10016, United States of America.

CIP data is on file at the Library of Congres
ISBN 978–0–19–006232–3 (pbk.)
ISBN 978–0–19–006231–6 (hbk.)

6 8 10 9 7

Paperback printed by LSC Communications, United States of America
Hardback printed by Bridgeport National Bindery, Inc., United States of America

*Dedicated to the Memory of*
*Allen S. Whiting*
*Professor, Mentor, Friend, and Pioneer*
*in the Study of China's Foreign Relations*

# CONTENTS

# PREFACE AND ACKNOWLEDGMENTS

Since the establishment of the People's Republic of China (PRC) seventy years ago, it has become a global actor and an increasing global power. China is impacting the world and international relations in multiple ways. It is only going to become more so over time. As such, the world needs to understand the dimensions and implications of the PRC's position in world affairs.

This volume attempts to be both timely and comprehensive in its coverage. With two exceptions (chapters 2 and 3), the following chapters are all quite contemporary in their focus, taking stock of China's foreign relations and roles in the world at the two-decade mark (2020) of the twenty-first century. They are written by many of the world's leading scholars of Chinese foreign policy. The volume is divided into six sections and sixteen individual chapters. The first section is an introductory one that attempts to summarize how the PRC's foreign relations have generally evolved over time during its seventy-year history; it identifies many of the drivers that have shaped China's policies and behavior, as well as identifying a number of patterns that have emerged over time. The second section considers myriad historical factors that continue to impact China's calculations and its "grand strategy." The third section evaluates a range of contemporary domestic factors (perceptual, social, institutional, leadership) that shape and contribute to the decisions and actions taken by China's policymakers. The fourth and fifth sections of the book consider China's position in the world along two distinct dimensions: first, China's international interactions across four distinct functional spheres (economic, cultural, global governance, and military/security); and, second, geographically. The latter includes China's relations with the world's other two major powers (United States and Russia) as well as China's relations across multiple regions and multilateral institutions (Europe, Asia, Middle East, Africa, Latin America, and regional multilateralism). There is then a concluding section/chapter that attempts to peer into the future by identifying the major challenges that may lie ahead for China's position in world affairs.

Taken together, the contributions to this volume should provide readers with a full understanding of how China is impacting the world (hence the title of the volume). The book is primarily intended as a textbook for students (undergraduate and graduate) in courses on Chinese foreign policy and international relations—but it is also simultaneously suitable for scholars and other professional analysts. As editor, I do not see this as a static volume—but rather a dynamic one that will evolve over time. We hope to update this volume every five to ten years, depending on developments, so as to take account of important changes in China's external relations.

There are several reasons I decided to undertake, compile, and edit this volume. The first is that, as a professor of university courses on China's foreign policy for more than three decades, I find that the existing textbooks are either out of date or limited in their coverage. This volume is very up-to-date and its organization parallels the way that I structure my own course syllabi on the subject. It is essentially an input-output schema: exploring the factors that shape policies and actions, and then investigating the various dimensions of China's behavior on the global stage.

With regard to the former, we need to better understand the historical factors and traditions that continue to impact contemporary calculations in Beijing. Chinese statecraft hardly began when the Chinese Communist Party (CCP) came to power in 1949, or when Deng Xiaoping reoriented the country's direction after 1978. As such, one needs to have a general understanding of the twists and turns and overall evolution of China's foreign relations up to the present—the first chapter provides a general overview of this over time. Also, as China itself has become a more pluralistic society over the past four decades, we need to better understand the linkages of domestic actors in shaping the country's external posture. While we need to "bring society back in" to the analysis of China's foreign policy (see chapter 4), at the end of the day Beijing's external policies are still made within a tightly coordinated Leninist bureaucratic system (even more so under Xi Jinping's rule)—and thus we need to understand, as best as possible, the institutional landscape in which policies are deliberated and executed (see chapter 5).

With regard to the latter, China's bilateral relations with the major powers and its regional relationships have all experienced significant evolution and changes in recent years—thus Section V contains contemporary assessments of these relationships. Yet, importantly, we need to look beyond China's bilateral and regional relationships to consider its behavior and interactions in and across specific operational domains—which not only provides greater depth of understanding in each area, but also facilitates identification of patterns across geographic regions. This is done in Section IV.

Having digested all of this, readers will naturally wonder, what about the future? What can be expected from China's interactions with the world? While I have no crystal ball, in the concluding chapter I speculate by identifying some of the main factors and variables that will likely shape China's global position and which analysts will do well to keep their eyes on going forward. From these sixteen chapters, readers will hopefully come away with a full and detailed understanding of the complexities of China's progressive integration into the international order, the factors that shape China's calculus and behavior, the contemporary status of China's position across multiple issue areas and regions, and possible trajectories of its future course.

I also wish to offer my deep personal and professional thanks to many who have helped bring this volume to fruition. Books like this don't just "happen." They take much planning and lengthy lead times, lengthy research and writing, meeting deadlines, constant checking of various data, attention to formatting, intellectual coherence and dialogue among the chapters, and perhaps above all: collegiality. It has been a real professional pleasure to work with the fifteen authors who have contributed chapters. They are all leading scholars of China's foreign relations in the world, and I am pleased to have been able to recruit so many from outside the United States to contribute (the volume thus has a true international "feel" to it). They have all taken considerable time in their extremely busy careers and personal lives to contemplate, research, and write their chapters over the course of more than a year (the project began in late 2017 and came to fruition in early 2019). They were all unfailingly cooperative and constructive in responding to my initial invitations, suggestions for how to structure their chapters, and my editing, queries, and occasional prodding. Each chapter went through multiple drafts, and the final products reveal these painstaking efforts.

Producing volumes like this also requires financial resources—and I would like to acknowledge the support of the China Policy Program (CPP) of the Elliott School of International Affairs at George Washington University, and particularly the generous contributions of Christopher J. Fussner of Singapore to support this and many other projects of the CPP over the past two decades. This is just one of many books and programs that would not have become realities if it were not for Chris' generous support and strategic foresight, for which I am most grateful.

While such volumes do not materialize without the contributors and financial supporters, they definitely do not become a reality without the publisher. I thus wish to deeply thank my editor David McBride at Oxford University Press in New York. This is the third book I have had the pleasure of working on with Dave and OUP, and each has been a professional pleasure. The OUP team is truly first-rate in all respects and phases of publication—from considering an initial book proposal and during the peer review process, throughout the entire production process from copyediting to proofreading, typesetting, and indexing—to final publication, launches, and marketing. OUP excels in all of these categories. OUP is also very much a *global* publisher, which is especially appropriate for a book on this topic. This I am most grateful to Dave and the whole team at OUP—in New York, Oxford, and worldwide.

Volumes like this also build on the previous work of others, and there is a rich existing literature in the field. But beyond these previous publications, those in any field are also deeply influenced by those who have trained us. I have been most fortunate during my university education (undergraduate and graduate) to have been taught and mentored by several leading scholars and trailblazers in the study of Chinese politics and PRC foreign relations, but none stands out more than Allen S. Whiting (1926–2018).[1] Although he recently passed away, Allen's professional legacy lives on and his cumulative impact on the field of China's foreign relations is substantial. Allen was much more than a China specialist— he was deeply engaged in studying the international relations of Asia writ large as well as American policy toward China and the region. He was an exemplar role model of an academic scholar who was simultaneously public educator and policy shaper. My admiration for him is enormous. Thus, I would like to dedicate this volume to the memory and contributions of Allen S. Whiting.

Finally, while much thought, preparation, and effort have gone into publishing this volume, and we have tried to produce as definitive a study as possible, it no doubt has its shortcomings. I therefore welcome all feedback from readers and professors who may assign this textbook in their courses. As noted above, we plan to publish updated editions periodically, and thus would be grateful for any and all suggestions for improvements in the future.

*David Shambaugh*
*Washington, DC*
*August 2019*

# Notes

1. Jonathan Pollack and David Shambaugh, "In Memoriam: Allen Suess Whiting," *The China Quarterly* 236 (December 2018): 917–929.

# ABOUT THE EDITOR

**David Shambaugh** is Gaston Sigur Professor of Asian Studies, Political Science, and International Affairs, and Director of the China Policy Program, in the Elliott School of International Affairs at George Washington University. He previously was Reader in Chinese Politics at the University of London School of Oriental and African Studies (SOAS), where he also served as Editor of *The China Quarterly*. An active public intellectual and frequent commentator in the international media, he serves on numerous editorial boards and has been a consultant to governments, research institutions, foundations, universities, corporations, banks, and investment funds. Educated at George Washington University (B.A.), Johns Hopkins SAIS (M.A.), and the University of Michigan (PhD), he has lectured worldwide and has been a visiting scholar or professor at universities and institutes in Australia, Austria, Brazil, China, Germany, Hong Kong, Italy, Japan, Russia, Singapore, and Taiwan. His scholarly work has focused on China's domestic politics, foreign relations, military and security, and the international relations of Asia. He has published more than thirty books—most recently, *China Goes Global* (2013), *Tangled Titans: The United States and China* (2013), *International Relations of Asia* (2014), *China's Future* (2016), *The China Reader: Rising Power* (2016), and *Where Great Powers Meet: America & China in Southeast Asia* (2020).

# ABOUT THE CONTRIBUTORS

**Shaun Breslin** is Professor of Politics and International Studies at the University of Warwick in the UK, and also Co-Editor of *The Pacific Review*. He currently holds a Leverhulme Major Research Fellowship to study the nature of China as a great power. He has also been a Distinguished Visiting Professorial Fellow at the Fudan University Institute for Advanced Studies in Social Sciences and held visiting positions at the China Foreign Affairs University, Renmin University, Peking University, City University of Hong Kong, and Nanyang Technological University in Singapore. His research focuses on China's domestic political economy, the politics of China's international economic interactions, and China's changing role and status in the global order. He also has a secondary interest in comparative studies of regional integrational processes. He is author of four books, including *China and the Global Political Economy* (2007), and has edited or co-edited sixteen books, readers, and special issues of journals.

**Joshua Eisenman** is Associate Professor at the Keough School of Global Affairs at the University of Notre Dame, and Senior Fellow for China Studies at the American Foreign Policy Council. His research focuses on the political economy of China's development and its foreign relations with the United States and the developing world—particularly Africa. With Eric Heginbotham, he co-edited *China Steps Out: Beijing's Major Power Engagement with the Developing World* (2018), and he co-authored *China and Africa: A Century of Engagement* (2012) with David H. Shinn. His most recent book is *Red China's Green Revolution: Technological Innovation, Institutional Change, and Economic Development under the Commune* (2018). Dr. Eisenman's work has been published in many academic journals including *World Development, Development and Change, Journal of Contemporary China,* and *Cold War History.* He is currently working on a book examining the China-Africa political and security relationship.

**Chas W. Freeman Jr.** is a Senior Fellow at Brown University's Watson Institute for International and Public Affairs. He is the former Assistant Secretary of Defense for International Security Affairs (1993–1994), Ambassador to Saudi Arabia (1989–1992), Principal Deputy Assistant Secretary of State for African Affairs (1986–1989), and *chargé d'affaires* at Bangkok (1984–1986) and Beijing (1981–1984). He served as Vice Chair of the Atlantic Council (1996-2008), Co-chair of the United States China Policy Foundation (1996–2009), and President of the Middle East Policy Council (1997–2009). He was the principal American interpreter during President Nixon's path-breaking 1972 visit to Beijing. His publications include the *Encyclopaedia Britannica* article on diplomacy, and *America's Continuing Misadventures in the Middle East* (2016); *Interesting Times: China, America, and the Shifting Balance of Prestige* (2013); *The Diplomat's Dictionary* (2nd ed. 2010); and *Arts of Power: Statecraft and Diplomacy* (2nd ed. 2010). A compendium of his speeches is available at chasfreeman.net.

**François Godement** is Senior Advisor to Institut Montaigne in Paris, a Non-Resident Senior Associate of the Carnegie Endowment for International Peace in Washington, DC, and an external consultant for the Policy Planning Staff of the French Ministry of Foreign Affairs. From 2008 to 2018 he was the director of European Council on Foreign Relations Asia and China Program and a Senior Policy Fellow at ECFR. He has been a professor at France's National Institute of Oriental Languages and Civilizations (1992–2006) and Sciences Po Paris (2006–2014). His most recent books are *La Chine à nos portes: une stratégie pour l'Europe* (2018) and *Contemporary China: Between Mao and Market* (2015). His publications at ECFR included *China's Promotion of New Global Values* (2019), *China at the Gates: A New Power Audit of EU-China Relations* (2017), and *Expanded Ambitions, Shrinking Achievements: How China Sees the Global Order* (2017). He is currently working on a project comparing digital privacy issues in Europe, China, and India. He is also a frequent contributor to media and academic debates on Asia and China.

**Peter Gries** is the Lee Kai Hung Chair and founding Director of the Manchester China Institute, and Professor of Chinese Politics at the University of Manchester. He previously was the Harold J. and Ruth Newman Chair and founding Director of the Institute for US-China Issues at the University of Oklahoma, and Assistant Professor of Politics at the University of Colorado, Boulder. He studies the political psychology of international affairs, with a focus on China and the United States. Gries is author of *The Politics of American Foreign Policy: How Ideology Divides Liberals and Conservatives over Foreign Affairs* (2014) and *China's New Nationalism: Pride, Politics, and Diplomacy* (2005), and co-editor of *State and Society in 21st-Century China* (2004) and *Chinese Politics* (2010), as well as dozens of academic journal articles.

**Eric Heginbotham** is a principal research scientist at MIT's Center for International Studies and a specialist on Asian security issues. Before joining MIT, he was a senior political scientist at the RAND Corporation. He co-edited *China Steps Out: Beijing's Major Power Engagement with the Developing World* (2018) with Joshua Eisenman, and coauthored *Chinese and Indian Strategic Behavior: Growing Power and Alarm* (2012) with George Gilboy. He was lead author of *China's Evolving Nuclear Deterrent* (2017) and the *US-China Military Scorecard* (2015). Heginbotham has published in *Foreign Affairs, International Security, Washington Quarterly*, and elsewhere, and he is currently working on a book on the prospects for a stable balance of power in East Asia.

**Srikanth Kondapalli** is Professor in Chinese Studies at Jawaharlal Nehru University, New Delhi, where he is also Chair of the Center for East Asian Studies in the School of International Studies. He taught at National Chengchi University, Taipei, in 2004 and has been a Visiting Fellow at China Institutes of Contemporary International Relations, Beijing, in May 2007; an Honorary Professor at Shandong University, Jinan (2009, 2011, 2013, 2015, and 2016); a Visiting Professor at Jilin University, Changchun (2014), and at Yunnan University of Finance and Economics, Kunming (2016); and a Non-Resident Senior Fellow at People's University since 2014. He has published two books: *China's Military: The PLA in Transition* (1999) and *China's Naval Power* (2001). Other volumes include: *Asian Security and China* (2004); *China and Its Neighbors* (2010); *China's Military and India* (2012), *China and the BRICS: Setting Up a Different Kitchen* (2016), and *One Belt One Road: China's Global Outreach* (2017).

**Katherine Morton** is the Chair and Professor of China's International Relations at the University of Sheffield, UK. Prior to her appointment she was the Associate Dean for Research at the College of Asia and the Pacific, Australian National University, and a Senior Fellow in the Department of International Relations. Her research addresses the domestic and international motivations behind China's changing role in the world and the implications for foreign policy and the study of International Relations. She has published widely on global governance, transnational security, the environment and climate change, food security, maritime security, and the South China Sea in numerous scholarly and public policy journals, including *Survival, International Affairs, Chinese Political Science Review, East Asia Forum, Asia-Pacific Review*, and the *Brown Journal of World Affairs*. Her forthcoming book examines the likely impacts of China's rising international status upon the evolving system of global governance. She previously published *International Aid and China's Environment: Taming the Yellow Dragon* (2005) and *China and the Global Environment: Learning from the Past, Anticipating the Future* (2009).

**Barry Naughton** is the So Kwanlok Professor at the School of Global Policy and Strategy, University of California, San Diego. His work on the Chinese economy focuses on market transition, industry and technology, foreign trade, and political economy. His first book, *Growing Out of the Plan,* won the Ohira Prize in 1996, and a new edition of his popular survey and textbook *The Chinese Economy: Adaptation and Growth* appeared in 2018. He has published in numerous scholarly journals, including *The China Quarterly* and *China Leadership Monitor,* and contributed numerous book chapters. He is currently working on a new book on China's industrial policy.

**Phillip C. Saunders** is Director of the Center for the Study of Chinese Military Affairs and a Distinguished Research Fellow at National Defense University's Institute for National Strategic Studies. He previously worked at the Monterey Institute of International Studies where he served as Director of the East Asia Nonproliferation Program from 1999 to 2003 and worked on Asia policy issues as an officer in the US Air Force. His research focuses on Chinese foreign policy, security policy, and military issues. Dr. Saunders is coauthor with David Gompert of *The Paradox of Power: Sino-American Strategic Restraint in an Era of Vulnerability* (2011), and co-editor of *Chairman Xi Remakes the PLA* (2019) and *PLA Influence on China's National Security Policymaking* (2015). He has also edited NDU Press books on Chinese contingency planning, China-Taiwan relations, the Chinese Navy, and the Chinese Air Force and published numerous articles and book chapters on China and Asian security issues.

**Robert Sutter** is Professor of Practice of International Affairs at the Elliott School of International Affairs at George Washington University, where he also is Director of the School's undergraduate program. Prior to his GWU appointment, he taught for a decade as Visiting Professor of Asian Studies at Georgetown University. Other previous teaching appointments include the University of Virginia and Johns Hopkins SAIS. In his thirty-three-year US government career, he served as Director of the Foreign Affairs and National Defense Division of the Congressional Research Service, the National Intelligence Officer for East Asia and the Pacific at the National Intelligence Council, and the China Division Director at the Department of State's Bureau of Intelligence and Research. Sutter's most recent books include *Axis of Authoritarians: Implications of China-Russia Cooperation* (2018) and new editions of *The United States and Asia: Regional Dynamics and 21st-Century Relations* (2015), *Chinese Foreign Relations: Power and Policy since the Cold War* (2016), *US-China Relations: Perilous Past, Uncertain Present* (2017), and *Foreign Relations of the PRC: The Legacies and Constraints of China's International Politics since 1949* (2018).

**Alexei D. Voskressenski** is Professor of Political Science at Moscow State Institute of International Relations (MGIMO University), where he also directs the Center for Comprehensive Chinese Studies and Regional Projects. He joined MGIMO after many years of work at the Russian Academy of Sciences as Head of the Department of Asian and African Studies (1999–2007), was Dean of the School of Political Affairs (2008–2017), and has served as Professor of Asian Studies, International Relations, and Comparative Politics at the School of International Relations (MGIMO) since 1999. He codirects the joint program "German Studies Russia" of MGIMO University/Freie Universität Berlin and is a founding editor-in-chief of the peer-reviewed journal *Comparative Politics Russia* (www.comparative politics.org), author, coauthor, and editor of fifty books—the most recent are *Non-Western Theories of International Relations* (2017); *Is Non-Western Democracy Possible?* (2017), *and The Regional World Order* (2019). He received two doctoral degrees, from Victoria University of Manchester, UK, and the Institute of Far Eastern Studies, Russian Academy of Sciences.

**Odd Arne Westad** is Elihu Professor of History and Global Affairs at Yale University. He has previously been School Professor of International History at the London School of Economics and Political Science, and S. T. Lee Professor of US-Asia Relations at Harvard University. Among his books are *The Global Cold War*, which won the Bancroft Prize, and *Decisive Encounters*, a history of the Chinese civil war. He also co-edited the three-volume *Cambridge History of the Cold War*. His most recent books are *Restless Empire: China and the World since 1750*, which won the Asia Society's Bernard Schwartz book award, and *The Cold War: A World History*. His new book, *Empire and Righteous Nation: 600 Years of China-Korea Relations*, will be published in 2020.

**Michael Yahuda** is Professor Emeritus in International Relations, the London School of Economics and Political Science, and Visiting Scholar at the Sigur Center for Asian Studies, George Washington University. For the past six decades his research and publishing has centered on China's foreign policy and on the international politics of East Asia. He has written eight books and edited or co-edited three more. These include *The Post-Cold War in Asia and the Challenge to ASEAN* (2006), *Sino-Japanese Relations after the Cold War: Two Tigers Sharing a Mountain* (2013), and *Hong Kong: China's Challenge* (2018). His latest is the fourth edition of the *International Politics of the Asia-Pacific* (2019). He has also published numerous book chapters and articles in leading academic journals.

**Suisheng Zhao** is Professor and Director of the Center for China-US Cooperation at Josef Korbel School of International Studies, University of Denver. He has also been a Campbell National Fellow at the Hoover Institution of Stanford

University, Associate Professor of Political Science and International Studies at Washington College in Maryland, Associate Professor of Government and East Asian Politics at Colby College in Maine, and Visiting Assistant Professor at the Graduate School of International Relations and Pacific Studies (IR/PS) at the University of California–San Diego. He is the founder and editor of the *Journal of Contemporary China* and the author and editor of more than a dozen of books and many articles on Chinese nationalism, Chinese politics/political economy, Chinese foreign policy, US-China relations, Cross–Taiwan Strait relations, and East Asian regional issues. These edited volumes include: *The Making of China's Foreign Policy in the 21st Century* (2018), *Chinese Foreign Policy: Pragmatism and Strategic Behavior* (2016), and *China and Democracy* (2014).

# SECTION I

# INTRODUCTION

# China's Long March to Global Power

### DAVID SHAMBAUGH

## Introduction

This volume catalogues multiple dimensions of China's foreign relations and interactions with the world at the outset of the third decade of the twenty-first century.

I use the term *foreign relations* instead of *foreign policy* intentionally. The latter is primarily composed of the declaratory policies of China's government on various issues, accordingly emphasizes diplomacy, and is at the national level of analysis. Foreign relations, on the other hand, encompasses a much broader range of a nation's interactions than official declaratory policy and diplomacy. Perhaps this is a semantic difference, but I think an important one. I have long believed that, when studying international affairs, analysts should look far beyond a nation's capital and official pronouncements and diplomatic engagements to take into account the broad range of a country's external engagement with foreign *societies* and international institutions (governmental and nongovernmental). It is important to delve beyond national state actors to consider the totality of a country's sub-national actors. We need to "bring society back in" to our analyses of international affairs. We similarly should take into account the actors and factors from *within* a nation's society, domestic institutions, national identity and perceptions, as well as historical legacies that shape and influence how a country presents itself and behaves beyond its borders. Observers and practitioners alike need to understand *why* a country behaves as it does as much as *how* and *what* it does in the international arena.

The four chapters in Sections II and III do an excellent job of exploring these historical and domestic contextual factors. Odd Arne Westad and Chas W. Freeman Jr.'s chapters both elaborate a number of China's historical experiences and how they have shaped China's contemporary identity, calculations, and "grand strategy." Peter Gries delves further into the issue of national identity,

David Shambaugh, *China's Long March to Global Power* In: *China and the World.* Edited by: David Shambaugh, Oxford University Press (2020). © Oxford University Press
DOI: 10.1093/oso/9780190062316.003.0001

particularly nationalism, and other social forces that condition China's perceptions of the world today. Suisheng Zhao takes readers inside the "black box" of China's foreign policymaking institutions and the roles that senior leaders (notably Xi Jinping) have in the policymaking process.

Thus, this is not simply a book about Chinese diplomacy or foreign policy narrowly defined. As China has "gone global," a wide array of Chinese actors ply the planet in search of opportunities. China is now deeply embedded on every continent and in every society (even the remaining seventeen nations with which it does not have official diplomatic relations), in space and cyberspace, in the Arctic and Antarctic, even on the moon. It is also embedded in international institutions—being a member of sixty-six intergovernmental organizations and an observer in nine others.[1]

China's sheer *presence* certainly qualifies it as a full international *actor* and many thus view China as an international *power*. However, I would still argue (as I did in my 2013 book *China Goes Global*) that China remains a "partial power."[2] That is, China's global power capabilities remain uneven; as the chapters in Sections IV and V illustrate, they are stronger in some areas and weaker in others.[3] This judgment is based on the two generally accepted definitions of power: *power as capabilities* (assets in different categories)[4] and *power as influence* (the ability to shape the behavior of others through a mixture of instruments).[5] Clearly, China's economic/commercial power is its strongest asset, while its scientific and technological power are now increasingly world-class. Beijing's diplomatic presence has also grown significantly in recent years. In 2017 the PRC had 264 diplomatic missions around the world (166 embassies, 90 consulates, and 8 permanent missions).[6] Bilaterally, no government is as diplomatically active as China's, with its leaders traversing all continents and hosting dozens of leaders in Beijing every year. One also notices Beijing becoming less reactive in its diplomacy (a long-standing tendency) and increasingly proactive during Xi Jinping's tenure. Consummate with this change, as Katherine Morton's chapter details, China has also become much more active and influential in international institutions and multilateral global governance. Beijing is no longer the "free rider" it once was and is increasingly behaving as a "responsible international stakeholder" (in Robert Zoellick's famous 2005 words),[7] contributing more proportionately to international public goods. China's military capabilities have also grown significantly, yet the People's Liberation Army remains primarily a regional Asian power in terms of its power projection (missiles and cyber capabilities notwithstanding). However, in terms of its international exchanges, as Phillip Saunders' chapter illustrates, the PLA is very much an international actor. As Shaun Breslin's chapter highlights, China's cultural and "soft" power remains quite limited on a global basis—despite the enormous resources that Beijing has invested in trying to improve China's international image and cultural ties. It is in this sphere where the distinction between *presence* and *influence* may be most stark: China definitely has a global cultural presence, but its soft power influence remains limited largely to developing countries (where it is also mixed).[8]

How these different instruments of power are wielded by China varies across regions of the world and with individual countries. The chapters in Section V survey China's relations with the world's other two major powers—the United States (Robert Sutter), Russia (Alexei Voskressenski)—and multiple regions: Europe (François Godement), Asia (Michael Yahuda), and Africa/ Latin America/Middle East (Joshua Eisenman and Eric Heginbotham). A final chapter in this section, by Srikanth Kondapalli, examines China's regional multilateralism.

In addition to the historical and contemporary chapters that follow, readers should also have some understanding of how PRC foreign relations have evolved over the past seven decades, what have been some of the key inflection points, and what have been the main "drivers" of China's policies and relationships over time. To be sure, this is no small task and countless volumes and articles have been published on the subject.[9] But that is what the remainder of this introductory chapter attempts to do—to provide thumbnail sketches of China's evolving engagement with the world over the past seven decades and to identify what has motivated China to act as it has.

# The 1950s: Isolation

The People's Republic began its existence in international isolation. The emerging Cold War bifurcation of the world into two competing camps definitely impacted "new China's" case for recognition as a sovereign member of the United Nations and international community. Only a dozen countries extended diplomatic recognition in 1949 and each was member of the Soviet bloc. In 1950 ten more nations recognized the PRC—four newly independent Asian countries and six Western countries. Even a decade after its founding, Beijing enjoyed diplomatic relations with only thirty-five nations.

Mao was fond of counting China's "friends" and "enemies"—the PRC had many more of the latter than the former in the early years of its existence. China was deeply isolated and cut off from ties with the West as well as many in the East. Facing this reality, Mao and the new PRC had little choice but to turn to Moscow for economic assistance and security. Mao traveled to Moscow in February 1950 and concluded the Sino-Soviet Treaty of Friendship, Alliance, and Mutual Assistance. For China, this was a move born both out of necessity and *choice*. That is, the PRC was ruled by a communist party, guided by Marxist-Leninist-Stalinist-Maoist ideology, it sought to construct a planned socialist economy, and was a regime committed to enlarging the number of communist party-states and countering "imperialism" around the world. The Soviet Union, therefore, offered the new infant People's Republic the only assistance available, and Moscow guaranteed the PRC's national security through a military alliance. But the USSR was also a *model* for the PRC, as the two communist party-states were political siblings and ideological soulmates (and, by extension, Moscow's other satellite regimes in Eastern Europe, Mongolia, North Vietnam, and North Korea). So, the Sino-Soviet relationship was not merely one of necessity and mutual convenience—it was one that Beijing *sought* and it was cemented in common Leninist political systems and worldviews.

The outbreak of the Korean War in June 1950 only served to solidify China's segregation from the non-communist world and ties to the communist camp, as well as increasing the threats to its national security. It also resulted in frustrating Beijing's opportunity to "liberate" Taiwan and seal the final chapter of its long-running civil war with the Kuomintang (Republic of China) regime—as the United States placed the Seventh Fleet in the Taiwan Strait just as Mao was preparing to cross the strait, attack the island, and forcibly conclude the civil war. Taiwan lay outside the US Far Eastern "defense perimeter" at the time and the Truman administration was uncertain of its continuing level of support for Chiang Kai-shek's rump regime. But with the outbreak of the Korean War and the extension of the Truman Doctrine from Europe to Asia, Washington began to guarantee Taiwan's security and the sustenance of the Republic of China on Taiwan. This was codified in a mutual security treaty with Taipei in 1954.

But with Stalin's death in March 1953, the fraternal dynamics of Sino-Soviet relationship began to progressively unravel. It took seven full years of progressive hemorrhaging, as Stalin's successor Nikita Khrushchev and Mao disagreed about one issue after another,[10] until July 1960 when the Soviet side decided to abruptly withdraw nearly 1,400 Soviet advisers and terminate cooperation on 200 joint industrial-technical projects.[11] Two more years of ideological acrimony would ensue, before the two fully broke off from one another. But the die was cast.

Thus, China's relations with the world during the 1950s were dominated by its international isolation and its relationship with the Soviet Union. The only significant exceptions were Beijing's involvement in two international conferences: the 1954 Geneva Conference and the 1955 Bandung Conference. Each international meeting allowed the PRC, and its premier and then foreign minister Zhou Enlai, to take its first steps on to the world stage.

After three years of horrendous war in Korea the battle lines stalemated near the 38th Parallel and an armistice was signed in 1953. Thereafter, the major powers convened in Geneva, Switzerland, from April through July 1954 to adjudicate the division of the Korean peninsula, as well as the future of Indochina.

These questions were treated separately: the two Korean regimes, the People's Republic of China, the Soviet Union, and the United States dealt with the Korean issue—while they were joined by France, the United Kingdom, and the Viet Minh to resolve the Indochina dilemma. The template for adjudicating both cases was the same: division of the countries into two zones with respective provisional governments, pending national elections under international supervision. The former occurred in each case (Korea was divided at the 38th Parallel and Vietnam at the 17th Parallel), but the latter never took place.

Zhou Enlai earned high marks for his calm demeanor, personal sophistication, and diplomatic acumen at the Geneva Conference. Zhou's performance stood in stark contrast to the more belligerent image the PRC had cast during its initial years. Although the Korean armistice negotiations had given PRC diplomats their first interactions with Americans since the 1949 revolution, the Geneva Conference offered more extended discussions and a more constructive atmosphere (nonetheless, John Foster Dulles famously refused to shake Zhou's hand in front on television cameras). Geneva also opened indirect channels of communication by Beijing with France, the United Kingdom, and United States (in the last case known as the "Warsaw channel").

The Bandung Conference of April 1955 in Indonesia offered the PRC another international platform, but with a different audience. Again, as at Geneva, Zhou Enlai played a prominent role and performed admirably. Also known as the Asian-African Conference, representatives of twenty-nine nations from these two regions gathered to offer a "third way" between the two competing Cold War camps (the socialist camp and the imperialist camp).[12] Mao himself declared this to be the "intermediate zone" in world affairs.[13] The Bandung Conference paved the path to the creation of the Non-Aligned Movement (in which China became an observer but not a member). It also offered the PRC the opportunity to advertise its "second identity" as a developing post-colonial nation (its first identity was as a socialist-communist state) and to begin to broaden its diplomatic ties with these countries. The declaration adopted by the conferees also reaffirmed many of the elements that China and India had incorporated the previous year into their Five Principles of Peaceful Coexistence.[14] This element in China's international identity—its connections to the developing world—has been one of the most consistent hallmarks of Chinese diplomacy throughout the history of the PRC. Most other elements of China's diplomacy have fluctuated considerably,[15] but Beijing's consistent identification with "third world," post-colonial, developing countries has been very consistent.

While the Geneva and Bandung conferences did offer the new PRC government useful opportunities to engage with international actors other than the Soviet Union and its satellite allies, China still remained relatively isolated in the world. By the end of the 1950s, it had formal diplomatic ties with only twenty-five nations. Moreover, as domestic Chinese politics became more radical beginning with the Anti-Rightist Campaign (1957), commune movement (1958), and Great Leap Forward (1958–1960), Sino-Soviet frictions also began to metastasize. Khrushchev criticized these Chinese policies. A significant additional element in the growing frictions with Moscow concerned Khrushchev's policy of "peaceful coexistence" with the imperialist United States, with which Mao profoundly disagreed. What seemed like an opening for Beijing following Geneva and Bandung was overwhelmed by a combination of Mao's lurch leftward domestically and his growing desire to confront the United States worldwide.

## The 1960s: From Bad to Worse

China entered the 1960s in an even more precarious position than it had begun the 1950s. Now devoid of its major patron and security guarantor, Beijing faced the world with two major enemies: the Soviet Union *and* the United States. Thus began a decade of Beijing's "dual adversary" strategy, struggling against the two "hegemons": the "imperialists" (United States) and the "social imperialists" (USSR). Even its relationship with neighboring nonaligned states, such as India and Indonesia, with whom it had gotten along during the 1950s, deteriorated badly during the 1960s. In the case of India, it resulted in a border war in 1962 (a conflict that colors their relationship to this day). In the case of Indonesia, the Chinese Communist Party (CCP) developed close ties with the Indonesian Communist Party (PKI), smuggling money and weapons to the PKI, and inviting its leader D. N. Aidit in Beijing on multiple occasions. On August 5, 1965, Aidit met with Mao in Beijing, who strongly encouraged him to move against "reactionary generals and officers in one blow."[16] In the same discussion, Mao promised to ship 30,000 light weapons to the PKI. These arms were delivered during September. As such, China was strongly suspected of helping to foment the (failed) September 30, 1965, coup attempt in Jakarta, and indeed was so accused by the surviving junta led by General Suharto. But subsequent information reveals no direct linkage—no proverbial "smoking gun"—between the CCP, PKI, and coup plotters.[17] Nonetheless, Jakarta blamed Beijing for helping to instigate the coup, and the junta's horrific post-coup massacre against ethnic Chinese, which claimed the lives of more than a million, fueled tensions. Relations subsequently became very strained before Indonesia officially suspended diplomatic ties with the PRC in 1967.

The CCP's support for the PKI was, in fact, a harbinger of the radicalization of China's foreign policy during the 1960s—most notably Beijing's attempts to "export revolution" by supporting communist parties and insurgency movements across Asia, Africa, and even in Latin America. The 1960s were definitely the revolutionary phase of China's foreign policy, as Beijing became a radical revisionist power seeking to overthrow established governments across these regions—all in an effort to foment global revolutions and a "united front" against the United States.[18] As Chairman Mao proclaimed in May 1960: "It is necessary to form a broad united front and unite with all forces, except the enemy, and continue to wage arduous struggles. . . . We should unite and drive US imperialism from Asia, Africa, and Latin America back to where it came from."[19] Mao's pronouncement was followed up by Zhou Enlai's tour of Africa in 1964, where he too proclaimed the continent "ripe for revolution." In September 1965, then Defense Minister Lin Biao codified Beijing's revolutionary mission in a much-publicized essay entitled *Long Live the Victory of People's War!*[20] Considered by some in the West (including US Defense Secretary Robert McNamara) as Beijing's blueprint for world conquest, Lin's treatise elaborated a scheme for "encircling" the "cities of the world" (North America and Western Europe) by the "rural areas of the world" (developing countries). This externalization of the CCP's own indigenous revolutionary strategy was viewed by many as a very aggressive articulation by a dangerous power now armed with nuclear weapons (following the October 16, 1964, detonation of China's first atomic bomb). Among other manifestations, Marshall Lin's manifesto caused the Johnson administration to increasingly view the war in Vietnam as directed by Beijing—thus catalyzing the dramatic buildup of American military forces in 1965.

China's image as a destabilizing and aggressive actor was only further fueled by the three-year (1966–1969) so-called Great Proletarian Cultural Revolution (无产阶级文化大革命).[21] Although primarily an effort by Mao to "cleanse the class ranks" and attack "revisionist elements" within the CCP, the GPCR was also a profoundly xenophobic and particularly anti-Western mass movement. Western leaders were burned in effigy by Red Guards in the streets of Beijing, the British Embassy was burned to the ground in August 1967, and the handful of foreigners remaining in China were subjected to persecution and imprisonment as an orgy of anarchic violence gripped the country. China's own Ministry of Foreign Affairs was disbanded, all ambassadors except one (Huang Hua in Egypt) were recalled, and MFA personnel were sent to labor in May Seventh Cadre Schools (五七干校). However, none of the chaos interrupted the support China was giving to various and sundry communist and socialist parties and their insurgent movements in the developing world (so-called "wars of national liberation"). Beijing continued to support such movements in *every* Southeast Asian country (except newly independent Singapore), as well as in many African states, and a few in Latin America. The International Liaison Department of the CCP (中共中联部) funneled money and weaponry to these groups.[22] Long-range transmitters in China's southwestern Yunnan Province beamed revolutionary propaganda 24/7 into Southeast Asian countries.

Thus, the decade of the 1960s was the most disruptive and destabilizing period in the history of the PRC's foreign relations. And it has been completely whitewashed and ignored in Chinese history books, as it is not consistent with the image of benign peaceful coexistence that Beijing seeks to project today.[23] But other nations, notably in Southeast Asia, have not forgotten this malign chapter in China's external behavior. By the end of the 1960s China remained quite isolated in the world, adding only twenty more nations with which it had diplomatic relations during the decade.

The decade of the 1960s also closed with increasing tensions in the Sino-Soviet relationship and pressure on China's national security. Following the Soviet Union's 1968 invasion of Czechoslovakia and pronouncement of the Brezhnev Doctrine (which held that Moscow reserved the right to intervene in any socialist state to prevent "counter-revolution"), China's leaders felt genuinely under existential threat. The tensions erupted into outright military conflict on the Ussuri River in the eastern sector of the disputed Sino-Soviet border in March 1969. Scores of soldiers were killed on each side, although the two sides' respective accounts of casualties vary. At the same time, the Soviet ambassador in Washington alerted the new Nixon administration that Moscow was seriously contemplating a "surgical" strike against China's nuclear weapons facilities at Lop Nor and Lanzhou.

Even to the ultra-confident Mao, who was now at the pinnacle of his power at the height of the Cultural Revolution, the situation looked increasingly concerning. One response of the Chairman's was to invoke the country to "dig tunnels deep, store grain everywhere, and never seek hegemony" (深挖洞，储粮食，不称霸)—an invocation that stimulated a mass civil defense project beneath China's cities. Mao's other response was to commission four military marshals (Chen Yi, Nie Rongzhen, Su Yu, Ye Jianying) to undertake a study of China's national security situation.[24] The marshal's study analyzed the potential for war with both the United States and the Soviet Union (as well as between the two)—it concluded that China's security was indeed under threat from both, that the Soviet Union was a slightly greater threat, yet they dismissed the possibility of an imminent attack on China by either the United States or USSR.

The marshals' assessment did not offer specific policy recommendations. But it certainly contributed to Mao's and Zhou Enlai's considerations of a possible opening to the United States. In good Marxist dialectical fashion, Mao had determined that the Soviet Union was the "main contradiction" (主要矛盾) while the Americans were a secondary threat. Unbeknownst to Mao and Zhou, halfway around the globe President Richard Nixon and his National Security Adviser Henry Kissinger were undertaking a similar assessment and contemplating exactly the same possibility, namely, that "the enemy of my enemy is my friend" and that "playing the China card" could enhance America's hand in its twilight struggle against the Soviet Union. Nixon also calculated that Beijing was central to his plans of a progressive drawdown of US forces in South Vietnam. Moreover, ironically, Nixon had begun to view China not so much as a rogue actor, but rather as in need of being "brought in from the cold" and integrated into the international community. In 1967, just prior to his presidency, Nixon published an article in the prestigious journal *Foreign Affairs*, in which he obliquely signaled a rapprochement with China. Eschewing the standard usage of "Red China" Nixon held out this olive branch:

> Taking the long view, we simply cannot afford to leave China forever outside the family of nations, there to nurture its fantasies, cherish its hates and threaten its neighbors. There is no place on this small planet for a billion of its potentially most able people to live in angry isolation.[25]

Thus, despite the internal chaos of the Cultural Revolution and the continuing external confrontations with the two superpowers, the new strategic rethinking taking place in both Beijing and Washington at the end of the 1960s presaged a new era in China's relations with the world.

## The 1970s: China Joins the World

The decade of the 1970s was characterized by three principal developments in China's foreign relations. The first was the dramatic opening with Canada in 1970,[26] and then the United States in 1971–1972. The second was the establishment of diplomatic relations with a number of countries (many of which the opening with the United States facilitated), and the PRC's admission to the United Nations in 1971. The third was increasing competition with the Soviet Union, in which Beijing tried to mobilize a broad "united front" (统战) against Moscow.

The opening with the United States not only ended two decades of enmity and non-contact, but also resulted in the creation of the so-called "strategic triangle" in world affairs (in fact the triangle had been created with the Sino-Soviet split, but now two parties were uniting against the third). Following Mao's and Nixon's independent decisions during 1968 and 1969 to explore the possibilities of an opening to the other, the two sides undertook a series of veiled moves in 1970 and 1971 to signal to the other that it was prepared to talk directly and at a high level. Neither Beijing nor Washington always read the other's oblique signals as intended, but by mid-1971 the message had gotten through three

principal channels (Warsaw, Budapest, Islamabad) and Henry Kissinger was
able to schedule his inaugural secret trip to Beijing (via Pakistan) in July 1971.
This and subsequent visits by Kissinger set in train President Nixon's own dramatic visit to China in February 1972. Nixon's trip was dubbed "the week that
changed the world," which was not an overstatement. Thereafter, not only did a
fundamentally new era in Sino-American relations open, but China also began
the lengthy process of coming out of its insular shell to "join the world." Two
decades of totalitarian isolation began to give way to tentative encounters with
the outside world. To be sure, China's radical domestic politics were still a constraint on its international interactions, as the so-called Gang of Four opposed
the opening to the United States and the West. But, with the dramatic Nixon
visit and the announcement of the "four modernizations" policy in 1973, China
had embarked on a new path.

It would take another seven years after the Nixon visit before full diplomatic relations were established between Beijing and Washington, but in the interim liaison
offices were established in each capital and a modicum of exchanges commenced.
Full normalization had to await the formal establishment of diplomatic ties on
January 1, 1979. Still, the Sino-American rapprochement had altered international
affairs.

It was also a critical step in Beijing's expansion of its foreign relations. By
the end of the 1960s, still only forty-five nations had diplomatic ties with the
PRC—by the end of the 1970s, 115 had established relations.[27] The opening
with the United States particularly facilitated establishment of ties with other
Western and Asian countries that were American allies. This, in turn, enabled
Beijing's coordination with these capitals to align against the Soviet Union. With
diplomatic relations in place, it also facilitated the opening of commercial and
cultural exchanges with Western countries. The Nixon opening likewise facilitated the PRC taking China's seat in the United Nations on November 15, 1971,
following the expulsion of the Republic of China (Taiwan).

The early part of the decade thus witnessed significant forward movement in
China's foreign relations. But, by mid-decade domestic considerations in China
began to impact China's nascent opening the world. Premier Zhou Enlai and
Chairman Mao Zedong both became terminally ill in 1975 and both passed
away in 1976. As their illnesses intensified, the struggle for political succession
heated up between the Gang of Four (led by Mao's wife Jiang Qing), moderate
cadres (led by Deng Xiaoping), and Mao's designated successor Hua Guofeng.
A month after Mao's death, the Gang were arrested on the authorization of Hua
and senior military leaders. This bold stroke brought great relief to the nation, as
Jiang Qing and her cronies were widely reviled, but it did not fully settle the succession question. Hua Guofeng still had to contend with the moderates led by

Deng Xiaoping (whom the Gang had managed to purge in the spring of 1976). Then ensued a period of delicate maneuvering until Deng was "rehabilitated" (平凡)and restored to his senior positions in the summer of 1977. It would take Deng five more years to fully isolate and ease Hua out of power—but by December 1978, and the famous Third Plenary Session of the Eleventh Central Committee, Deng was solidly in control.[28]

The Third Plenum changed everything in China—and in China's relations with the world. Now, "economics was in command." For foreign relations this meant an emphasis on developing ties with advanced countries that could contribute technology, investment, aid, and expertise to China's drive for modernization. Countering the Soviet "polar bear" and its client states (including Vietnam) remained Beijing's prime geostrategic challenge—but henceforth China's economic development became the sine qua non for all Chinese policies.

## The 1980s: From Optimism to Pessimism

China thus started out the decade with a new optimistic spirit about "reform and opening" (改革与开放)—but by decade's end it had been dashed on the rocks of the June 4, 1989, Tiananmen Incident. In between China underwent enormous changes domestically and externally. These were heady days, and the daily demonstrations in Beijing during the spring of 1989 only fueled enthusiasm inside and outside of China that the PRC was finally throwing off the shackles of political totalitarianism, economic commandism, and social strictures left over from the Mao era. But Deng's decision to use lethal force against the demonstrators in June 1989 set China back and badly tarnished its international reputation, attenuating its ties with Western countries for a number of years.

During this decade China opened its doors to foreign investment, rapidly expanded its foreign trade (based on an import substitution strategy), engaged in educational and other cultural exchanges with a variety of countries, eagerly studied other (and more liberal) political systems, began interactions with Western militaries (which sold it weapons), and began to open China itself to foreign visitors. Beijing further developed diplomatic ties, establishing diplomatic relations with an additional nineteen countries. China even normalized its ties with its erstwhile adversary the Soviet Union. It also embarked on the early stages of joining international organizations, such as the World Bank and International Monetary Fund. All in all, the PRC was headed in a very positive direction—until the tanks rolled into Tiananmen Square and killed an estimated 1,500–2,000 civilians on the streets of Beijing on June 4.

## The 1990s: From Isolation to Rehabilitation

These events left the PRC isolated yet again—at least as far as the West was concerned, which invoked multiple sanctions on the Chinese government and military. Public condemnation and outrage was prevalent throughout Western societies, governments, and media. Yet, the rest of the world remained relatively silent over the tragic events in Beijing. Japan joined in the G-7 sanctions, but within a year wriggled out of them. The South Korean government only noted that it was a "regrettable incident." Southeast Asian states were circumspect. On the one hand, Singapore's senior statesman Lee Kuan Yew issued a public statement saying: "My cabinet colleagues and I are shocked, horrified, and saddened by this disastrous turn of events." This was, in Lee's view, a simple statement of fact, but not a condemnation. In his memoirs, Prime Minister Lee observed: "I did not condemn them. I did not regard them as a repressive communist regime like the Soviet Union."[29] Subsequently, Lee led the way among Asian states in maintaining contact with Beijing, arguing that it would be counterproductive in the long term to isolate China. Lee's view at this troubled time was consistent with his overall strategy of integrating and binding China positively into the East Asian region. Elsewhere in the world other governments remained silent about the events in Tiananmen and did not suspend or severe ties. Thus, as traumatic as the events of June 1989 were for China's reputation internationally, Beijing's isolation was far from total.

It took about five years before the G-7 countries lifted most of their sanctions and re-engaged with China. The EU and United States maintained an arms embargo and drastically attenuated its exchanges with the PLA, while the American Congress also kept other economic sanctions in place. But by 1995 China had emerged from the isolation imposed in 1989.

In the interim, the leadership in Beijing watched in political horror as one communist party-state after another fell from power in Eastern Europe. And then in August 1991 the unthinkable occurred: the Soviet Union itself disintegrated and Soviet Communist Party rule along with it. Paranoia and trepidation gripped the CCP leadership in Beijing, as they feared a repeat in China. But the security lockdown that followed June 4 permitted no such thing. In this atmosphere, an aging Deng Xiaoping took two important steps. Although he had formally retired from all positions and was in failing health, in 1990 Deng first enunciated the "grand strategy" of *taoguang yanghui* (韬光养晦), that is, that China should keep a low profile and remain calm in the face of such pressures and uncertainties. Second, in early 1992 Deng took his famous "southern sojourn" (南巡), which rebooted economic reforms.

With these acts and changes in the Chinese leadership, the PRC began to re-engage with the world. As shocked as the Chinese leadership was by the collapse of the Soviet Union, Beijing quickly pivoted to establish diplomatic ties with the new Russian Federation as well as the fourteen other newly independent former members of the USSR. Ties with the European Union began to blossom after 1995 as well. The return of Hong Kong to Chinese sovereignty in 1997 was also an important step. By the late 1990s, Beijing also began to participate in various Asian regional multilateral institutions—presaging a decade-long period of intensified engagement with its Asian neighbors.[30] Its helping hand to Southeast Asian states in the wake of the 1997 Asian Financial Crisis contributed to this trend. Even relations with the United States began to rebound in 1997 and 1998 with the exchange of state visits between Presidents Jiang Zemin and Bill Clinton.

Thus, the decade of the 1990s was one in which China's foreign relations ricocheted from one extreme to another—from being seen as an international pariah and outcast (at least in the West) to a more normal nation that was becoming ever more integrated into the regional and international systems. During the decade Beijing added another thirty-two nations with which it established formal diplomatic relations. As the new millennium approached, Beijing had weathered significant storms and was facing the future with increased confidence.

## The 2000s: Omnidirectional Diplomacy

Having forged formal relations with most nations in the world and broadening its international footprint, while becoming gradually more comfortable in multilateral diplomacy, the task before China was to give greater depth to its presence around the world. Thus China embarked on the policy of "going out" (走出去) or "going global" (走向世界). First enunciated by Jiang Zemin in mid-1990s, it wasn't until the 2000s that a broad range of Chinese actors—companies, localities, educational and other institutions, media, and individuals—really began to establish a presence across the globe.[31] During this decade, these Chinese actors fanned out across Africa, Europe, and Latin America. China's footprint became truly international for the first time. While some of this activity was undertaken by private actors, government state-owned enterprises (SOEs), national oil companies (NOCs), and state media were the predominant players. China's escalating economic appetite for raw material commodities and energy supplies drove much of this dynamic.

Beijing also deepened its ties with Russia and broadened its ties with the Shanghai Cooperation Organization countries in Central Asia. Sino-Indian ties also stabilized and improved. Within East Asia, China enjoyed probably its best decade ever—seen by some observers as a "golden decade" (1999–2009) in China's relations with its periphery.[32] Following the EP-3 incident in early 2001, Sino-American relations also enjoyed stable development throughout the remainder of the presidency of George W. Bush.

Thus, during the period of Hu Jintao's rule, a relative shift in China's foreign relations occurred when compared to the Jiang Zemin era: a shift from prioritization on relations with the main powers (United States, Russia, EU) to more variegated and omnidirectional diplomacy with a new emphasis on the Global South. This was evident on regional, bilateral, and multilateral levels. As Srikanth Kondapalli's chapter illustrates, it was during this decade that China established a wide range of regional multilateral institutions and dialogue groupings with every continent. During Hu Jintao's reign we also witnessed the Chinese recognition and embrace of "soft power." It was in Hu's speech to the 17th Party Congress in 2007 that the term "soft power" (软实力) was first officially used. Thus began a major effort by Beijing to go on offense in the international information domain, in attempts to improve China's global image and influence international narratives about China. As Shaun Breslin's chapter elucidates, this is a huge, multifaceted, and extremely well-resourced effort.[33] It has, however, had very uneven results. Various polls show that China's reputation remains relatively high south of the equator but equally low north of it. Given the enormity of its expenditures on soft power related activities (estimated in the $10–$20 billion per annum range), the return on Beijing's investments have not been great.

While this decade was on balance quite positive for China's foreign relations, toward the end of the decade a new—and more ominous—shift in China's external relations became evident. The year 2009–2010 thus became known as China's "year of assertiveness."[34] While some scholars dispute that there was any appreciable change in China's behavior,[35] many observers noted a more caustic and confrontational approach. In rapid succession Beijing confronted many of its neighbors over seemingly innocuous events. It threatened Tokyo with diplomatic and economic retaliation over the arrest of a drunken Chinese fisherman who had strayed into Japanese waters near the disputed Senkaku/ Diaoyu islands. It did the same against the Philippines over conflicting claims in the South China Sea. It irritated South Korea by blocking a resolution in the UN Security Council condemning the North Korean sinking of the ROK Navy submarine *Cheonan*, taking forty-six sailors to their deaths. It escalated China's claims to disputed territory with India and beefed up military units in these contested zones. It arrested and imprisoned Australian businessmen, allegedly in response to Canberra's blocking of a mega-merger of Chinese and Australian energy giants Chinalco and Rio Tinto. It put Denmark in the diplomatic deep freeze for a year in retaliation for hosting the Dalai Lama in Copenhagen. It did the same to Norway for seven years after imprisoned Chinese intellectual and dissent Liu Xiaobo was awarded the Nobel Prize for Peace. Multilaterally, China's diplomats undermined the Copenhagen Climate Change Conference by blocking a final agreement and communique. Beijing became very testy with the EU over several issues, and gave the cold shoulder to new American president Barack Obama when he paid a state visit to Beijing in November 2009.

All of these "assertive" moves transpired over the course of an eighteen-month period during 2009–2010. So, what was quite a successful decade in China's ties with the world ended on a series of bad notes. This trend carried over into the next decade, although by 2011–2012 Beijing recalibrated and sought to ameliorate strains with a number of the aforementioned countries. But, for many, the damage was done. While the previous decade had infused a sense of China as an increasingly productive partner—particularly in Asia and Europe—Beijing's behavior during 2009–2010 resurrected bad memories from the past and caused many countries to be more wary of China.

## The 2010s: Increased Confidence and Prominence

Since Xi Jinping's ascension to power in 2012, China has exhibited increased confidence and proactiveness on the world stage. As noted, Xi has replaced Deng Xiaoping's prescription for passive diplomacy—"bide time, hide brightness, do not take the lead" (韬光养晦不当头) with his more activist dictum "striving for achievement" (奋发有为). Xi has also emphasized China's "great rejuvenation" (大复兴), the "Chinese Dream" (中国梦), and a "community of a shared future for mankind" (人类命运共同体). Xi has prioritized foreign policy, he has asserted that China should practice "major country diplomacy" (大国外交), and he has advocated a "new type of major power relations" (新型大国关系). He has convened several high-level central work conferences on foreign policy and peripheral diplomacy (周边外交), and (as Suisheng Zhao's chapter delineates) Xi has reorganized and centralized the foreign policy making institutional process. He has been personally very active in diplomacy, visiting all continents and many countries. His signature "Belt and Road Initiative" (一带一路) has drawn much international attention, with 123 countries and 29 international organizations having signed on as of 2019, according to China's Foreign Minister Wang Yi.[36] Xi has notably emphasized that China should play a more prominent role in global governance (全球治理) and multilateral diplomacy (多边外交). Xi has also advocated improving China's "external propaganda" (对外宣传) and by "telling China's story well."

Taken together, these concepts and initiatives have characterized China's proactive diplomacy under Xi Jinping.[37] Even Yang Jiechi, China's senior and seasoned diplomat who also holds a position on the ruling Politburo, gushed in an article that:

We should have a keen appreciation of the profound significance of General Secretary Xi Jinping's thought on diplomacy to our times. . . . We should have a keen appreciation of the spirit of innovation embodied in General Secretary Xi Jinping's thought on diplomacy. . . . We should have a keen appreciation of the strategic wisdom underpinning General Secretary Xi Jinping's thought on diplomacy. . . . We should fully appreciate the great political, theoretical, practical and methodological significance of General Secretary Xi Jinping's thought on diplomacy. We should, with a keen sense of mission, responsibility, purpose and commitment, work hard to study this thinking and implement it earnestly, systematically and thoroughly. We should strive to gain a deep understanding of the essence and core of this thinking, so that it will become a powerful source of inspiration and strength that guides us in conducting major-country diplomacy with distinctive Chinese features.[38]

Such sycophancy aside, there is little doubt that China's foreign policy has assumed a new and more forthright stance under Xi Jinping. This has made some other countries nervous. Yet Xi sought to reassure the world in his landmark speech to the 19th Party Congress in 2017 that: "China's development does not pose a threat to any other country. No matter what stage of development it reaches, China will never seek hegemony or engage in expansion."[39]

This meme is a regular refrain heard since Zhou Enlai first enunciated it in the 1970s—perhaps precisely because Beijing has thus far failed to reassure others of its benign intensions and "peaceful rise." The stronger China becomes, seemingly the greater the skepticism—hence the ever-increasing need for reassurances. It is true that China has not fought a war since 1979, has not engaged in overt military expansion or foreign conquest, engages in a variety of confidence-building dialogue mechanisms with other countries, and Beijing goes out of its way to counter what it describes as the "China threat theory" (中国威胁论). Yet, the sheer size of China's population and economy, its rigid political system, its rapidly modernizing military, and other features of its growing material power, all contribute to increasing uncertainties and suspicions among other nations. Therefore, China's greatest challenge in its foreign relations in the future may well lie in the information domain and realm of public diplomacy.

As China enters the second decade of the millennium, China's power and position in the world has never been greater. This is an inexorable trend and is not likely to recede. When considered against the backdrop of the seven decades of the PRC's fluctuant encounter with the world, as outlined in this chapter, Beijing's current position is really remarkable. China has had—and will continue to have—many successes in its interactions with the international community. This is not to posit, however, that China will not encounter difficulties in its foreign relations going forward. This is inevitable, and is already occurring. The following chapters in Sections IV and V of this volume identify and elaborate, in considerable detail, the growing complexities in China's foreign relations across all continents and multiple spheres. The operative questions, however, are: what will likely be the inevitable challenges and how will China likely respond to them? I offer some of my own speculations in the concluding chapter.

# Notes

1. George Mason University Index Mundi, "China's International Organization Participation": https://www.indexmundi.com/china/international_organization_participation.html.
2. David Shambaugh, *China Goes Global: The Partial Power* (New York: Oxford University Press, 2013).
3. The China Power Project at the Center for Strategic and International Studies (CSIS) in Washington, DC, offers the best multidimensional assessment of China's power: https://www.csis.org/programs/china-power-project.
4. The classic exposition of this view remains Hans Morgenthau, *Politics Among Nations: The Struggle for Power and Peace* (New York: McGraw-Hill, multiple editions).
5. See Joseph Nye, *The Future of Power* (New York: Public Affairs, 2011).
6. China ranks second globally in the 2017 Global Diplomacy Index, a survey designed to compare diplomatic networks. See: https://globaldiplomacyindex.lowyinstitute.org/#.
7. Robert Zoellick, "Whither China: From Membership to Responsibility," Remarks to the National Committee on US-China Relations, September 21, 2005: https://2001-2009.state.gov/s/d/former/zoellick/rem/53682.htm.
8. Pew Research Center, "Five Charts on Global Views of China," October 19, 2018: https://www.pewresearch.org/fact-tank/2018/10/19/5-charts-on-global-views-of-china/.
9. For the best-integrated overview volumes, see: John W. Garver, *China's Quest: The History of the Foreign Relations of the People's Republic of China* (New York and Oxford: Oxford University Press, 2016); Robert G. Sutter, *Chinese Foreign Relations: Power and Policy since the Cold War* (Lanham, MD: Rowman and Littlefield, fourth edition 2016); Robert G. Sutter, *Foreign Relations of the PRC* (Lanham, MD: Rowman and Littlefield, second edition 2019); Henry Kissinger, *On China* (New York: Penguin Press, 2011); Samuel Kim, ed., *China and the World: Chinese Foreign Policy Faces the New Millennium* (Boulder, CO: Westview Press, fourth edition 1998); Thomas W. Robinson and David Shambaugh, eds., *Chinese Foreign Policy: Theory and Practice* (Oxford: Clarendon Press, 1996); Michael H. Hunt, *The Genesis of Chinese Communist Foreign Policy* (New York: Columbia University Press, 1998); John Garver, *Foreign Relations of the People's Republic of China* (Englewood Cliffs, NJ: Prentice Hall, 1993); Xue Mohong et al., *Diplomacy of Contemporary China* (Hong Kong: Horizon Press, 1990); Harry Harding, ed., *China's Foreign Relations in the 1980s* (New Haven: Yale University Press, 1984); John Gittings, *The World and China, 1922–1972* (New York: Harper & Row, 1974); Harold C. Hinton, *China's Turbulent Quest: An Analysis of China's Foreign Policy since 1949* (New York: Macmillan, 1970); Michael B. Yahuda, *China's Role in World Affairs* (London: Croom Helm, 1978); and Harold C. Hinton, *Communist China in World Politics* (London: Macmillan, 1966).
10. The other causes of the split included Moscow's failure to support China's bombardment of Taiwan's offshore islands and brinksmanship vis-à-vis Washington; criticism of Mao's agricultural collectivization and Great Leap Forward; failure to provide China with the promised sample atom bomb; and demands to establish a longwave radio facility and provide access for Soviet submarines to Chinese naval bases. For China's part, Beijing (and particularly Mao) was critical of Khrushchev's 1956 "secret speech" denunciation of Stalin; approach to the

1956 uprisings in Hungary and Poland; and his 1958 "peaceful coexistence" policy toward (and visit to) the United States. There were other ideological issues as well, as well as the personalities of Mao and Khrushchev, which all collectively served to drive the two apart. The best studies of the Sino-Soviet relationship split are: Odd Arne Westad, ed., *Brother in Arms: The Rise and Fall of the Sino-Soviet Alliance, 1945–1963* (Washington, DC, and Stanford, CA: Woodrow Wilson Center Press and Stanford University Press, 1998); Austin Jersild, *The Sino-Soviet Alliance* (Chapel Hill: University of North Carolina Press, 2014); Donald Zagoria, *The Sino-Soviet Conflict, 1956–1961* (Princeton: Princeton University Press, 1962); Herbert Ellison, ed., *The Sino-Soviet Conflict* (Seattle: University of Washington Press, 1982); Lorenz M. Luthi, *The Sino-Soviet Split* (Princeton: Princeton University Press, 2008); and Sergey Radchenko, *Two Suns in the Heaven: The Sino-Soviet Struggle for Supremacy, 1962–1967* (Washington, DC, and Stanford, CA: Woodrow Wilson Center Press and Stanford University Press, 2009).

11. See "Note from the Soviet Embassy in Beijing to the Ministry of Foreign Affairs of the People's Republic of China," July 18, 1960, available at: https://digitalarchive.wilsoncenter.org/document/117052.

12. See David Kimche, *The Afro-Asian Movement* (New Brunswick, NJ: Transaction Books, 1972).

13. Mao perceptively first used this term in an August 1946 interview with the American correspondent Anna Louise Strong, to refer to those countries that lay between the emerging Soviet and American camps. See Chen Jian, "Bridging Revolution and Decolonization: The 'Bandung Discourse' in China's Early Cold War Experience," *The Chinese Historical Review* 15, no. 2 (fall 2008): 212.

14. Agreement between the Republic of India and the People's Republic of China on Trade and Intercourse between the Tibet Region of China and India, April 29, 1954, available at: https://digitalarchive.wilsoncenter.org/document/121558.

15. The characteristic of diplomatic vacillation is the principal argument in Robert Sutter's *Foreign Relations of the PRC*.

16. Cited in John W. Garver, *China's Quest*, 221.

17. As Garver concludes, following an exhaustive examination of the available evidence: "It is virtually certain that CCP and PKI leaders discussed strategy for the Indonesian revolution, and Beijing lauded and encouraged the PKI struggle. Yet there is no evidence that Beijing knew of it, let alone helped plan, the calamitous PKI coup attempt that soon occurred." See Garver, *China's Quest*, 222. Also see Devina Heriyanto, "Was China Behind the September 1965 Failed Coup?" *The Jakarta Post*, October 20, 2017: https://www.thejakartapost.com/academia/2017/10/20/qa-was-china-behind-the-sept-30-1965-failed-coup.html. This article and other recent scholarship that comes to similar conclusions is based largely on declassified US government documents available through the National Declassification Center and National Security Archive at George Washington University: https://nsarchive.gwu.edu/briefing-book/indonesia/2017-10-17/indonesia-mass-murder-1965-us-embassy-files.

18. For a useful discussion of this period see Michael B. Yahuda, *China's Role in World Affairs*, chapter 5.

19. *Chairman Mao Tse-tung's Important Talks with Guests from Asia, Africa, and Latin America* (Beijing: Foreign Languages Press, 1970), 5–6.

20. Lin Piao, *Long Live the Victory of People's War!* (Beijing: Foreign Languages Press, 1965).

21. Chinese officials and historians claim that the GPCR lasted a full decade, from 1966–1976, but in fact the "active phase"(积极阶段) only lasted three years until the Ninth Party Congress in 1969.

22. The classic study of this subject remains Peter Van Ness, *Revolution and Chinese Foreign Policy: Peking's Support for Wars of National Liberation* (Berkeley: University of California Press, 1970).

23. For example, one official history undertaken by the Ministry of Foreign Affairs contains only two brief chapters on this period entitled "Promotion of Unity and Cooperation with Asia, African, and Latin American Countries and People" and "Pursuance of Good Neighborly Policy and Gradual Settlement of Questions Left Over from History." See Editorial Board, *Diplomacy of Contemporary China* (Hong Kong: New Horizon Press).

24. The text can be found at: https://digitalarchive.wilsoncenter.org/document/117146.pdf?v=
fa3a7c3c65e5433277128b2427a6702a.

25. Richard M. Nixon, "Asia after Viet Nam," *Foreign Affairs* 46, no. 1 (October 1967): 111–125.

26. For excellent surveys of Canadian-China relations dating back to the Trudeau opening, see
Paul Evans, *Engaging China: Myth, Aspiration, and Strategy in Canadian Policy from Trudeau
to Harper* (Toronto: University of Toronto Press, 2014); and David Mulroney, *Middle
Power, Middle Kingdom: What Canadians Need to Know About China* (Toronto: Penguin
Canada, 2015).

27. "Dates of Establishment of Diplomatic Relations with the People's Republic of China," available at: https://en.wikipedia.org/wiki/Dates_of_establishment_of_diplomatic_relations_
with_the_People%27s_Republic_of_China#1960s.

28. For studies of this transitional period see Roderick MacFarquhar, ed., *The Politics of China*
(Cambridge: Cambridge University Press, third edition 2011), chapter 4; and Robert
Weatherley, *Mao's Forgotten Successor: The Political Career of Hua Guofeng* (London: Palgrave
Macmillan, 2010).

29. Lee Kuan Yew, *From Third World to First: The Singapore Story, 1965–2000* (Singapore: Times
Media, 2000), 693.

30. See David Shambaugh, "China Engages Asia: Reshaping the Regional Order," *International
Security* 29, no. 3 (winter 2004/2005): 64–99, and *Power Shift: China and Asia's New Dynamics*
(Berkeley: University of California Press, 2005).

31. See Shambaugh, *China Goes Global.*

32. See Shambaugh, *Power Shift* and "China Engages Asia."

33. See Shambaugh, *China Goes Global*, chapter 6; and Shambaugh, "China's Soft Power Push: The
Search for Respect," *Foreign Affairs* (July–August 2015): 99–107.

34. See, for example, Michael D. Swaine, "Perceptions of an Assertive China," *China Leadership
Monitor* 32 (2010), available at: http://media.hoover.org/sites/default/files/documents/
CLM32MS.pdf.

35. See Alastair Iain Johnston, "How New and Assertive Is China's New Assertiveness?"
*International Security* 37, no. 4 (spring 2013): 7–48.

36. "Full Text of Foreign Minister Wang Yi's News Conference at Second Session of 13th NPC
2019," Xinhua, March 8, 2019.

37. See Jianwei Wang, "Xi Jinping's 'Major Country Diplomacy': A Paradigm Shift?" *Journal of
Contemporary China* 28, no. 115 (January 2019): 15–30.

38. Yang Jiechi, "Study and Implement General Secretary Xi Jinping's Thought on Diplomacy
in a Deep-going Way and Keep Writing New Chapters of Major-Country Diplomacy with
Distinctive Chinese Features," Xinhua, July 19, 2017: http://www.xinhuanet.com/english/
2017-07/19/c_136456009.htm.

39. Xi Jinping, "Secure a Decisive Victory in Building a Moderately Prosperous Society in All
Respects and Strive for the Great Success of Socialism with Chinese Characteristics for a New
Era," speech at the 19th National Congress of the Communist Party of China, October 18,
2017, 53.

# SECTION II

# HISTORICAL SOURCES

2

# Legacies of the Past

ODD ARNE WESTAD

As with all countries and societies, China's present is determined by its past. Current leaders are of course at liberty to make their own decisions in order to improve their country, and the best among them do. But they do so within a framework of mind and territory that has been bequeathed them by the past. In China's case, it is often argued that the past carries even more of weight than elsewhere, simply because there is more of it: China's history, particularly in intellectual terms, goes back several thousand years. It could, however, as easily be argued that it is the significance that history is given inside Chinese culture that provides it with remarkable power in the present. Many countries, after all, can in some form or another claim thousands of years of history without that longevity becoming a staple of their political and ideological discourses. The sharp centrality of history to China may therefore as easily be seen as an ideological construct in itself rather than something given by chronology or continuity.[1]

For China's foreign affairs today there are two aspects of the past that matter more than others. One is the legacy of empire. Today's China, both in shape and content, grew out of the Qing empire and has taken over a number of that empire's characteristics. The other is authoritarianism, which—as is the case in many places—comes out of the deeper past, but in China has become a default mode of government, to the extent that a large number of Chinese believe that their country is uncommonly suited for authoritarian government (and the other way around). Recently, many Chinese (and some non-Chinese) have started celebrating autocratic government as part of a successful model of development, especially well suited to Chinese conditions. Both of these features of China's past are in need of further investigation as they pertain to the present.

Odd Arne Westad, *Legacies of the Past* In: *China and the World*. Edited by: David Shambaugh, Oxford University Press (2020). © Oxford University Press
DOI: 10.1093/oso/9780190062316.003.0002

# Empire

Empire was the main form of political organization on a global scale before the mid-twentieth century. In what we know as China, empires were distinguished by their size and their cohesion. Over the past two thousand years, China has seen a number of empires that, at their peak, were able to expand their territory, integrate their populations, and control the wider region from the Himalayas to Central Asia, Korea, and Vietnam. There have also been times when Chinese states have been smaller in size and formed state systems not unlike what happened in Europe over the past five hundred years. But, in overall terms, it is the legacies of empire that have shaped China today, not least because the last of the Chinese empires, the Qing, at its height was such a powerful and pervasive entity. Since Chinese empires, like European or South Asian empires, were different in character and orientation, it is very important to note that when we speak about the direct impact of empire on China today, we are mainly speaking about the Qing, which ruled China from 1644 to 1912.[2]

Even if it is right to focus on the Qing empire, there are of course deeper legacies from the past that influence Chinese foreign affairs today. Making these too specific makes no sense: strategists who believe that current People's Republic of China (PRC) strategies can be constructed from reading Sun Zi or Meng Zi are certainly mistaken, just as their Chinese counterparts would be if they thought that US policies are derived from Thucydides or Xenophon. What is at work are rather broad trends, especially in terms of self-perception. Two are particularly important: a concept of cultural cohesion and a concept of centrality. These concepts have shaped China's interaction with the world for a very long time.[3]

China's cultural cohesion emerged from the written Chinese language, which gradually became the means of interaction for large numbers of elites inside the empire and outside. By the end of the first millennium after the founding of the Han empire, the command of written Chinese was used as a key cultural marker in eastern Asia—whoever mastered it was on the inside of an increasingly complex cultural web. It gave the users, whatever state they found themselves within, a particular connection to and affinity for Chinese culture. The written language served as a great conveyor belt of ideas and technologies, not only from whatever empire controlled China and toward the rest of eastern Asia, but often in other directions as well. It created a pervasive cultural cohesion that defined a region.[4]

Instead of a claim to universal political centrality, which it often has been seen as constituting, in historical terms Chinese elites have asserted the superiority of their states in a cultural sense: China was at the center of a common culture because it was the origin, the root, of its manifestations, of which the superiority of the empire and the person of the emperor—over time known as the "son of heaven"—was one. Of course, imperial centrality was much more immediate when the emperor had a great deal of physical power to back up his position. And the cultural zone in which such claims had validity was limited to some areas immediately adjacent to China itself, first and foremost Korea and Vietnam, and to some extent Japan. Even so, it would be wrong to write off Chinese centrality simply as an ideologized version of China's military power. For a very long time, it was a concept that others bought into as well as Chinese.[5]

The long-term consequences of these concepts are fairly clear and also visible today. Among many Chinese, they have led to an immense cultural pride: I am among the many who have witnessed how barely literate Chinese delight in their country being the root of a regional (and today increasingly global) culture. But as with all concepts of centrality, their practices can go in different directions: they can justify attempting to dominate a region (as Germany did in Europe prior to 1945) or integrate a region (as Germany has done in Europe after 1945). But, however they are practiced, concepts of centrality often give rise to a sense of exceptionalism with regard to others.

The inheritance from China's deeper past is therefore significant but malleable. What the People's Republic of China inherited from the Qing empire seems more hard-wired, both in terms of perceptions and institutions. Some historians of China see this as ironic, since so much energy has been spent in Chinese nationalist historiography after 1912 on denouncing the empire's "foreign" Manchu rulers and denying its significance for China.[6] But in many ways denying the fluidity and changeability of empire and stressing the break between imperial and post-imperial institutions are common positions across post-imperial space, both in former peripheries and former metropoles. The Chinese distaste for the Qing is echoed in most other settings where a collapsed empire serves as a useful foil for glorification of the present (or at least as an excuse for contemporary imperfections).[7]

Instead, what stands out in China today are the multiple ways in which today's People's Republic has inherited Qing notions and practices. Many of the concepts of extreme centralization are from the Qing era, as are institutions such as the hukou (户口), the household registration system by which Chinese are permitted or denied the right to settle outside the region of their birth.[8] In overall terms, the PRC's current authoritarianism, its state reverence, its methods for controlling and fashioning private enterprise, organizations, and religious communities all come out of the Qing (although many of them, of course, have deeper roots). China today has done away with less of its imperial legacies overall than most other post-imperial states.

For the purposes of understanding the PRC's international affairs, grasping this relative continuity and its effects is central. It has a strong effect both on what China is and how it constructs its outer worlds. The Qing empire expanded

China's borders into Mongolia, the Dzungar and Tarim basins, Tibet, the north-east (Manchuria), and the southwestern Hmong and Lolo areas. Even more important, it carried out large-scale Chinese colonization of these regions, start-ing the trend toward complete Sinification that the PRC has put into high gear today. The expansion of China is therefore in many ways similar to that of Russia or the United States, with large increases in contiguous territory and the accom-panying assimilation or extermination of other groups within defined borders. Even the 92 percent within the PRC who identify as Chinese (or Han, as the official designation goes) compares with the 81 percent Russians in Russia, and 85 percent Euro or African Americans in the United States.

The borders that the PRC have today are largely the ones it inherited from the Qing empire. Outer Mongolia (today's Mongolian republic) has been shaved off, as has large chunks of land in the far northeast (to Russia)—Mao Zedong used to say that China had not yet presented the bill to Moscow for these acqui-sitions. Other than that, China's borders have been remarkably stable since the empire was abolished in 1912. China is therefore the only empire that has man-aged the transition to a nation-state without a significant loss of territory, and this determines not just its internal composition but its foreign affairs to a very high extent.[9]

The Qing empire attempted to regulate its relationships with surrounding states in ways that secured the ideological centrality of the empire while also looking after its security and economic interests. On occasion, historians refer to these policies as "the tribute system," though tribute was only a part of the rela-tionships and the content of each country's links with Beijing was distinct and specific (and often remarkably varied). The common element was the Qing's insistence that all surrounding countries were in principle subservient to the empire and that their representatives ought to show up in the imperial capital at regular intervals to proclaim this deference. Other than that, relationships differed widely, dependent on cultural connections, historical ties, and local needs.[10]

The two countries that in Qing protocols had the closest ties with the empire, while still not being a part of it, were Korea and Vietnam. Korea had interacted with China for a very long time, and during the Ming era the Korean state became a vassal of the empire, a relationship that continued more or less intact through Qing times. Korean rulers always guarded their freedom of action jeal-ously, and Qing political influence within Korea was very limited, even if Korean kings accepted the Qing emperor as suzerain. The relationship was deeply cul-tural. Korean elites viewed themselves as part of a common culture centered on China, even when they found the Qing empire's Manchurian roots insufficiently Confucian.[11]

Vietnam, and to a lesser extent the rest of Indochina, also stood in a direct relationship with the Qing empire that went beyond anything seen elsewhere, except in Korea.[12] It was sometimes a troubled relationship: the fact that the Vietnamese king regarded himself to be a vassal of the emperor also meant that the Qing reserved the right to determine matters such as the correct succession. And, unlike Korea, the turbulent politics of Vietnam, especially from the late eighteenth century on, meant numerous Chinese attempts at intervening in Vietnamese affairs. Ironically, the somewhat more remote relationship compared to Korea meant more intervention, because the two political cultures were less immediately aligned. The interventions gave rise to long-term resentments in Vietnam, some of which have lasted up to our own time.[13]

Japan was partly inside and partly outside the inner Chinese cultural circle. In spite of having formed much of their cultural and political framework under the influence of China (often through Korea), Japanese states were generally outside of direct Chinese imperial control. The Qing empire never attempted to dominate Japan in the way it dominated its other neighbors, and its elites generally looked down on the Japanese as piratical troublemakers beyond the immediate realm of civilization. And as Japan became unified under the Tokugawa shogunate from the early seventeenth century on, Japanese leaders feared all forms of direct Chinese leverage, much as they feared other forms of foreign power.

For Turks and Persians beyond the Qing's "new frontier" (Xinjiang), for peninsular Southeast Asia and the islands, and for South Asia beyond the Himalayas, Chinese attempts at regulating its neighborhood meant even less. In Chinese terms, at least, most of the states in these regions were connected to the empire in some form of vassalage, but the relationships were not close and in some cases entirely theoretical, since leaders in Beijing had only the vaguest sense of what kind of entities they were dealing with at the other end. In these cases the ideology of empire easily superseded any form of practice, and the discourse of imperial control within the Qing state was far more significant than any attempts at exercising concrete supremacy abroad.[14]

This, then, is what the China-centered imperial regional order of the Qing looked like before its collapse in the late nineteenth century. Unlike what is sometimes prophesied, this order is unlikely to make its return. It remains, of course, in historical echoes and more or less constructed memories, some of which are very powerful tools in Asian politics. Beyond that, a Chinese sense of centrality also remains, made more powerful by the country's recent economic success. And in the neighboring countries a fear of Chinese domination lingers, alongside (at least in Korea and Vietnam) a sense of cultural interconnection. The rise of domestic nationalisms is a new phenomenon (except, perhaps, in Korea) that makes the return of a China-centered system less likely.

Ever since the collapse of imperial China, some scholars have theorized sets of distinctions between assumed "Western" and "Eastern" approaches to international relations. One thread in these discourses has been the notion that "Eastern" interactions, when freed from European international control, are by themselves more peaceful and less confrontational than those of the "West."[15] There is very little in the historical record that gives credence to such views. Chinese empires (and certainly the Qing) were expansionist and assertive, and so were other states within the region. When we speak of the legacies of empires within Asia, we need to count the effects of Asia-based empires as well as Europe-based ones.

Denying such a qualitative difference between European and Asian state systems is not, of course, the same as denying difference altogether. There were very significant differences between European arrangements (often, with a certain amplification, referred to as "Westphalian" orders) and those that have existed in eastern Asia since the Ming era. While the European state system indicated the potential for legal and diplomatic equality among states, the eastern Asian one emphasized hierarchy, with the China-based empire at least conceptually on top. Sovereignty was more diffuse in eastern Asia, and smaller states had more of an ability to trade aspects of sovereignty for practical concessions from the empire.[16] There was also a much wider variety of informal exchanges and diffuse positions, to which official proclamations spoke in ways that were intended to be read in different ways by different groups. While empire was at the heart of the eastern Asian international order, it was never universal in jurisdiction, capability, or competence.

## Authoritarianism

Most empires are authoritarian because of their very nature: in order to rule over many different groups, elites assert the need for repressive and illiberal institutions and policies. That Chinese empires have been authoritarian in their political composition is therefore more in line with what other empires have been in the past than different from them. What *is* different is that today's China has taken over and to some extent celebrates the authoritarianism of the past. Participatory democracy is not suited for China even today, the Chinese Communists' argument goes, because it is a big and diverse country that needs a firm hand at the tiller to secure social stability and economic growth. The problem with pro-authoritarian arguments is not just that they are used as an excuse for bad governance at home. It is also that they create an image of China abroad that dents its reputation for technological progress and commercial success. For many people around the world, and not least in Asia, the threat from China is not its size nor its power, but its defense of one-party rule and authoritarian government.[17]

It is therefore of key importance to understanding China's contemporary foreign relations to understand where the country's authoritarianism comes from. There are of course several sources for it. Some are based on forms of Neo-Confucian thinking that have been influential in China for around 1,000 years. Some come out of imperial practices, especially as employed by the Qing empire. And some originate in the twentieth century with the birth of Chinese Communism. Let us deal with each of these in turn.

All Confucian thinking is hierarchical, but not all of it is authoritarian. At its best, Confucianism sets out assortments of duties and obligations that are valid up and down the rungs of hierarchies, from the emperor to the humblest of servants. When carefully adhered to in society and craftily employed within the state, Confucianism can create a remarkably cohesive social environment, in which individuals may feel both empowered and secure. The form of Confucianism most in vogue in China since the Song empire, often called Neo-Confucianism, emphasizes self-improvement as the only way of producing a better society. This form of thinking has often led to an emphasis on personal qualities over popular support. Especially during the Qing empire, the idea that it was the rectitude and sagacity of an official, above even his proven results, that qualified for high office, was hardwired into the imperial system of preferences. And such qualities were more likely to be found among officials whose families had served the empire for generations, thereby replacing the concept of a meritocracy with that of favoritism or even nepotism, not unlike China today.[18]

The emphasis on elite selection and heredity was probably stimulated by the Qing being led by families, including the imperial family, who were non-Chinese in origin. The Manchu roots of the dynasty, and the outsider quality that much of the Qing enterprise had, even after it had ruled China for a century, contributed to a sense of exclusivity and distinctiveness among the elite. The Qing were never quite able to relinquish the sense, inwardly and outwardly, that they were a small elite, which had conquered China by force and ruled it through a combination of purpose and fear.[19] Again, the similarities with Communist rule are striking, even if the Communists have different purposes and very different origins.

One aspect of its rule that the CCP has taken over from the Qing is its totalitarian presumptions. The Chinese preoccupation with a strong state goes much further back than the last dynasty, but it was the Qing which expanded and perfected China's state veneration. For the Qing, the alternative to authoritarian government was not freedom, but chaos. The need to regulate the population, sometimes in minuscule detail, was therefore obvious to them. The ideal, never implemented in practice, was government as a machine led by incorruptible idealists who worked for the best of the state. All other aspects of social life

had to be subsumed under the workings of the state: religion, business, education, entertainment, even family affairs. Dictatorship was the will of Heaven and
heavy regulation the duty of the regime.[20]

The past hundred years in Chinese history has been a battle over whether the
country can banish these ghosts of the past and move on. There have been times
when the future seemed wide open, and other times when it seemed very closed
and reflective of the Qing era. The direction that China seems to go in domestically matters intensely for its foreign affairs, as is the case with any other country.
Nobody among China's neighbors, or further afield, believes that a China that
oppresses its own population, treats minorities harshly, and subsumes all activities to the needs of a centralized and dictatorial state will work with them in set-
tling bilateral or multilateral matters fairly and promptly. They may be wrong
about this, but such are the assumptions and China's more recent actions in eastern Asia seem to confirm them.

# The "Century of Humiliation"

For the Chinese Communist state, the concept of China being weak and
exploited before the Communist conquest is an article of faith. The "century of humiliation," which is assumed to have lasted from the first Opium
War in 1839 to the end of the Chinese civil war in 1949, is the reason, it
claims, the CCP and, eventually, the PRC came into being. The Chinese
Communist state is the Chinese people's response to being humiliated
by foreigners after the Qing government started getting into trouble in
the mid-nineteenth century. If China today is nationalist, centralist, and
authoritarian, this was caused by the terrible attacks on China that foreign
imperialists, from the British to the Japanese, carried out. In other words,
the CCP dictatorship is necessary to set things right and make China rich
and strong again.[21]

This version of history is not only untrue but also unhelpful for China in
finding its place in the world. The late Qing empire did lose its wars against
stronger empires that encroached on its territory. And Europeans behaved, and
sometimes still behave, with racist condescension toward Chinese, not least
in the zones they took control of along China's coast and main rivers. Japan
launched an all-out attack against China in 1937 and its forces committed
terrible crimes thereafter. But China as a whole was never colonized, and the
borders of China today are therefore remarkably similar to those of the Qing
empire. The Western concessions in China were returned to Chinese jurisdiction well before the CCP took over. China suffered under foreign attacks, but it
was never under foreign direction, at least not for very long.

But what is really untrue about the "humiliation" story is that it introduces an image of Chinese as passive victims of foreign aggression until they were rescued by the Communist Party. Instead, what happened as the Qing empire got into trouble was that Chinese from all walks of life, as others within the empire, used the opportunity to break out from the stranglehold that the imperial state had had on them. They migrated, worked, traded, invented, believed, and studied in ways that the state had tried to prevent them from doing. They cooperated with foreigners. They experimented with new forms of political representation and new forms of culture or gender relations. In short, they attempted, as best they could, to take control of their own lives.[22]

Not all was well in China in the late imperial and republican eras. The weakening of the central state opened up for rampant forms of exploitation, especially in the countryside, and capitalism undercut many social ties that people had depended on in the past. But, during the early twentieth century, China avoided the stifling oppression of the Qing or the murderous campaigns of the early Communist period. This may not be good news for those who believe that the purpose of Chinese society is to produce a strong state. But it did provide people in China with opportunities that they did not have before or after, or at least not until the era of economic reform in the 1980s and 1990s.

## The Past in the Present

Today's Chinese government has inherited the legacies of empire and especially the last empire's authoritarianism. It has also constructed a version of recent history that emphasizes past Chinese victimhood as a justification for Communist control. The only alternative to CCP rule, according to this version of Chinese history, is domestic chaos and a return to humiliation at the hands of foreigners. The fact that the political theory the party represents, communism, was developed by a German, Karl Marx, and first implemented by a Russian and a Georgian, Lenin and Stalin, is often conveniently forgotten by today's party leaders. The strengthening of one-party rule, which is the main aim of General Secretary and President Xi Jinping, is first and foremost justified by Chinese nationalism and China's national needs.

The CCP version of history is of course strengthened by China's recent economic success, which are outlined elsewhere in this volume. The growth of the Chinese economy and its increasing internationalization have created links with the world that China's Communist leaders find difficult to manage. But it has also supplied a story about Chinese successes that can be used to present a positive image of the country abroad. China is genuinely admired by many in Asia and Africa who themselves dream of high growth rates and high-tech production lines, and it is acclaimed and feared in equal amounts by Westerners who are anxious about their own displacement as global leaders. Most Chinese are understandably proud of their economic achievements, and many are still willing to give the Communist Party at least the benefit of the doubt for having presided over such a period of extraordinary growth.

It may be that China's economic advance together with the historical legacies of empire and authoritarianism, now mixed with more recent nationalism, will make compromise abroad more difficult. That will lead to problems for China, because it is on such compromise that the country's further rise depends. Those, be they in Beijing or Washington, who believe that eastern Asia will return to its international state of around 1750 with China as an uncontested hegemon, or that China as a new great power will get its way by behaving like other rising powers have in the past—by throwing its weight around and alienating others— are almost certainly wrong. Eastern Asia, and the world, are more complex than before, and nationalisms and quests for sovereignty more widespread. Even if China overcomes its domestic challenges and continues its rise, it will not be able to dictate its will to others. Unless the whole international system, region-ally and globally, changes dramatically, China will be dependent on compromise to further its own interests, whatever way its government perceives them.

This is where China may face its biggest foreign policy challenges. The con-structed history of China as ever peaceful and accommodating is not only untrue, it is also rejected by China's neighbors and unhelpful to the processes of Chinese foreign policy making. The more China defines itself as a normal country (albeit a very big one) with limited but clear foreign policy interests, the better it is both for China and its neighbors. But China's imperial heritage stands in the way of such forms of thinking. So does its authoritarianism, which frightens others else-where in Asia and beyond. Although there is no absolute rule that authoritarian governments are more aggressive than democratic or pluralistic ones, it is hard to convince other countries that China's authoritarianism stops at home. As long as China remains a repressive authoritarian state, its diplomatic, military, business, and cultural initiatives abroad will always be regarded with suspicion by others who do not share these values. A more attractive China, for Chinese and foreigners alike, will mean that the country has to overcome its past and present itself in a new light. The tremendous changes it has gone through over the past generation shows that such a different China is possible, even if it is not very likely in the short run.

# Notes

1. The classic discussion is Prasenjit Duara, *Rescuing History from the Nation: Questioning Narratives of Modern China* (Chicago: University of Chicago Press, 1995). See also Julia C.

Schneider, *Nation and Ethnicity: Chinese Discourses on History, Historiography, and Nationalism (1900s–1920s)* (Boston: Brill, 2017).

2. For an overview of empire in Asia since the early modern era, see the two-volume work Brian P. Farrell and Jack Fairey, eds., *Empire in Asia: A New Global History*, vol. 1, and Brian P. Farrell and Donna Brunero, eds., *Empire in Asia: A New Global History*, vol. 2 (both London: Bloomsbury, 2018). For a discussion of imperial interactions, see Odd Arne Westad, "Empire in Asia: The Long Nineteenth Century?," in Farrell and Brunero, vol. 2.

3. See Odd Arne Westad, *Restless Empire: China and the World since 1750* (New York: Basic Books, 2012).

4. A good overview is in Hongyuan Dong, *A History of the Chinese Language* (London: Routledge, 2014).

5. See Alexander Woodside, *Lost Modernities: China, Vietnam, Korea, and the Hazards of World History* (Cambridge, MA: Harvard University Press, 2006); and Alexander Woodside, "The Centre and the Borderlands in Chinese Political Theory," in *The Chinese State at the Borders*, ed. Diana Lary (Vancouver: UBC Press, 2008).

6. The degree to which the Qing should be understood as a Chinese empire, a Manchu one, or as an amalgam of Manchu, Central Asian, and Chinese influences is still a hotly debated topic; see Ding Yizhuang and Mark Elliott, "How to Write Chinese History in the Twenty-first Century: The Impact of the 'New Qing History' Studies and Chinese Responses," *Chinese Studies in History* 51, no. 1 (January 2, 2018): 70–95.

7. For its origins, see Wang Chunxia, *"Pai Man" yu minzu zhuyi* ["Anti-Manchuism" and Nationalism] (Beijing: Shehui kexue wenxian chubanshe, 2005).

8. For an overview, see Wang Weihai, *Zhongguo huji zhidu: lishi yu zhengzhi de fenxi* [China's Huji System: A Historical and Political Analysis] (Shanghai: Shanghai wenhua chubanshe, 2006).

9. For the southwest and Tibet, see Charles Giersch, *Asian Borderlands: The Transformation of Qing China's Yunnan Frontier* (Cambridge, MA: Harvard University Press, 2006); and Yingcong Dai, *The Sichuan Frontier and Tibet: Imperial Strategy in the Early Qing* (Seattle: University of Washington Press, 2009). A good overview of conceptual issues is James Leibold, *Reconfiguring Chinese Nationalism: How the Qing Frontier and Its Indigenes Became Chinese* (New York: Palgrave Macmillan, 2007).

10. The contributions in Dittmar Schorkowitz and Ning Chia, eds., *Managing Frontiers in Qing China: The Lifanyuan and Libu Revisited* (Leiden: Brill, 2017) take us a bit of the way in understanding how Qing foreign relations were actually managed.

11. See Odd Arne Westad, *Empire and Righteous Nation: Six Hundred Years of China-Korea Relations* (Cambridge, MA: Harvard University Press, forthcoming).

12. For an overview, see Jaymin Kim, "The Rule of Ritual: Crimes and Justice in Qing-Vietnamese Relations during the Qianlong Period (1736–1796)," in *China's Encounters on the South and Southwest: Reforging the Fiery Frontier over Two Millennia*, ed. James A. Anderson and John K. Whitmore (Leiden: Brill, 2014).

13. Tuong Vu, "The Party v. the People: Anti-China Nationalism in Contemporary Vietnam," *Journal of Vietnamese Studies* 9, no. 4 (2014): 33–66.

14. For a view of changes from the mid-eighteenth century to the early nineteenth, see Matthew W. Mosca, *From Frontier Policy to Foreign Policy: The Question of India and the Transformation of Geopolitics in Qing China* (Stanford, CA: Stanford University Press, 2013).

15. Some have even started using the term "Eastphalia" as a contrast to the Westphalian order in Europe (Sung Kim, David Fidler, and Sumit Ganguly, "Eastphalia Rising? Asian Influence and the Fate of Human Security," *World Policy Journal* 26, no. 2 (2009): 53–64). The term is unlikely to catch on, since there is an actual Eastphalia in eastern Germany, unrelated to current debates in international relations theory.

16. For general perspectives, see Zvi Ben-Dor Benite, Stefanos Geroulanos, and Nicole Jerr, eds., *The Scaffolding of Sovereignty: Global and Aesthetic Perspectives on the History of a Concept* (New York: Columbia University Press, 2017); for East Asia in the nineteenth century see Junnan Lai, "Sovereignty and 'Civilization': International Law and East Asia in the Nineteenth Century," *Modern China* 40, no. 3 (2014): 282–314, and Tong Lam, "Policing the Imperial Nation: Sovereignty, International Law, and the Civilizing Mission in Late Qing China," *Comparative Studies in Society and History* 52, no. 4 (2010): 881–908.

17. For the early modern era, see Michael Ng-Quinn, "The Normative Justification of Traditional Chinese Authoritarianism," *Critical Review of International Social and Political Philosophy* 9, no. 3 (2006): 379–397. Current affairs are covered in Wenfang Tang, *Populist Authoritarianism: Chinese Political Culture and Regime Sustainability* (New York: Oxford University Press, 2016) and Daniel Koss, *Where the Party Rules: The Rank and File of China's Communist State* (Cambridge: Cambridge University Press, 2018). For an alarmist international view, see Stefan Halper, *The Beijing Consensus: How China's Authoritarian Model Will Dominate the Twenty-first Century* (New York: Basic Books, 2010).

18. For an overview, see Peter Bol, *Neo-Confucianism in History*, Harvard East Asian Monographs 307 (Cambridge, MA: Harvard University Press, 2008).

19. For a brilliant discussion of Manchu identities, see Pamela Kyle Crossley, *A Translucent Mirror: History and Identity in Qing Imperial Ideology* (Berkeley: University of California Press, 1999).

20. See Willard J. Peterson, "Dominating Learning from Above During the K'ang-Hsi Period," in *The Cambridge History of China: Volume 9: The Ch'ing Dynasty to 1800*, ed. Willard J. Peterson, vol. 9 (Cambridge: Cambridge University Press, 2016), 571–605 and Wang Fan-sen, "Political Pressures on the Cultural Sphere in the Ch'ing Period," in Peterson, 606–48. See also Jonathan D. Spence, *Treason by the Book* (New York: Viking, 2001), and for an overview of the late Qing era that stresses the collapse of the Qing authoritarian order, see Zhongguo shehui kexueyuan jindaishi yanjiusuo and Suzhou daxue shehui xueyuan, eds., *Wan Qing guojia yu shehui [State and Society in Late Qing]* (Beijing: Shehui kexue wenxian chubanshe, 2007).

21. See William A. Callahan, *China: The Pessoptimist Nation* (Oxford: Oxford University Press, 2010), especially 31–60; Zheng Wang, *Never Forget National Humiliation: Historical Memory in Chinese Politics and Foreign Relations* (Columbia University Press, 2014); and Jonathan Unger, *Chinese Nationalism* (London: Taylor and Francis, 2016).

22. See Westad, *Restless Empire: China and the World since 1750*, 19–52.

# 3

# China's National Experiences and the Evolution of PRC Grand Strategy

CHAS W. FREEMAN JR.

China is both a civilization and a state. States often have strategies. Civilizations do not, but their experiences inform the priorities of the states that rule them. As a civilization, China is a cultural entity of remarkable antiquity and continuity whose distinctive characteristics include:

- the use of ideograms rather than an alphabet or syllabary to write;
- a preference for hierarchical, meritocratic systems of governance;
- esteem for the educated who compete to man the state and deprecation of those in other walks of life;
- an obsession with "face" (面子—prestige, dignity, status, and influence derived from the esteem of those one respects);
- reverence for age and ancestry;
- an elite bias toward agnosticism rather than religiosity;
- an emphasis on communal propriety rather than law to maintain order, resolve disputes, and preserve social tranquility; and
- culinary traditions based on food sized for extremely fuel-efficient cooking and consumption with chopsticks.

Chinese civilization is associated with unusually high population density that enables labor-intensive agriculture (in Western terms, more like gardening than farming). The Chinese agricultural economy depends on recycling animal (especially swine) and human waste to cultivate grains and vegetables and raise fish and fowl. The environmental requirements for this sort of agriculture have long limited Chinese civilization to much the same area in East Asia it now occupies,[1] though many of China's neighbors have selectively adopted elements of its culture.

Chas W. Freeman Jr., *China's National Experiences and the Evolution of PRC Grand Strategy* In: *China and the World.* Edited by: David Shambaugh, Oxford University Press (2020). © Oxford University Press DOI: 10.1093/oso/9780190062316.003.0003

Mountains, deserts, forests, and seas confine the Chinese. They are not effective barriers to assault by uncivilized nomads or seaborne foreigners. Still, they long insulated China from other advanced societies. China's geographic distance from societies with equivalent capabilities fostered smug complacency about Chinese cultural superiority. Chinese were aware of the existence of competing civilizations but dismissed them as irrelevant to their own well-being and domestic tranquility. Ingrained disdain for foreigners magnified the trauma for the Chinese elite as the West imposed escalating losses of "face" on them from the sixteenth century through the twentieth.

## State Identities

Many different states, each with its own personality and worldview, have governed all or part of China. The earliest were indigenous. More recently, invaders have often imposed new states on China. The first historically attested unification of China occurred in 221 BCE under the Qin, one of seven competing states in the territories that constitute modern China. Like Macedon in classical Greece, Qin was a partially assimilated state on the periphery of the higher but less warlike civilization over which it achieved hegemony, then conquest. Qin rule lasted only fourteen years,[2] ending in 207 BCE. But it set patterns in Chinese political culture that have persisted for more than two millennia.

Even before Qin, Chinese saw unity as their country's natural and only legitimate order.[3] Each new state established to govern all of China thought of itself as defining a new era and constitutional reality that separated its order from those of the past.[4] In the past millennium, this was true for the Yuan (the state within the Mongol Empire that Genghis Khan's grandson, Kublai Khan, imposed on China in 1271), for the Ming (founded by insurgent Chinese peasants in 1368), and for the Qing (imposed on China in 1644 by its Manchu conquerors).

Similar claims to discontinuity in state identity characterized the Republic of China (ROC—founded on October 10, 1911) and the People's Republic of China (PRC—established on October 1, 1949).[5] Each repudiated key elements of its predecessor regimes, while retaining other of their features.

The PRC has passed through several phases in its evolution as a state. As it has matured, both its consciousness and its embrace of its connections to China's cultural past have grown. But, like previous Chinese states, the PRC continues to see itself as unique—not just the latest regime to govern "China," but one that has transformed China's political order into something entirely new. In part, this self-image reflects the PRC's roots in Marxism-Leninism, which originated in Europe, not China.

Significantly, unlike previous Chinese states (including the ROC), the PRC did not establish a calendar linked to its reign over China. It accepted the internationally ubiquitous Gregorian calendar as its own. In retrospect, like the ROC and unlike the Qing, the PRC sought acceptance rather than isolation from the international state system, but this could not become fully apparent until the PRC was admitted to that system. It then proved to be a cautious student and conservative supporter of the existing order, to which it rapidly assimilated itself. This is especially notable because, for over two decades, a vigorous US effort to ensure that the PRC could not join the United Nations or other elements of the American-led world order had left it on the outside, looking in.

## The Imperative of a Peaceful Order

For 365 or 542 of the past thousand years, depending on how you define "China," foreign conquerors (Qiang, Jurchen, Mongols, and Manchus) governed much or all of it. For another 107 years (from the end of the first "Opium War" in 1842 to the founding of the PRC in 1949), European, American, and Japanese imperialists invaded China from the South and East China Seas. These foreign intruders humiliated both the Qing and the ROC. They posed what appeared to be an existential menace to the rule of China by Chinese themselves.

In the nineteenth century, the Qing state proved incapable of defending Chinese society against Western domination or maintaining domestic order. This set the stage for the death by violence of at least 50–60 million Chinese.[6] In the twentieth century, Chinese weakness reduced the national security policy of the ROC (1911–1949) to the adoption of postures calculated to recruit foreign patrons for resistance to China's warlords, Japanese invaders, and insurgent Communists. ROC policy was tactical and temporizing rather than outward-looking or strategic.

To defend his state's existence, Chiang Kai-shek found himself forced to balance his nationalism against the imperative of appeasing the European and American imperialist presences on Chinese soil. He had no power to project beyond the ROC's borders, and therefore no strategy for doing so. Instead, he focused on conserving his forces and exploiting China's continued cultural attractiveness to both overseas Chinese and China-connected foreigners. This, and the geopolitical importance of denying China strategically to the Japanese empire, enabled him to secure American military aid, subsidies, and political protection against both his foreign and domestic enemies. But his ROC performed satisfactorily against neither.

Defeated on the Chinese mainland, the ROC was ultimately forced to retreat to Taiwan, an island province of China it had just recovered from Japan. Chiang's regime was able to stand its ground in Taiwan only after the US Navy intervened in the Chinese civil war to prevent its final defeat by the then-Soviet-aligned PRC. (Behind its American shield, the ROC on Taiwan then began a long evolution that resulted in its becoming the first liberal democracy ever to flourish on Chinese soil.)

Memories of protracted Chinese impotence scar Chinese nationalism—now incarnated in the roughly 90 million members of its ruling Chinese Communist Party (CCP). The anarchic carnage of the "Cultural Revolution" (1966–1976) just consolidated an already well-developed Chinese obsession with the maintenance of a stable order on their periphery and domestic tranquility in their country. Almost without exception, Chinese believe that a strong state and a centralized political order are necessary both to restore China's wealth and international status and to defend the Chinese people against the persistent threat of foreign aggression.

The international state system established after World War II sought to protect the weak from the strong by subjecting both to rules and standards of conduct. Given their country's history, Chinese have had ample reason to favor such protections. Fostering a "peaceful international environment" on China's periphery that would allow it to concentrate on its domestic development has been a seminal objective of the PRC's grand strategy. Beijing has come to see peace on the PRC's borders as the essential prerequisite for the achievement of both prosperity and immunity from foreign aggression.

## Governance under the PRC

After time lost and much suffering due to the erratic and sometimes delusional policies of its founder and first leader, Mao Zedong, and amid a protracted US effort to destabilize and overthrow it, the People's Republic of China broadly conformed to the expectations Chinese culture has established for a Chinese state. The PRC:

- retained but (as a new state setting new standards) idiosyncratically simplified China's ideographic writing system and other aspects of its cultural identity;
- after a false start, merged Leninism with the Chinese tradition of examination-based meritocracy to create a modernized form of China's traditional, bureaucratic governance;
- after initially repudiating the traditional Chinese linkage between education, expertise, and prestige, reinstated it;
- oppressed China's religions before condescending to tolerate them;[7] and

- struggled with mixed and varying success to introduce rule by law as an alternative to bureaucratic interpretation of policy.

These evolutions echoed China's past, but the newly founded PRC broke with major elements of the Chinese heritage by imposing Soviet-style industrial feudalism and its own disastrous form of rural collectivization.

The PRC's approach to its foreign relations also differed from that of its predecessors. In the 1950s, under Soviet influence, the PRC embraced Moscow's views of the post–World War II international order. It also adopted norms of international law associated with the sovereign equality of states, a concept foreign to the Chinese tradition of statecraft. It did so in part because these norms were both an apparent rebuke and an antidote to China's recent experience of disgrace and domination at the hands of outside powers.

It soon appeared that the USSR wanted to subordinate the PRC to its ideological leadership. By the 1960s, the PRC had reason to fear a Soviet attempt to subjugate it militarily. Premodern Chinese regimes had insisted on international acceptance of an international hierarchy, with the Chinese state at its apex. Now the USSR seemed to have a similar view of how international affairs should be organized, but with itself at the top of the heap. The PRC rejected this.

## China Embraces the Westphalian Order

The PRC has its own distinctive personality, preferences, and modus operandi, all of which differ from those of its imperial predecessors. The tributary system, with its elaborate rituals aimed at giving China's rulers "face" and its thinly disguised potlatch-like state trading practices, has been replaced with a new Chinese code of propriety that stresses the inherent equality of states as independent political entities.

The "Five Principles of Peaceful Coexistence" (or "Panchsheel" and codified in a bilateral agreement between China and India in 1954) are a succinct summary of the precepts of the Westphalian order:

- mutual respect for each other's territorial integrity and sovereignty;
- mutual non-aggression;
- mutual non-interference in each other's internal affairs;
- equality and cooperation for mutual benefit; and
- peaceful coexistence.

They were formulated in the context of the Cold War, which began in Asia with the Korean War of 1950. They were, in part, a Chinese, Indian, and Indonesian answer to the perceived effort by the contending American and Soviet super-powers to subordinate smaller states and incorporate them into their competing spheres of influence. (In Asia, this process took the form of the US and Soviet conclusion of "alliances" that were in fact extensions by the superpowers of "pro-tectorate" or "client state" status[8] to the states of the region not in the other's sphere of influence.)

Among other things, the five principles represent a definitive repudiation of the pre-colonial, Sinocentric order in East Asia. (Many in the West have pre-ferred to interpret PRC behavior through the prism of the Sinocentric tributary systems established by the Yuan, Ming, and Qing. But this is profoundly mis-leading. It overlooks the many changes that have occurred in both China and in Asia as a whole.) The five principles are key guidelines of PRC foreign pol-icy, reliably predicting much of its behavior. The PRC accepts the Westphalian notion of states acting as nominal equals in their exclusive control of territories and their inhabitants. It does not espouse the premodern Asian notion of loyalty to a hierarchy of authority with China (or a duopoly—"G2"—of China and the United States) at its apex.

Instead, Beijing insists on the sovereign equality of all states as the key to assured national independence and self-determination in a world of ideological diversity and varying political and socioeconomic systems. This explains why the PRC goes to almost ludicrous lengths to honor visitors from small nations with symbolic and protocolary treatment equal to that it bestows on those from the largest and most powerful. Its stand on international law also rests on the centrality of sovereignty. Beijing has strongly opposed Western efforts to qualify the immunities inherent in sovereignty through proposals like "humanitarian intervention" or the "right to protect."

## Insecurity on the Borders and
## Sino-American Confrontation

Soon after the proclamation of the People's Republic on October 1, 1949, Kim Il-sung, the Soviet-installed founder and leader of the North Korean "Democratic People's Republic of Korea," persuaded a skeptical Stalin and reluctant Mao Zedong to back his attempt to unify Korea by force. On June 25, 1950, Kim sent his divisions into the US-aligned Republic of Korea. The United States viewed this as an effort by the USSR and PRC to use a Korean proxy to break out of con-tainment. Washington responded militarily—not just in Korea, but in the Taiwan Strait.

In Korea, US intervention menaced China's borders and threatened to destroy the buffer state in north Korea. This triggered counterattack by elements of the

Chinese People's Liberation Army. North and South Korean, US, and Chinese forces fought to a standstill.[9] Korea remained divided.

The deployment of the US Navy to the Taiwan Strait precluded an otherwise inevitable final PRC victory over the ROC on Taiwan in the Chinese civil war. This divided China and gave rise to the "Taiwan problem": the question of Taiwan's political relationship with the rest of China.

The face-offs in Korea and the Taiwan Strait cemented a twenty-year-long state of geopolitical hostility between the PRC and the United States. In short, despite the political bump-up its military performance gave to the PRC, the war sparked by Kim Il-sung's aggressive Korean nationalism was a strategic disaster not just for him and his country but for both the PRC and United States.

## Containment vs. Revolution

Throughout the 1950s and 1960s, the US policy of containment, though directed mainly at the USSR, also applied to the PRC. The PLA continued to put pressure on Taiwan and the US forces assisting in its defense,[10] while the United States patrolled the Chinese coasts and conducted covert operations in the PRC designed to destabilize and distract it.[11] To counter "containment," Beijing advanced a global strategy of revolutionary incitement and anti-Western destabilization with a focus on Southeast Asia. It declared that "countries want independence, nations want liberation, and people want revolution," called for the overthrow of the American-led international order, and condemned the multilateral organizations created after World War II at Bretton Woods. American diplomacy successfully excluded the PRC from participation in the United Nations and all other international forums. The United States worked hard to prevent recognition of the PRC by other nations.

The PRC supported communist insurgencies in Malaya and the Philippines as well as the communist participants in the independence struggles and civil wars in Indochina (Laos, Vietnam, and ultimately Cambodia as well). It cultivated the non-aligned movement, made common cause with post-colonial India and Indonesia against both Washington and Moscow, identified itself with the "Third World," and began a program of foreign aid in East Africa. The United States felt sufficiently threatened by these activities to sponsor the creation of the Southeast Asian Treaty Organization (SEATO), intensifying its embargo on trade with China in dollars. President Kennedy proposed the "Peace Corps" in part as a response to allegedly effective PRC grass roots influence-building in developing nations.

## The PRC as US Protectorate and Entente Partner

For two decades, the United States found both Chiang Kai-shek's ROC's pre-
tension that it was still the de jure government of China and Taiwan's de facto
separation from the rest of China useful in containing the PRC and frustrating
Soviet diplomacy. But in 1971–1972, America abandoned its use of Taiwan to
contain the PRC and turned to using the PRC to contain the Soviet Union.
The Shanghai Communiqué (issued in 1972 at the end of President Richard
Nixon's diplomatically extraordinary travel to the capital of a state the United
States did not recognize)[12] enabled geopolitical cooperation between the
United States and PRC. In it, both sides candidly stated their differences,[13]
before agreeing that, notwithstanding these, they could cooperate strategi-
cally. And so, to a limited extent, they did, even though the major utility of the
PRC to the United States was simply its continued existence as an indigestibly
independent, anti-Soviet state.

   Nearly seven years later, within the course of a few days in mid-December
1978, Deng Xiaoping both opened China to learning from America and the
West and cast off many of the ideological strictures that Soviet tutelage and
Mao's ascendancy had put in place.[14] The PRC set aside its policy of liber-
ating Taiwan by force and replaced it with a "fundamental policy of striving
for peaceful reunification." It abandoned its revolutionary rhetoric about a
new world order and began the process of integrating itself into the existing,
US-dominated international system. Instead of trying to transform the world
to conform with Marxism-Leninism-Mao Zedong thought, the PRC sought
to transform itself through eclectic borrowing of ideas and practices from
overseas Chinese and the West. The children of the PRC elite crowded into
America's universities.

## Dengist Grand Strategy

Grand strategies set long-term objectives and align policies with political, economic, informational, cultural, and military resources to support their implementation.[15] In combination, Deng's revised political, economic, and national
security policies constituted a new grand strategy for China's return to wealth
and power through domestic "reform and opening" to the capitalist world. The
strategy sought to ease China's restoration to wealth and power by concentrating single-mindedly on its economic development while avoiding antagonism,
controversy, or conflict with the United States and other great powers. To these
ends, under Deng, the PRC resolved to:

- establish and sustain a peaceful environment on China's borders and in the approaches to them;
- avoid forming alliances, making enemies, or taking sides in other countries' quarrels;
- keep a low political and military profile;
- cultivate friendship and trade with all nations regardless of their ideology; and
- Minimize friction with other countries by reacting to perceived slights and insults with restraint.

China has the longest land borders in the world—over 22,000 kilometers or nearly 14,000 miles—abutting fourteen countries, including several that have invaded it or been at war with it. The PRC's "four modernizations" nevertheless gave priority to agriculture, industry, and science and technology. National defense was last on the list. (PRC defense spending fell from 16 percent of the state budget in 1980 to about 8 percent in 1987.) But Deng believed that to focus on economic development, the PRC needed effective assurance of its security from attack by a hostile power. To this end, that is, to achieve long-term peace and security on its frontiers, Deng judged, the PRC had first to mitigate and, if possible, eliminate the threat of an apparent Soviet attempt at encirclement of it. He saw the Soviet alliance with Vietnam, whose control of Laos and Cambodia Moscow was then backing, as the *Schwerpunkt* (key link) in this threat.

In February 1979, having put the USSR off balance through his January 1 breakthrough in relations with Washington and subsequent triumphal visit to the United States, Deng launched a military campaign against Vietnam. His objective was to teach Vietnam that it could not afford to build an empire in Indochina in association with the PRC's Soviet enemy.

Years of war had equipped Vietnam with perhaps the world's most formidable infantry. The PLA's performance against it revealed serious weaknesses in its warfighting capabilities. The PRC's "lesson" to Vietnam proved far more militarily costly than Beijing had expected. But the Vietnamese got the point. Over time, they withdrew from Cambodia, loosened their control in Laos, and attenuated their alignment and cooperation with Moscow. A decade later in 1991 the Soviet collapse eliminated the threat of encirclement by it. This facilitated a wary Sino-Vietnamese rapprochement and mutual accommodation.

The USSR's December 24, 1979, occupation of Afghanistan galvanized a US-PRC entente (limited partnership for limited purposes) directed at actively countering the Soviet presence in that neighbor of both China and the USSR. Over the course of the 1980s, the United States bought billions of dollars of Chinese weapons for the Afghan *mujahideen*,[16] and hundreds of millions of dollars' worth of Chinese-manufactured, Soviet-designed equipment against which to train the US armed forces.[17] US assistance helped modernize PRC aircraft,[18] anti-tank weapons, torpedoes, artillery shell production, and counter-battery radar systems. The two countries cooperated in the collection of strategic and tactical intelligence on the Soviet military and its weaponry by establishing a network of jointly managed listening posts at key locations near the PRC's borders. The fruits of Sino-American entente played an essential role in the pressure on the USSR that ultimately ended the Cold War.

Beijing's entente with Washington was the exception to its aversion to foreign entanglements. It came to an end in 1989, with the fall of the Berlin Wall, which marked the end of the Soviet empire. This deprived Sino-American relations of their strategic rationale at precisely the moment that Chinese domestic unrest drained it of all psychological warmth.

## PRC Grand Strategy After 1989

A year after the PRC's June 1989 suppression of the student uprisings in Beijing and other cities had soured the West on China and emboldened his domestic critics, Deng memorialized his recommendations for PRC foreign policy in six phrases, consisting of twenty-four ideograms:

- 冷静观察—observe [trends and events] dispassionately;
- 站稳脚跟—stand firm;
- 身着警付—cope [with challenges] calmly and deliberately;
- 韬光养晦—avoid the limelight, cultivate obscurity;
- 善于守拙—focus on remaining humble; and
- 决不当头—in no way take the lead.

These six phrases have usually been translated (not very accurately) as "observe calmly; secure our position; cope with affairs calmly; hide our capacities and bide our time; be good at maintaining a low profile, and never claim leadership." Later, Deng added the phrase 有所作为, translated as "and make some contributions" or "accomplish some things" to make it clear that caution and a low profile should not preclude making gains where the PRC could.

Some have made much of the sinister deception they see as implicit in the fourth of Deng's phrases, 韬光养晦 [taoguang yanghui], which has usually been translated into English as "hide our capacities and bide our time." But in Chinese, this phrase (an idiom (成语)] referring to an able official in retirement) has no implication at all of "biding time until one can act"; quite the opposite. It is more accurately translated as above ("avoid the limelight, cultivate obscurity") or as "hide one's light and live in seclusion."[19]

## Toward a More Peaceful Periphery

Beijing reacted to dissolution of the Soviet Union itself in accordance with Deng's guidelines. It immediately mounted an effort to normalize relations with its largest and historically most predatory neighbor, the Russian Federation, as well as with the Soviet Union's suddenly independent, former Central Asian satrapies. Beijing's aim was to establish peace on its western borders but, even more, to ensure that when Russia inevitably again rose in power, the PRC would have a friendly relationship with it.

The PRC did not limit its push for a peaceful international environment to Russia. Over the course of a decade, the PRC negotiated border settlements with Laos (1992), the Russian Federation (1994), Kazakhstan (1994–1995), Kyrgyzstan (1996), and Tajikistan (1999, but not ratified by the Tajiks until 2011). Beijing and Hanoi settled their land borders (1999) and agreed on a division of exclusive economic zones (EEZs) in the Gulf of Tonkin (2000). They then quietly began bilateral negotiations on their respective claims in the South China Sea. These talks were unhinged by Secretary of State Hillary Clinton's unexpected insertion of the United States into the dispute during a July 2010 Asian security forum in Hanoi. (After a long hiatus, bilateral Sino-Vietnamese talks have recently resumed.)

## Unsettled Frontiers

Despite the PRC's demonstrated willingness to negotiate border settlements with its neighbors, some remain unresolved. Primary among these is the border with India. In 1996, the PRC and India agreed to resolve their border dispute, initiate confidence-building measures, and demarcate the line of actual control. (India contests China's borders with Bhutan, Myanmar, Nepal, and Pakistan as well as its own.) The two sides had discussed their border intermittently since the 1950s, when PRC premier Zhou Enlai first offered to swap PRC claims in one sector of the Tibet border with those of India in another. Zhou's offer was rebuffed by Indian prime minister Jawaharlal Nehru. In 1962, the PRC and India fought a brief border war in which the PLA advanced well beyond the line of control and then voluntarily withdrew to it. The line of control remains the scene of occasional military confrontations.

The PRC's borders with north Korea, Mongolia, and Myanmar are undisputed but those with its maritime neighbors have yet to be defined. The PRC disputes sovereignty with Japan over the Senkaku Archipelago or Diaoyu Islands, which it claims are part of Taiwan. Inasmuch as the relationship of Taiwan to the rest of China itself remains in question, Beijing is unable to negotiate a resolution of this dispute with Tokyo. It has sought indefinitely to defer consideration of the issue by the two sides. Since 2010, however, the tacit understanding that neither side would make an issue of the dispute has given way to paramilitary confrontation between the two nations' coast guards. The United States has pointedly backed Japan on the issue.

Many claimants dispute sovereignty over the islets, rocks, reefs, and adjoining seabed resources of the South China Sea (both Beijing and Taipei on behalf of "China," as well as Hanoi, Kuala Lumpur, and Manila). Taipei has held one islet in the Spratly Islands for "China" since the Japanese surrendered it in 1945. The PRC has occupied most of the Paracel (西沙) Islands since 1949 and all of it since 1974.

In the 1970s and 1980s, the non-Chinese claimants seized and garrisoned most of the land features in the Spratly Islands. (Malaysia acquired five outposts, the Philippines nine, and Vietnam forty-eight.) The PRC did not react until the late 1980s, when it took possession of seven rocks and reefs. After 2010, this excited increasingly strident opposition from the United States. In 2014, the PRC transformed its holdings into artificial islands and garrisoned them. The US Navy stepped up "freedom of navigation operations" to challenge this. There is no diplomatic process in place to mitigate the escalating confrontation between the United States and PLA navies there, with each side objecting to how the other exercises its presence.

A naval confrontation with the United States over Taiwan in 1995 and 1996,[20] and an apparent move by Taiwan toward permanent separation from China in 1999,[21] had persuaded the PRC that it needed to acquire the military capability to subdue Taiwan against US military opposition. It had not previously had such a program. China's leaders set a target of 2008 for achieving this capability, thus both raising the priority assigned to military modernization programs and making preparation for Taiwan contingencies involving the US armed forces their core purpose. (At the same time, Chinese leaders authorized a major expansion in united front work directed at lessening Taiwanese opposition to peaceful reunification with the China mainland.)

## PRC Reactions to Close Encounters with the US Military

## and to Developments in Taiwan

True to its grand strategy of avoiding confrontation, the PRC did not change course in response to two incidents that would have justified military retaliation by it against the United States.

- On May 7, 1999, a US Air Force B-2 bomber struck the PRC embassy in Belgrade with precision-guided munitions, killing three Chinese and wounding twenty. President Clinton apologized, and US officials explained that the bombing was due to a map error. No one in China believed (or believes) that the bombing was accidental.

- On April 1, 2001, a US Navy spy plane and a PLA Air Force interceptor collided off Hainan Island, killing the pilot of the Chinese aircraft and forcing the American plane into a surprise landing at a PRC airbase on the island. Each side attributed the accident to reckless flying by the other.

Meanwhile, Beijing had come to see Taipei rather than Washington as the key to resolving the issue of Taiwan's relationship with the PRC. (It viewed the United States as playing a spoiler role in this through continuing arms sales and salami-slicing moves toward greater "officiality" in its relations with Taipei.) The PLA met its 2008 deadline for building a capability to keep the United States at bay if it finds it necessary to use force to compel Taiwan's reunification with it. Over the first two decades of the twenty-first century, Taiwan's politics first shifted toward support for independence, then toward cross-Strait rapprochement, before shifting back again. Tensions waxed and waned as the PLA demonstrated its new capabilities. By 2018, though intermittently challenged by the United States, the PRC had achieved effective military dominance of the Taiwan area.

# PRC Disillusionment with America and Pride in Its Own Achievements

For three decades after the inception of "reform and opening" in 1978, the PRC was an avid student and emulator of American institutions and practices. In many respects, Chinese saw America as the primary model for the modernization of their financial system, including banking, insurance, stock markets, and "wealth management." American influence slowly became apparent in almost all aspects of Chinese daily life, even the Chinese military establishment. (In 1997, just in time for the debut of its Hong Kong garrison, the PLA donned spiffy American-style uniforms.)[22] But the financial crisis of 2008–2010, for which American financial elites were responsible and in which they performed poorly compared to their Chinese counterparts, convinced many Chinese that they had little or nothing more useful to learn from the United States. For a time, as Chinese faith in the American model ebbed, their self-confidence verged on hubris.[23]

As the second decade of the twenty-first century nears a close, China's economy has become the second largest or, by some measures, the largest in the world. Its defense spending has remained somewhat less than 2 percent of GDP—leaving lots of room for a surge, if necessary—but, by 2018, the PRC defense budget had risen to $175 billion (from $14.6 billion in 2000). China's scientific, technological, engineering, and mathematical (STEM) workforce is now by far the largest in the world, dwarfing that of other countries.[24] The PLA has acquired a credible capacity to defend itself against the world's most modern and competent armed forces, including those of the United States. It is also increasingly engaged internationally, contributing significant funds and forces to UN peacekeeping operations.[25]

Under the PRC, China has displaced America from many of the first-place global rankings it has held for over a century. China is now the world's largest manufacturer (accounting for 25 percent or more of global goods production) and its mightiest trading economy. The Chinese economy generates 30 percent of global growth. As the United States has lost enthusiasm for and declined to reform or reinvest in the international financial institutions it created at Bretton Woods, the PRC has stepped forward to meet unmet needs by organizing new financial institutions to supplement, complement, and cooperate with legacy organizations. These are independent of the United States and not subject to its control. The PRC has also stepped cautiously into the vacuum left by the US withdrawal from the effort to battle global climate change.

## American Estrangement from the PRC

The increasing relevance of China to issues of international governance that the United States once commanded discomfits Americans, who have seized on both the perceived Chinese eclipse of American influence abroad and objectionable Chinese business practices as explanations for their own discontents. Most Americans reject the widespread view abroad that the causes of the current American malaise are primarily homegrown and cannot be laid at the feet of China or other foreigners.

Like the United States in the nineteenth century and Japan in the twentieth, the PRC has used both fair means and foul to acquire the intellectual property of foreign countries and companies and apply it to the modernization of its industrial base. China's growing weight in the global economy and the scale of its efforts to acquire technology clandestinely through cyber operations have made such technology acquisition an increasing irritant in US-China relations. Many Chinese technological advances are now homegrown rather than imported from abroad. But most Americans erroneously attribute the PRC's progress almost entirely to the theft of US-originated technology.

Meanwhile, the PRC's emergence as a major military power (with the world's second largest defense budget) has alarmed the US armed forces. Over the seven decades since World War II, especially after the end of the Cold War, the United States had no credible military competitor on the Eurasian landmass. Now China has returned to a position of power in its own region and, increasingly, beyond it. Americans fear that their "allies"[26] will doubt the US ability to protect them from intimidation by China.

In a classic example of a "security dilemma," the US military-industrial-congressional establishment has interpreted PRC efforts to develop credible defenses against foreign attacks of the kind China experienced in recent centuries as heralding aggressive intent and requiring a US response in kind. PRC defense modernization has become the main driver of increases in the already enormous US defense budget and American efforts to develop new classes of weaponry. Similarly, US military operations on the PRC periphery are now the main drivers of changes in PLA force structure and weaponry.

As the PRC economy grew and its armed forces became more capable, the premises on which the grand strategy advocated by Deng Xiaoping had rested became untenable. China's rise has provoked an obsessively hostile American response that is unlikely to be reversed anytime soon. The PRC is no longer just an observer of trends and events internationally. It is both an active participant in them or their object. China can no longer avoid the limelight. It has become the focus of attention from both its neighbors and the United States. Others look to the PRC to fill the leadership vacuum left by the current, surly US retreat from active engagement in world affairs. Beijing has slowly begun to do so.

In East Asia, the clear trend has been toward an increasingly Sinocentric economic order. China is where the world's supply chains converge. Over the course of the Obama administration (2009–2017), American disillusionment with the PRC and suspicion of it steadily increased. But US efforts to demonstrate America's continuing primacy in the Indo-Pacific region through a largely rhetorical military "pivot to Asia" and the formation of a US-led "Trans-Pacific Partnership" (TPP) failed to gain traction. Few presidential candidates in the 2016 elections mentioned the "pivot." All opposed TPP while expressing concern about Chinese economic rivalry with the United States. One of incoming president Donald Trump's first actions was to withdraw the United States from TPP.

## Toward a Revised PRC Grand Strategy

By 2013, rising distrust in Sino-American relations as well as the sense that the PRC's growth in wealth and power now entitle it to deal with the United States as an equal led General-Secretary Xi Jinping to propose that the United States and PRC craft a "new type of great power relationship" (新型大国关系). As Xi explained it, the benefit of the concept would be the moderation of rivalry between the two as well as between the PRC and other great powers. He called for the abandonment of any zero-sum calculus in Sino-American relations and advocated its replacement with dialogue based on mutual respect by each party for the other's core national interests.

Xi's proposal was entirely consistent with the world order Americans had conceived and institutionalized in the United Nations after World War II. It was an offer to live with the post–World War II American presence in Asia *if this was not directed against China.* But his initiative was received cynically in post–Cold War Washington, where a majority saw it as a Chinese effort to elevate the PRC to equal status with the United States and thereby undermine US primacy in both the Indo-Pacific and globally. Rather than seeing the very vagueness of the proposal as an opportunity to make something of it, the United States brushed it aside. Washington thereby confirmed Chinese suspicions that the purpose of the US presence in Asia was to oppose the rise of China rather than to facilitate its accommodation by other Asian countries.

The "new type of great power relations" motif ended up as the stated basis of Sino-Russian relations. In part as a result of US strategic hostility, military pressure, and economic warfare on both, relations between these two Eurasian giants are now the best they have ever been.

## Sino-American Rivalry Becomes Adversarial Antagonism

Once the Trump administration took office in 2017, the United States continued and rapidly completed a decade-long transition in US-China relations from cooperative transactionalism through rivalry to adversarial antagonism, positioning itself as the PRC's global opponent:

- geopolitically (with special reference to Africa and Latin America as well as to China's growing partnership with Russia and presumed ambition to organize a new, non-American-led world order);
- diplomatically (through an effort to exclude the PRC from a significant role in managing affairs in its region, on the Eurasian landmass and adjacent areas through the Belt and Road Initiative, or in the global commons);
- economically (through bilateral economic warfare, including sanctions, investment restrictions, tariffs and import quotas, intervention to halt the legal transfer of intellectual property to Chinese licensees, and efforts to bar Chinese high-tech companies from penetrating markets abroad traditionally dominated by American or US-friendly multinational companies);

- informationally and culturally (through attacks on PRC foreign relations with third countries and alleged PRC influence operations in both the United States and abroad);
- militarily (through naval and intelligence collection operations in the PRC's maritime near abroad and efforts to complicate PRC power projection from its coastlines or offshore island bastions); and
- competitively, in other militarily and economically relevant strategic domains like cyber and outer space.

American hostility to the continuing rise of China under the PRC has invalidated Beijing's previous accommodationist grand strategy. In 2019, the PRC confronts an unpalatable choice between: (1) capitulation to Washington's demands that it abandon its heretofore successful approach to assuring Chinese prosperity and security; (2) attempting, over US opposition, to preserve and even strengthen the institutions and practices of the American-created order that have facilitated its prosperity and security; or (3) responding forcefully and in kind to the perceived American attempt to sabotage China's growing wealth and power and to change its regime.

Forty years ago, the PRC's adoption of "reform and opening" under Deng Xiaoping's guidelines transformed global geopolitics and economics. The PRC's adjustment of its grand strategy to cope with the American return to pre-1970s strategic antagonism promises to do the same. Beijing has signaled a willingness to accommodate some US demands—but made it clear that it will not capitulate to those requiring fundamental changes in China's political economy. The US presence in Asia is now explicitly directed at countering the PRC and undermining its economic growth, military security, and prospects for consolidating its sovereignty and territorial integrity, especially by reuniting Taiwan with the mainland, whether peacefully or by force.

## Alternative Strategic Responses to US Hostility by the PRC

Even if bilateral economic tensions can be cooled by diplomatic negotiation, Beijing must still adjust its policies to deal with an assertively antagonistic United States. China does not need to match US global capabilities, still less US global responsibilities. All it needs to do is defend itself against attack.

This means that the PRC will seek to dilute and, in some areas, eliminate reliance on US high-tech products and commodities. It may recognize that elements of its current business practices irritate key trading partners and need adjustment. But it faces a choice between a cautious effort to counter or displace American regional and global leadership or an aggressive campaign to reduce US regional and global influence and hamstring American power. There are Chinese advocates of both alternatives.

In this context, a *relatively restrained* PRC response to the threats it now faces from the United States could conceivably include policies designed to:

- open Chinese financial markets, but only to non-American banks, brokerages, and insurance companies;
- conclude bilateral investment treaties to promote cross-investment, but only with countries other than the United States;
- work with other nations offended by US unilateral sanctions to accelerate the development of a banking system disconnected from the United States that can end global dollar supremacy;
- cooperate with the EU, Japan, and others to reform and reinforce the WTO, strengthen other multilateral institutions, and form new institutions to supplement those earlier created and dominated by the United States.

Alternatively, if Beijing wished to make life tough(er) for Washington, it could adopt any number of counteractions, for example:

- adopt a policy of aiding any country subject to unilateral US sanctions or ostracism—actively seeking to exploit any vacuum the US ostracism creates, not just moving into it;
- cooperate with others to undercut US efforts to pressure Cuba, Iran, North Korea, Venezuela, etc.;
- work with other autocracies to set standards for cyberspace that support sovereign rather than multilateral control of cyberspace and the use of artificial intelligence and other applications of digital technology to maintain domestic tranquility by controlling political expression and maximizing immunity to cyberattack;
- mount a worldwide campaign against US unilateralism, unreliability, and interference in other countries' politics, including support for regime change;
- in cooperation with Russia, Iran, north Korea, and other countries subject to US threats, encourage movements in nations allied or aligned with the United States to protest any further US military presence or use of facilities on their territory;
- support South-North unification and post-unification strategic neutrality in Korea;
- intensify efforts to strip Taiwan of its remaining diplomatic recognition or constrict its semi-official representation abroad;
- seek amendments to the UN Convention on the Law of the Sea (which the United States has not ratified) to enact the PRC (and probable majority

international) view on baseline-drawing to delimit sovereignty and the right to restrict naval activities near coastlines; and

- step up the campaign to convince Taiwan that the United States is unreliable, and that time is running out for it, in the absence of some form of reunification with the rest of China.

An even *more aggressive Chinese response* to the United States might add policies that:

- directly or indirectly sanction US banks and companies in retaliation for US unilateral sanctions;
- aggressively sue the United States in the WTO and call it out in the United Nations;
- seek to persuade members of the Paris Climate Accords to place tariffs on imports from non-members or to tax carbon imports from countries that have not themselves taxed them;
- join trade liberalization and tariff reduction arrangements, like the Japanese-led version of TPP, that the United States has not joined or from which it has withdrawn;
- adopt export controls banning the export of China's increasingly sophisticated technology to the United States;
- criminalize foreign IPR theft from China;
- modify the PRC's "no-first-use" nuclear doctrine to define limited circumstances in which Beijing might order a first strike;
- expand the PRC's nuclear arsenal and step up construction and deployment of submarines and long-range bombers that can hold the continental United States at risk;
- reciprocally exclude the United States from participation in its space program, while using it to secure relations with others;
- join North Korea in offering a peace treaty to South Korea that does not include the United States and report this to the United Nations along with a demand for the dissolution of the "United Nations Command" in Korea;[27]
- conclude a multiparty agreement on the South China Sea that provides that every claimant can keep what it already has without regard to how it acquired it, pending a negotiated settlement of disputes over sovereignty;
- mine the approaches to PRC holdings in the South China Sea's Paracel and Spratly Islands to inhibit any approach to them by the US Navy inconsistent with the PRC interpretation of international law;
- renounce its commitment to follow the Missile Technology Control Regime (MTCR) and export missiles capable of striking and deterring the

United States to anti-American regimes, including those in the Western
Hemisphere;

- establish a military presence, including naval bases, in Latin America and
  northwest Africa to support of missile-launching submarines targeting the
  United States;
- develop joint security operations and exercises aimed at securing strategic
  lines of communication with Japan, South Korea, Indonesia, and others; and
- step up military pressure on Taiwan in preparation for making it "an offer it
  can't refuse" through an escalating program of military exercises designed to
  demonstrate a capacity to devastate the island regardless of any US response.

In other words, China now has the capacity to inflict serious pain on the United
States and its interests, should it so choose. The advantages the PRC will bring
to any contest with the United States are more formidable than most Americans
realize:

- China's manufacturing capacity is over 50 percent larger than that of the
  United States.
- Its STEM workforce is at least eight times larger than that of the United States
  and growing much faster.
- Its defense expenditures are modest in relation to its national budget and
  GDP and could easily be doubled or even tripled.
- The PLA is on the defensive, with short lines of communication to its front
  lines, while the US armed forces must project power and sustain operations
  at a great distance from their homeland.
- Beijing has no clear commitments to any foreign "ally" and is free to act with-
  out regard to the short-term impact of doing so on third countries.
- Lacking third country "allies," there are none that can easily embroil China
  in war with America, whereas the opposite is not true for the United States
  vis-à-vis China.
- China is the major trading partner of almost every country on Earth.
- China is seen as the country of the future and no country wants to choose
  between it and the United States.
- The PRC's internal security and counterintelligence systems are far less pen-
  etrable than those of the United States.

The outcome of a protracted confrontation between the PRC and the United
States is far from certain. The outbreak of such a confrontation is a world-altering
event that will determine the course of the twenty-first century and the shape of
the world to come.

# Conclusion

As it celebrates the seventieth anniversary of its founding in 1949, the PRC has not accomplished the essential tasks of previous newly established Chinese states—restoring territorial integrity and establishing agreed borders for China. These tasks continue to define the PRC's "core interests" and will remain its central objectives. But the rise of Chinese wealth, power, and technological competence once again faces active American opposition. Despite not having sought global or regional leadership, the PRC has little choice but to seek it. It needs a reordering of regional and global geopolitics and institutions to counter US adversarial antagonism.

China has risen peacefully—so far—by practicing Dengist passivity and restraint. It can no longer expect to be able to do so. The PRC has institutionalized an entente with the Russian Federation that augments its ability to counter US efforts to dominate global and regional affairs. China's Belt and Road Initiative promises to expand its economic influence in a wide swath of the Eurasian landmass and possibly throughout the entire Eastern Hemisphere. The United States is the declared adversary of both these elements of Chinese grand strategy.

China is now fully integrated into the American-sponsored globalized order. In the context of American hostility, the US retreat from that order and alienation of its international partners give the PRC a strong incentive to expand and reshape world affairs in ways that defend and advance Chinese interests. To do this, the PRC must make common cause with a substantial majority of the world's nations, including great and medium-ranked powers in Europe, Latin America, and Africa. Most of these countries have long been aligned with the United States. To enlist their support, China must not just court them but modernize its diplomacy to acquire the ability to manage coalitions of the like-minded. Such diplomacy demands a level of empathy for foreign interests that has not been much in evidence in the PRC's conduct of foreign affairs to date.

The challenges before Chinese grand strategy are clear. The ability of the PRC to meet them is not.

# Notes

1. The traditional Chinese agricultural economy is not suited to places in which dams, terracing, and other feats of engineering cannot recreate conditions suitable for intensive agriculture. As in the Middle East, geographic as well as cultural factors thus divide those who live in villages and depend on farming from nomadic herdsmen. The Chinese have always been vulnerable to invasions and pillaging by warriors from the mountainous, arid, and forest zones

that surround them. This vulnerability has forced them into a traditionally defensive posture focused on inner Asia.

2. Slightly longer than the thirteen years of Alexander the Great's empire, 336–323 BCE.

3. China has, however, often been divided between competing sovereignties.

4. Each dynasty can be thought of as a constitutional order. Traditional Chinese historiography predicts that such orders have a longevity of about 225–275 years, after which they either reconstitute themselves, collapse, and disappear, or are overthrown by invaders. Usually such invaders have been semi-Sinicized. The Mongols were established as Chinese-style dynasties in north China before they took the whole country. The Manchu court in Shenyang was a copy of the Ming court in Beijing. From the Chinese perspective, the semi-Sinicized Japanese, who attempted to conquer China in the mid-twentieth century, fit the same distressing pattern.

5. When the author first encountered officials of the PRC in Beijing in 1972, he was stunned to discover that they did not think of the state for which they worked as having anything very much in common or representing continuity with "China." They made it clear that they saw the PRC as a new order that had decisively broken with China's past.

6. The Taiping and Nian rebellions took 20–30 million lives. The Tongzhi Hui revolt resulted in the death of 8–12 million. About 45,000 died in the first Sino-Japanese War. About 40,000 Chinese were killed in the foreign response to the Boxer rebellion. Japan's invasion of China (1931–1945) is estimated to have resulted in about 20–25 million deaths. 8–11 million died in the Chinese civil war (1945–1949).

7. In 2018, the PRC reverted to an oppressive campaign to "Sinicize" minorities and religions of foreign origin like Islam.

8. An "alliance" embodies broad mutual commitments by the parties to aid each other in time of need. An "entente" is a limited commitment by the parties for limited purposes and some-times a limited time. A "protectorate" is a one-sided commitment by a stronger to a weaker state to ensure its continued independence and territorial integrity because these are of stra-tegic importance to the protector, not because the protected party has undertaken any recip-rocal commitment. A "client state" relationship is an exchange of benefits between a superior and an inferior strategic partner. A "transactional" relationship rests on specific bargains in which each side trades something for what it gets from the other on a basis of equality.

   By way of illustration, At the outset of their relationship, the USSR and PRC were allies. North Korea was their supposedly joint protectorate. As their sense of common interests decayed, they became entente partners against the United States. Their relationship then passed through phases of transactionalism and rivalry before becoming adversarial. The United States has had only protectorates and client states in Asia. The ROC was a US protec-torate during World War II and Japan became one after its defeat. South Vietnam, Cambodia, South Korea, and Taiwan were (and in the case of Korea and Taiwan remain) protectorates. The Philippines and Thailand were client states. Over the past eighty years, China has been a protectorate, an enemy, again a protectorate, an entente partner, a transactional partner, a rival, and now an adversarial antagonist.

9. Operating as the "Chinese People's Volunteer Army."

10. This was reflected in several "offshore island crises" in the Dachen Archipelago (1854–1955); Jinmen and Mazu (Quemoy and Matsu) (1955); Jinmen and Mazu (1958).

11. These operations included fomenting a revolt in Tibet and escorting the Dalai Lama in 1959 to pre-prepared political asylum in India (where he has remained in exile). The PRC retali-ated by offering (far less effective) symbolic encouragement to Puerto Rican independence advocates, the American Indian Movement, and other radical dissident groups in the United States.

12. Text at: https://history.state.gov/historicaldocuments/frus1969-76v17/d203.

13. The purpose of doing so was to reassure each side's diplomatic partners that neither the Untied States nor the PRC was selling out their interests.

14. Sino-American "normalization" was announced in Beijing on December 16, 1978. On December 18, Deng opened the 3rd Plenum of the 11th Chinese Communist Party Central Committee, at which he proclaimed policies of "reform and opening."

15. For other studies of China's grand strategy see: Michael D. Swaine and Ashley J. Tellis, *Interpreting China's Grand Strategy: Past Present, and Future* (Santa Monica, CA: Rand

Corporation, 2000); Avery Goldstein, *Rising to the Challenge: China's Grand Strategy and International Security* (Stanford, CA: Stanford University Press, 2005); Ye Zicheng, *Inside China's Grand Strategy: The Perspective from the People's Republic* (Lexington: University of Kentucky Press, 2010); Henry Kissinger, *On China* (New York: Penguin Press, 2011); Michael Pillsbury, *The Hundred Year Marathon: China's Secret Strategy to Replace America as the Global Superpower* (New York: St. Martin's Griffin, 2016); Sulmaan Wasif Kahn, *Haunted by Chaos: China's Grand Strategy from Mao Zedong to Xi Jinping* (Cambridge, MA: Harvard University Press, 2018); and Wang Jisi, "China's Search for a Grand Strategy: A Rising Power Finds Its Way," *Foreign Affairs* 90, no. 2 (March/April 2011): 68–70.

16. Bruce Reidel, *What We Won: America's Secret War in Afghanistan, 1979–1989* (Washington, DC: Brookings Institution Press, 2014).

17. https://acesflyinghigh.wordpress.com/2015/02/25/usaf-aggressor-squadrons/. See also the description of the overall "Constant Peg" program at: https://www.globalsecurity.org/military/systems/aircraft/constant-peg.htm.

18. Though extrapolated from a Soviet design, the J-8 was the first indigenously designed Chinese high-speed, high-altitude aircraft. The USAF program devoted to modernizing it was called "Peace Pearl." The "J" in "J-8" is from the Chinese word "Jian" (歼), which means "annihilate." The English equivalent of "F" for fighter/interceptor and the J-8 is sometimes referred to as the F-8.

19. 韬光养晦is a fixed four-character phrase (成语) from a poem by Kong Rong (孔融) (153–208 CE). Chinese dictionaries offer "韬晦隐居" ("to hide one's light and live in seclusion") as a synonym. This was Kong's advice to a minister dismissed by the emperor: to withdraw from view and refrain from agitating for reinstatement in power. Ironically, Kong Rong was executed by Cao Cao for violating his own advice. Contemporary Sinophobes' transformation of Kong's advice to retire from the fray into alleged evidence of a diabolical scheme to regain power is a final irony.

20. For an account of this crisis, see "Preventing War in the Taiwan Strait," *Foreign Affairs* 77, no. 4 (1998).

21. Taiwan's leader, Lee Teng-hui, proclaimed his 两国论 ("two state doctrine") on the Deutsche Welle on July 9, 1999, in effect declaring Taiwan independence without using the word.

22. The PLA has since adopted many American-originated practices, including the presentation of coins to recognize superior service or to commemorate visits to military units.

23. But Chinese parents continued to seek to send their children to American universities and the PLA continued to look to the US armed forces as embodying the professionalism they aspired to emulate.

24. As of 2016, the PRC had 4.7 million STEM workers; the United States had 568,000.

25. The PRC is the second largest funder of peacekeeping operations (after the United States and ahead of Japan) and has committed to provide up to 8,000 troops to them.

26. In reality, protectorates and client states, none of which have reciprocal obligations to protect the United States from its enemies.

27. Technically, the United States was never at war with North Korea; the United Nations was. The United Nations, not the United States, joined China and North Korea in signing the Korean Armistice Agreement (1950).

# SECTION III

# DOMESTIC SOURCES

# 4

# Nationalism, Social Influences, and Chinese Foreign Policy

PETER GRIES[*]

> Although domestic aid is needed, foreign aid is important as well . . . it projects a positive national image, and international influence. (Weibo user, May 2017)[1]

> The government should stop wasting money on foreign countries! They will turn their back on China once aid is delivered. The Chinese government should focus on those who really need help: [Chinese] children in remote areas who cannot afford food and clothes! (Weibo user, May 2017)[2]

The "One Belt, One Road" Initiative (OBOR; 一带一路) is Chinese president Xi Jinping's signature foreign policy initiative. Closely associated with Xi's promised "China Dream" (中国梦) of national rejuvenation, the Chinese Communist Party (CCP) promotes OBOR aggressively both home and abroad.

As the epigraphs above reveal, however, the Chinese people are divided over the international megaproject. "Linking the world together in a positive way is a great idea," a Zhihu (a popular Chinese version of Quora) blogger wrote in 2017, "unlike how America gains allies through war." Not all agree, however. "It's too risky," another Zhihu user wrote. Terrorists will disrupt Chinese infrastructure projects, and "America will try to disrupt it as well."[3]

Do these Chinese bloggers and their debates matter for China's foreign policy? Many mainstream international relations theorists would argue that they do *not*. For structural realists and neoliberal institutionalists, domestic society and politics do not matter: it is the system-level relations among nations, such as the balance of power, that drive foreign policy.[4] Other IR theorists counter, however, that what occurs within states *does* shape international affairs. Democratic and capitalist peace theorists contend that the nature of their domestic political and

Peter Gries, *Nationalism, Social Influences, and Chinese Foreign Policy* In: *China and the World.* Edited by: David Shambaugh, Oxford University Press (2020). © Oxford University Press
DOI: 10.1093/oso/9780190062316.003.0004

economic systems powerfully shapes the prospects for war and peace between nations.[5]

In the next chapter, Suisheng Zhao examines how China's political elite makes foreign policy. He rightly notes that although foreign policy expertise has grown dramatically in China, Xi has consolidated too much decision-making authority into his own hands. This increases the odds of miscalculation and conflict.

Where Zhao's chapter examines the Chinese party-state top-down, this chapter looks from the bottom-up, interrogating the broader social context within which Chinese foreign policy is made. Its overarching argument will be that *social influences matter*: because Xi and the CCP stake their legitimacy in large part based on the claim that they are "making China great again," social actors in China can and do make nationalist counterclaims about how China's foreign policy should be conducted—and often press for tougher foreign policies. The CCP pays close attention to social influences on Chinese foreign policy—and so should we. The chapter will also explore: (1) *what* different groups of Chinese people feel and think about the world; (2) the *origins* of their worldviews in state socialization about China's past encounters with the world; and (3) the foreign policy *consequences* of nationalism and other social influences.

Mainland Chinese are socialized into a social Darwinian view of the world as both hierarchical and competitive. There are three major ways socially appropriate worldviews are learned. First, the CCP's revival of Confucianism in China today promotes a Sinocentric view of China's past encounters with the world, with China at the top of a hierarchical "All under Heaven" (天下). Second, as Odd Arne Westad's chapter in this volume also stresses, enduring party-state and popular narratives about the more recent "Century of Humiliation" (百年国耻) promote resentment toward Japan and the West: China was unfairly knocked off its rightful place at the top of international affairs in the mid-nineteenth century, and will retake it. Third and finally, for forty years now, China under Reform has been a place of ruthless capitalist competition, and the world outside is depicted as little different: it's us or them, and only the toughest and fittest survive. Whether Chinese or foreign, few can be trusted.

Two responses to this perceived global jungle predominate: nationalist and cosmopolitan. The *nationalist* response goes beyond the love of China (*patriotism*) to assert China's *superiority over other nations*. The cosmopolitan or more worldly response takes two forms: a rejection of parochialism in favor of universalism, and identifying with a modern West rather than a backwards China. The latter pro-Western cosmopolitanism appears to predominate, and shares with the nationalist response a social Darwinian view of the world. It inverts the hierarchy, however, placing the West at the top. Such cosmopolitanism admires and consumes America, Europe, and their sociocultural products.

China's rise and globalization have led to greater direct and indirect contacts between China and the world, as young Chinese travel more and are more engaged with global popular culture. But the effect of increasing international contacts on Chinese foreign policy is contingent: globalization can foster either inclusionary *or* exclusionary reactions to the foreign—an embrace of cosmopolitanism *or* nationalism.[6] A perceived Western insult to China's dignity can instantaneously transform cosmopolitan young Chinese in Paris or Shanghai into nationalists. We thus need to be cautious about reifying the views of distinct social groups, as their identities and attitudes can vary dramatically from moment to moment.

Although complex, these international attitudes vary in systematic ways that can be studied. Not all Chinese are the same, and different groups can exhibit different attitudes. The weight of the limited evidence to be reviewed in this chapter suggests that, on average, younger, southern, and more urban Chinese tend to be more pro-Western than older, northern, and more rural Chinese, who tend to be more nationalistic. But CCP socialization powerfully constrains how all Mainland Chinese view the world.

The chapter will also suggest—but not prove—that the Chinese public shapes Chinese foreign policy. The relationship between the party-state and society is reciprocal. The CCP plays a critical but distal role, through its control of the education, media, and entertainment industries, in socializing Mainland Chinese into a social Darwinian view of a world—especially the West—that is hostile toward China. But the Chinese people can have a proximal impact on Chinese foreign policy—especially when nationalist opinion and street demonstrations are widespread, and demand tougher foreign policies. When it comes to nationalist foreign policy issues, from Japan to Taiwan, the Chinese society matters—a lot.

The chapter begins by arguing that social influences matter: the CCP has inextricably linked itself, society, and foreign policy by staking its domestic right to rule upon its foreign policy performance. The chapter then turns to the thorny empirical question of *what* we know about Chinese feelings and attitudes toward different parts of the world, from China's Asian neighbors, to the admired *and* resented Euro-American First World, to Russia, and the dark and backwards Third World of Africa and Latin America. It then turns to the causes/drivers (*why?*) of these worldviews, arguing that both demographics (e.g., age and location) and individual predispositions (e.g., nationalism and cosmopolitanism) matter, but that political and peer socialization has a powerful constraining effect on the international attitudes of the Chinese people. Specifically, it explores: (1) the revival of the traditional Confucian notion of "All under Heaven"; (2) the enduring narrative of the "Century of Humiliation"; and (3) how life in China under Reform powerfully shapes Chinese worldviews today. The chapter then turns to the consequences of Chinese worldviews, exploring the contested issue of the impact of popular nationalism on Chinese foreign policy. It concludes with thoughts on the implications of this analysis for the future of China's engagement with the world.

A note of caution: even our best evidence on this topic is imperfect and partial, so many of the issues discussed in this chapter are contested. There are real limits on what we can confidently say about social influences on Chinese foreign policy. Intellectual humility is therefore vital.

## The Nationalist Politics of State Legitimation in China

A widespread view has long held that democracies are at a diplomatic disadvantage compared to dictatorships, which are seen as free of the domestic constraints that hamstring statesmen in democracies. "In the conduct of their foreign relations," US secretary of state Dean Acheson lamented during the Cold War, "democracies appear to me decidedly inferior to other governments."[7] This section will argue, however, that it is precisely because China today is a dictatorship, lacking the procedural legitimacy afforded to democratically elected governments, that when making foreign policy, President Xi and his CCP must be particularly responsive to social influences like popular nationalism.

"The Chinese people have stood up!" Mao Zedong is widely remembered to have declared at the founding of the People's Republic of China (PRC) in Tiananmen Square on October 1, 1949. Mao had a thick Hunanese accent, and the audio in the archival footage is terrible, so it is impossible to know if Mao actually said those words. Regardless, that is what Mainland Chinese are taught that he said—*not* "Workers of the World Unite!" or another Marxist slogan. Mao and the CCP, from the very inception of the PRC, have staked their claim to rule less on communist than on nationalist ideology: the CCP should rule China because it led the fight against Western imperialists and Japan, especially the "War of Resistance against Japan" (抗日战争) of the mid-twentieth century. The CCP won the late 1940s civil war against their Nationalist rivals, who retreated to Taiwan, in large part because they convinced the Chinese people that they were *more nationalist than the Nationalists.*[8]

Nationalism has only become *more* central to the CCP's claim to rightful rule in the seventy years since then. First the Cultural Revolution (1966–1976) and then the Tiananmen Massacre (1989) discredited communism as a legitimating ideology. The CCP therefore increasingly turned to nationalism to legitimize its rule. In the early 1990s it launched a "Patriotic Education" (爱国主义教育) campaign to solidify its shaken legitimacy after Tiananmen.

With Xi's "China Dream," over the past decade the CCP has doubled down, becoming further dependent on its nationalist credentials to rule. A Shanghai banner pairing "China's Dream, My Dream" with "Wealth and Power" (see Figure 4.1)blends the contemporary (Xi Jinping's signature slogan) with the past (the hallmark slogan that motivated the Qing Dynasty Self-Strengthening Movement, 1861–1895). The national goal of achieving "wealth and power" (富强)has been a long-standing and powerful narrative in modern China.

In today's China, the accent in "socialism with Chinese characteristics" (有 中国特色的社会主义) is decidedly on the "*Chinese.*" The "Beijing Consensus" or "China model" is nationalist by definition: based on Confucian meritocracy, is now widely depicted as superior to the "Washington Consensus" of market-friendly economics, portrayed as in decline since the Global Financial Crisis (GFC) of 2008. Patriotism has been reduced to nationalism. For the CCP, "loving China" normally requires resenting the foreign. "Self-glorification usually rides in tandem with demonization of the threatening Other," Lutgrad Lams writes in a thoughtful analysis of strategic communication in Xi's China, "the negative mirror of the self."[9]

*Figure 4.1* "China Dream, My Dream: Rich and Powerful." Source: Author photo, Shanghai, 29 November 2017.

Nationalism is a double-edged sword in China today. The CCP constructs and uses it to sustain its rule, but bottom-up nationalist pressures increasingly challenge the CCP's legitimacy. And those pressures tend to be aggressive. Chinese nationalism can no longer be described as a purely "state" or "official" top-down affair.[10] Aware that popular nationalists now command a large following, China's elite must appease them. China's elite do not enjoy a "nondemocratic advantage" over their counterparts in democracies; as they make foreign policy, they too must be responsive to social influences.

## Studying Chinese Worldviews

*What* do different groups of ordinary Chinese feel and think about the world, and China's place in it? Unfortunately, there are no easy answers to even such seemingly simple questions. There are both conceptual and empirical challenges.

Conceptually, there are two major challenges. First, feelings and attitudes toward the world are contingent, the product of both the individual and the situation, so they are fluid. Second, while some person variables, like gender and race, are relatively stable over time, other predispositions, like nationalism/cosmopolitanism, can vary substantially from moment to moment. It is useful, therefore to distinguish between relatively enduring levels of a predisposition, and temporary levels affected by a recent event. For instance, Iain Johnston may or may not be right that enduring levels of nationalism are decreasing among Beijing residents.[11] But that will not matter if an international incident has spiked temporary levels of nationalism. Indeed, it is usually China's most cosmopolitan social group—urban youth—that is at the forefront of nationalist street demonstrations against foreign countries.

The empirical challenge is also formidable. In China today, there are still no nationally representative surveys that directly and systematically measure politically sensitive questions about the Chinese people's worldviews. The best we can do, therefore, is to make careful inferences from the available evidence, partial as it may often be. These include surveys, texts (e.g., social media posts, television, movies), and behaviors (e.g., street demonstrations, boycotts).

Surveys are one way to capture *what* the Chinese people feel and think about the world and their place in it. Extant surveys, however, suffer from problems of both measurement and generalizability. When questions are poorly worded, or answer categories poorly designed, the meaning of answers to the questions can be difficult if not impossible to interpret.

When samples are not representative of the full population, furthermore, one cannot generalize results to all Chinese. Most surveys of Chinese worldviews are limited to university students,[12] or one city,[13] or online convenience samples,[14] so are limited in their ability to provide broad generalizations about the absolute levels of either ideological predispositions like nationalism, or specific international attitudes, like toward United States or Japan.

So what can existing surveys tell us? The questions about trust in foreign countries in the 2012 *US-China Security Perceptions Survey*, carried out by the Carnegie Endowment for Peace in tandem with the Research Center for Contemporary China (RCCC) at Peking University, are about as good survey data as we have. The ten countries included were measured on a continuous four-point scale from "completely trust" to "don't trust at all," reducing the measurement error common in questions with fewer or categorical response choices. And the sample of 2,597 adults utilized GPS Assisted Area Sampling to allow for generalization to China's *urban* population.[15] Results cannot, however, be generalized to all Chinese.

Of the ten countries, Figure 4.2 reveals, Russia and Pakistan were trusted the most, while Japan, the Philippines, and the United States were trusted the least. Notably, even Russia and Pakistan were not trusted, with mean scores of just 2.6 and 2.4 on a 1–4 scale where the midpoint was 2.5.

In short, some of the best survey evidence available on feelings/attitudes toward foreign countries suggests that urban Chinese do *not* trust foreign countries. It also reveals that urban Chinese dislike some countries (e.g., Japan, India, the Philippines, United States, Vietnam) much more than others.

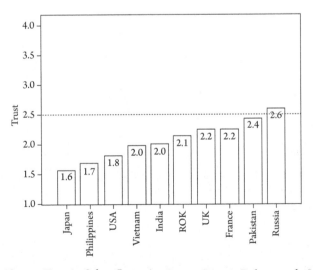

*Figure 4.2* Chinese Trust in Other Countries. Source: Carnegie Endowment for International Peace, 2012 US-China Security Perceptions Survey.

## Writing the World

Chinese-language texts also provide valuable evidence about how ordinary Chinese feel about foreign affairs. Textual analysis can take both qualitative and quantitative forms. Most qualitative work involves content analysis: summaries and interpretations of what people write. For instance, in an early use of the nascent Chinese Internet, I read 281 condolence letters, essays, and poems that were emailed, faxed, and mailed to the *Guangming Daily* from across China following the 1999 Belgrade bombing. The newspaper then posted them to a special page on their embryonic website commemorating their reporters Xu Xinghu and Zhu Ying, who died in the bombing.[16] These texts provided an early window into the worldviews of a broad (but not representative) sample of Chinese.

With the rapid growth of the Internet and proliferation of social media over the past twenty years, opportunities for qualitative content analysis of the feelings and attitudes of ordinary Chinese toward the world have grown exponentially. For instance, Miao Feng and Elaine Yuan have conducted a sentiment analysis of Weibo tweets during the 2012 Diaoyu Island protests, exploring the roots of middle-class Chinese anti-Japanese rage.[17]

Formal discourse analysis of Chinese texts provides a deeper dive into the assumptions that underpin Chinese worldviews. For instance, Lutgard Lams conducted a semantic analysis of official PRC newspaper coverage of Chinese diplomatic standoffs with the United States (in 2001) and Japan (in 2010). She shows how the CCP uses various linguistic techniques to naturalize its narrative of American/Japanese aggression and Chinese victimization.[18]

Quantitative content analysis is also becoming more widespread. For instance, Zhang, Liu, and Wen coded the content of over 6,000 tweets from 146 Chinese opinion leaders on Weibo, China's largest social media platform. They then argue for a "liberal nationalism" in which Weibo elites "question, rather than defend, the legitimacy of the Chinese regime."[19]

Today, the challenge is making sense of too much text in Chinese cyberspace, especially given the role of censorship in distorting what we can see after the fact.[20] Gary King and his students at Harvard utilized computer-assisted text analytic methods to compare the content of censored and uncensored social media posts, and argued that CCP censorship is directed at forestalling any social mobilization that might threaten its rule.[21] This is consistent with this chapter's overarching argument that social influences matter for Chinese foreign policy because the CCP seeks to maintain its nationalist claim to rightful rule.

## Acting on the World

How ordinary Chinese act is also indirect evidence of their views of the world. The Chinese people, I will argue in the penultimate section of this chapter, are no mere puppets of the state, but possess their own independent subjectivity. For instance, urban Chinese take to the streets to demonstrate not just over labor and NIMBY (not in my back yard) disputes, but also over foreign affairs. Ethnographies of street protests have yielded valuable insights into Chinese worldviews. For instance, Nyiri and Zhang thoughtfully explore the "cosmopolitan nationalism" of young Chinese students in 2008 Sydney and Canberra protesting Western media coverage of rioting in Tibet.[22]

But ethnographies sometimes tell us more about the ethnographer than their subjects. James Farrer participated in the spring 2005 anti-Japanese protests in Shanghai. Although he acknowledges witnessing widespread "anti-Japanese racism" and "militant Chinese nationalism,"[23] his desire to identify with the Chinese protestors against Japan leads him to sweep their racism under the rug.[24]

Chinese consumers also boycott foreign goods and services, revealing their displeasure toward specific countries and companies. Chinese tourism to South Korea plummeted in 2017 following Seoul's decision to install a US-made THAAD anti-missile system. Dolce and Gabbana earned the ire of Chinese consumers following the 2018 airing of a racist promotional video. These protests, boycotts, and associated discourse online provide a valuable window into the feelings that ordinary Chinese have toward countries from Australia to Japan, South Korea, and Italy.

## China's World

So what do these various types of evidence suggest about Chinese views of their Asian neighbors, the West, Russia, and the Third World? I now hazard a few generalizations, fully aware of their limitations.

In 2012, Figure 4.2 suggests, urban Chinese did *not* trust China's East (Japan and South Korea), Southeast (Philippines and Vietnam), and South (India) Asian neighbors.

Mainland Chinese today hate Japan. While there are small groups of young Japanophiles (哈日族) who enjoy Japanese manga and cosplay, and a minuscule group of "spiritually Japanese" (精神日本人) provocateurs who reject their Chineseness to identify with Japan, the average Mainland Chinese person appears to view Japan today as little different from the Imperial Japan that invaded and occupied China seventy years ago. In 2003, when Ma Licheng appealed on humanist grounds for his compatriots to stop hating Japan, and Shi Yinhong reasoned in realpolitik terms for rapprochement with Japan to drive a wedge in the US-Japan alliance, both were excoriated in social and public media.[25] Anti-Japanese sentiment was if anything worse a decade later during the Diaoyu Islands demonstrations of 2012–2013, which rocked scores of cities.[26] While British and American "devils" (鬼子) must be specified, every Mainland Chinese knows that, unmarked, "devils" are Japanese. "Japanese devils" is redundant in Chinese.

Mainland Chinese today are more ambivalent toward the Koreas. One might argue that there are two competing perceptions of North Korea in China today. On the one hand, Chinese liberals view North Korean backwardness as an annoying reminder of China's Maoist past—a dark period many would prefer to forget. On the other hand, many Chinese conservatives view North Korea as a socialist Holy Land, uncorrupted by capitalism and its inequalities. For them, a paternalistic fondness remains for a "little brother" North Korea that China saved during the "War of Resistance against America to Aid Korea" (抗美援朝战争).

Chinese today are also of two minds when it comes to South Korea. Young urban Chinese tend to be captivated by K-pop, from fashion to music to TV soap operas. For instance, an online survey of 1,413 Chinese netizens in 2010 and 2011 revealed that exposure to South Korean TV dramas was associated with warmth toward South Korea. Chinese nationalists, meanwhile, both admire Korean nationalism—especially when directed against Japan—and revile it, as when South Koreans refuse to acknowledge their historical and cultural indebtedness to China.[27]

Many Mainland Chinese today view Southeast Asian nations like Vietnam and the Philippines as recipients of Chinese beneficence in the past. They are therefore easily enraged by the perceived ungratefulness of their southeast Asian neighbors. "China is a big country and other countries are small countries," Foreign Minister Yang Jiechi famously fumed at the 2010 ASEAN Regional Forum in Hanoi. "And that is just a fact." Most Mainland Chinese today would likely agree with Yang's paternalistic indignation: children should respect their elders.

In South Asia, Chinese continue to distrust India, seen as an ally of the United States and potential rival blocking China's rise. As Figure 4.2 reveals, Chinese feel more positively toward Pakistan. A shared antipathy toward India—the enemy of my enemy is my friend—appears to contribute to a comradeship with "iron Pakistan" (巴铁).

The West is both resented and admired. A superpower rivalry with the United States likely contributed to greater urban Chinese mistrust of the United States than the UK and France in 2012 (see Figure 4.2). But the major Western European powers are also associated with narratives of the "Century of Humiliation," to be discussed in the next section, likely explaining why they too are mistrusted. While resentment centers on the West's foreign policies, admiration for their domestic politics, societies, and culture seems widespread. For instance, Chinese vlogger "itsRae" posted a video of twenty-four hours in New York. "To tell you the truth, the reason I like New York the best is because it's full of freedom," one viewer commented. "I haven't been yet, but I definitely will."[28]

A pro-Western cosmopolitanism coexists with an anti-Western nationalism among Chinese today, especially urban youth. Figure 4.2 reveals that urban Chinese in 2012 were ambivalent toward Russia, but trust it more than any of the other ten countries asked about. The Russian invasion of Manchuria during the "Century of Humiliation," and the Sino-Soviet split during the 1960s, which included a border clash on Zhenbao Island in 1969, contribute to Chinese suspicions toward Russia. On the other hand, many Chinese today admire Putin's strong leadership, and may overestimate Russia's global influence. Gilbert Rozman argues that a shared communist legacy, and opposition to the West, pulls Chinese and Russians together today.[29]

Anecdotal evidence suggests that Mainland Chinese today largely look down on Africa and the Third World as colored and backwards.[30] The 2018 Chinese lunar New Year show, the most watched television program in the world, included a lengthy skit about Chinese in Africa that included Blackface and a monkey suit. An implicit "Yellow Man's Burden" narrated China's paternalistic duty to bring prosperity to the "Dark Continent."[31] Racism shapes Chinese worldviews, as it does in America and elsewhere.[32]

## How Socialization Shapes Chinese Worldviews

What drives these broad worldviews (nationalism/cosmopolitanism) and specific international attitudes (e.g., toward Asia, Africa, Russia, and the West)?

Demographics matter, but not much—and the evidence is extremely mixed. The weight of our limited data suggests that, on average, younger, southern, and more urban Chinese tend to be slightly more cosmopolitan/pro-Western than older, northern, and more rural Chinese, who tend to be more nationalistic. Johnston argues, based on surveys of Beijing residents from 1998 to 2015, that older Beijingers are more nationalistic than Beijing's youth.[33] Based on a 2007 survey of university students in Beijing, Elina Sinkkonen argues that rural Chinese are more nationalistic.[34] These empirical findings make intuitive sense: older Chinese, having experienced poverty personally, may on average evince greater pride in China's accomplishments under "Reform and Opening"—and greater anger against foreigners who do not appear to affirm them. Many younger urban

Chinese, by contrast, take prosperity for granted, and are more likely to have traveled to the West and identify with it.

The effects of gender, education, and income are less clear. Based on a field experiment conducted in a Ningbo shopping center in 2009, Hoffman and Larner argued that women, the elderly, the less affluent, and more rural and educated respondents are more nationalistic. But their measure of nationalism was actually closer to patriotism.[35] Comparing Carnegie's 2012 US and Chinese surveys of mutual attitudes, Gries and Sanders found that while seven demographic variables accounted for a substantial 9 percent of variation in American trust in foreign countries, a similar analysis of their Chinese survey data revealed *no variation at all.*[36]

Political and peer socialization appears to matter more in China than the West, powerfully constraining how Mainland Chinese view the world. Statistical analysis of Carnegie's 2012 Chinese survey data suggests that the CCP is successfully teaching the Chinese people what and how to think about foreign countries.[37]

Existing qualitative scholarship also suggests that the CCP successfully utilizes its propaganda and educational systems, old and new media, and the entertainment industries to socialize Mainland Chinese to mistrust a "dog-eat-dog" world. Anne-Marie Brady showed how the CCP has intensified its propaganda and ideological work since the Tiananmen Massacre.[38] Interpreting a wide variety of texts, Bill Callahan has argued that "patriotic education" in China today is actually highly nationalistic, teaching the Chinese people both how to view foreigners—"as barbarians: the United States as the evil hegemon, Japanese as devils"—and "what to feel" about them: "humiliation, hatred, and revenge."[39] Kirk Denton has similarly explored the role of Chinese museums in shaping Chinese views of their past encounters with foreigners. He concludes that the "CCP exerts a profound influence over the memoryscape and mediascape of China."[40] And Annie Nie has documented how the CCP came to embrace and nurture the Chinese computer game industry to promote anti-Japanese nationalism.[41]

Two historical narratives are central to the socialization of Mainland Chinese into a social Darwinian worldview: "All under Heaven" (天下) and "The Century of Humiliation" (百年国耻).

## "All under Heaven"

During the Cultural Revolution attacks on the "Four Olds" in 1966, Red Guards vandalized the Cemetery of Confucius in his hometown of Qufu in Shandong Province. The corpse of a seventy-sixth-generation descendant of Confucius was removed from its grave and hung naked from a tree. Confucianism was dead.

Like a zombie, fifty years later Confucianism is back from the dead in China. As early as 1994, Xiao Gongqing advocated the use of a nationalism derived from Confucianism to fill the ideological void after the Tiananmen Massacre. "Since the Chinese Communist Party is no longer communist," Tom Christensen succinctly explained the logic, "it must be even more Chinese."[42] The Confucian revival has accelerated over the past decade. "Socialist ideology has given way to the notion of Chineseness," Kelvin Cheung persuasively argues, "a new source of legitimacy in China's modernization." Confucianism has become the "new nationalist discourse."[43] Symbolic of this shift, socialist holidays like International Workers/May Day have been shortened to lengthen more traditional Chinese holidays.

The idea of "All under Heaven" (天下) has been central to this project. In a thoughtful recent analysis, Xie Shaobo argues that when used to name the entire world, "All under Heaven" (天下) can transcend parochialism in favour of a genuinely universalist cosmopolitanism. When placed within the framework of a Confucian moral order, however, it becomes Sinocentric and nationalistic. "There was throughout the history of imperial China an unrelenting emphasis on *yixia zhibian*—distinction between Chinese and non-Chinese."[44]

Like the "White Man's Burden," the "Yellow Man's Burden" is based upon difference and superiority—decidedly *not* cosmopolitan.[45] "Confucian nationalism" is not an oxymoron.[46] It allows for the reinforcement of cultural and racial boundaries when barbarians do not accept Chinese values. It also contributes both to a racialized view of the world, that places darker-skinned Africans at the bottom and Chinese toward the top. It also depicts China's East Asian neighbors as former tributary states and therefore indebted to China. In this view, these neighbors benefited from a millennia-old Pax Sinica.

## "The Century of Shame and Humiliation"

The historical narrative of "The Century of Humiliation" (百年国耻) also socializes Chinese to view the world as a jungle where only the fittest survive. It powerfully shapes Chinese views of the "West," which in this context largely refers to those seen as exploiting China during the century following the Opium Wars, such as Britain, France, the United States, and of course Japan.[47]

The weight of extant evidence suggests that Mainland Chinese have been taught to hate Japan. "Decades of centralized school education and official propaganda in China," He Yinan argues, has created "pernicious myths" about the past that contribute to "visceral" anti-Japanese nationalism in China today.[48] Annie Nie similarly shows how the CCP nurtured the development of a gaming industry that constructs Japan as hated devils.[49] "War of Resistance against Japan" TV dramas are also ubiquitous in China today, depicting Japanese as one-dimensional villains. More thoughtful, humanist treatments of wartime Japanese soldiers, like Jiang Wen's movie *Devil on the Doorstep* (鬼子来了), have been censored and drowned out.

The "Century of Humiliation" continues to shape Chinese views of the United States and Western Europe as well. The 1993 television drama *A Beijinger in New York* (北京人在纽约) marked the emergence of anti-American sentiment in the post-Tiananmen and "patriotic education" campaign China of the early 1990s. It contained repeated racist comments about Americans. The protagonist, played by Jiang Wen, fulfilled a male Chinese nationalist fantasy by defeating his male American rival and having his way with white women. The TV show was a hit.

Depictions of revenge are no longer hidden. 2017's *Wolf Warrior II* (战狼II) is an action film in which director and lead actor Wu Jing plays a Chinese Rambo, Leng Feng, who kills American mercenary "Big Daddy" in the finale. One promotional poster features Leng's middle finger, and the slogan, "Anyone who offends China, no matter how far, will be exterminated" (犯我中华者，虽远必诛). It remains the highest-grossing Chinese film ever released.

Some scholars would disagree that Chinese are socialized into a nationalist worldview. Based on a 2013 survey in four Chinese cities, Qian, Xu, and Chen argue that history textbooks do *not* contribute to nationalism among high school students.[50] Two of their three measures of "nationalism" (superiority over other nations) actually measure patriotism (love of China), however, and they do not cohere well. Measurement error, therefore, has likely contributed to a false negative. Their qualitative data are more informative. Interviews with high school students who had visited museums and "patriotic education bases" suggested a contingent impact upon their nationalism. When they were poorly designed, like in the small town of Pingbei, they were boring. But when the patriotic education sites were well designed, as in the Memorial Hall of the Victims of the Nanjing Massacre, they successfully inculcated anti-Japanese hatred.

## Capitalism and Competition

Forty years of "Reform and Opening" has also likely shaped Chinese views of the world today. Unlike the state-led, top-down socialization involved in the "All under Heaven" and "Century of Humiliation" narratives about China's past encounters with the world, this peer-to-peer socialization is more horizontal. As capitalism has turned China into a place of cutthroat competition, and pervasive exploitation, many Chinese have learned not to trust their fellow Chinese—and likely project such mistrust onto foreigners.

A social Darwinian view of the world as a dog-eat-dog place of competition appears to powerfully shape Chinese views of the world (see Figure 4.3). Chinese

*Figure 4.3* Capitalism and Competition: *"Time is money, efficiency is life."* Source: Author photo, National Museum of Art, Beijing, 30 September 2018.

immigrants in Africa, Wang Zhihang argues, are neither neo-colonialists or racists. Instead, "their need to survive and succeed at all costs is internalised as part of their Chinese national identity."[51] All three may actually shape Chinese views of Africa. The "Yellow Man's Burden" not only elevates Confucian Civilization as superior, but racializes the African Other as inferior. Meanwhile, narratives of the "Century of Humiliation" have socialized Chinese to view themselves as the eternal victim of colonialism, blinding them to the possibility that Africans may view China's activities in Africa as exploitative neo-colonialism. And Wang is likely also right that Chinese don't just mistrust Africans—cutthroat capitalist competition has socialized them to mistrust each other as well.

In short, Mainland Chinese today appear to be triply socialized into a social Darwinian view of the world as hierarchical and competitive, where only the fittest survive. These socialization influences promote nationalism, but cosmopolitan responses are also possible.

## Cosmopolitan Shanghai?

Is there space for a universalist cosmopolitanism that rejects parochial nationalism in China today? Sheldon Lu traces the roots of Chinese cosmopolitanism to early twentieth-century Shanghai, where Chinese writers like Zhou Zuoren and Lin Yutang both constructed and inhabited a "middling modernity," "between the extremes of nationalism and all-out Westernization, between traditionalism and radical anti-traditionalism."[52] Compared to Beijing, the political capital in the north, Shanghai, as China's cultural and commercial capital, remains more cosmopolitan today as well.

Has a universalist cosmopolitanism survived Maoism and the Cultural Revolution? In China today, the sprouts of cosmopolitanism tantalize. Young Chinese grow up watching American, British, and Korean TV shows, from *The Big Bang Theory* to *Sherlock*. Thoughtful young Vloggers like "KatandSid" provide a virtual space for the negotiation of East/West similarity/difference—and the construction of an equal (not hierarchical) global citizenship. Meanwhile, artists like Zhu Jingyi and sporting goods brands like Lining fuse Chinese and Western elements into their artistic and commercial products, hinting at the emergence of a cosmopolitanism of equals.

The CCP has long limited foreign films and shows on Chinese TV, however. And in the name of promoting "correct values" (正确价值观), it is increasingly regulating their presence online as well.[53] Furthermore, there is substantial backlash against universalist content. For instance, while some comments to "KatandSid" videos embrace a cosmopolitanism of equal global citizenship, others reveal deep-rooted hierarchical worldviews, whether a pro-Western cosmopolitanism or an anti-Western nationalism. Pro-Western cosmopolitans distinguish themselves as modern and Western from their more traditional and backwards Chinese compatriots through the conspicuous consumption and display of the West. But when the referent is the West, the same young Chinese can also depict themselves as superior, having overtaken a West seen as lagging since the 2008 Global Financial Crisis.

## Does Popular Nationalism Shape Chinese Foreign Policy?

Do these worldviews of the Chinese people matter? Specifically, does popular nationalism shape Chinese foreign policy?

First, a comparative perspective: Does public opinion shape foreign policy making in democracies? In the study of American foreign policy, Aaron Wildavsky's "two presidencies" thesis was dominant up until the Vietnam War. It held that the US Congress largely deferred to the president on foreign—but not domestic—policy.[54] With the Vietnam War, however, partisanship over foreign policy became more apparent. In a longitudinal analysis of survey data, Benjamin

Page and Robert Shapiro found that changes in public opinion on international events regularly *preceded* changes in American foreign policies.[55] A new thesis emerged to explain this finding: since the United States is a democracy, and the elected officials who make foreign policy generally desire re-election, they are attuned to what the public wants. In a comprehensive review of this "electoral connection" argument, Duke's John Aldrich concluded that "The potential impact of foreign policy views on electoral outcomes is the critical mechanism linking public attitudes to elite behaviour."[56]

But does public opinion shape foreign policy making in non-democracies like China, where there is no "electoral connection"? This issue is highly contested. For instance, Duan Xiaolin claims that it does not: Chinese nationalism is not rising and the CCP has it in check.[57] Liao Ning disagrees, arguing that it does. "Constrained by high domestic audience costs," Liao argues, the CCP foreign policy elite "is often compelled to adopt an uncompromising stance."[58]

James Reilly and Jessica Chen Weiss are two of the more prominent critics of the idea that popular nationalism shapes Chinese foreign policy. Reilly's 2012 *Strong Society, Smart State* examines the relationship between public opinion, mass mobilization, and the Chinese state in the context of China's Japan policy. Reilly argues that the CCP has become an "adaptive authoritarian" regime, responding adeptly to public discontent, rationally managing popular nationalists and then quickly returning to pragmatic Japan policies. The state uses propaganda campaigns to reshape public attitudes in a manner consistent with its goals. The Chinese state is "smart."[59]

Is the CCP really as adroit at blending responsiveness, repression, and persuasion as Reilly suggests? Is it "smart," or was it just lucky that the events that Reilly chose to re-examine were relatively manageable? The viciousness and violence of the 2012 Diaoyu/Senkaku Islands protests, and the PLA military escalations that followed them, appear to undermine Reilly's claim that Sino-Japanese relations are "relatively stable," and that 'The likelihood of China going to war with Japan is no greater in 2011 that [*sic*] it was in 2000."[60] The Diaoyu Islands protests of 2012–2013 strongly suggested otherwise.

Jessica Chen Weiss makes a different argument. She applies international relations bargaining theory to China, claiming that Chinese leaders strategically manipulate popular nationalists to signal either resolve (e.g., the Belgrade bombing of 1999) or a willingness to cooperate (e.g., the Hainan EP-3 spy plane incident of 2001) in their diplomacy toward the United States. When a major event occurs, which mobilizes Chinese nationalists and creates the necessary conditions for mass protest, the CCP *chooses* to either "nip protests in the bud" by giving a "red light" to domestic nationalists, thus reducing domestic audience costs, or *allow* protests to develop, giving a "green light" to domestic nationalists, tying their own hands and communicating resolve to their diplomatic foes.[61] Nationalist politics within China, she argues, are driven by leadership decisions about what messages to signal to the external world.

Applications of rationalist bargaining theory to Sino-American relations today, however, suffers from many of the same empirical problems that it does in explaining international crises elsewhere. Jack Snyder has convincingly argued that bargaining theory is little more than "conjecture," failing to survive a real-world reality check. For instance, historical analysis reveals that leaders rarely issue "bridge burning ultimatums" to increase audience costs and signal resolve. Instead, they usually seek the opposite: flexibility through ambiguity so that they are not forced into a corner from which they cannot retreat.[62]

In the case of Sino-American relations, Jessica Weiss claims that the CCP allows or forbids domestic protests primarily on the basis of its strategic interests. For instance, she asserts that the Chinese government permitted anti-American protests in 1999 to gain the "international benefits of signalling resolve." Another possibility, of course, is that with the death of three Chinese and the visible anger of vast segments of Chinese society, the CCP elite may have realized that it would be too costly to its nationalist legitimacy to suppress the protests. They gave a "green light" to domestic nationalists not because of its "international benefits," but because CCP regime legitimacy was at stake.

Indeed, the predominant view in the field is that popular nationalism *does* increasingly shape Chinese foreign policy. The late Allen Whiting first described Chinese nationalism as "assertive," and suggested that Chinese domestic and foreign policy were intertwined.[63] In the 1990s, Sam Zhao argued that nationalism in China was "state-led" and "pragmatic"—under control.[64] Analysis of the strident turn in Chinese foreign policy after 2008 led him to reconsider, however: "the government is increasingly responsive to public opinion," Zhao concluded in 2013.[65]

Because the CCP makes nationalist claims to rightful rule, the Chinese people can utilize the state's own nationalist grammar to make counterclaims—and pressure the CCP to take tougher policies.[66] Gries, Steiger, and Wang showed how the toughening of China's Japan policy during the Diaoyu Islands protests of 2012–2013 *closely followed* public expressions of anti-Japanese sentiment both online and on the streets of Chinese cities.[67] Given that a cause must precede an effect, this research provided strong circumstantial evidence that popular nationalism did indeed shape China's Japan policy. They also found that popular anger was directed not just at Japan, but also at the CCP for being too soft on Japan. In an independent analysis of the same protests, Cairns and Carlson also found that "micro-bloggers' harshest nationalist invective was directed not towards Japan but at a Chinese state they characterized as ineffectual and corrupt."[68]

The view that popular nationalism has contributed to a greater assertiveness in Chinese foreign policy over the last decade is now widespread. "China's contentious diplomacy," Robert Ross wrote in 2013, reflected "increased pressures" on the CCP leadership. Tom Christensen similarly argued in his 2015 *The China Challenge* that popular nationalism shaped the "acerbic turn" of Beijing's US policy in 2010.[69]

## Chinese and the World

Globalization today, Xie Shaobo thoughtfully laments, exhibits a "dismaying antimony": both increased "understanding, acceptance, and mutual respect . . . between peoples and cultures," and "various forms of xenophobia, hostility towards cultural and ethnic others, and ethnocentric arrogance."[70] Twenty-first-century China is no exception. As direct (e.g., travel) and indirect (popular culture) contacts between Chinese and the world increase, both inclusionary and exclusionary reactions are possible, promoting either cosmopolitanism or nationalism.

This chapter has argued that such social influences matter for Chinese foreign policy. China may not be a democracy, but because the CCP claims rightful rule based on a promise to "make China great again," it is highly attuned to domestic nationalist opinion. For Beijing, therefore, foreign policy is a two-level game: both the geopolitics of responding to other states *and* responding to domestic social groups.

It has also argued that the CCP actively utilizes its educational, media, and cultural systems to socialize the Chinese people into a social Darwinian worldview of international hierarchy and competition. Today's Confucian revival promotes not patriotism but nationalism, with its emphasis on moral and racial superiority. More often than not, "All under Heaven" implies a "Yellow Man's Burden" little different from Kipling's 1899 "White Man's Burden"—both rationalizations for colonialism. The so-called anti-imperialist patriotism that flows from narratives of the "Century of Humiliation" promotes desires for revenge and restitution: a decidedly *nationalist* desire that China be restored to its proper place at the top of the international hierarchy—*not* for the equality of nations. Finally, the cutthroat capitalist competition so central to life within China today is likely projected onto the foreign as well, again contributing to a dog-eat-dog view of the world.

As a result, on average Chinese today do not appear to trust many foreign countries. As in much of the post-colonial world, the West is both admired and resented, promoting both a pro-Western cosmopolitanism, *and* an anti-imperialist nationalism. Many Chinese today enjoy K-pop, but China's East

Asian neighbors are largely seen as former tributary states that have benefited from Chinese beneficence, generating anger when they are "ungrateful"— suspicious of China's regional intentions. And Africa and the Third World are largely looked down upon as colored and backwards.

This is not a pretty picture. As China's relative economic and military power increase, we can expect elite and popular Chinese nationalists to increasingly push China's leadership to take tougher foreign policy positions. And President Xi Jinping appears receptive, eager to leave a legacy befitting an emperor through the "forceful reunification" of Taiwan.[71] To make matters worse, the growing influence of popular Chinese nationalists comes at a time when populism and nativism are on the rise around the world. To avoid conflict, therefore, building mutual understanding and trust are more urgent than ever.

# Notes

\* The author would like to thank Ye Junyan, Tang Yanqi, and Song Jingyi for their research assistance, and Wang Tao, Shogo Suzuki, and Elena Barabantseva for their comments.

1. https://www.weibo.com/2150758415/F2WZElGl5?type=comment.
2. https://www.weibo.com/5682172050/D1YvYaj6d?type=comment#_rnd1541643724719.
3. https://zhuanlan.zhihu.com/p/26905507.
4. On structural realism and liberalism, see Ken Waltz, *Theory of International Politics* (Long Grove, IL: Waveland Press, 1979); and Robert Keohane and Joseph Nye, *Power and Interdependence: World Politics in Transition* (Boston: Little, Brown, and Company, 1989).
5. See Michael Doyle, "Kant, Liberal Legacies, and Foreign Affairs, Part I," *Philosophy and Public Affairs* 12, no. 3 (1983): 205–235; and Erik Gartzke, "The Capitalist Peace," *American Journal of Political Science* 51 (2007): 166–191.
6. Chi Yue Chiu, Peter Gries, Carlos Torelli, and Shirley Cheng, "Toward a Social Psychology of Globalization," *Journal of Social Issues* 67, no. 4 (2011): 663–676.
7. Peter Hays Gries, *The Politics of American Foreign Policy: How Ideology Divides Liberals and Conservatives over Foreign Affairs* (Stanford, CA: Stanford University Press, 2014), 22–25.
8. Chalmers A. Johnson, *Peasant Nationalism and Communist Power: The Emergence of Revolutionary China, 1937–1945* (Stanford, CA: Stanford University Press, 1962).
9. Lutgard Lams, "Examining Strategic Narratives in Chinese Official Discourse under Xi Jinping," *Journal of Chinese Political Science* 23, no. 3 (2018): 387–411.
10. Peter Hays Gries, *China's New Nationalism: Pride, Politics, and Diplomacy* (Berkeley: University of California Press, 2004); Peter Hays Gries, "Chinese Nationalism: Challenging the State?" *Current History* 104, no. 683(2005): 251–56.
11. Neither the original Chinese language wordings nor many statistics are presented, making it difficult to evaluate Johnston's claims. See Alastair Iain Johnston, "Is Chinese Nationalism Rising? Evidence from Beijing," *International Security* 41, no. 3 (2016): 7–43.
12. See, for example, Peter Hays Gries, Qingmin Zhang, H. Michael Crowson, and Huajian Cai, "Patriotism, Nationalism, and China's US Policy: Structures and Consequences of Chinese National Identity," *China Quarterly* 205 (2011): 1–17.
13. See, for example, Alastair Iain Johnston, "Is Chinese Nationalism Rising? Evidence from Beijing," *International Security* 41, no. 3 (2016): 7–43.
14. See, for example, Peter Hays Gries, "Disillusionment and Dismay: How Chinese Netizens Think and Feel about the Two Koreas," *Journal of East Asian Studies* 12 (2012): 31–56.
15. Pierre F. Landry and Mingming Shen, "Reaching Migrants in Survey Research: The Use of the Global Positioning System to Reduce Coverage Bias in China," *Political Analysis* 13, no. 1 (2005): 1–22.

16. Peter Hays Gries, "Tears of Rage: Chinese Nationalist Reactions to the Belgrade Embassy Bombing," *The China Journal* 46 (2001): 25–43.
17. Miao Feng and Elaine J. Yuan, "Public Opinion on Weibo: The Case of the Diaoyu Islands Dispute," in *The Dispute over the Diaoyu/Senkaku Islands: How Media Narratives Shape Public Opinion and Challenge the Global Order*, edited by Thomas A. Hollihan, 119–140 (New York: Palgrave, 2014).
18. Lutgard Lams, "Othering in Chinese Official Media Narratives During Diplomatic Standoffs with the US and Japan," *Palgrave Communications* 3, no. 33 (2017), 1–11.
19. Yinxian Zhang, Jiajun Liu, and Ji-Rong Wen, "Nationalism on Weibo: Towards a Multifaceted Understanding of Chinese Nationalism," *The China Quarterly* 235 (2018): 772.
20. See, for example, Rongbin Han, "Defending the Authoritarian Regime Online: China's 'Voluntary Fifty-Cent Army'." *The China Quarterly* 224 (2015): 1006–1025; Florian Schneider, *China's Digital Nationalism* (New York: Oxford University Press, 2018).
21. Gary King, Jennifer Pan, and Margaret E Roberts, "How Censorship in China Allows Government Criticism but Silences Collective Expression," *American Political Science Review* 107, no. 2 (2013): 1–18.
22. Pál Nyíri, Juan Zhang, and Merriden Varrall, "China's Cosmopolitan Nationalists: 'Heroes' and 'Traitors' of the 2008 Olympics," *The China Journal* 63 (2010): 25–55.
23. James Farrer, "The Multiple Contexts of Protest: Reflections on the Reception of the MIT Visualizing Cultures Project and the Anti-Right Japanese Demonstration in Shanghai," *Positions: Asia Critique* 23, no. 1 (2015): 59–90.
24. Kevin Carrico and Peter Gries, "Race, Knowledge Production, and Chinese Nationalism," *Nations and Nationalism* 22, no. 3 (2016):428–32.
25. Peter Hays Gries, "China's 'New Thinking' on Japan," *The China Quarterly* 184 (2005): 831–850.
26. Peter Hays Gries, Derek Steiger, and Tao Wang, "Popular Nationalism and China's Japan Policy: The Diaoyu Islands Protests, 2012–2013," *Journal of Contemporary China* 25, no. 98 (2015): 264–276.
27. See, for example, Peter Hays Gries, "Disillusionment and Dismay: How Chinese Netizens Think and Feel about the Two Koreas," *Journal of East Asian Studies* 12 (2012): 31–56.
28. See http://n.miaopai.com/media/933BEna5-gOn98iioZ22FfRhytagKvts.
29. Gilbert Rozman, *The Sino-Russian Challenge to the World Order: National Identities, Bilateral Relations, and East Versus West in the 2010s* (Stanford, CA: Stanford University Press, 2014).
30. Frank Dikotter, *The Discourse of Race in Modern China* (Hong Kong: Hong Kong University Press, 1992).
31. Pál Nyíri, "The Yellow Man's Burden: Chinese Migrants on a Civilizing Mission," *The China Journal* 56 (2006): 83–106.
32. Gries, *Politics of American Foreign Policy*.
33. Johnston, "Is Chinese Nationalism Rising?"
34. Elina Sinkkonen, "Nationalism, Patriotism, and Foreign Policy Attitudes among Chinese University Students," *The China Quarterly* 216 (2013): 1045–1063.
35. It also had a subject matter confound, as their foreign charity was Médecins Sans Frontiers, and the Chinese was Hope Project, so interest in helping a medical versus a poverty charity presents an alternative explanation for why participants chose one over the other. See Robert Hoffmann and Jeremy Larner, "The Demography of Chinese Nationalism: A Field-Experimental Approach," *The China Quarterly* 213 (2013): 189–204.
36. Peter Hays Gries and Matthew Sanders, "How Socialization Shapes Chinese Views of America and the World," *Japanese Journal of Political Science* 17, no. 1 (2016): 1–21.
37. Ibid.
38. Anne-Marie Brady *Marketing Dictatorship: Propaganda and Thought Work in Contemporary China* (Lanham, MD: Rowman & Littlefield, 2008).
39. Bill Callahan, *China: The Pessoptimist Nation* (Oxford: Oxford University Press, 2010), 194.
40. Kirk Denton, *Exhibiting the Past: Historical Memory and the Politics of Museums in Postsocialist China* (Honolulu: University of Hawaii Press, 2014).
41. Annie Hongping Nie, "Gaming, Nationalism, and Ideological Work in Contemporary China: Online Games Based on the War of Resistance Against Japan," *Journal of Contemporary China* 22, no. 81 (2013): 499–517.

42. Tom Christensen, "Chinese Realpolitik," *Foreign Affairs* 75, no. 5 (1996): 37.
43. Kelvin Chi-Kin Cheung, "Away from Socialism, Towards Chinese Characteristics: Confucianism and the Futures of Chinese Nationalism," *China Information* 26, no. 2 (2012): 206.
44. Shaobo Xie, "Chinese Beginnings of Cosmopolitanism: A Genealogical Critique of *Tianxia Guan*," *Telos* 180 (2017): 17.
45. Nyíri, "The Yellow Man's Burden."
46. Prasenjit Duara, "Nationalists among Transnationals: Overseas Chinese and the Idea of China," in *Ungrounded Empires: The Cultural Politics of Modern Chinese Trans-nationalism*, edited by Aihwa Ong and Donald Nonini (London: Routledge, 1997).
47. Gries, *China's New Nationalism*; Callahan, *China: The Pessoptimist Nation*.
48. Yinan He, "History, Chinese Nationalism, and the Emerging Sino-Japanese Conflict," *Journal of Contemporary China* 16, no. 50 (2007): 2.
49. Nie, "Gaming, Nationalism, and Ideological Work in Contemporary China."
50. Licheng Qian, Bin Xu, and Dingding Chen, "Does History Education Promote Nationalism in China? A 'Limited Effect' Explanation," *Journal of Contemporary China* 26, no. 104 (2017): 199–212.
51. Zhihang Wang, "Understanding Chinese Immigrants in Africa from the Perspective of National Identity," *Asian Ethnicity* 20, no. 1 (2019): 31.
52. Sheldon Lu, "Cosmopolitanism and Alternative Modernity in Twentieth-Century China," *Telos* 180 (2017): 110.
53. http://www.sohu.com/a/159392388_674734.
54. Aaron Wildavsky, "The Two Presidencies," *Transaction* 4, no. 2, (1966): 162–173.
55. Benjamin Page and Robert Shapiro, "Effects of Public Opinion on Policy," *The American Political Science Review* 77, no. 1(1983): 175–190.
56. John Aldrich et al., "Foreign Policy and the Electoral Connection," *Annual Review of Political Science* 16, no. 3 (2006): 477–502.
57. Duan Xiaolin, "Unanswered Questions: Why We May Be Wrong about Chinese Nationalism and Its Foreign Policy Implications," *Journal of Contemporary China* 26, no. 108 (2017): 886–900.
58. Liao Ning, "Presentist or Cultural Memory: Chinese Nationalism as Constraint on Beijing's Foreign Policy Making," *Asian Politics & Policy* 5, no. 4 (2013): 543–565.
59. James Reilly, *Strong Society, Smart State: The Rise of Public Opinion in China's Japan Policy* (New York: Columbia University Press, 2011), 6–7.
60. Ibid.
61. Jessica Chen Weiss, "Authoritarian Signaling, Mass Audiences, and Nationalist Protest in China," *International Organization* 67, no. 1 (2013): 26–27.
62. Jack Snyder and Erica D. Borghard, "The Cost of Empty Threats: A Penny, Not a Pound," *American Political Science Review* 105, no. 3 (2011): 437, 439.
63. Allen S. Whiting, "Assertive Nationalism in Chinese Foreign Policy," *Asian Survey* 23, no. 8 (1983): 913–933; and Allen Whiting, "Chinese Nationalism and Foreign Policy after Deng," *The China Quarterly* 142 (1995): 295–316.
64. Suisheng Zhao, "A State-led Nationalism: The Patriotic Education Campaign in Post-Tiananmen China," *Communist and Post-communist Studies* 31, no. 3 (1998): 287–302.
65. Suisheng Zhao, "Foreign Policy Implications of Chinese Nationalism Revisited: The Strident Turn," *Journal of Contemporary China* 22, no. 82 (2013): 536.
66. Gries, *China's New Nationalism*; Gries, "Chinese Nationalism."
67. Gries, Steiger, and Wang, "Popular Nationalism and China's Japan Policy."
68. Christopher Cairns and Allen Carlson, "Real-World Islands in a Social Media Sea: Nationalism and Censorship on Weibo during the 2012 Diaoyu/Senkaku Crisis," *The China Quarterly* 225 (2016): 24.
69. Thomas Christensen, *The China Challenge: Shaping the Choices of a Rising Power* (New York: W. W. Norton, 2015), 259. Cited in Xiaolin Duan, "Unanswered Questions," 896.
70. Shaobo Xie, "Chinese Beginnings of Cosmopolitanism," 8.
71. Peter Gries and Tao Wang, "Will China Seize Taiwan? Wishful Thinking in Beijing, Taipei, and Washington Could Spell War in 2019," *Foreign Affairs* snapshot, February 15, 2019.

# 5

# China's Foreign Policy Making Process

*Players and Institutions*

SUISHENG ZHAO

For many years after the founding of the PRC, China's foreign policy making process, especially on national security issues, was a black box for outside observers. While the Chinese people learned about China's foreign policy decisions and outcomes primarily from the official news and announcements, scholars and analysts had to piece together snippets of information to identify the actors and institutions in China's foreign policy apparatus. China's reform and opening to the outside world, which began in the 1980s, have greatly expanded China's international involvement and have provided new opportunities for scholars to study China's foreign policy making process. While the lack of transparency remains a barrier, scholars have been able to collect more information from Chinese publications and interviews with retired Chinese diplomats to construct the increasingly accurate picture of the foreign policy makers and their interactions with bureaucratic institutions.[1] Among these efforts, David Shambaugh has usefully conceptualized five concentric circles in China's foreign policy making: the highest-level decision-making authorities; ministries; intelligence and research institutions; local governments and corporations; and the society.[2]

While the five circles have represented a more or less complete picture, this chapter focuses on the top echelon of the foreign policy decision makers and institutions and some new players in the foreign policy arena. China's foreign policy making power is extremely concentrated in the hands of the Chinese Communist Party (CCP) and its paramount party leader, with the assistance of the central foreign policy coordination and elaboration organs (协调议事) such as the CCP Foreign Affairs/National Security Leadership Small Groups

Suisheng Zhao, *China's Foreign Policy Making Process* In: *China and the World*. Edited by: David Shambaugh, Oxford University Press (2020). © Oxford University Press
DOI: 10.1093/oso/9780190062316.003.0005

and Commission. The paramount leader and other senior leaders at the apex of the power hierarchy have always played a crucial role in setting China's overall foreign policy direction, determining China's national security strategy, and managing international crises. But they have to rely on the opaque and behind-the-scenes coordination organs to work through a large number of bureaucratic agencies of the state, party, and military, whose primary roles are information gathering and the implementation and recommendation of policy. In addition, some new players, such as think tanks, media, local governments, and transnational corporations, have played a variety of roles to influence China's foreign policy. This chapter will examine the evolving role of the paramount leader, the foreign policy coordination and elaboration organs, the bureaucracies, and the new players in the making and transformation of China's foreign policy. Providing a historical overview, it also observes how President Xi Jinping has centralized and personalized foreign policy making power in the name of strengthening a unified party leadership.

## Leaders Matter:

## From Revolutionary to Low-Profile Diplomacy

China's authoritarian political system gives the party-state and its paramount leader immense power in the making of policy, including foreign policy. The CCP Central Committee is ostensibly the highest policy making institution. As the Central Committee meets only once a year, its Politburo and Politburo Standing Committee (PSC) meet more frequently (although their meeting dates and their agendas are very rarely made public), and these bodies make decisions on behalf of the Central Committee. The paramount leader normally holds the position of the CCP general secretary (previously chairman), has the authority to call Politburo meetings, and has been actively involved in foreign policy making. The paramount leader's personality, personal policy preferences, vision, and decision-making style are, therefore, important in the making of China's foreign policy. Mao Zedong, Deng Xiaoping, and Xi Jinping are the three most powerful paramount leaders in PRC history and they have played critical roles in the transformation of China's foreign policy over time—from revolutionary diplomacy, to developmental diplomacy, and to big-power diplomacy.

As the founder of the PRC, Mao Zedong was a charismatic and revolutionary leader who tried to stifle all opposition and dissent, and often made decisions alone. Challenging institutional and any other constraints according to his belief system, Mao acted on the basis of his own views and made decisions personally and top-down. China's decision to enter the Korean War was a classic example. Mao's resolve, in spite of the considerable doubt and opposition within the CCP leadership, was decisive to dispatch Chinese troops to the Korean War in 1950.[3] Mao also dominated China's decisions in the Taiwan Strait crises of 1958 and 1960, the Sino-Indian border war in 1962, the China-Soviet border war in 1969, and even the rapprochement with the United States in 1971.

Believing in the inevitable victory of anti-imperialism, socialist revolution, and national liberation struggles, Mao insisted that the main theme of China's diplomacy was war and revolution—because as long as imperialism existed, war was inevitable and would inevitably lead to revolution (according to classic Leninist theory). He was also convinced that "the East wind was prevailing over the West wind" (the socialist world was rising while the capitalist world was declining). Acting upon the beliefs, Mao aligned with the Soviet Union against the US-led capitalist world and exported the Chinese model of socialism to third world countries in the 1950s and 1960s. After the Sino-Soviet split, Mao stood firm in confronting both superpowers, the United States and the Soviet Union, during the 1960s and 1970s.[4]

But an all-powerful leader is at odds with the reality of the compromises and flexibility necessary in policy making to best serve China's national interests. Mao as a strongman and crusader in the struggle for the leadership of international socialist movement not only put China in a possibly dangerous position of fighting wars against both superpowers, but also effectively isolated China from the larger world in the 1960s, which were enormously costly for the Chinese people and for the world at large. Launching the Cultural Revolution in 1966, Mao plunged China into national calamity and mayhem and had to start normalization of relations with the United States to pull China out of international isolation in the 1970s.

Coming out of the chaos of the Cultural Revolution, Deng Xiaoping emerged in the 1980s to reform and modernize the economy and open China from the isolated revolutionary state into an active member of the international community. Seeing peace and development as the two big trends in the world and believing that a new world war could be postponed or avoided, Deng shifted Chinese foreign policy from Maoist ideological inclinations toward policies based on practical issues and challenges. Less of a crusader and more of a pragmatic leader than Mao, Deng was receptive to new information and demonstrated great flexibility. Actively involved in foreign policy making processes, particularly in handling China's foreign relations with the United States, Japan, and other major countries, Deng respected constraints and tried to accomplish his goals through a gradual and institutionalized policy process.

The most important foreign policy decision reflecting Deng's pragmatism was the *taoguang yanghui* (韬光养晦) dictum—to hide China's strength, take a low-key posture to minimize external attention, bide its time, and never take the lead—which Deng invoked in the wake of the Tiananmen crisis in 1989, as China was condemned by much of the international community and placed under sanctions by the United States and other Western countries. Tiananmen was followed by the end of the Cold War. A diverse array of economic, human rights, and other political issues came to the fore and complicated Beijing's relations with Western countries. With a sober assessment of China's global position and the challenges ahead, Deng focused on China's economic development and reforms and proposed three addenda to China's *taoguang yanghui* policy: (1) carefully assess the situation (冷静观察); (2) consolidate China's positions (稳住阵脚); and (3) calmly cope with the challenges (沉着应付).[5] This strategic decision guided China through the shadow of Tiananmen and the end of the Cold War.

As the paramount leader making strategic and critical foreign policy decisions, and following his return to power in 1977, Deng Xiaoping never held the party general-secretary/chairman or top government positions, although he controlled the military as the chairman of the CMC. Deng's authority came from his personal stature, connections, and breadth of experience. Making important decisions personally and in a top-down manner, Deng initiated a decentralization process to delegate authority to the bureaucracy and tried to build a collective leadership (集体决策) with a group of senior leaders jointly making decisions, as the reform and opening up expanded the Chinese foreign policy agenda and brought an increasing number of players in the foreign policy process.

Although Deng Xiaoping promoted the collective leadership to replace the one-man decision model under Mao, key national security decisions remained a privilege reserved for him personally throughout his reign. A true collective leadership was implemented only after Deng's retirement in the early 1990s. Deng's successors Jiang Zemin and Hu Jintao did not have the personal authority that Deng held. They played the role of the paramount leaders mostly as the top office holders. As such, they were the first among equals of the PBSC members. Jiang Zemin summarized the rules of collective leadership in terms of individual preparation (个别酝酿), division of responsibility (分工负责), and decisions made at meetings (会议决定).[6] In other words, significant issues must be discussed among all members at each level and information should be prepared and distributed and opinions exchanged prior to the meetings. Decisions must be reached only at formal meetings and approved by a consensus or at least the majority of all participants.

As the PSC's designated leader in charge of foreign and national security affairs, Jiang and Hu still had the final authority in the making of the strategic and national security decisions because they could initiate, veto, or ratify foreign policy decisions under the principle of collective leadership. Other PSC members must respect their policy preferences and give them special consideration in exchange for the general-secretary's support of their preferences on issues under their purview. Deference to the general-secretary was politically expedient. Additionally, the principle of collective leadership in national security affairs was confined to the strategic issues to be brought to the PSC for collective decision-making. Routine and daily national security matters were primarily the responsibility of the general-secretary.[7]

Different from the transformational leaders of Mao and Deng, Jiang and Hu were transactional leaders, following the foreign policy directions set by Deng. Concentrating on China's economic development, they worked hard to integrate China into the broader international economy and create a stable and peaceful external environment over a prolonged period for China's modernization.[8] Placing primacy on China's domestic economic development and reflecting realist balance-of-power geopolitics and international economic interdependence, Jiang and Hu offered the opportunity for China to maintain continuity of its foreign policy and made China's international behavior pragmatic and predictable.

Jiang made public Deng's three principles for China's low-profile foreign policy at his meeting with a US congressional delegation in Beijing in November 1992.[9] Following Deng's principles and avoiding confrontation with the United States, Jiang proposed a set of sixteen character principles in dealing with Sino-US relations—"enhancing confidence, reducing troubles, expanding cooperation, and avoiding confrontation" (增加信任, 减小麻烦, 加强合作, 不搞对抗)—at his first meeting with US President Clinton in Seattle in 1993.[10] Promoting a multipolar world, Jiang tried "learning to live with the hegemon" and made adaptation and policy adjustments to the reality of the US dominance in the international system.[11]

During Hu Jintao's tenure, Beijing became increasingly confident and even assertive on some international issues, especially after the global financial crisis started in 2008. But Hu continued Deng's *taoguang yanghui* policy to reassure other countries of China's intention of peaceful rise when a rising China sparked anxieties over an emergent China threat. Hu endorsed the concept of China's "peaceful rise" originally put forward by his aide Zheng Bijian, but this was quickly changed to "peaceful development" because of the concerns that using the word "rise" could intimidate some of China's Asian neighbors and might imply attaining superpower status. Hu continued to focus on domestic stability (内政主导), emphasizing the principles of maintaining status quo (维护现状) and averting crisis (危机规避) in order to extend a period of strategic opportunity (战略机遇期), in which a benign external environment would allow China to pursue its modernization programs.[12]

## Xi Jinping and China's Big-Power Diplomacy

Xi Jinping came to office in October 2012 and quickly concentrated immense power in himself as the "core" of the leadership. Reducing the PSC from nine to seven members at the 18th Party Congress in 2012, Xi successfully amended the PRC constitution at the National People's Congress in 2018 to abolish the term limit on his presidency. Through the anti-corruption campaign to eliminate his rivals, Xi has successfully restored the strong-man leadership and centralized power, with the assistance of a small circle of trusted allies, making the "collective leadership" a remote memory. Unlike his predecessors Jiang Zemin and Hu Jintao, who largely focused on domestic affairs, Xi has taken a stronger personal interest in foreign policy issues and devoted at least equal amount of time and energy, if not more, on diplomacy—traveling all over the world and ushering in new foreign policy initiatives, concepts, and discourse with dazzling speed.[13] In an expression of Xi's personal leadership temperament, which is impatient with the incremental bureaucratic process, Xi has emphasized the "top-level design" (顶层设计) and bottom-line thinking (底线思维) to develop strategic visions, conduct strategic planning, and make tough decisions.

Making foreign policy decisions based on his interpretation of China's national greatness and power with the intent of shaping international affairs according to China's own visions and priorities, Xi has steered Chinese foreign policy away from Deng Xiaoping's low-profile diplomacy toward proactive big-power diplomacy (大国外交) with Chinese characteristics, which is to transform the mission of China's diplomacy from seeking a peaceful environment conducive to domestic development to one that puts expanding China's global reach as a linchpin to achieve the so-called China dream of the great rejuvenation of the Chinese nation. Xi has redefined and expanded the function and purpose of Chinese diplomacy to effectively apply the growing Chinese power and influence in support of a more ambitious foreign policy agenda.[14]

To pursue "big power diplomacy," Xi has introduced idealistic and moralistic elements into China's diplomacy. The underlying assumption is that a big country or major power cannot just pursue its interests, but must also pursue justice. In the past, Chinese foreign policy was often criticized as strong in opposing others' world visions without offering much of its own. Xi realized that as a superpower in the making, China needs to offer its vision of the future world. He came up with the concept of "community of shared future for mankind" (CSFM). While the CSFM is an idealistic vision for the future, he proposed to establish a "new type of international relations" underlined by some new universal norms to move the world closer to such a destiny. Among other things, Xi and his associates trumped the norm of "win-win cooperation" as a pillar for his major country diplomacy.[15] Xi has thus brought China's external relations to a new height of activism and a much broader scope of operation, putting forward a series of Chinese proposals and initiatives for the reform of global governance and exerting China's clout overseas, such as the Belt and Road Initiative (BRI) and the Asian Infrastructure Investment Bank (AIIB).

Incorporating idealism into his major country diplomacy, Xi continued to stick to realism in managing China's foreign and security relations with the outside world. Distinguishing himself from Mao and Deng, he stated at the 19th Party Congress in October 2017 that while Mao made the Chinese people to stand up (站起来) and Deng made the Chinese people to prosper (富起来), he was going to make China strong (强起来).[16] Given Mao's lamentable record, many Chinese people still seem to have an appetite for the strong, omnipotent leader because Xi displayed self-confidence that matches the mood of the times in China, one of renewed nationalism and self-assertion. Pledging to return China to the glory of the past at the center of the world stage, Xi Jinping, upon coming to office in 2013, introduced the slogan "Chinese Dream" to inspire the Chinese people. While previous Chinese leaders largely considered China at the periphery or semi-periphery of the world stage, Xi announced at the 19th Party Congress in 2017 that China had come to the center stage of the world.

Presenting himself as a leader absorbing global respect like never before, Xi has emphasized bottom-line thinking, which means China should draw red lines that should not be crossed under any circumstances. With bottom-line thinking, Xi declared that while China will stick with the path of peaceful development, other countries should do the same. Only when all countries pursue a path of peaceful development can they jointly develop and enjoy peaceful coexistence.[17] In other words, China's peaceful development is not unconditional and is contingent upon whether other countries' behavior is reciprocal with respect to China's core national interests, implying that there is a possibility for a non-peaceful rise if other countries pursue non-peaceful policies toward China.[18] This dual stress on peaceful development and the protection of national interests is a hallmark of Xi's big-power diplomacy.

Xi has increasingly used China's growing power to advance China's interest, including large-scale building of militarized artificial islands in disputed water of the South China Sea. Advancing the big-power diplomacy, Xi has challenged American primacy in the Asia-Pacific with the attempt to establish a China-centric alternative. Although the ingredients and the strategic rationale for China's more assertive international behavior were there before, Xi has seized opportunities to extend and capitalize on its clout, and bolster China's external position in response his perception of China's power and the external environment. Such things as the BRI, the AIIB, and the buildup in the South China Sea would not have arisen at the time if a different leader was in his place.

## Foreign Policy Coordination

For many years, the Central Foreign Affairs Leading Small Group (FALSG) and the Central National Security Leading Small Group (NSLSG) were the two standing and sometimes ephemeral interdepartmental committees for foreign policy coordination and elaboration. The FALSG was long-standing, dating to its establishment in 1956. The NSLSG was created in 2000 after the NATO bombing of the Chinese embassy in Belgrade in 1999. These two LSGs shared the same administrative staff in the Foreign Affairs Office (FAO) of the CCP Central Committee and relied on the FAO "for staff work and to exercise overall sectoral coordination."[19] The head of the FAO is usually a vice premier or state councilor in charge of foreign affairs. The members of NSLSG/FALSG consisted of all agencies involved in foreign and national security policy arenas.

The NSLSG and FALSG were empowered by the Politburo to make decisions on certain regular policy issues. What LSGs could or could not decide depended on the issue, the confidence and power of its leader, and the circumstances such as crisis or routine decisions. Their primary responsibility was to provide a forum for the members of the central leadership in charge of foreign affairs to meet face-to-face with the top bureaucrats to hash out priorities and make recommendations to the Politburo. Without a fixed meeting schedule, they convened when a foreign affairs or a national security issue arose where the paramount leader wanted to coordinate with the stakeholders. Using LSGs to coordinate foreign policy making served the objective of division of responsibility among the top leaders, as it allowed the paramount leader to control policy formulation and coordinate policy implementation and overcome the bureaucratic barriers, thus perpetuating personal authority of the paramount leader.

The policy preferences and recommendations by the LSGs were likely to have an important impact on the final outcome of the decision making process because their recommendations were often taken to represent a consensus among stakeholders. Reaching a consensus or the perception of consensus among the key stakeholders is extremely important for the maintenance of political unity. According to one scholar, "Once a consensus is reached at the FALSG on the pending issues, it is submitted to the unwieldy Politburo for pro forma approval. This modus operandi is further reinforced by the facts that the head of the FALSG is the paramount leader himself and the 'recommendations' were supported by their own colleagues in the Politburo with foreign policy responsibilities."[20] The ratification of these decisions by the PSC was most times simply a formality also because most PSC members were not well versed in the details of complex foreign policy issues and had to rely on the expertise in the LSGs.

The FALSG/NSLSG's remit for foreign and national security policy coordination and elaboration was constrained somewhat by the shortage of the full-time policy staff. While they were high ranking and broadly representative, they could not function regularly for selecting, summarizing, and judging all types of policy suggestions and could work only on critical and strategic issues while most of the routine foreign and national security policy issues were left to the autonomy of each line agency. As a result, they were more of reactive crisis-management mechanisms than daily policy coordination and elaboration institutions based on consistent, effective, and efficient information processing and agency coordination. By presenting their specific perspectives and missions as China's top priority, the fragmented bureaucratic agencies often manipulated decision-making by recommendations with selective information that supported their particular policy positions.

Since President Xi came to office, he has strengthened all existing LSGs and set up new LSGs with himself as the head of most of the LSGs, in order to bypass entrenched interests and cut through bureaucratic roadblocks (known as relying on LSGs to rule the country, 小组治国). The most important new LSG is the State Security Commission (SSC), established in 2013 as a decision-making, elaboration, and coordination organization (决策和议事协调机构). Claiming that China faced a more complicated internal and external security environment than at any other time in history, at the first SSC meeting in April 2014 Xi Jinping proposed a concept of the "overall national security outlook" (总体国家安全观) to cope with an array of eleven areas of security threats—including the threats to Chinese culture, cyberspace, ideology, and political security (code words for regime security and ideological security). Before the SSC, Chinese leaders tended to handle domestic and international security issues in ad hoc leading groups. The overall national security mandate gives the SSC comprehensive authority to consolidate the party core and Xi's personal control of China's vast security apparatus and to cope with both domestic and external security issues, both traditional and non-traditional security issues, and both development and security issues.[21]

Functioning behind the scenes, the SSC has kept a low profile. But President Xi announced at the second SSC meeting in April 2018 that "the SSC has solved many problems that had long remained unsolved and achieved tasks that had long remained undone."[22] He specifically mentioned four aspects of accomplishments: the construction of main architecture of the national security system; the formation of the national security theory system; the improvement of the national security strategy system; and the establishment of a national security coordination mechanism. In particular, the SSC guided the making and implementation of the State Security Law and State Security Strategy Outline in 2015.

Unlike the US National Security Council, the SSC showed a marked orientation toward the regime security, including domestic threats with foreign connections. Because of the SSC's internal security focus, the FALSG was upgraded to Central Foreign Affairs Commission (FAC) in the overhaul of the party and state institutions in March 2018. While the precise difference between the LSG and the commission remains unclear, commissions are more formalized and possess more bureaucratic power to guide policy. Commissions were prevalent and powerful during the period of Soviet planning in China during the 1950s–1970s. The "upgrade" represents the rising status of foreign affairs in the Chinese political hierarchy and also sends a clear message that the Party alone controls China's foreign affairs.[23] President Xi's speech at the FAC inaugural meeting on May 15, 2018, confirmed that the upgrade is to enhance the centralized and unified leadership of the CCP over foreign affairs. With President Xi as head of the new Foreign Affairs Commission, and Premier Li Keqiang the deputy head, the newly promoted Politburo member and former state councilor in charge of foreign affairs, Yang Jiechi, was appointed as the secretary-general and chief of its General Office.[24]

High-level foreign affairs work conferences (工作会议) have also helped bring together the senior bureaucrats and other players germane to the general foreign policy or a given foreign policy subject. These conferences are authoritative gatherings of the entire leadership to build policy consensus on China's national security strategy and foreign policy agenda while synthesizing China's official analysis of international trends and assessing how China should anticipate and respond to them in furthering its own national interests. President Xi has convened the work conferences much more often than his predecessors.

Soon after coming to office, Xi convened a Central Work Conference on Peripheral Diplomacy in October 2013, the first high-level conference on China's relations with neighboring countries since the founding of the PRC. In a lengthy speech to outline the importance and direction of China's periphery diplomacy, President Xi asserted that while China wanted to maintain good neighborly relations based on amity, sincerity, mutual benefit, and inclusiveness (亲诚惠容), China can sacrifice its core interests under no circumstances. Drawing a "red line" for neighbors, Xi demanded the periphery policy safeguard China's core interests, particularly sovereignty and territorial integrity in the attempts to reclaim the territories that belonged to China since "ancient times."[25]

President Xi held the Fourth Central Foreign Affairs Work Conference in November 2014, of which there had previously been only three in 1971, 1991, and 2006. The conference was to establish "the guidelines, basic principles, strategic goals and major mission of China's diplomacy in the new era." The central theme was big-power diplomacy with Chinese characteristics. Calling on China's diplomats to "develop a distinctive diplomatic approach befitting its role as a major power and show salient Chinese features, Chinese style and Chinese confidence," Xi explicitly stressed that these diplomatic undertakings were designed to effectively use its strength in achieving the China dream.[26] The conference statement represented the official funeral of Deng Xiaoping's *tao-guang yanghui* policy and heralded the beginning of "big power diplomacy." Xi placed an unprecedented emphasis on advancing and protecting China's "legitimate rights and interests" in addition to the statement of peaceful development. Xi's linkage of China's diplomacy with its rising importance in the world and the need to use its growing strength to advance its interests was a new facet of Chinese foreign policy.[27]

While Presidents Jiang Zemin and Hu Jintao each had only convened one such work conference and on a much smaller scale, Xi held another Central Foreign Affairs Work Conference in June 2018, attended by the entire PSC, plus ex-officio member Vice President Wang Qishan, together with all other eighteen Politburo members, and the senior officials in the entire Chinese foreign, security, military, economic, trade, finance, cyber, intelligence community, as well as the central think tank community and nearly all Chinese ambassadors. Although the entire deliberations of the conference were not made public, China's official *Xinhua* News Agency published a 3,000-plus word story on this meeting. A strong sign of Xi's consolidation of power and in a visible break from past practice, state media reports failed to mention previous leaders and their foreign policy concepts, but were full of references to foreign policy projects and concepts developed under Xi. Calling to lead the reform of global governance, Xi emphasized that "diplomacy represents the will of the state, and diplomatic power must stay with the CCP Central Committee and consciously be consistent with the Central Committee on ideology and on action."[28] The emphasis on the party's absolute control over foreign policy is new. In the recent past, the country's foreign policy establishment had seen themselves and been seen by the political establishment as a technocratic elite. That is now changing in foreign policy as much as it has already changed in economic policy.[29]

## State Diplomacy and Bureaucracy

In China's party-state, the CCP has authority over the government. The State Council is the executive organ in charge of implementation of policies made by the Chinese Communist Party. The People's Liberation Army (PLA) is an armed wing of the Party rather than a state military. Over time, the state bureaucratic apparatus has been at the forefront of Chinese diplomacy, although their responsibilities are circumscribed to information gathering and analysis, as well as policy implementation and recommendations. As China has been involved

deeply and broadly in international affairs, an increasing number of stakeholders from the party, government, and military have developed interests in foreign
affairs. China's foreign and national security bureaucracies have been expanded
to conduct state diplomacy as well as the so-called party diplomacy and military
diplomacy.

In the meantime, a proliferation of policy issues such as military relations,
science and technology, education and culture, foreign expertise, intelligence
and information, foreign publicity, trade, and technology transfer have required
professional and specialized knowledge for the management of the foreign relations. As a result, the paramount leader and his lieutenants have to rely more and
more on the support of bureaucratic agencies and delegate authority to a large
number of bureaucratic institutions with multiple voices to handle routine and
technique issues.[30] Competing for their voices to be heard, the institutional status of bureaucratic agencies has evolved on the crowded stage of Chinese diplomacy. Since President Xi come to office, he has streamlined the state diplomacy,
elevated the CCP's party-to-party diplomacy, and strengthened the civilian control over the military diplomacy.

The Ministry of Foreign Affairs (MFA) is the government agency responsible
for state diplomacy. But its function and bureaucratic status have experienced
significant changes due to the development of specialization and professionalism. Although Chinese diplomats, like all Chinese officials, have to demonstrate their political loyalty to the Communist Party, they have been primarily
composed of graduates from elite universities trained in foreign languages and
specialized knowledge; as a result of this recruitment, over time the MFA has
become increasingly professionalized. As sizable transfers of middle-ranking
officials from other ministries or provincial governments to the MFA have rarely
taken place since the mid-1960s, the foreign affairs professionals with relatively
narrow expertise have dominated the MFA.[31]

Adapting to the development of specialization and professionalism, the Jiang
Zemin and Hu Jintao leadership increasingly relied upon officials in the MFA,
which "has a reputation of being the most professional among its bureaucratic
equals."[32] The development, however, produced a paradoxical transformation
of the political status of the MFA: the more specialized and professionalized
of the Chinese diplomats, the less important their political status. As career
professionals, top diplomats could hardly make it to the top level of the political hierarchy in the CCP leadership before the 19th CCP Congress in 2017.
The post of foreign minister diminished from a Politburo member and vice
premier to vice premier only and to state councilor during the Jiang and Hu
administrations. In contrast, as the economic reform and open-door policy
empowered the Ministry of Foreign Economic Relations and Trade/Ministry
of Commence (MFERT/MOC), two MFERT ministers rose to the ranks of

national leadership: Li Lanqing became a member of the standing committee of the Politburo (1997–2002) and vice premier (1998–2003) and Wu Yi became a vice premier (2003–2008).[33]

After many years' decline, the political status of MFA was enhanced, symbolized by the promotion of Yang Jiechi, China's top-ranking career diplomat, to the Politburo in October 2017, the first former foreign minister to reach that level in two decades. Yang was also appointed as the head of the newly established Foreign Affairs Commission, which could provide him with great bureaucratic power to help set FAC meeting agendas and control the flow of documents to the top leaders. Wang Yi, the sitting foreign minister, was appointed as the state councilor at the NPC session in March 2018, another first time in decades.

While the elevation of two career diplomats raised eyebrows, the promotion of stellar, seasoned career diplomats aligns with President Xi's vision to consolidate foreign policymaking at the top level of the Party. Speaking at the meeting of Chinese diplomatic envoys to foreign countries in December 2017, Xi required them to remain "absolutely loyal to the Party," the country, and the people, and also to enhance their professional ability and keep their knowledge up to date.[34] In a sweeping reform of the MFA, which started in early 2017, the MFA was urged to "forge a politically resolute, professionally exquisite, strictly disciplined foreign affairs corps." The reform was to create a more empowered diplomatic corps and more consolidated diplomatic structure better representing China's interests with one voice as China approached the center of the world stage. One of the results of the reform is that the MFA has gained a centralized authority over financial and personnel managements at Chinese missions overseas. These reforms have stabilized the personnel in the MFA.[35]

In addition to the MFA, many other government agencies have taken on responsibility of specialized aspects of foreign affairs. The Foreign Affairs Committee of the National People's Congress (NPC), China's legislature, has played a role of foreign policy consultation and parliamentary diplomacy. The Foreign Affairs Office of the State Council is primarily an administrative setup to supervise local foreign affairs offices and coordinate routine matters involving foreign affairs for the top leaders. The Ministry of Commerce is responsible for foreign trade, foreign direct investment, consumer protection, market competition and negotiating bilateral and multilateral trade agreements. The People's Bank of China and the Ministry of Finance have served as the official windows working with the International Monetary Fund and the World Bank respectively. The National Development and Reform Commission supervises bilateral and multilateral economic cooperation and exchanges, serving also as an official coordination agency for BRI projects. The Ministry of Education is in charge of international education exchanges, including (via the Hanban) all Confucius Institutes abroad. The Ministry of Culture has the responsibility to promote international cultural exchanges. The Information Office of the State Council is in charge of China's overseas propaganda work (对外宣传). The Ministry of State Security is for intelligence collection and analysis, counterintelligence (including countering terrorist groups or dissidents with foreign connections), cybersecurity, and other domestic intelligence missions. The Xinhua News Agency and other national news agencies have responsibilities for information gathering and reporting through their internal channels to policymakers.

As new issues have arisen that fall between the cracks of the existing foreign affairs bureaucracy, new agencies have been formed in recent years. Two important agencies established in March 2018 are the State Immigration Administration (SIA), which took over exit and entry, customs, and immigration affairs from the Ministry of Public Security, while the International Development Cooperation Administration (CIDCA) is supposed to centralize control over China's massive and opaque foreign aid programs that the Ministry of Commerce and Ministry of Foreign Affairs previously competed over, in an attempt to balance short-term commercial benefit and longer-term strategic interests as Beijing has shifted from foreign aid recipient to one of the world's biggest donors.

## Party Diplomacy and the CCP Bureaucracy

Along with evolving state diplomacy, party-to-party relations (党际关系) has been elevated since President Xi came to office. The PRC as a party-state has always relied on non-traditional means for its diplomacy. The departments under the CCP Central Committee such as the International [Liaison] Department (ILD),[36] the Propaganda Department,[37] and the United Front Work Department (UFWD) have always played an important part in Chinese diplomacy.[38] They supplement and extend and sometimes override the work of the MFA and other state bureaucratic agencies involved in China foreign affairs.

The ILD is the official agency for party-to-party diplomacy (政党外交). It was established in 1951 with an initial mandate to oversee relations with foreign communist and socialist parties, especially the Communist Party of the Soviet Union. After the Cold War, the ILD's mission broadened to include cultivating relations with non-communist parties and serving as the official conduit to handle North Korean issues. As most of its activities were not covered in the media, the ILD's role in China's external relations has long been underappreciated by foreign observers.[39]

But since President Xi came to office the media exposure of the ILD has increased significantly (showing its growing importance), as he has emphasized that China is a socialist country and bound together with other socialist countries by shared socialist values. The ILD has been an active and alternative channel to state-to-state diplomacy, boasting ties that span over the globe and the full political spectrum. Keeping regular contacts with more than 600 political parties and organizations in about 160 countries, the ILD has taken more active role in building and maintaining relations with other socialist countries such as Vietnam, Laos, Cambodia, and Cuba.[40] The ILD distinguishes its diplomatic role from that of the MFA as being more long-term-oriented, more flexible, and especially focused on helping rectify foreigners' "incorrect ideas" of the Party and country.[41]

Dispatching and receiving several hundred delegations annually, the ILD has taken on the responsibility to promote China's experiences in socialist development, known as the "China model," by launching the annual "CCP and the World Dialogue" in 2014. This dialogue was upgraded into the CCP in Dialogue with World Political Parties High-level Meeting in 2017. Over 600 representatives from nearly 300 political parties and organizations of 120 countries attended the meeting, including Burmese leader and state counselor Aung San Suu Kyi, President of the Cambodian People's Party and Prime Minister Hun Sen, and President Choo Mi-ae of South Korea's Democratic United Party. The Dialogue was for the first time that the CCP held a high-level meeting with such a wide range of political parties from around the world. In the keynote speech President Xi suggested the Dialogue be institutionalized and developed into a high-level political dialogue platform of broad representation and international influence. The Dialogue issued the Beijing Initiative, which praised China's contributions to the world and endorsed Xi's concept of "community of a shared future for mankind and of a better world."[42] As follow-ups, the ILD organized several thematic party dialogues, including the commemoration of the 200th birthday of Karl Marx in May 2018, attended by leaders of seventy-five Communist and Workers Parties across the globe, the first time the CCP hosted a conference of communist parties in China. The ILD also hosted the African Dialogue in July 2018, attended by more than 100 leaders of over 40 political parties in 40-plus African countries.[43]

In addition to the ILD, other CCP central departments have also been active in party diplomacy. While the Department of Propaganda has long carried out international propaganda (外宣) aimed mostly at the non–ethnic Chinese public overseas, the United Front Work Department (UFWD) has become increasingly visible in working on sympathetic foreign celebrities and professional groups with a focus on Chinese diaspora communities. Since China's opening up in 1978, a large number of Chinese have gone to study and work abroad. Many stayed, becoming citizens of foreign countries but retaining varying degrees of ties with their native land. Appealing to patriotism to bolster its legitimacy at home and abroad, the UFWD has cultivated overseas Chinese communities, particularly the more recent migrants (新侨), winning their hearts and minds in the support of the CCP and its policies. As a result, the UFWD, which President Xi referred to as a "magic weapon" (法宝)for the rejuvenation of the Chinese nation,[44] has become increasingly active in using community associations and harnessing overseas Chinese, particularly businessmen, community leaders, and students, to project CCP's influence abroad. Non-Chinese, particularly those who enjoyed positions of respect in their communities and varying amounts of wealth, are sought out as well. The UFWD has emerged stronger than ever after the 2018 government reshuffle, which put the Party at the front and center of centralized power. The State Council Overseas China Affairs Office and Religious Affairs Office were merged into the UFWD in the reshuffle. The UFWD has also taken on responsibility for minority groups, religious management, and Taiwan, Hong Kong, and Macao affairs.[45]

## Military Diplomacy and Civil-Military Coordination

The PLA is in charge of "military diplomacy" (军事外交), as the term appeared officially in *China's National Defense White Paper* for the first time in 1998.[46] Focusing primarily on major powers such as Russia and the United States and on Asian countries, military diplomacy seeks to advance China's national defense goals by establishing a variety of communications and crisis management mechanisms with foreign militaries, including senior-level visits, security dialogues, nontraditional security cooperation, military exercises, functional exchanges, and port calls.[47] Participating in UN peacekeeping operations since 1990, the PLA has contributed more troops than any other permanent member of the UN Security Council.

Military diplomacy is managed top-down by the Central Military Commission (CMC), chaired by the paramount leader. With the exception of the party-state leader, all CMC members are senior generals handpicked by the civilian leadership on the basis of their proven political and personal loyalty. Acting as the nexus between the military and civilian decision making apparatuses, the CMC is to ensure the "absolute loyalty" of the armed forces to the Party. Although the PLA's influence in the national policymaking process is strong, its ability to be heard at the very top levels of the political leadership cannot be taken for granted.[48]

The PLA retains a powerful voice at the highest levels of China's foreign and security decision-making process through an institutional arrangement whereby top military officers are members of the Politburo and the central leading groups and coordination organs.[49] The military delegates are also an important bloc at the National People's Congress.[50] But the military has not had a representative in the Politburo Standing Committee since 2002. The PLA is influential only in shaping China's defense and security policies, such as policies toward Taiwan and maritime sovereignty disputes.[51] The civilian foreign policy establishment remains dominant in advancing China's diplomatic and economic agenda. The MFA, for example, has assumed a leading role in international arms control negotiations.[52] Focusing mostly on defense and security issues, the PLA has consciously backed civilian leaders' foreign policy at the strategic level and kept a distance from civilians' making of foreign policy since the end of the Cultural Revolution in the 1970s.

Civil-military coordination, however, has not been easy because the PLA has its own institutional interests, which sometimes are in conflict with that of the civilian leadership. For example, while Chinese civilian leaders believe that the imperative of maintaining economic development as the principal means of regime survival dictates strategic restraint, the PLA may prefer a more confrontational security posture because tensions with foreign countries would support more defense spending. In addition, military officers tend to perceive the world differently than do diplomats and other civilian bureaucrats,[53] because the PLA demographics continue to be predominantly rural and the military claims a high ideological ground and its indoctrination more nationalistic. By contrast, the civilian bureaucrats are full of college graduates from China's elite universities, who are more cosmopolitan, urban, fluent in foreign languages, and well-versed in diplomatic protocols.[54]

Presidents Jiang and Hu both followed a formula of reigning without overt rule (统而不治). During their watches, the PLA had autonomy in running military administration and operations, including security-related foreign affairs. Effective channels of consultation exist between civilians and generals at the apex of power over strategic foreign policy guidance, but the lack of a coordinated system that provided oversight over PLA actions with national security consequences was a problem for both Jiang and Hu. Such examples were prominent, highlighted by the collision between a Chinese jet fighter with an American naval surveillance plane near Hainan Island in April 2001, the surprise anti-satellite missile (ASAT) test in January 2007 (which the MFA was not able to verify or provide any comment until more than a week later), and the rollout of the J-20 stealth fighter during the visit by US secretary of defense Robert Gates in January 2011. In all these cases, Presidents Jiang and Hu were not informed in advance.

Without effective oversight, some PLA officers tried to influence the public debate about national security issues and became media sensations. General Zhu Chenghu in the PLA National Defense University told international media in 2005 (without authorization) that if the Americans aim their missiles and position-guided ammunition to target China's territory, China would have to respond with nuclear weapons. Zhu's comments caused a media stir because it was against China's official "no-first use" policy.[55] President Hu had to intervene to calm the international community. Zhu was transferred from a first-line position at the Institute for Strategic Studies to the second-line Department of Military Training for Foreigners at the NDU so that he would have less opportunity to express his hawkish opinions publicly.[56] Although hawkish remarks by PLA figures did not represent official policy or imply divisions within the policy makers, they have often caused frictions.

The lack of civil-military coordination was in part because the military is not subject to the leadership of the State Council. Instead of being a part of the State Council, the PLA ranks parallel to it. The PLA only reports to the CMC through a closed system and independently makes decisions on defense-related foreign affairs. With a completely different governance structure than other areas of the Chinese state, and a good deal of autonomy over its own professional and operational activities, the PLA has its own department of foreign affairs, think tanks for strategic research, and intelligence agencies. Given the PLA's special political status in the polity and military secrecy and sensitivity, generals do not normally feel obliged to inform their civilian counterparts and tend not to share specific and high-stake undertakings with government agencies, even though they may have international repercussions. The lack of institutional channels of communication is not only due to organizational barriers, but also to political taboos. Unauthorized contact between civilians and generals easily cause serious suspicion. In addition, neither Jiang nor Hu had the military background and personality that would confer the absolute authority over the PLA.[57]

After President Xi came to office, he was determined to more firmly establish both the Party and his personal authority over the military. Launching unusually lengthy and intense anti-corruption campaigns and enforcing ideological orthodoxy in the Party and military, Xi purged many senior military officers, including Guo Boxiong and Xu Caihou, two CMC vice chairmen under President Hu. The two generals were charged with bribery, but state media later accused them of political misconduct. Subsequently, two other CMC members—Generals Zhang Yang and Feng Fanghui—were also removed on corruption charges. General Zhang committed suicide by hanging. These high-ranking generals were just the tip of the iceberg, as more than 13,000 officers have been investigated, according to the *PLA Daily*.[58]

To make sure the military is under the absolute control of the Party, President Xi also undertook a drastic reorganization of the PLA in January 2016. This shakeup was—by far—the most thoroughgoing reorganization of the armed forces since the establishment of the PRC in 1949. It represented an organizational shift from the Soviet to the American model, shifting from a hierarchical to a more horizontal and "joint" model. Xi's military reform also reestablished the CMC chairman responsibility system, which stresses the chairman's dominant role. An editorial in the *PLA Daily*, the mouthpiece of China's military, required that "The armed forces of China shall be under the unified leadership and command of the CMC chairman.... All significant issues regarding national defense and military development shall be decided and finalized by the CMC chairman and the overall work of the CMC shall be presided [over] and taken charge of by the CMC chairman."[59] Xi has therefore taken greater control of the military than almost any of his predecessors.

## New Players in the Foreign Policy Process

As China's international activities have increased, many new players have entered the foreign policy arena, "licensed" in corporatist fashion to serve China's overall foreign policy objectives.[60] The most notable new players are foreign policy think tanks, the informed and increasingly active social groups and netizens, local governments, and transnational corporations.[61]

"Think tank" (智库)is a new term in China to refer to policy research centers and institutes. The term has gained popularity since President Xi came to power and called for building "Chinese-style think tanks." The "Decision of the CCP Central Committee on Comprehensively Deepening Reform for Several Major Issues" adopted at the Third Plenary Session of the 18th CCP Central Committee in November 2013 called for strengthening a "new-style think tank with Chinese characteristics" (中国特色新型智库) and improving the policy advisory system (决策咨询制度).This was the first time that the term "think tank" as a concept appeared in a CCP official document.[62]

Most of the important foreign policy think tanks in China have operated within the bureaucratic hierarchies.[63] The premier and most comprehensive think tank is the Chinese Academy of Social Sciences (CASS). A cabinet-level government institution to "provide important research papers and policy suggestions to the CCP Central Committee and the State Council,"[64] CASS runs many international and area studies institutes, including the Institute of World Economic and Politics; Institute of American Studies; Institute of European Studies; Institute of Latin America Studies; Institute of Asia-Pacific Studies; Institute of Japanese Studies; Institute of Russian, East European, and Central Asian Studies; Institute of West Asian and African Studies; Institute of Peaceful Development Studies; and the Institute of Taiwan Studies. Each of these institutes undertakes both scholarly and policy-oriented research and publishes journals in their subject areas.

The most influential foreign and national security policy think tank is the China Institutes of Contemporary International Relations (CICIR) under the auspices of the Ministry of State Security (MSS). CICIR is staffed with more than 300 researchers and covers a wide range of strategic, political, economic, and security issues as well as country and regional studies. The China Institute of International Studies (CIIS) under the Ministry of Foreign Affairs is the longest-standing foreign policy think tank in China (established 1958), but with only a few dozen researchers, CIIS has less comprehensive influence than CICIR. The military also has a range of its own think tanks and research institutes.[65] The Shanghai Institutes for International Studies (SIIS) is the most influential foreign policy think tank outside of Beijing. Nongovernment think-tanks have also emerged in recent years, but they have tried to undertake government-commissioned research projects and serve the government needs. The most influential one is the Center for China and Globalization (CCG), founded in 2008 by Wang Huiyao, a scholar returned from overseas.

The primary function of Chinese think tanks is to submit internal reports and references (内部报参和内批) to the top leaders and party-state agencies and present in-person advice through lectures and briefings. Think tank specialists have been successful in raising their academic profile and are emerging as key players in their fields after their reports received top leaders' comments (示办).[66] It is important to understand that China's think tanks are not independent. Their government affiliation and orientation have limited their ability to provide objective policy recommendations, especially when the research results may go against the official policy lines.[67] By and large, universities and professors do not play much of a role in advising the government on foreign policy issues, although there are some exceptions and the academic fields of international relations (and its subfields) have made significant advances since the 1980s.[68]

The second type of new players are informed and increasingly active citizens. China's greater involvement in the world has helped Chinese people become more aware of and interested in international affairs. Interested citizens have become actively involved in the debate over foreign policy issues by writing comments to newspapers or posting messages online. To stay commercially viable and politically correct, the media have appealed to the nationalistic or even the xenophobic taste of their potential audiences. *Global Times*, a nationalist newspaper devoted to international affairs and owned by the *People's Daily*, is very popular throughout the country. In addition, social media are a powerful platform for discussing heated international issues, effectively allowing growing numbers of Chinese people to be part of the national foreign policy conversation. As the top officials are no longer the exclusive holders of policy-related information, the media has communicated the public opinion back to the upper tiers, exacerbating public emotion toward certain news items, and even mobilizing collective actions in response to some news.[69]

The third type of new players is local governments. The decentralization of foreign trade and investment power from the central to local governments has brought local governments into direct interaction with foreign countries and produced local liberalism by which local governments strive to push for transnational collaboration and cooperation in the economic, social, cultural, and nontraditional security arenas. For example, local governments in Yunnan and Guangxi provinces have played an important role in cementing the relations between China and the mainland ASEAN countries, which have increasingly been brought into the Chinese orbit while the maritime ASEAN members are still uncertain about their future relations with China.[70] Liaoning and Shandong provinces, which are strategically situated adjacent to South Korea, competed in opening up to South Korea and attempted to make arrangements for the first South Korean trade mission to China in the late 1980s and helped establish Beijing's formal diplomatic relationship with Seoul in 1992.

The fourth type of new players are China's transnational corporations, particularly the state-owned enterprises (SOEs) and government banks. The global expansion of Chinese companies has generated their overseas interests, which they want policymakers to be aware and considerate of. As a result, the extensive overseas activities of Chinese companies have become a consideration in the making of Chinese foreign policy. In the meantime, the state has often relied on commercial engagement to advance broader foreign policy and security agendas. Large SOEs in strategic industries such as petroleum, minerals, nuclear power, electronics, and defense tend to have close ties with Beijing's political elite. In certain cases, such as in the making of China's energy security policy, the energy SOEs can exert a limited influence because their executives are consulted for their expertise and are sometimes present when relevant foreign issues are deliberated. The SOEs, such as energy companies and financial institutions, have opposed Beijing joining the United States and other countries in the sanctions against Iran and North Korea because the sanctions would hurt their commercial interests. Such commercial interests have certainly become an important consideration in China's foreign policy process. After the arrest of the chief financial officer of Chinese electronic giant Huawei by the Canadian government in the request of the US government in December 2018, the entire Chinese foreign policy establishment punished the Canadian government in retaliation.

## Conclusion

The increasing number of stakeholders and the requirement of specialized knowledge have produced the need to solicit, digest, bargain, and balance a

greater number of interests and views and meld them into a coordinated foreign policy process—yet, the paramount leaders have retained absolute latitude
in shaping China's overall foreign policy direction. Presidents Jiang Zemin and
Hu Jintao continued Deng Xiaoping's pragmatic and modest foreign policy,
although they remained firm on sensitive issues involving China's vital national
interests. Sharpening their learning curve from China's participation in international affairs and relying on policy advisers, bureaucrats, and experts to provide
information and intelligence and draw on broad knowledge and experience in
international transactions, they were sensitive during the period to China's relative strength and weaknesses with respect to the international context in which
they operated. Throughout the period from Deng through Hu, think tanks and
research organs came to play a significant role in advising the top leadership on
foreign affairs—but since Xi came to power the roles and influence of these institutions have been redefined to serve his diplomatic priorities.

President Xi has single-handedly committed to a fundamental change in
course from Deng's low-profile foreign policy. Believing that strongman rule is
what China needs when it faces grave challenges, Xi has declared China's "big-
power diplomacy." While Xi's predecessors had walked a difficult tightrope,
trying to maintain both modest policy and nationalist fervor among Chinese
people, the balance has been lost under Xi. The moderate China has disappeared as China has moved more firmly toward nationalistic power politics.
Recentralizing foreign policy making power and taking personal command of all
of the foreign policy coordination bodies, Xi's ability to make policy decisions
remains hindered by the information provided by many stakeholders competing for his limited attention. Xi's top-down style has made it more hazardous for
Beijing's opaque bureaucratic agencies to provide him with objective information. Moving away from collective leadership, Xi has minimized the opportunities for his wrong decisions to be corrected. The chance of mistakes in China's
policymaking process has increased.

# Notes

1. See David M. Lampton, ed., *The Making of Chinese Foreign and Security Policy in the Era of
   Reform* (Stanford, CA: Stanford University Press, 2001); Gilbert Rozman, ed., *China's Foreign
   Policy: Who Makes It and How Is It Made?* (London: Palgrave Macmillan, 2013); Lu Ning, *The
   Dynamics of Foreign Policy Decision Making in China* (Boulder, CO: Westview Press, 1997);
   and Carol Lee Hamrin and Suisheng Zhao, eds., *Decision-Making in Deng's China: Perspectives
   from Insiders* (Armonk, NY: M. E. Sharpe, 1995).
2. David Shambaugh, *China Goes Global: The Partial Power* (New York: Oxford University Press,
   2013) 62.
3. 沈志华(ShenZhihua)，最后的天朝：毛泽东，金日成与中朝关系[The Last Heavenly
   Dynasty: Mao Zedong, Kim Il-Sung, and Sino-North Korean Relations] (Hong Kong,
   Chinese University Press, 2018), 217–229.

4. Qingmin Zhang, "Towards an Integrated Theory of Chinese Foreign Policy: Bringing Leadership Personality Back In," *Journal of Contemporary China* 23, no. 89 (September 2014): 902–922.

5. Deng Xiaoping, *Deng Xiaoping Wenxuan* [Selected Works of Deng Xiaoping] (Beijing: Renmin Publishing House, 1993), 321.

6. Angang Hu, 中国集体领导体制 [The System of Collective Leadership in China] (Beijing: Zhongguo Renmin Daxue Chubanshe, 2013).

7. Yun Sun, *China's National Security Decision-Making: Processes and Challenges*, The Brookings Institution, Center for Northeast Asian Policy Studies, May 2013, http://www.brookings.edu/research/papers/2013/05/chinese-national-security-decision-making-sun.

8. H. Lyman Miller and Liu Xiaohong, "The Foreign Policy Outlook of China's Third Generation Elite," in David M. Lampton, *The Making of Chinese Foreign and Security Policy* (Stanford, CA: Stanford University Press, 2001), 138.

9. Chen Youwei, 天安门事件后中国与美国外交内幕 [Inside Story of China's Diplomatic Relations with the US after the Tiananmen Incident) (Taipei: Zhongzheng Shuju, 1999), 100.

10. Liu Liandi and Wang Dawei, eds., 中美关系的轨迹-建交以来大事纵览 [The Trajectory of the Sino-American Relations—A Survey of Major Events since the Normalization of Diplomatic Relationship] (Beijing: Shishi Chubanshe, 1995), 470.

11. Jia Qingguo, "Learning to Live with the Hegemon: Evolution of China's Policy toward the US since the End of the Cold War," *Journal of Contemporary China* 14, no. 44 (2005): 395.

12. You Ji, "The PLA and Diplomacy: Unraveling Myths about the Military Role in Foreign Policy-Making," *Journal of Contemporary China* 23, no. 86 (2014): 240.

13. Zhimin Lin, "Xi Jinping's "Major Country Diplomacy": The Impacts of China's Growing Capacity," *Journal of Contemporary China* 28, no. 115 (2019).

14. Weixing Hu, "Xi Jinping's 'Major Country Diplomacy': The Role of Leadership in Foreign Policy Transformation," *Journal of Contemporary China* 28, no. 115 (July 2018): 1–14.

15. Jianwei Wang, "Xi Jinping's 'Major Country Diplomacy': A Paradigm Shift?" *Journal of Contemporary China* 28, no. 115 (2018): 15–30.

16. Xi Jinping's Report at the 19th CPC National Congress, October 18, 2017, *Xinhua*, http://news.xinhuanet.com/english/special/2017-11/03/c_136725942.htm.

17. *Xinhua*, "Xi Vows Peaceful Development While Not Waiving Legitimate Rights," January 29, 2013, http://en.people.cn/90785/8113230.html.

18. Jianwei Wang, "Xi Jinping's "Major Country Diplomacy: A Paradigm Shift?"

19. Lu Ning, *The Dynamics of Foreign Policy Decision Making in China* (Boulder, CO: Westview Press, 1997), 12.

20. Taeho Kim, "Leading Small Groups: Managing All under Heaven," in *China's Leadership in the 21st Century: The Rise of the Fourth Generation*, edited by David M. Finkelstein and Maryanne Kivlehan, 127–128 (Armonk, NY: M. E. Sharpe, 2003).

21. Weixing Hu, "Xi Jinping 'Big Power Diplomacy' and China's Central National Security Commission (CNSC)," *Journal of Contemporary China* 25, no. 98 (March 2016): 163–177; David M. Lampton, "Xi Jinping and the National Security Commission: Policy Coordination and Political Power," *Journal of Contemporary China* 24, no. 95 (September 2015): 959–777.

22. "十九届中央国安委首会，习近平压实责任" [First Meeting of the Central National Security Commission, President Xi Pushed for Taking Responsibilities], 新华网 (Xinhuanet), April 18, 2018, http://politics.people.com.cn/n1/2018/0418/c1001-29935332.html.

23. Helena Legarda, "In Xi's China, the Center Takes Control of Foreign Affairs," *The Diplomat*, August 1, 2018, https://thediplomat.com/2018/08/in-xis-china-the-center-takes-control-of-foreign-affairs/.

24. "习近平主持召开中央外事工作委员会第一次会议" [Xi Jinping Hosts the First Meeting of the Central Foreign Affairs Commission], 新华社 (Xinhua News Agency), May 15, 2018, http://www.gov.cn/xinwen/2018-05/15/content_5291161.htm.

25. "习近平在周边外交工作座谈会上发表重要讲话" [President Xi Made an Important Speech at the Central Work Conference on Peripheral Diplomacy], Xinhua, October 25, 2013, http://www.xinhuanet.com/politics/2013-10/25/c_117878897.htm.

26. "习近平出席中央外事工作会议并发表重要讲话" [Xi Jinping Attended the Central Foreign Affairs Work Conference and Made an Important Speech], November

29, 2014,新华网 (Xinhuanet), http://news.xinhuanet.com/politics/2014-11/29/c_1113457723.htm.

27. Michael D. Swaine, "Xi Jinping's Address to the Central Conference on Work Relating to Foreign Affairs: Assessing and Advancing Major-Power Diplomacy with Chinese Characteristics," *China Leadership Monitor*, Issue 46 (Winter 2015), https://www.hoover.org/sites/default/files/clm46ms.pdf.

28. "习近平,努力开创中国特色大国外交新局面" [Xi Jinping Urges Breaking New Ground in Major Country Diplomacy with Chinese Characteristics], Xinhua, June 23, 2018, http://www.xinhuanet.com/politics/2018-06/23/c_1123025806.htm.

29. Kevin Rudd, "Xi Jinping, China, and the Global Order: The Significance of China's 2018 Foreign Policy Work Conference," Speech at the Lee Kuan Yew School of Public Policy, National University of Singapore, June 26, 2018, http://kevinrudd.com/portfolio-item/kevin-rudd-speaks-to-the-lee-kuan-yew-school-of-public-policy-xi-jinping-china-and-the-global-order-the-significance-of-chinas-2018-central-foreign-policy-work-conference/.

30. David M. Lampton, "China's Foreign and National Security Policy Making Process: Is It Changing and Does It Matter?" in David M. Lampton, *The Making of Chinese Foreign and Security Policy* (Stanford, CA: Stanford University Press, 2001), 2.

31. George Yang, "Mechanisms of Foreign Policy-Making and Implementation in the Ministry of Foreign Affairs," in *Decision-Making in Deng's China: Perspective from Insiders*, edited by Carol Lee Hamrin and Suisheng Zhao, 91–100 (Armonk, NY: M. E. Sharpe, 1995)..

32. Lu Ning, *The Dynamics of Foreign Policy Decision Making in China*, 20.

33. Jing Sun, "Growing Diplomacy, Retreating Diplomats—How China's Foreign Ministry Has Been Marginalized in Foreign Policymaking," *Journal of Contemporary China* 26, no. 105 (May 2017): 419–433.

34. "习近平对中国外交人员提四点要求" [Xi Jinping Made Four Requirements for Chinese Diplomats], December 28, 2017, http://www.chinanews.com/gn/2017/12-28/8411832.shtml.

35. 王逸舟 (Wang Yizhou) and 李欣达 (Li Xinda), "从外交官数量的历史变迁谈我国外交能力建设新课题" [The Historical Evolution in the Number of Chinese Diplomats and the New Agenda in the Building of Chinese Diplomatic Capacity], 人民网-国际频道 (People.com-international channel), September 13, 2017, http://world.people.com.cn/n1/2017/0913/c1002-29533476.html.

36. Concerning the International Department, see Julia G. Bowie, "International Liaison Work for the New Era: Generating Global Consensus?" *Party Watch Annual Report 2018*, https://docs.wixstatic.com/ugd/183fcc_687cd757272e461885069b3e3365f46d.pdf.

37. Concerning the Propaganda Department, see David Shambaugh, "China's External Propaganda Work: Missions, Messengers, and Mediums," *Party Watch Annual Report 2018*, https://docs.wixstatic.com/ugd/183fcc_e21fe3b7d14447bfaba30d3b6d6e3ac0.pdf.

38. Concerning the UFWD, see Anne-Marie Brady, *Magic Weapons: China's Political Influence Activities under Xi Jinping* (Washington, DC: Kissinger Institute on China and the United States, Woodrow Wilson Center, September 18, 2017), https://www.wilsoncenter.org/article/magic-weapons-chinas-political-influence-activities-under-xi-jinping; and Anne-Marie Brady, "Exploit Every Rift: United Front Work Goes Global," *Party Watch Annual Report 2018*, https://docs.wixstatic.com/ugd/183fcc_5dfb4a9b2dde492db4002f4aa90f4a25.pdf.

39. See David Shambaugh, "China's Quiet Diplomacy: The International Department of the Chinese Communist Party," *China: An International Journal* 5, no. 1 (March 2007): 26–54.

40. 中共中央对外联络部官网 [The CCP Central Committee International Liaison Department Introduction Official Website], http://www.idcpc.org.cn/gywb/wbjj/.

41. David Gitter and Leah Fang, "The Chinese Communist Party International Department: Overlooked Yet Ever Present," *The Diplomat*, August 8, 2016.

42. "2017年中国共产党与世界政党高层对话会" [The CCP in Dialogue with World Political Parties High-level Meeting in 2017], 人民网 (People.com), December 3, 2017, http://cpc.people.com.cn/GB/67481/415498/index.html.

43. "中国共产党与世界政党高层对话会非洲专题会为中非交流合作注入强劲动力," [The African Special Subject Conference of the CCP in Dialogue with World Political Parties High-level Meeting Have Motivated the Exchange and Cooperation between China

and Africa], China-Africa Forum, July 23, 2018, https://www.fmprc.gov.cn/zflt/chn/zxxx/t1578642.htm.

44. 冯海波 (Feng Haibo), "十八大以来习近平总书记对统一战线理论的丰富和发展" [Enrichment and Development of the United Front Theories by General-Secretary Xi Jinping after the 18th Party Congress], 荆楚统战 (Jinchu United Front), January 5, 2018, http://www.zytzb.gov.cn/tzb2010/wxwb/201801/243f42014b5f4f2bad384e47d-22f23cc.shtml.

45. 康琪雪 (Kang Qixue), "部委撤并10天后，部长转任" [Ten Days after the Merger of the Ministries and Commissions], 新京报 (New Beijing News), April 2, 2018, http://news.sina.com.cn/c/nd/2018-04-01/doc-ifysuzkc3090348.shtml.

46. Information Office of the State Council, the People's Republic of China, *China's National Defense in 1998*, September 1998, https://jamestown.org/wp-content/uploads/2016/07/China%E2%80%99s-National-Defense-in-1998.pdf?x87069.

47. Kenneth Allen, Phillip C. Saunders, and John Chen, "Chinese Military Diplomacy, 2003–2016: Trends and Implications," *China Strategic Perspectives*, no. 11, July 17, 2017, http://ndupress.ndu.edu/Media/News/Article/1249864/chinese-military-diplomacy-20032016-trends-and-implications/.

48. See Michael Swaine, Zhang Tuosheng, and Danielle Cohen, *Managing Sino-American Crises: Case Studies and Analysis* (Washington, DC: Carnegie Endowment for International Peace), 2006.

49. See Phillip C. Saunders and Andrew Scobell, eds., *PLA Influence on National Security Decision Making* (Stanford, CA: Stanford University Press, 2015).

50. You Ji, "The PLA and Diplomacy: Unraveling Some Myths About Civil Military Interaction in Chinese Foreign Policy-Making," *Journal of Contemporary China* 23, no. 86 (March 2014): 236–254.

51. Tai Ming Cheung, "The Influence of the Gun: China's Central Military Commission and Its Relationship with the Military, Party, and State Decision-Making Systems," in David M. Lampton, *The Making of Chinese Foreign and Security Policy* (Stanford, CA: Stanford University Press, 2001), 61–90.

52. Jing-dong Yuan, "China's Pragmatic Approach to Nonproliferation Policy in the Post-Cold War Era," in *Chinese Foreign Policy, Pragmatism and Strategic Behavior*, edited by Suisheng Zhao, 151–178 (Armonk, NY: M. E. Sharpe, 2004).

53. On PLA perceptions see David Shambaugh, "China's Military Views the World: Ambivalent Security," *International Security* 24, no. 3 (Winter 1999/2000): 52–79.

54. Jing Sun, "Growing Diplomacy, Retreating Diplomats—How Chinese Foreign Ministry Has Been Marginalized in Foreign Policymaking," *Journal of Contemporary China* 26, no. 105 (May 2017): 419–433.

55. Joseph Kahn, "Chinese General Threatens Use of A-Bombs if US Intrudes," *New York Times*, July 15, 2005.

56. Personal interview with Major General Zhu Chenghu, Denver, May 2015.

57. Yun Sun, *China's National Security Decision-Making: Processes and Challenges* (Washington, DC: Brookings Institution Center for Northeast Asian Policy Studies, May 2013): http://www.brookings.edu/research/papers/2013/05/chinese-national-security-decision-making-sun; and You Ji, "The PLA and Diplomacy: Unraveling Some Myths about Civil Military Interaction in Chinese Foreign Policy-Making."

58. Cited in Charles Clover, "Xi Takes Aim at Military in Anti-Graft Drive," *Financial Times*, February 11, 2018.

59. Liu Zhen, "Xi Jinping Shakes Up China's Military Leadership," *South China Morning Post*, October 26, 2017, https://www.scmp.com/news/china/diplomacy-defence/article/2116856/what-changes-top-mean-chinas-military.

60. David M. Lampton, "China's Foreign and National Security Policy-Making Process: Is It Changing and Does It Matter?" in David M. Lampton, *The Making of Chinese Foreign and Security Policy* (Stanford, CA: Stanford University Press, 2001), 12.

61. Also see Linda Jakobson and Dean Knox, *New Foreign Policy Actors in China* (Stockholm: SIPRI Policy Paper No. 26, September 2010); Yufan Ho and Lin Su, eds., *China's Foreign Policy Making: Societal Forces* (Aldershot, UK: Ashgate, 2005).

62. 缘书何 (Zhu Shuyuan), "习近平为？特别强调"新型智库建设" [Why Has Xi Jinping Stressed the Construction of Think Tanks]闻中国共产党新告网 cpcnews.com, October 29, 2014, http://theory.people.com.cn/n/2014/1029/c148980-25928251.html.

63. On the role of think tanks in China's foreign policy process, see David Shambaugh, "China's National Security Research Bureaucracy," *The China Quarterly* 110 (June 1987): 276–304; David Shambaugh, "China's International Relations Think Tanks: Evolving Structure and Process," *The China Quarterly* 171 (September 2002): 575–596; Bonnie S. Glaser and Phillip C. Saunders, "Chinese Civilian Foreign Policy Research Institutes: Evolving Roles and Increasing Influence," *The China Quarterly* 171 (September 2002): 597–616; and Bates Gill and James Mulvenon, "Chinese Military Related Think Tanks: Their Changing Role in the 1990s," *The China Quarterly* 171 (September 2002): 617–624.

64. PRC State Council Official Website, Chinese Academy of Social Sciences, http://www.gov.cn/english/2005-12/02/content_116009.htm.

65. See Bates Gill and James Mulvenon, "Chinese Military Related Think Tanks: Their Changing Role in the 1990s," *The China Quarterly* 171 (September 2002): 617–624.

66. Wen-Hsuan Tsai and Liao Xingmiu, "Concentrating Power to Accomplish Big Things: The CCP's *Pishi* System and Operation in Contemporary China," *Journal of Contemporary China* 26, no. 104 (March 2017): 297–310.

67. Xue Li, "One Belt, One Road and Change in China's Foreign Policy Decision Making Structure," *Dong Nan Ya Yanjiu*, No. 2 (2016), http://www.cnki.com.cn/Article/CJFDTotal-DNYY201602007.htm.

68. See David Shambaugh, "International Relations Studies in China: History, Trends, and Prospects," *International Relations of the Asia-Pacific* 11, no. 3 (September 2011): 339–372.

69. Jianwei Wang, "Chinese Media and Foreign Policy," *Journal of Contemporary China* 23, no. 86 (March 2014).

70. Mingjiang Li, "Local Liberalism: China's Provincial Approaches to Relations with Southeast Asia," *Journal of Contemporary China* 23, no. 86 (March 2014).

# DOMAINS OF CHINA'S GLOBAL INTERACTIONS

# 6

# China's Global
# Economic Interactions

BARRY NAUGHTON

China's extraordinary economic growth has changed every aspect of the global economy. China has become, since 2010, the world's second largest economy, and since 2013, the world's largest trading economy. Many other indicators rank China first or second in the world. Size and growth give China economic "clout" that the Chinese government seeks to exploit both for economic benefit and to derive influence in many spheres of international relations. But to really understand China's global economic roles and impact, it is crucial to understand the evolving nature of the domestic Chinese economy.

The growth process that has given China such economic heft has also made China a middle-income country. But with the onset of economic "middle age," a set of regular structural changes have followed. As outlined in the first section of this chapter, in response to these structural changes China would inevitably have changed the scale and character of its economic interactions with the rest of the globe.

However, China's policy response to the new challenges and opportunities presented by these structural changes has been dissimilar from that of earlier developing countries and different from what most economists expected. Indeed, since 2009–2010, China has developed a distinctive set of international economic policies that were by no means inevitable. These policies grew out of the unusual economic events that marked the first part of the twenty-first century—including the Global Financial Crisis (GFC)—and from the determination the Chinese leaders displayed thereafter to exert worldwide global economic influence.

The broad policy orientation that grew from these forces can be best considered by examining two complex policy initiatives: renminbi (RMB) internationalization and the Belt and Road Initiative. I examine both: each can be seen as a

Barry Naughton, *China's Global Economic Interactions* In: *China and the World*. Edited by: David Shambaugh, Oxford University Press (2020). © Oxford University Press
DOI: 10.1093/oso/9780190062316.003.0006

response to the surplus of domestic saving that emerged in the wake of sustained rapid economic growth, and they are to a certain extent competing strategies. The final section of the chapter assesses China's overall international economic position as of 2018. It concludes with some prognostications about the future of China's position in the global economy.

# The Maturation of the Chinese Economy

China has reached middle-income status: in 2018, China's GDP per capita was almost exactly equal to the global average at $16,000 per capita, measured at purchasing power parities (PPP).[1] From 1978 through 2010, China grew at an average rate of 10 percent per year, but this era of "miracle growth" is now over. The 6.4 percent growth rate in the final quarter of 2018 reflects the "new normal" of medium- to high-speed growth. This new normal is the result of a host of intersecting factors: labor force growth has slowed (and now is begin-ning to reverse); the flood of rural to urban migration has begun to ebb; and many domestic industries have reached maturity with abundance capacity and saturated markets. These long-run structural changes have occurred in regular patterns of change that are similar to those in earlier developing economies.

These domestic structural changes drive important changes in China's global economic interactions. It is important to note at the outset that slower growth does not mean diminished global impact, because the base from which annual growth is calculated is much bigger today than it was in the years of "miracle growth." In the 1980s, China's GDP growth made up about 7 percent of total world GDP growth, and by the first decade of the new century, this had increased to 19 percent. But from 2010 to 2017, China accounted for 28 percent of world GDP growth. Thus, China's global economic interactions will change in char-acter but continue to increase in overall impact, and China's growing market demand will continue to be highly attractive to other global players.

## The "Miracle Growth" Policy Package

During the 1978–2010 "miracle growth" phase, rapid growth was fueled by the availability of seemingly endless supplies of cheap labor. As China opened up, its latent comparative advantage in labor-intensive manufactured exports was real-ized and exports took off. Enabled to become a large importer, especially of raw materials, China became the largest customer for the world's iron ore, copper, and oil. Foreign trade was explained by a comparative advantage framework, and trade was the most important of China's global economic interactions.

It was not easy to change the inherited command economy system, but China ultimately carried out successful economic reforms that in turn facilitated policies supporting rapid economic growth. As employment expanded, the barriers that hindered rural-to-urban migration were gradually lowered. Exchange rate policy emphasized finding a low and stable RMB value, furthering exports. Incoming foreign direct investment was welcomed, along with the creation of private domestic firms. On the financial side, a mostly state-run banking system was used to channel credit to large firms and exporters, leaving small firms to informal financial markets ("shadow banking"). The system was inefficient and had few linkages to world financial markets, but it was adequate to provide resources for urbanization, industrialization, and rapid infrastructure development. In the mid-1990s international finances were liberalized on the current account—transactions involving payments for real goods and services—which was adequate to support growing trade.

On top of these policy changes, China's entry into the World Trade Organization (WTO) in 2001 then gradually ignited what was perhaps the greatest export boom the world has ever witnessed: between 2002 and 2007, China's exports *quadrupled*, and exports soared to 34 percent of GDP (Figure 6.1), very high for a large, continental economy. Through a successful program of economic reform and opening, China had unleashed a powerful, export-driven growth surge. This export surge powered the final period of China's "miracle growth."

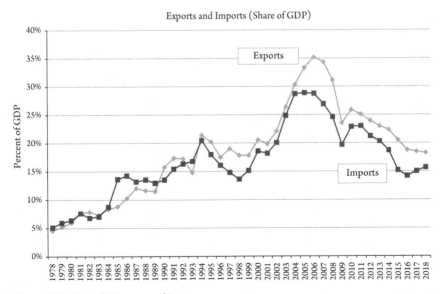

*Figure 6.1* China 's Exports and Imports

However, as of 2007, China was still far from being an open economy. Most domestic service markets were highly protected, even after WTO provisions kicked in.[2] The capital account was still closed to the outside world, meaning that firms could not freely move funds in or out of the country or convert RMB into foreign currencies (except as needed for import and export transactions). China generally controlled outgoing direct investment, relaxing the prohibition only for a few firms to "go on out" and invest and operate internationally. These were generally state-owned enterprises (SOEs), of which the most significant were China's three state-owned oil companies. As China became a net oil importer after 1993, China displayed great sensitivity to the specter of energy dependency. The state-owned oil companies were allowed and encouraged to develop new sources of oil supplies, and to take stakes in foreign oilfields ("equity oil"). This stimulated Chinese national oil companies (NOCs) to diversify their sources of supply away from the Middle East, and meant that natural resources accounted for the bulk of China's early outward investment.

### The Structural Changes

Then everything began to change. Two domestic changes have been most fundamental for the international economy: labor market changes that are driving a loss in competitiveness in labor-intensive exports; and the increase in domestic saving available for international investment. Most fundamental have been the changes in labor market conditions. As the once seemingly inexhaustible supply of underemployed rural workers was drawn down, the flood of rural-to-urban migration began to ebb, and wages began a long steady increase. Rising wages for migrant workers in export factories in Guangdong attracted widespread attention in 2004. Today, total labor supply has already plateaued, and the slight declines registered through 2018 will accelerate rapidly after 2029. China has begun to grow out of the phase of exporting labor-intensive manufactures. Exports as a share of GDP have declined steadily since their 2005–2007 peak (at first sharply in the GFC, then steadily and inexorably; see Figure 6.1).

Rapidly increasing wages imply a better-off population. Indeed, given that the Chinese labor force has already stopped growing, output per worker is still growing at 6 percent per year, which is compatible with highly visible improvements in living standards and a steadily expanding middle class. With increasing income, Chinese households, businesses, and government began to accumulate wealth: aggregate domestic saving reached an extraordinary 50 percent of total national income. This massive saving effort naturally created a surplus of saving available for investment abroad as well, despite an extraordinary domestic investment effort.[3] At first, those capital outflows (equal to the current account surplus) were channeled into increases in official foreign exchange reserves, as Chinese policymakers kept the RMB value low to sustain the labor-intensive export-driven growth strategy. However, after a few years, it became clear that this policy was costly, unnecessary, and unsustainable over the long term. If China was losing competitiveness in labor-intensive exports anyway, and had ample saving to invest overseas in multiple forms, there was no point in buying up low-return US Treasury bills in order to keep the RMB inexpensive. The old export-promotion policies, based on cheap labor and large—but relatively shallow—integration with the world, were steadily becoming less appropriate for China's needs.

### The Policy Challenge: Options and Expectations

A great deal was at stake in China's economic transformation. As China began to move up and out of labor-intensive manufactures after 2007, it opened up space lower down the ladder for countries such as Vietnam, Indonesia, and Bangladesh to grow their export industries. The anticipated increase in China's outward investment had the potential to increase investment in other developing countries, which—unlike China—were held back by inadequate total saving and investment. As a rising middle-income, middle-tech economy, there was enormous potential for deeper integration with technology leaders, especially those in the United States and East Asia. While it was impossible to predict the specific policy configuration China would adopt, it seemed likely that China would become more open as it responded to these opportunities and to the booming global economy of the 2003–2008 period.

In fact, most economists and businessmen expected that China would respond to new conditions by pursuing further policies of market-oriented economic reform and deeper integration with the global economy. These expectations were partly based on China's past trajectory and objectives. As far back as 1996, China officially declared to the International Monetary Fund (IMF) that it would open its capital account as promptly as possible, and allow money to move in and out of China, even if not tied to imports and exports. Although the policy had been repeatedly deferred, it was still on the agenda. Moreover, the growth China had experienced was clearly due to the successful reform program, so it was reasonable to assume that pragmatic policymakers would learn the lesson and push forward with further rounds of reform. Finally, forerunner economies, such as Japan, Korea, and Taiwan, had all moved to more open economies (and less government steerage) after the end of their own "miracle growth" periods. There was little expectation of a sudden, "big bang" adoption of radical openness, but many expected a continuation of China's adaptive, two-steps-forward-one-step-back approach. China would respond to short-run challenges and opportunities, and make gradual progress toward a more open economy.

## How China Got from There to Here

China's actual policy trajectory was shaped by two dramatic economic events. The first was the emergence of an enormous trade surplus in 2006–2007, and the second was the Global Financial Crisis (GFC) of 2008–2009. The rapid growth of China's exports led to enormous trade surpluses equaling 7 percent of China's GDP for the three years 2006–2008 (the gap between the export and import lines in Figure 6.1). Generally, anything over 3–4 percent of GDP is considered a "large" and destabilizing surplus. Chinese policymakers had begun to let the RMB appreciate in 2005, but at first they chose to encourage trade surpluses by maintaining a very slow pace of appreciation.

The result was the rapid accumulation of official foreign exchange reserves, shown in Figure 6.2. Bear in mind that additions to official reserves always mean the central bank is buying up foreign currency with domestic currency, preventing the full appreciation of the currency that would have occurred in the absence of intervention. By the end of 2007, it was inescapable that China's imbalances

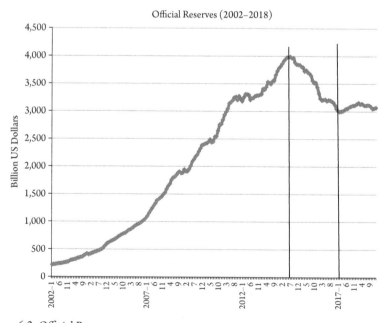

*Figure 6.2* Official Reserves

were serious and unsustainable. China's official reserves had reached $1.5 trillion, already equal to 150 percent of annual imports and thus adequate for precautionary purposes, and policymakers were facing accelerating inflation and increasing trade frictions. China finally shifted policy, raised interest rates, and began allowing the RMB to appreciate much more rapidly than before.

In reality, a completely unanticipated external event drove China's adjustment: the GFC emanating from New York forced a peculiar kind of rebalancing on China. As China's exports went into free fall at the end of 2008, China's trade surplus naturally dropped, and China undertook a massive domestic stimulus program to offset the sharp drop in external demand. China thus relied on a huge increase in investment (mainly by the government) to increase domestic demand, thus "rebalancing" the economy in terms of its global economic interactions. This choice contributed significantly to the global recovery from crisis. However, the cost was that, domestically, China's economy became even more unbalanced and that it is more reliant than ever on domestic investment, rather than consumption, to drive growth. For the six years from 2009 through 2014, gross fixed capital formation was above 45 percent of GDP, far higher than any other economy in the world, and after 2014 declined only very gradually to 42.7 percent of GDP in 2017. The GFC thus changed China's economic trajectory in important ways that continue through the present.

The global crisis also changed China's perception of its place in the world economy. The GFC had been created by regulatory and policy failures in the United States—thus greatly impairing the appeal of the US model of the financialized, market economy. Moreover, China's decisive stimulus program was seen to have contributed to managing the fallout from the crisis. Did this not signify that the Chinese government could and should be bolder in using its newfound economic strength to achieve both political and economic objectives at home and abroad? Further market-oriented reforms seemed less urgent, and a leadership consensus emerged that the government could "concentrate forces to accomplish big things" (集中力量播大事).[4]

Domestically, this leadership consensus led to a steady increase in the Chinese government's commitment to technology-oriented industrial policies, which increased direct government intervention in the economy (and led to subsequent friction with the United States and other trade partners). Internationally, the feeling that China's international influence had failed to keep up with its growing economic strength led to a search for new initiatives and instruments. As he prepared to hand off power to Xi Jinping in 2012, Hu Jintao pointed to multiple factors in the global environment that would work in China's favor, including "multi-polarity, the deepening of globalization . . . new breakthroughs brewing in the technological revolution, growing multi-layered and comprehensive global cooperation, and the growing real strength of emerging market economies and developing countries."[5] Crisis had led to opportunity, but what policies would be adopted to capitalize on this opportunity?

## Wielding Economic Influence

As the global and Chinese economies began to stabilize in 2009, Chinese policymakers sought to restructure foreign economic policy to take into account the new reality. Chinese official foreign exchange reserves continued to grow, notwithstanding the reduction of the trade surplus to a more reasonable, but still large, 3 percent of GDP. Reserves surpassed $3.2 trillion by late 2011 before stabilizing. Chinese policymakers were proud of their huge reserve stockpile, but these reserves were inevitably invested in low-return (but safe) fixed-income securities, especially US Treasury bonds. Policymakers began looking for ways to convert low-yielding official assets into higher-yielding assets that could be owned by Chinese banks, state-owned firms, or even private businesses and individuals. China was looking for new policies that suited its status as a high-saving, middle-income economy.

The first step was to increase lending to developing countries. In just two years from the end of 2008 to 2010, China extended $51 billion in credit to Latin American countries, with just over half going to Venezuela. The instrument of this largesse was the China Development Bank (CDB), the giant "policy bank" created in 1994. CDB already played an important role in China's domestic economy, and it now stepped forward as a major international actor as well. To be sure, there were precedents for CDB's lending, smaller in scale and more directly tied to China's quest for energy (oil) security. In Africa, China's national oil companies (NOCs) had begun to play an important role, especially in Sudan and Angola. The China-Africa Development Fund was set up under CDB auspices after a summit in Beijing in November 2006, and in 2007 a China-Venezuela Development Fund was created. These funds were set up to support direct Chinese investments in the partner countries, unlocking CDB funds to support specific projects. CDB also developed the "Angola model" to increase lending to petro-states, again including Venezuela. In this model, oil serves as collateral, and actual repayment is made and denominated in barrels of oil, not in dollars.

Chinese policymakers convinced themselves that there was a natural complementarity between China and the world's big oil exporters, underpinned by the security presumed to come from taking repayment in tangible barrels of oil. In actuality, by taking repayment in physical quantities of oil, China was implicitly betting on rising oil prices. Since the growth of Chinese demand was the largest factor pushing up oil prices, this meant that Chinese policymakers were hitching their international investment strategy to their own domestic economy, the opposite of diversification. In any case, the policies applied only to a handful of oil exporters and traditional client states, revealing that these actions did not yet add up to a general strategy. How could China craft a broader set of policies that would convert its external saving from low-yield US Treasury bills into higher-yielding investments overseas, while also using its economic clout to exercise more influence internationally? Two different approaches emerged. Competing philosophies lay behind the two approaches, and each approach led to policies with distinctive, and even idiosyncratic, Chinese characteristics.

## RMB Internationalization and Capital Account Liberalization

The first broad approach was "internationalization" of the RMB. The policy is generally traced back to a speech made by Zhou Xiaochuan, the head of the People's Bank of China (PBC), in March 2009 at the height of the GFC. Zhou's speech did not even mention the RMB (or China, for that matter), but it became the cornerstone of an ambitious policy to extend the reach of the RMB and China's international financial influence. Zhou pointed out that in the wake of the GFC, the world was suffering from inadequate liquidity due to the failures of the US financial system and the inherent defects of a national currency serving as global money. Zhou advocated an increased role for a "super-sovereign" (or international) money.[6] The IMF already had a type of super-sovereign currency, the Special Drawing Right (SDR), but it played an insignificant role in the global financial system. Zhou's proposal was immensely timely, since there was a broad international consensus on the need to increase liquidity to fight the GFC, and the creation of more SDRs would certainly help. In fact, in August 2009 a new allocation of SDRs equal to about $250 billion was made, which increased the total supply of SDRs tenfold. While making only a modest contribution to global liquidity, it came at a crucial time. It also cemented the good relations between the PBC and the IMF, which had been casting around for a positive new role in the global system and was delighted to be able to step up with an increased role for the SDR.

Yet far more important was the new positioning of the PBC that emerged in the wake of Zhou's speech. While Zhou was careful to argue that a super-sovereign currency would be good for everyone, including the United States, the speech was clearly critical of the US dollar's dominant role in global finance. Moreover, Zhou advocated expanding the number of currencies included in the SDR's "reference basket," and China's RMB would the obvious candidate for such an expansion. From this point on, the PBC transformed into a consistent

advocate for "internationalization of the RMB." The PBC took immediate concrete steps to encourage the use of the RMB in trade settlement and encouraged the development of RMB markets in offshore financial centers. Reversing
past policies, the PBC approved the accumulation of pools of RMB held outside
China (and outside the control of Chinese regulators). The implied positioning of the RMB as a rival to the mighty US dollar clearly appealed to Chinese
leaders. Indeed, Zhou made his long-standing objective of RMB capital account
convertibility more attractive to the political leadership by tying it to China's
global influence and prestige. Despite the nationalistic overtones, the basic philosophy behind RMB internationalization was clearly one of liberalization: ultimately, full RMB internationalization would require further domestic financial
reform, opening of the capital account, and integration with global markets.
Zhou intended for RMB internationalization to be a driver of further financial
reform and opening in China.

For several years, RMB internationalization proceeded smoothly. Use of the
RMB to settle trade transactions grew to a third of all Chinese trade in mid-
2015. In Hong Kong, RMB deposits grew steadily to 1 trillion RMB in mid-
2015, equal to 10 percent of all Hong Kong bank deposits.[7] At the same time, by
the end of 2015 the PBC had signed "swap agreements" with thirty-four central
banks, providing access to emergency liquidity, and encouraging foreign banks
to hold RMB in their official reserves. PBC policy was given urgency by an external deadline: in October 2015, the IMF would hold a regular five-year review
that would decide whether to include the RMB in the reference basket for the
SDR. PBC strategists aimed to carry out several steps of liberalization and reach
this mainly symbolic milestone. The highest hurdle was the requirement that
SDR currencies be "freely usable." The PBC pledged to meet specific bench-
marks related to international use of the RMB, and looked forward to its inclu-
sion in the SDR basket. In and of itself, this was of little economic importance,
but the PBC would receive the IMF's imprimatur for RMB internationalization
and be that much closer to capital account convertibility.

In truth, beyond this deadline, the PBC did not have a specific concrete strategy. For Zhou Xiaochuan and the PBC, the ultimate end state of RMB internationalization was an open capital account, in which money could flow relatively
freely in and out of China. They were not purists: PBC officials rejected the idea
of a completely unfettered capital account, since they argued that the Asian and
global financial crises had shown that countries needed to maintain some emergency controls over capital flows. Still, they looked forward to a set-up in which
investment capital could flow in and out of China in response to differential
opportunities and interest rates. This would make macroeconomic policy more
straightforward and efficient, increase the return to Chinese investment, and
improve the efficiency of the domestic economy. PBC officials argued that the

steady buildup of overseas RMB would create new and more efficient markets. As domestic financial liberalization proceeded, domestic and overseas markets could gradually be linked up, they hoped, with minimum disruption.

This dream was rudely interrupted by events that began in August 2015. Suddenly, after years of expecting that the RMB would steadily appreciate over the long run, market sentiment turned sharply negative after a modest PBC move and began to incorporate the possibility of significant depreciation in the short run. The capital account had already been liberalized enough to allow some outflows of capital: these now accelerated. Official foreign exchange reserves fell by almost exactly $1 trillion from the peak of $4 billion, hitting bottom at $3 trillion at the end of 2016. Outflows were concentrated in the six months between July 2015 and January 2016. The PBC was forced to retreat: controls were reimposed on capital outflows, and strong measures taken to stabilize the RMB.

Ironically, the decision to include the RMB in the IMF's SDR basket was made and implemented on schedule, but it was a Pyrrhic victory. Depreciation of the RMB—combined with renewed controls—soured outside holders on RMB assets. Once that one-sided expectation of RMB appreciation was overturned, RMB deposits in Hong Kong declined by 40 percent, and the share of China's trade denominated in RMB dropped in half (since merchants were no longer interested in building up offshore RMB positions). Moreover, to combat speculation against the RMB in Hong Kong, regulators severely squeezed RMB credit access in Hong Kong. RMB internationalization went into reverse.[8]

These dramatic events also ultimately drove major shifts with respects to outgoing direct investment. Figure 6.3 shows both the long-term decline in the

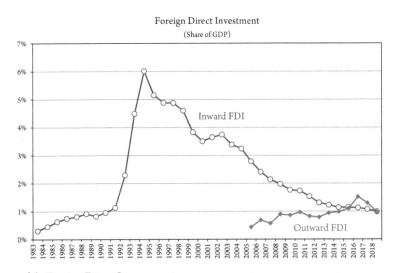

Figure 6.3  Foreign Direct Investment

importance of foreign direct investment (FDI) to the Chinese economy, and the dramatic short-term increase and fall of outgoing FDI (OFDI) in the years 2015–2018. The liberalization of the capital account in 2014–2015 applied also to OFDI, and, for the first time, private companies began to develop large overseas investment programs. OFDI surged—in 2016 and 2017 exceeding incoming FDI for two years. But as China retreated from opening the capital account, it inevitably placed renewed controls on OFDI. In the event, it turned out that a mere four firms had accounted for $55 billion, about a third of the total private OFDI in 2015–2016, and these were soon made the object of enhanced regulatory scrutiny and forced to unwind many investments. China's arrival as a major source of global FDI had turned out to be premature.

The PBC's dream of using RMB internationalization to drive a broader process of financial liberalization thus came to an ignominious end. RMB internationalization has failed for now, but it is not entirely dead. RMB internationalization is kept alive by, among other things, the intensified efforts of the United States to use control of the financial "plumbing"—the global payments system—to sanction rogue states and strategic foes. Beginning with Iran in 1979, US financial sanctions have spread to cover North Korea, Russia, and Venezuela, and in December 2018 were responsible for the arrest in Canada of Meng Wanzhou, chief financial executive of what is arguably China's best tech company, Huawei. These actions make it inevitable that China will continue to build its own international payments system, and also gives other countries some interest in supporting RMB internationalization.

In the broader context, the failure of RMB internationalization has instead pushed Chinese policymakers back to a slower, more orthodox path. During the years of RMB internationalization, domestic financial reforms proceeded, albeit without any dramatic breakthroughs. In 2018, in response to the pressures of the US-China "trade war," China made new commitments to eliminate restrictions on foreign financial firms operating in China. China's domestic bond market has grown steadily over the past decade, and now incremental steps are being taken to attract foreign investors. A similar effort is at work with the Chinese stock market, pioneered by the "Hong Kong-Shanghai Connect," which allows investors to purchase stocks on the Shanghai market through Hong Kong brokers. These experiments are being expanded and broadened, in a way that contributes moderately to both domestic financial reform and capital market opening. In the long run, these may bring capital account opening back onto the agenda.

## The Belt and Road Initiative

Even as RMB internationalization was undergoing its rise and fall, a conceptually completely different program was being developed. The Belt and Road Initiative

(BRI), originally dubbed as One Belt, One Road (OBOR), was launched as a concept by Xi Jinping in twin speeches in Astana, Kazakhstan, in September 2013 and Jakarta, Indonesia, in November of that year. The former launched the "New Silk Road" across Central Asia, while the latter initiated the "21st Century New Maritime Silk Road." They have subsequently been combined and built into a comprehensive and high-profile program, promoted by Xi Jinping as one of his signature initiatives.

At its core, BRI is a program of infrastructure construction that links China to its neighbors and beyond, but it has many other features that add complexity and sometimes misconceptions. BRI can be considered the successor of the influence efforts begun after the GFC in 2009–2010. Unlike those efforts, BRI is wrapped in a philosophical framework and is sometimes presented as an alternative Chinese model of development. At its heart, however, are a series of bilateral agreements signed between China and individual economies, successors to the joint "Development Funds" set up with Africa and Venezuela in 2006–2007. Despite its name, the BRI is not restricted to any particular geographic area, and eight Latin American countries and many more African countries are associated with BRI. According to Beijing, eighty-two countries have signed on to BRI. Despite the general developmental overtones, the basic philosophy behind the BRI is one of exercising greater international influence by providing benefits to a broad range of developing economies and tying them more closely to China.

## Key Features of the Belt and Road Initiative

The BRI is a bundle of bilateral agreements signed between China and individual countries, especially neighboring countries. These agreements specify a wide variety of infrastructure projects—ranging from ports to rail lines to electric grids to IT networks—and make financing arrangements for them. The BRI envisages six land corridors linking China with neighboring regions (Figure 6.4). Of these, the China-Singapore Corridor through Southeast Asia is by far the most economically significant, and the China-Pakistan Economic Corridor is the most advanced, due to the close strategic partnership between China and Pakistan. Complementing these spokes is a global port network that links China's highly developed ports with a string of ports through the Indian Ocean to Europe, currently to Piraeus in Greece. Thus, one of the most fundamental objectives of the BRI is to improve the infrastructure linking China to its neighbors. Transport infrastructure—highways and railroads, including high-speed railroads—will reduce transaction costs and pull nations closer together economically. Communications infrastructure is also an integral part of many BRI initiatives, designed to unite neighbors in common information standards and, not incidentally, improve the competitive position of Chinese hardware and service providers. This infrastructure diplomacy is thus the functional equivalent

The Belt and Road Initiative: Six Economic Corridors Spanning Asia, Europe, and Africa

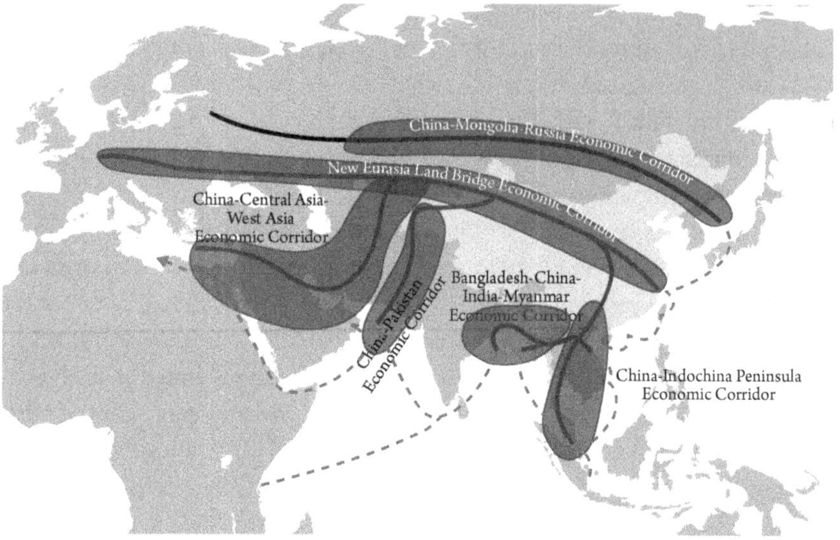

*Figure 6.4* The Belt and Road Initiative

of a trade pact: It draws countries closer together, and implicitly creates higher economic barriers to countries outside the "club."

Equally important to understanding BRI, though, is that it is not a multilateral organization. Although countries are said to "join" BRI, that simply means that they negotiate a bilateral deal with China. They get benefits and promise to do things in return, but these are negotiated bilaterally. Chile "joined" Belt and Road in 2018, but this means nothing except that Chile intends to bargain with China to get a good deal as a "club member." A key objective of BRI is thus to strengthen policy coordination between China and other nations, especially those on its periphery. This coordination can range from comprehensive joint planning—as in the China-Pakistan case—to agreement on a few pilot projects. This bilateral flexibility means that the geographic coherence of BRI can be discarded whenever convenient: obviously Chile has nothing to do with "silk roads," land or maritime, historical or contemporary. Metaphorically, BRI is like the canopy of an umbrella: the six land-based corridors, like the ribs of an umbrella, give it structure; but the canopy itself can accommodate any country.

The key Chinese agency implementing BRI is the China Development Bank. This should not be surprising, given that the major motivation for countries to associate with BRI, besides the intrinsic benefit of the infrastructure, is the promise of financing from China. However, CDB's role goes well beyond finance: CDB is a kind of lead planning agency, interfacing with foreign planning and project agencies. CDB drew up the 2013 road map to guide collaboration on the China-Pakistan Economic Corridor, and then took over as the lead agency. CDB is in charge of long-range planning for three of the six economic corridors, as well as for bilateral coordination with Kazakhstan, Laos, and Cambodia.[9] CDB has developed project planning and finance expertise over the past twenty years; in the BRI it builds on this expertise to create regional infrastructure programs.

## Outcomes of BRI

BRI can provide significant economic benefits to China and to its neighbors. The fact that the regions on both sides of China's land borders are sparsely connected to infrastructure is largely the result of historical accident. With the important exception of the China-Pakistan link, the border terrain is not overwhelmingly rugged. Rather, the pre–World War I wave of globalization stalled out before it could connect these regions, and China's retreat from global interactions after 1949 postponed any further development until recently. The states on China's periphery are generally small, with weak development capabilities and limited capital markets, so they can benefit from the finance and planning assistance.

The most important type of infrastructure will, of course, be transport infrastructure—including both road and rail. The crown jewel of BRI will eventually be a high-speed rail network extending down through Southeast Asia, linking China and Singapore. Communications infrastructure, including fiber-optic cable, will be included in the package. China is seeking both to increase bandwidth and to reorient the architecture of the system to reduce dependency on a limited number of Western-controlled nodes and channels. Finally, "soft infrastructure," including harmonization of technical standards, harmonization of financial regulation, and customs and trade facilitation, has been part of BRI since the beginning.[10]

Besides the general economic benefits, individual Chinese companies will profit from the program. Most obvious are the Chinese international construction companies, already some of the biggest and most competitive in the world. A few Chinese heavy industry companies might be able to offload some of their excess capacity to BRI neighbors, but given the size disparities, this is unlikely to amount to more than a nice business for a handful of companies. BRI includes the construction of China-assisted industrial parks that will provide a base for "convoys" of large state-owned enterprises leading private firms into new business opportunities.

## The Asian Infrastructure Investment Bank (AIIB) and BRI Financing

China offers other countries access to finance as an incentive to join the BRI. It is not surprising, therefore, to find that China has established a number of new financial institutions to facilitate BRI. A "Silk Road Fund" was established in November 2014 with a commitment of $40 billion, mostly from China's foreign exchange reserves. Designed to take equity positions in promising BRI businesses, the Silk Road Fund has undergone several sharp turns in management strategy since. The most eye-catching initiative is the Asian Infrastructure Investment Bank (AIIB).[11] Born at almost the same time, and intertwined ever since, AIIB and BRI are actually very different and not formally tied together. AIIB is very tightly constructed, while BRI is baggy and imprecise. AIIB is quite transparent, whereas BRI is realized through bilateral agreements that are almost never public. AIIB has clear ground rules and a multinational governance structure, all of which BRI lacks. They are an odd couple.

AIIB is often thought of as "China's multilateral development bank." Although the bank had 57 founding members, and 93 at the end of 2018, the initiative came from China, the bank is headquartered in Beijing, and China put up 30 percent of the share capital. Voting rights are weighted to benefit small members, but China still has 26 percent of the vote, enough to block any important decision it disagrees with. Members have subscribed $100 billion in capital, of which they put up 20 percent, borrowing money in credit markets to make up the rest. This is the same model followed by the World Bank and other multilateral development banks (MDBs). Indeed, AIIB is in most respects quite similar to the regional MDBs, such as the Inter-American Development Bank and the Asian Development Bank. Like them, it was set up on the initiative of a large, growing regional power (Brazil and Japan, respectively).

The AIIB is an advocate for high-quality rules and institutions. AIIB head Jin Liqun was selected for his extensive international experience and high credibility within the multilateral development bank community. Jin has promoted transparency, the use of English to promote international cooperation, and the use of the US dollar as the currency, in order to minimize financial costs and risks. Moreover, AIIB carefully studied the other MDBs, in order to follow best practice: for example, environmental assessments are routine; procurement rules specify open, competitive, and transparent bidding; and there is a policy on public information. There are a few modest differences, such as the absence of a resident board of directors, and slightly more flexibility to engage in different types of investment, but these are straightforward positive adaptations to today's more flexible finances and better communications. AIIB, in other words, is designed to be a demonstration project, an effort to show the world that China can run a world-class institution with full transparency. It is also intended to give China experience in establishing, guiding, and running a top-tier institution.

The United States and Japan are not members of the AIIB, although after the UK became a founding member, most other developed countries, including Canada, Germany, and South Korea, joined. The US knee-jerk hostility to the

AIIB has gained it little advantage. After all, if the world can support an Asian Development Bank, with a dominant Japanese voice, it can certainly support an AIIB with a dominant Chinese voice. In fact, about two-thirds of AIIB's lending through the end of 2018 has been joint with other MDBs, including the World Bank and the ADB, with which the AIIB has excellent relations. India is the largest recipient of AIIB loans. If there is one caution to be raised about the AIIB, it is the reminder that AIIB is not the main funding source for the BRI. Indeed, at the end of September 2018, the AIIB had only $3.3 billion in investments on its balance sheet. By comparison, the CDB had $240 billion in foreign exchange loans on its balance sheet at the end of 2017. AIIB lending is only 1.5 percent that of the CDB. To be sure, AIIB is young and its portfolio will grow. But it will never approach the CDB in size or importance.

## Trade, Trade Wars, and China's Outward Direct Investment

As China has moved out of its comparative advantage in labor-intensive manufactures, its trade has become more diversified geographically and in terms of commodity composition. At its peak, in 1999, the US market accounted for 42 percent of China's exports.[12] In subsequent years, China expanded its export markets around the world, and by 2013, the US market had fallen below 20 percent of Chinese exports, before rebounding slightly. One thing that has not changed, however, is that the US trade deficit with China has remained approximately the same size as China's overall trade surplus. That is to say, Chinese trade with the rest of the world is roughly balanced, while it runs a chronic huge surplus with the United States. Although China's overall surplus has fallen as a share of GDP, the surplus with the United States has remained stubbornly above 3 percent of China's rapidly growing GDP. The US trade deficit with China has thus continued to grow, and in 2018 reached a record $419 billion. This imbalance inevitably contributes to tensions between the two powers.

To be sure, the bilateral trade pattern to some extent follows from China's overall pattern of trade, in which it imports large quantities of raw materials (including energy, metals, and agricultural materials) and exports manufactured goods. China is drawn by ties of complementarity to two groups: raw material exporters, such as Australia and Brazil; and suppliers of intermediate goods and components, such as Korea, Taiwan, and Japan. China runs bilateral deficits with all of these except Japan. The problem for the United States is not that it absorbs an enormous quantity of Chinese exports, but rather that it does not figure very prominently as a supplier of sophisticated goods to the China market. The contrast with the European Union is striking. Overall, the EU runs a large deficit with China. However, it is only about $200 billion, half the size of the US deficit, and it has been relatively stable since 2013, while the US deficit has grown steadily. Moreover, one obvious reason for this divergent performance is that Germany has emerged as China's supplier of choice for precision machinery and automobiles. Germany still has a deficit with China, but it is modest ($20 billion), scarcely noticeable next to Germany's massive overall surplus.

By contrast, the United States has clear comparative advantage in a number of high-technology sectors, particularly information technology hardware. However, those manufacturing sectors have already been restructured in close partnership with companies in East Asia and China. Thus, US companies maintain their headquarters and core research and design functions in the United States, but outsource production to East Asia and final assembly to China. The income earned by these companies does not show up in the trade data at all. The obvious example is Apple, which imports tens of billions of dollars worth of iPhones from China every year, profiting tremendously. In short, the US trade deficit with China is partly the result of the deeper integration between the United States and China in high-tech sectors. As a result, China's shift to aggressive techno-industrial policy over the last ten years threatens US interests much more than it threatens most other countries. Add to this the high degree of protection of China's service sectors—in which the United States also has comparative advantage—and it is easy to see the deep roots of economic friction between the two economies and the sources of the US-China "trade war."

As with trade, so has China's outward foreign direct investment (OFDI) become completely globalized. Figure 6.5 shows that the total of $1.14 trillion cumulative Chinese OFDI from 2005 through 2018 reached every region of the globe.[13] Developed countries are the biggest recipients, accounting for almost two-thirds of cumulative investment. Europe attracts the most Chinese investment ($343 billion), but the largest single-country recipients are the United States ($180 billion), Australia ($94 billion), and the UK ($80 billion). The Belt and Road clearly does not dominate Chinese OFDI overall. China's OFDI has many motives, but acquisition of technology has been a significant driver of OFDI in developed countries, and it has been a growing source of friction, particularly in the United States and Germany. While the reduction in OFDI in 2017 and 2018 was primarily driven by domestic Chinese policy, restrictions on acquisitions of high-tech firms in both Germany and the United States was a significant contributing factor. When benchmarked against the size of host country GDP, a different picture emerges: while cumulative Chinese direct investment in most developed economies was under 2 percent of 2017 GDP, for Sub-Saharan Africa as a whole the figure was 5.2 percent. This figure helps explain why the Chinese economic presence in Africa is so controversial. Moreover, while natural resource–seeking investment has become less dominant as a motive for

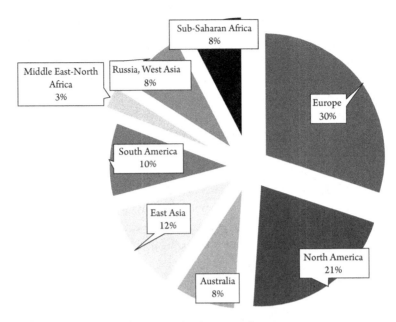

*Figure 6.5* Regional Composition of China's Outward Foreign Investment

China's OFDI, it has certainly not disappeared. China's cumulative investment in Australia was 7 percent of 2017 GDP, a response both to Australia's abundant minerals and to its excellent property rights regime. In recent years, China has used a combination of OFDI and loans to finally bring Russia's abundant oil resources into China's emerging continental pipeline network.[14] If China moves forward with liberalization of its capital account, we should expect OFDI to once again increase and flow toward a wide variety of developed and developing countries.

## Taking Stock

This chapter began with a discussion of structural changes reshaping the Chinese economy. Here we return to evaluate the extent to which changes in China's global economic interactions have been effective responses to those changes.

### A Creditor Nation

China is today a significant creditor nation, holding net foreign assets of about $2 trillion. However, the world has so far not been flooded with Chinese capital. Rather, China's net international assets have been stable since 2013, as both assets and liabilities have increased by about $1 trillion since. Most of China's immense savings is used at home, as China has pursued an historically unprecedented high investment policy. In addition, reforms that would have unleashed capital outflows largely failed and controls have been reinstated. As China now begins to age, we can expect that the domestic saving rate will begin to decline, but this may take a long time. In the meantime, major shifts in policy could still unleash a significant capital outflow.

China has so far not gained clear benefits from its status as a global creditor. Economically, China's foreign assets earn a rate of return much lower than what China pays foreigners for their assets in China. This was true in 2005–2007, and it is still true today, even though China has sought, since the GFC, to increase the rate of return of its external investments by moving away from low-yielding official reserves. A very rough rate of return can be calculated by dividing international investment income in the balance of payments by aggregate foreign assets at the end of the previous year. By this measure, China's aggregate rate of return was 3.4 percent in 2016–2018, while it paid foreign holders of Chinese assets 5.9 percent over the same period. On balance, China still borrows expensive money and loans it out cheaply.[15]

China's effort to gain influence by providing capital has been marked more by missteps than by notable successes. Among BRI countries, China's influence efforts collapsed in Malaysia, the Seychelles, and Sri Lanka when democratic elections evicted corrupt elites who had taken China's BRI money and profited from it. Yet surely the saddest story is that of Venezuela. By the time China began massive loans to Venezuela, it was obvious that the Venezuelan economy was heading for severe difficulties. The fact that Hugo Chávez proposed a socialist, revolutionary, and anti-American "Bolivarian" agenda obviously added to his attraction and may have blinded China to the gathering peril. In the event, much of the money in the China-Venezuela Development Fund was stolen, and a score of ambitious, unfinished projects, including a major railroad line, now lie abandoned and rusting in jungle. There is little doubt that China's generosity enabled irresponsible policymaking by the Chávez and Maduro governments. Hard currency loans (all in US dollars) provided the regime access to crucial imports, and facilitated widespread corruption among the Bolivarian elite. Very little was spent on vital investments in the oil sector. As the slow-motion Venezuelan collapse gathered momentum after 2016, China throttled back new lending, but by that time it had already extended $62 billion in cumulative lending to Venezuela. Estimating from the trade accounts, China could have been repaid a maximum of $40 billion, leaving it exposed to at least $20 billion in potential losses, only a small portion of which it is likely to get back. As Ferchen puts it, the China-Venezuela relationship became "completely dysfunctional for the governments, businesses and citizens of both countries."[16]

While no developing country fully escapes the dangers of debt diplomacy, experiences have varied substantially. For a number of countries, debt sustainability may become an issue, particularly if interest rates rise while raw material prices stay low. China's credit diplomacy has certainly increased its influence with Pakistan, tiny Laos and Cambodia, and neighboring Kazakhstan, among others. Many African countries have accepted Chinese aid and loans, and many have benefited from the developmental opportunities created. All that can be said is that the use of credit to generate international influence has led to a lower economic rate of return and uncertain diplomatic gains.

## Opening to the World

China reached a significant developmental turning point after 2010, but without becoming substantially more open. This is most obvious with respect to capital account liberalization and direct investment. Capital account opening failed once again in 2015–2016, after having been on the agenda, unrealized, for more than twenty years. In some cases, the absence of liberalization and further opening has been due to the real technical challenges of difficult reforms, but in other cases, it is the result of interest group influences and the reluctance of top policymakers to surrender direct control over the economy. The barriers on foreign company participation in many service sectors certainly fits in this latter category. As a result, China's opening is still very limited, controlled, and highly differentiated by sector.

This policy bias creates many problems for China and the world. In the first place, it creates friction with potential economic partners who increasingly perceive Chinese policy as mercantilist and designed to limit the benefits they get from economic interchange. It also limits China's options. For example, capital account opening could be achieved more easily if private parties could be attracted to participate more fully in China's stock and bond markets. However, right now, private foreign capital inflows are limited, because investors lack confidence in China's legal and regulatory framework. This makes it more difficult for China to open up and allow capital outflows. Further steps in domestic reform would make it easier to open up, because offsetting two-way capital flows would follow as investors on both sides diversified.

A strong security consideration has continued to be a major feature of China's international economic relations. Energy insecurity has lately been somewhat ameliorated by the completion of a pipeline network connecting China with Russia, Kazakhstan, and Turkmenistan. However, security considerations still limit China's willingness to import food grains (other than soybeans). Moreover, lately an entirely new concept of semiconductor insecurity has been introduced by US-China frictions. These limitations are likely to be just as salient for the foreseeable future.

## China's Relationship with International Economic Organizations

As Katherine Morton's chapter in this volume also argues, China's relationships with international organizations—including international economic organizations—are generally quite good. China often supports the agendas of those organizations, participates constructively and actively, and in return is treated generously by the organizations. The IMF, as discussed earlier, is a perfect example. China supported the IMF's redefinition of mission after the GFC, and the IMF in turn wishes to bring in China as a supporter in order to consolidate its own global legitimacy. To be sure, China has been frustrated by the slow pace of governance reform at the IMF, designed to increase the influence and voting weight of China and other fast-growing developing countries. For years the Europeans dragged their feet, unwilling to accept the decline in their collective voice, despite American prodding; then after agreement was finally reached in 2010, the US Congress refuse to ratify it, holding out for five more years even though every other nation had agreed. However, relations between China and the organization itself have generally been good. The same could be said about the World Bank.

More broadly, China maintains relatively good relations with quasi-governmental organizations and public bodies. The positive relations established with foreign central banks during the RMB internationalization campaign has encouraged China to allow foreign central banks into the domestic bond market. Foreign central banks are much more patient investors than private firms, and are therefore less sensitive to restrictions on liquidity and unclear regulation (they also have greater top-level bargaining power). This may encourage China in the next stage of market liberalization, to proceed with a partial opening of financial markets.

Despite its relatively good relations with multinational organizations, China never commits itself fully to their agendas. As Srikanth Kondapalli's chapter in this book illustrates well, China prefers to set up parallel organizations in which it has more direct influence, and is extremely hesitant to bind itself to the rules and principles of any single multinational organization. With "growing multilevel cooperation," China is able to play off different options in different situations. AIIB, for example, is a parallel structure to the World Bank and the ADB, but in another sense is parallel to CDB. Another example would be China's management of its government wealth portfolio. The China Investment Corporation (CIC) functions as a traditional sovereign wealth fund, committing itself to a portfolio approach of seeking financial return without interfering in governance.

At the same time, a parallel organization, Buttonwood Investment, wholly owned by China's State Administration of Foreign Exchange, functions as a parallel sovereign fund with much greater flexibility and less transparency, sometimes engaging in quick financial transactions and complex deals.

## Relations with Developed Countries

Since the beginning of the Trump Administration in 2016, US-China economic relations have taken a pronounced negative turn, culminating in the "trade war" of unilateral tariffs and mutual retaliation. What seems clear is that the economic relationship between China and most developed countries is deteriorating. There are strong economic reasons why the United States is at the forefront of this development: the large trade deficit the United States runs, the close integration of the two countries' high-tech sectors, and the frustration of U.S. service companies who would like entry into the China market. Along with these economic factors, there are of course also noneconomic factors, including strategic rivalry. Yet for all that, the main reason for deteriorating relations is the glaring lack of reciprocity in relations between China and other large economies.

As China has become a middle-income country, and as its pretensions to technological leadership have become more prominent, the need for a set of rules to govern head-to-head competition has become more pressing. Further market liberalization—as originally anticipated—would of course imply commitment to a new set of rules for deeper integration. In the absence of that liberalization, however, the developed countries face a newly assertive China without any clear mutually agreed principles to govern that competition. Without faith in the trajectory of China's market-oriented reforms, it is no wonder that developed economies look at China's policies with increasing unease.

China's dramatic growth has changed every aspect of the global economy. Yet China's policy adaptation to these changes seems incomplete and not yet successful. In its quest for greater international influence, China has opted for grand schemes of government activity rather than deeper integration. These choices have surprised outsiders and undermined the acceptance of China's rise that was founded on the success and dynamism of its reform process. It has also set the stage for an extended period of economic friction between China and, especially, the United States.

## Notes

1. PPP figures in constant 2011 dollars from World Bank, *World Development Indicators*, at https://databank.worldbank.org/data/reports.aspx?source=world-development-indicators.

2. Dollar, David. "Forty Years of Opening Up," in *Forty Years of Reforming China*, edited by Jacques deLisle and Avery Goldstein (Washington, DC: Brookings Institution Press, 2019).

3. Total domestic saving minus domestic investment equals "surplus saving" or capital outflows. Capital outflows—including accumulation of reserves by the central bank—must be equal to the current account surplus. The trade surplus is by far the largest component of the current account surplus for China.

4. Wen Jiabao, "Report on the Work of the Government (2010)," Third Session of the 11th National People's Congress, March 5, 2010, accessed at http://www.npc.gov.cn/englishnpc/Speeches/2010-03/19/content_1564308.htm.

5. Hu Jintao, "Resolutely Advance on the Road of Chinese-style Socialism and Struggle for a Well-off Society—Report to the 18th Congress of the Chinese Communist Party," November 8, 2012. Accessed at http://news.china.com.cn/politics/2012-11/20/content_27165856.htm.

6. Zhou Xiaochuan. "Reform the International Monetary System," March 23, 2009. Accessed at https://www.bis.org/review/r090402c.pdf.

7. Zhang Ming and Zhang Bin, "The Boom and Bust of the RMB's Internationalization: A Perspective from Cross-Border Arbitrage," *Asian Economic Policy Review* 12 (2017): 237–253.

8. Ibid.; Eswar Prasad, *Gaining Currency: The Rise of the Renminbi* (New York: Oxford University Press, 2016).

9. China Development Bank, "Serve OBOR Construction with Developmental Finance," Xinhua May 8, 2017. Accessed at http://news.xinhuanet.com/money/2017-05/08/c_129594753.htm; H. Sanderson and M. Forsythe, *China's Superbank: Debt, Oil, and Influence—How China Development Bank Is Rewriting the Rules of Finance* (Singapore: John Wiley & Sons, 2013).

10. Zu Fu, "In Planning for the Six Economic Corridors in OBOR, "Soft Connection" Is Receiving Attention," *21st Century Economic Herald*, May 28, 2015 (in Chinese), accessed at http://finance.ifeng.com/a/20150528/13737982_0.shtml.

11. Lichtenstein, Natalie. *A Comparative Guide to the Asian Infrastructure Investment Bank* (New York: Oxford University Press, 2019).

12. This comparison uses US import data from the Department of Commerce, accessed at https://www.census.gov/foreign-trade/balance/c5700.html, juxtaposed with Chinese export data. The US import data include the large volume of Chinese exports to Hong Kong that are re-exported to the United States, and include freight and insurance charges. Neither of these are included in Chinese export data. This imparts a small upward bias to the comparison, but allows us to show long-term trends accurately.

13. American Enterprise Institute and Heritage Foundation, "China Global Investment Tracker." https://www.aei.org/china-global-investment-tracker, accessed March 10, 2019.

14. Downs, Erica, "China-Russia Energy Relations: Better than Ever," in Erica Downs et al., *The Emerging Russia-Asia Energy Nexus* (Washington, DC: The National Bureau of Asian Research, NBR Special Report 74, December 2018), 17–31.

15. This analysis follows Prasad, *Gaining Currency*, 61–64, updated through 2018.

16. Ferchen, Matt. "Venezuela and China: A Risky Story of Oil and Money," *Open Democracy*, February 6, 2019. Accessed at https://www.opendemocracy.net/democraciaabierta/matt-ferchen/venezuela-and-china-perfect-storm.

# 7

# China's Global Cultural Interactions

SHAUN BRESLIN

The English town of Bicester has a population of just over 32,000 and lies roughly halfway between London and Birmingham. It is very much like any of the other smallish market towns that are a feature of the English countryside—with one important exception. On any given day, a visitor to the local outlet mall at Bicester Village will hear as much Chinese being spoken as English, often even more. Only the royal residence of Buckingham Palace in London is now thought to attract more Chinese visitors every year, and such is the importance of these visitors—both tourists and day-tripping UK-based Chinese students—that the shops employ native Chinese-language speakers, and signs at the local railway station are in Chinese as well as English.

While the small and charming size of Bicester makes its experiences rather unique, residents of university towns and cities across the world (and particularly in the English-speaking world) have also become more used to interacting with Chinese visitors on a daily basis. In a number of cases the growth in student numbers has been significant enough to result in changes to the structural basis of local "host" economies, either through a desire to attract Chinese to come or as a consequence of their arrival (or both). As student numbers have grown (now nearly one million worldwide), Chinese shops, restaurants, and other service providers have opened to serve their needs, either filling a pre-existing gap or adding new varieties to the Chinese goods and cuisines set up by longer-established communities of Chinese immigrants. In some cases, the construction of student-targeting housing projects has revitalized declining urban centers, and also has shifted local demographics (both in terms of ethnicity and age distribution).

Through both personal interactions and material change, the increased ability and desire of sections of the Chinese population to have international experiences has resulted in a growing awareness of Chinese preferences, expectations, and habits in recipient countries. Indeed, these individuals might have

Shaun Breslin, *China's Global Cultural Interactions* In: *China and the World*. Edited by: David Shambaugh, Oxford University Press (2020). © Oxford University Press
DOI: 10.1093/oso/9780190062316.003.0007

collectively (and inadvertently) done more to increase knowledge of China and its very broadly defined culture(s) than the massive amount of time, energy, and money that the Chinese state has spent on promoting itself overseas through explicit and deliberate cultural promotion projects. Yet it is perhaps too simplistic to argue that more people-based forms of cultural interaction are perceived positively (and thus are successful) and more state-directed ones negatively (and thus unsuccessful). Complaints about the behavior of some Chinese tourist groups provides one corrective to this view,[1] and the rather positive perception of official Chinese state projects in some developing countries—particularly, but not only, in Africa—provides another. It is also important to note that responses to China and its rise vary not just among countries, but within individual polities as well. This is true in general responses to growing Chinese presence as well as in response to specific individual projects, such as the way that different Confucius Institutes (CIs) are perceived in different places.[2] Moreover, it is rather difficult to take the Chinese state out of the equation in any area given the permissions and permits that are often required for international travel and contacts. And while it might be possible to try to gauge foreign opinions of China and how they have changed, it is all but impossible to separate out one individual causal source of this change. Nevertheless, there is a case for saying that, in general, the more the Chinese state is identified with a project the more suspicious target audiences (and particularly Western governments) are about the project's intentions, and thus perhaps the less successful it is likely to be.

This chapter proceeds by very briefly tracing the historical precedents behind the contemporary promotion of Chinese culture abroad, before moving to outline the various answers to the obvious first question: why bother? Given the focus that has been placed on major state projects—for example, mega events such as the Shanghai Expo or the Olympics, the promotion of Confucius Institutes (CIs) and classrooms, and the internationalization of the Chinese media—it makes sense to then turn to these questions: what has been done, why, and with what results? The final section will return to the importance of the more people-based forms of interaction with a specific focus on students and education. Here, I suggest that rather than just think about the specific promotion of Chinese culture itself, it is also important to consider the indirect cultural consequences of the growth of material resources and financial power.

The concept of "soft power" is often invoked when it comes to discussing the sort of issues that are considered in this chapter, not least within China itself where the term has gained popularity among both academics and politicians. While it is important to distinguish between different types and sources of global power, it seems somewhat odd to refer to a concerted and well-funded state project as being "soft." Moreover, it is used to refer to so many different types of activity by different analysts—including at times some distinctively hard features like strategic financial relations—that it is losing intersubjective meaning.[3] While drawing from a number of sources that frame themselves as the study of Chinese soft power,[4] this chapter will instead use the broader concept of "international cultural communications" to allow it to cover a range of both soft and somewhat harder ways in which a range of different Chinese actors try to promote a preferred story of China—what it is and what it wants—to international audiences.

## Selling China

The use of culture and media by the Chinese Communist Party (CCP) to try to influence others and win friends is nothing new. The establishment of the Chinese People's Association for Cultural Relations with Foreign Countries in May 1954 was an explicit attempt to use people-to-people exchanges to build sympathy and support for China in other countries at a time when the still rather new People's Republic did not have diplomatic relations with a number of states.[5] Four years later, *The Peking Review* was established to provide a Chinese view of Chinese developments in English (and later German, French, and Japanese) to an international audience. Alongside the *China Daily* (established in 1981), the now renamed *Beijing Review* continues to be a major print and web-based source of how China wants its news to be reported today. China set up its first overseas Cultural Centers in Mauritius and Benin in the 1980s,[6] around the same time that African students started studying in China in largish numbers on lengthy scholarships provided by the Chinese government.[7] And "sports diplomacy" (in the form of the Chinese team's participation in the 1971 world ping-pong championship in Tokyo and the subsequent invitation for the US team to visit China) facilitated the Sino-US rapprochement and the normalization of Sino-Japanese diplomatic relations.[8]

Although a central-level Foreign Propaganda Group (外宣领导小组) had existed since the 1980s, the origins of the contemporary formal state-led organizational approach to promoting Chinese culture and interests overseas can perhaps be dated to the establishment of a new Leading Group for Propaganda and Ideology work in 1990, and its subordinate, the State Council Information Office (国信办or SCIO) the following year.[9] This was a period when China's overseas reputation was still very much shaped by the Tiananmen Incident, and it is notable—though not surprising—that the central propaganda machinery has more control over national image promotion overseas than the Foreign Ministry and other government agencies.[10]

In 1991, the SCIO published the first Chinese White Paper on China's understanding of human rights, which perhaps marked the start of the official attempt to disseminate official counter-narratives to challenge dominant Western understandings by explaining Chinese goals and policies across a range of issue areas.[11] As the 1990s progressed, this effort began to expand as the "China Threat Theory" gained increasing popularity in China (the idea that foreigners were trying to paint a picture of a dangerous and revisionist China that would destabilize the existing global order). As a result, it became ever more important to find ways to "refute the 'China threat' thesis, facilitate a better understanding of China's domestic socio-economic reality, and persuade the outside world to accept and support China's rise."[12]

The first academic paper on Chinese soft power was written by then Fudan University academic (and now Politburo Standing Committee member) Wang Huning in 1993,[13] the same year that China was not awarded the millennium Olympic Games as had been widely expected (not least within China itself). If further evidence was required that China's international political standing could harm its increasingly globally interdependent growth prospects, it was provided in 1995 when what had become an annual vote condemning China's human rights record was only defeated by a single vote. Moreover, until 1999, Chinese access to the US market with "Most Favored Nation" status was dependent on approval via an annual Congressional vote in Washington that provided a ritualized opportunity for criticism of China to come to the fore.

Wang Huning swapped an academic career for a political one in 1995, and it is probably no mere coincidence that this second career coincides with the growth of policy interest in soft power and international cultural interactions. Wang started working in the Central Policy Research Office in 1995, became head of it under Hu Jintao in 2002, was appointed head of the Leading Group for Propaganda and Ideology Work in 2017 under Xi Jinping, and was appointed to the Politburo Standing Committee in the same year. It was under Hu Jintao that the promotion of what he explicitly referred to in his address to the 17th Party Congress in 2007 as Chinese "soft power" (软实力) entered a new period of study of how to improve it, supported by centrally mandated and funded projects to expand it. For the first time a specific Plan for National Cultural Development was developed domestically, and substantial funds began to be allocated for the promotion of Chinese culture abroad.[14] While not explicitly termed so, the establishment of the concept of the "peaceful rise" of China became a sort of official soft power state mantra, designed to act as a direct antidote to the idea of a China threat.

However, as with many issue areas, things that started with earlier leaders have been taken to a new level and a new intensity under Xi Jinping. His stated goal is to "increase China's soft power, give a good Chinese narrative, and better communicate China's messages to the world" and to turn China into a "socialist cultural superpower."[15] The method is to establish a new "go-global, multi-platform, national and international strategic communication strategy."[16]

## Goals and Drivers

The obvious first question to ask is why spend so much time, effort, and money trying to promote these visions of China and Chinese culture given what appears to be their rather partial success (at best) in influencing others and creating a popular global image of China (perceptions of China in global public opinion polls remain decidedly mixed)? One motivation is that this is simply the sort of thing that Great Powers do (and a number of not so great ones as well). Or put another way, if China is to be—and seen and believed to be—a truly global actor and global power, then it is incumbent that the government project itself as a global cultural actor in ways commensurate to its overall comprehensive national power. This entails doing some of the things that the British Council, the Goethe Institute, or the Cervantes Institute does. Holding high-profile global events like the World Expo in 2010 and the China International Investment Expo in 2018, both in Shanghai, also serves a sort of global power benchmarking purpose, while the 2008 Beijing Olympics also played a signaling role as a "'coming out party' for a rising China."[17]

The idea that states (particularly, but not only, emerging great powers) are driven by the desire for status has a relatively long tradition in international relations studies, and China has been depicted as not so much one example, but arguably the most status-driven of all contemporary powers.[18] The desire to gain status is intertwined with, but not identical to, the importance of respect;[19] status is about having a recognized position and respect is about a positive external appreciation of how that status was achieved. Although the focus of this chapter is on the external projection of China, it is important to acknowledge that both status and respect play important domestic roles too. Being *seen* to be a global power fits with the people's own image of what China is (or should be).[20] This potentially generates gratitude to the Party for delivering China back to its rightful position (status), while the recognition of and admiration for this re-emergence by others (respect) provides further external validation for the Party's policies and strategies, reinforcing its "moral authority" to rule.[21]

Either through ignorance or through the deliberate misrepresentation of China by those who want to check its rise, debates about China's rise in other countries are believed to be often based on fundamental misunderstandings of what China is, what it will be, and what it will want to be in the future.[22] Hence the need for China to try and control the way that that China is understood by changing the way that people come into contact with China, telling different stories of China to those that are usually told in the international media (or telling those existing stories in different ways), and *controlling the international narrative* on the consequences of China's rise. Above all else, this is the main objective of China's intercultural communications. This entails establishing an idea of the "Chinese difference"—a country that will not simply act as other previous and contemporary Great Powers acted because it has a fundamentally different set of belief systems that emerge from a different set of histories and experiences and different philosophical precedents. It is an exercise in the promotion of difference and exceptionalism.

To this end, the very public embrace of the promotion of soft power by the Chinese leadership is in itself a tool of persuasion; that is, the very act of talking about soft power is important in itself. Just as the European Union has a self-identity as a "normative power" that is a different type of global actor than traditional powers, so China's leaders are attempting to establish the identity of a "soft power great power" in contrast to the hard power preferences, historical actions, and the "outdated Cold-War mentality and zero-sum mindset" of Western Great Powers.[23] Moreover, this is depicted not just as a matter of choice, but is embedded in China's historical and cultural traditions found in Confucianism, Taoism, Buddhism, and other classics[24] (there isn't space here to interrogate the way in which a range of different and often competing philosophical traditions have been bundled together to form a single Chinese cultural tradition). It is not just in China that histories and traditions have been redefined to serve current political needs. Nevertheless, the way that what "was once believed to be the major obstacle to economic development in Asia" and a source of many of China's problems has become the cultural bedrock of a new "era of Sino-centred economic prosperity and alternative Chinese modernity" is rather noteworthy.[25] So too is the fact that while there are some who think that there is global appeal in China's modern political structures and thinking, there is a broad consensus that it makes more sense to focus on "China's vast historical and cultural tradition . . . as a rich resource to be used to attract foreigners to learn more about the country and to improve China's status in the eyes of the world."[26]

One key implication is that this is not just about China—it is also about the way that international relations and the global order are organized, or more correctly *should* be organized. At the very least, we can argue that China is engaged in an attempt to block the dominance of Western discourses and thinking by taking the lead in providing "a discourse on international affairs, as an alternative to a 'Western' discourse."[27] For example, China was one of the promoters of UNESCO's Convention on the Diversity of Cultural Expressions in 2005 that protects the rights of governments to protect and promote their indigenous cultural goods and services,[28] and has been one of the major funders of its International Fund for the Cultural Diversity.[29]

## Tools and Mechanisms

Much of what is done to facilitate global cultural interactions and sell the preferred self-image of China looks like straightforward old-fashioned diplomacy.

### Forums and Networks

This includes a wide range of summits, conferences, and global events either organized by China or, as in the case of the Olympics, allocated to China by a global organization—which are specifically used by the Chinese government to try and influence a wider global audience. Even China's hosting of peripatetic global meetings such as the G-20 are often thought of as soft power tools in China, in the way that "host diplomacy" allows China to exert influence by setting agendas and through the collateral contacts with journalists and researchers that usually accompany these events.[30]

The relationship between research institutions and the party-state is another example of how China seeks to project official policies abroad. International interaction between researchers is normally thought of as being something separate from formal diplomacy, conducted by people who are not direct agents of the state. In the Chinese case, there is more to the role of think tanks than just repeating the official line, and as a number of universities and enterprises have now set up their own think tanks as ways of packaging and disseminating academic research, the Chinese think tank community has grown and become more diverse in terms of funding and direct affiliations. That said, many of them remain close to their Party or state patrons—not least some of the more influential ones—as Wang and Xue find that even independent think tanks tend to follow government policy rather than try to be innovative (let alone to challenge existing policy).[31] Indeed, the expansion of think tanks was a result of a central initiative enunciated by Xi Jinping, and a national steering group exists to ensure that they become "an intelligence platform for China's international strategy in the new era."[32]

Two more recent developments of semi-formal exchanges warrant special attention. The first is the development of a range of China-led think tank networks: the China-Latin America and Caribbean Think Tanks Forum was set up in 2010, the China-Africa Think Tanks Forum in 2012, the Silk Road Think Tanks Forum and the China-East and Central European Countries Think

Tank Network both in 2015, and the China Council for BRICS Think Tanks Cooperation in 2016.[33] These individual networks combine to create a bigger Sinocentric hub-and-spoke complex that has considerable potential to facilitate the promotion of Chinese interests.

The second relates to the Belt and Road Initiative (BRI). This is a project that lends itself to cultural interactions. It is, after all, supposedly built on historical precursors, historical roots, the replication of historical patterns of trade, and also the historical movement of people—the old and ancient Silk Road combined with the idea of a pacific (in more than one way) maritime history perhaps best epitomized by the voyages of Zheng He. It is perhaps no surprise that these precedents have been emphasized through the funding of "museums, expos, festivals, and countless intangible heritage initiatives," and a concerted attempt to promote the BRI as being more than just about economics, but having a shared cultural basis as well.[34]

## The Media

Explaining and promoting the BRI has also become a major task for China's foreign language media, with China Global Television Network (CGTN), for example, carrying a number of specials on various BRI projects. As CGTN produces and broadcasts some of its daily output from its Nairobi office and has a strong Africa focus, reports on BRI projects on the continent are particularly prominent. CGTN is the inheritor of the English-language television output first broadcast by CCTV (China Central Television) on Channel 9 from 2000, with a claimed international viewership of 200 million in 2017 (outside China) in six different languages.[35] Along with China Radio International (CRI), the inheritor of the New China News Radio first broadcast from Yan'an during the revolution, CGTN and the other foreign-language services provided by CCTV are charged with enhancing China's "communication capacity" (传共能力)—increasing the appeal, impact, and credibility of China's media output.[36] In addition to English, CCTV broadcasts ten channels internationally including content in French, Arabic, Spanish, Russian, and Japanese (as well as, of course, Chinese). According to Thussu, "in 2017, China Radio International was broadcasting in 61 languages via its six overseas regional hubs and 32 bureaus. It had affiliations with 70 overseas radio stations and 18 global internet radio services."[37]

While originally separate organizations under the National Radio and Television Administration (and its various predecessors), their administration and leadership were combined along with the domestic China National Radio into a single new centralized Voice of China in March 2018 in a very obvious echo of the Voice of America, which at the time of writing had the capacity to broadcast in forty-three languages having (in contrast to CRI) cut a number of services since the turn of the millennium. This new initiative is under the direct leadership of the Central Propaganda Department. It is important to note that the Chinese term for propaganda (宣传) does not have the same connotation of forced thought change or brainwashing that is often the case in English.[38] Indeed, it can also mean "publicity" or "advocacy" in Chinese, and the Propaganda Department is often called the Publicity Department in English (including in official Chinese sources).

It is fair to say that if this administrative reorganization was not important, then there would have been no need for it to happen. It is also fair to say that it creates something of a tension in the dual objectives of these overseas media actors. There is, of course, a specific China focus to their broadcasting, and propagating the preferred narrative of China is their main task. However, there is also an aspiration to become a credible source of global news reporting, something akin to the way that Al Jazeera has come to challenge the dominance of the traditional Western broadcasters,[39] not just to explain China to the world but also "to explain the world to the world."[40] In particular, the official Chinese media has self-avowedly positioned itself as a voice of the Global South as a whole, "claiming to articulate a Southern news agenda" rather than just a Chinese one, and an antidote to what is depicted as mainstream negative reporting of Africa in particular.[41] The challenge, then, is how they can both be a credible international news source, and a voice of China at the same time?

One solution is presentation. CGTN has an immediate look and feel of familiarity and conformity, as much of its output is fronted by non-Chinese anchors (including from its foreign bureaus), and its promotional links for later programs and trailing of upcoming stories use graphics, videos, and station IDs that will be very familiar to consumers of international news networks. To be sure, many of the programs are specifically about China, and there are more Chinese academics, analysts, and experts in the interview chair than would be the case with other channels. But it is entirely possible to turn to CGTN when surfing through channels and not immediately realize that it is a Chinese news channel at all— particularly if you are expecting to see the CCTV logo in the corner.

The original Chinese source of material might not also be clear to the casual viewer when it appears on other stations' outputs through content swaps, such as the one CCTV signed with Sky News Australia in 2011,[42] or the multifaceted exchange agreed by the Media Group and Argentinian broadcasters in 2018. Such formal collaborations are also a feature of the print media, with the UK *Daily Mail*, for example, agreeing to swap content with the *People's Daily* in 2016. The *China Daily* also pays for its English-language monthly *China Watch* to be inserted into major outlets like the *Washington Post*, *Sydney Morning Herald*, and the *Daily Telegraph* in the UK.[43] Paid *China Daily* advertising inserts into regional newspapers in the United States that looked at first sight very much like news articles on the Sino-US trade dispute were used as evidence by President Trump of China's attempt to influence the midterm US elections in 2018.[44] A *Financial Times* investigation also found that around 200 nominally independent Chinese-language media providers were using (often free) content provided by the *People's Daily* or the Xinhua News Agency,[45] while CRI both has bought radio stations overseas and has controlling interests in others that broadcast "China-friendly news and programming."[46]

All of this is in addition to what the various foreign-language versions of the *People's Daily, China Daily, Global Times,* and the Xinhua News Agency publish themselves in print and online. *People's Daily,* for example, has an online presence in Arabic, French, Russian, Spanish, Japanese, and English as well as Chinese and claims to be "one of the largest comprehensive internet media sources in the world" with over 50 million social media followers. This includes the claim that its 44.4 million Facebook followers is the largest active followership of any print newspaper in the world on Facebook; which is somewhat ironic given Facebook's inaccessibility in China itself.[47] *China Daily* claims a daily circulation of 900,000 (a third in China itself) and a total readership of 45 million either in print or online.[48] As with the broadcast media, the print media has globalized its operations at a time when some longer-standing Western newspapers are reducing their presence. In South Africa, this entailed the *China Daily* simply picking up the staff, print, and distribution arrangements of the *Financial Times* as it ceased its local print run.[49]

Xinhua, or the New China News Agency, remains China's main state news agency, providing content for the major newspapers and for its own website. It is also a global media player, providing content in English, Spanish, Portuguese, Arabic, Russian, French, and Chinese from its 170 Chinese and overseas bureaus to over 200 international clients. While it is still very much a political actor, holding a ministerial-level rank in the Chinese administrative hierarchy, it has also become a profitable commercial media actor.[50] In this respect, Xinhua perhaps represents the biggest success of China's media based international cultural communication strategy.

## Art and Film

One area where even the exposure—let alone the impact—has been less than expected is in terms of the external penetration of Chinese popular cultural products. This might sound strange given the vast amounts of money that have been spent on funding a range of different types of cultural exchanges over the years. These range from specially themed China Cultural Years and exchanges,[51] to short individual-focused events like the EU-China Literature Festival first held in 2017. Indeed, China has become host to some of the biggest book festivals in the world as well as a regular high-profile attender at similar events overseas. It might sound even stranger when one considers that when a small part of the Terracotta Army was loaned to the British Museum in 2007 it had to change its opening hours to try to accommodate the demand, or the argument that the increased popularity of Chinese lantern and food festivals in the United States has increased "China's soft power."[52]

All of this is true, and there is no denying the pull that China's history, culture, and food has outside the country. And it feeds into the pull of China in other ways as well—most notably in terms of inward tourism. Whether this pull translates to sympathy or support for China's present and political structures and objectives is, of course, still very much open to question, and the single biggest question facing the architects of the promotion of China's overseas cultural presence.

But when it comes to modern popular culture, the record is rather different, particularly when compared to the popularity across the Asian region of, for example, soap operas, pop music, and comics from Japan, South Korea, and Taiwan[53]—or even when comparing the reach of the Chinese film industry into its global diaspora when compared to output from India. Moreover, Chinese cultural products and producers that have gained fame and recognition overseas have not always been that popular (or even well known) with domestic audiences or the Chinese state. This is particularly so when the political message of the art or artist does not coincide with state interests. The most obvious example is a comparison between the international reputation of Nobel Prize winner Liu Xiaobo and his domestic treatment as a political dissident. The work and reputation of Ai Weiwei is also a good example. And while Chen Kaige's *Farewell My Concubine* shared the 1993 Palme d'Or at Cannes with *The Piano*, it was banned by the state (before later being re-released in cut form).

Kung Fu films have been popular outside China for decades. But while they do present one vision of China, their global reach originates from the Hong Kong film industry, which still represents a "different" China from the PRC, and has a distinct and separate media industry.[54] Moreover, many of the more financially successful Chinese-language films have been either produced, funded, and distributed by mainstream US studios, or at least had significant involvement by them in partnership with Chinese (and often other) interests.[55] Dreamworks-produced Kung Fu Panda films were heavily criticized by some in China for appropriating and using Chinese cultural icons and presenting an American version of China to a global audience rather than a Chinese one,[56] but both still broke box office records in China itself (for animated movies) and prompted much debate as to why China could not reproduce its own cultural heritage in such entertaining and profitable ways. While some Chinese films like *The Mermaid, Wolf Warrior,* and *The Detective* films have had some overseas impact, this tends to be in countries with sizeable Chinese-speaking communities. For the time being, the main market for Chinese-made films remains overwhelmingly within China itself.

Disney, Sony, Warner Bros, and Dreamworks have now all developed various forms of collaboration with Chinese actors (including the Ministry of Culture). Though these are designed in part to increase the global penetration of Chinese output,[57] the desire of key global media actors (and some governments) to collaborate with Chinese partners is largely driven by the desire to open the still relatively closed domestic Chinese market, in the first instance to break the strict limitations on distribution of foreign films in China, with an eye to being able to participation in Chinese online media more generally in the longer run.[58] The casting of some films also seems to have been influenced by a search for a Chinese release and a Chinese market, as has also been the case in the ways films have been cut and edited. Here the source of the power that China seems to have when it comes to the film industry lies not so much in its culture as in the preferences of Chinese consumers combined with the Chinese government's ability and willingness to ration access to some key sectors.

## Education and Exchanges

The promotion of Chinese language teaching was identified by the Ministry of Culture in 2003 as a key means of increasing China's global voice by facilitating "friendship and mutual understanding."[59] Building on this understanding, the Ministry of Education produced a Plan for Study in China in 2010 that outlined the goal of China becoming the world's biggest destination for students going abroad by attracting half a million of them by 2020. These students, the plan argues (or hopes), will "both understand China and contribute to connecting China to the rest of the world."

The Institute of International Education's Project Atlas reports 442,773 overseas students in China in 2017, up from 328,330 when they started recording Chinese statistics in 2013 and just under 200,000 in 2007.[60] This placed China behind only the United States (just over one million incomers in 2016) and the UK (501,045 in 2017) as the world's third biggest destination for overseas students. Of these, almost one in six came from South Korea (70,540), and although the United States is the second largest origin of students with 23,838, it is instructive that this is only slightly more than from Thailand. Overall, seven countries in China's "back yard" (those that might expect to be most directly influenced by China's continued rise) provided 37.6 percent of all international students in 2017, and the same states have been the biggest source of international students in China for a number of years.[61] Perhaps more surprising, in

2016 there were more students from Anglophone Africa studying in China than in either the United States or the United Kingdom, and the Chinese government has formally committed itself to training more African future elites.[62]

The majority of the work that has been conducted on the consequences of the growth of international education for China has tended to focus on Chinese students going overseas rather than vice versa. Though some have found that studying overseas does lead to a more positive impression of the host country,[63] other studies show more mixed findings,[64] with one study of Chinese students returning from South Korea suggesting that the shorter the stay, the more positive the outlook.[65] And while in general there is a consensus that "international academic exchange does provide increased intercultural understanding," understanding is not always the same as liking and liking a country is not always the same as supporting that country's government's policies.[66]

While the numbers of foreigners studying in China each year might not be that large, there is a relatively large stock of ex-students now who occupy high-level positions in business, academia, and government around the world. But it is fair to say that they do not form a single cohesive group with a shared positive view of China and its objectives. The reality is that many of those who have studied in China find much to love and admire and much to be critical of at the same time.

## Confucius Institutes

Of course, one does not have to physically go to China to study Chinese language, culture, and history. If the teaching is available, you can do it at home as well. Through the promotion of Confucius Institutes (CIs), Confucius Classrooms, and other cultural projects overseas, the Chinese state has been more than happy to provide these opportunities. CIs fall under the control of the Ministry of Education–affiliated Hanban, officially translated in English as the Office of Chinese Language Council International. Having set up the first CIs in 2004, over 500 were in operation at the end of 2018 (137 in Asia and Oceania, 173 in Europe, 54 in Africa, 110 in the United States, and 51 in the rest of the Americas and the Caribbean). There were also over 1,000 smaller Confucius Classrooms providing some form of Chinese language or cultural training in schools, just under half of them in the United States.[67] As each of these 1,500 or so projects entails a collaboration between at least one Chinese and one foreign institution, there is now an extensive network of international institutional partnerships as well as the delivery of courses, resources, and language testing as a result of this rather rapid expansion.[68]

On the face of it this all sounds rather positive, particularly given the oft-repeated argument in large parts of the world that we need more people with Chinese language skills to deal with the consequence of a more globally active China. Yet the CIs have become one of the most closely observed and intensely debated instruments of Chinese cultural interactions. The most commonly voiced criticism is that they go further than simply promoting Chinese culture and/or positive (in Chinese views) stories and counternarratives to the dominantly negative foreign ones. In addition, so the argument goes, they control what can and cannot be said and debated about China in the universities that host them, either through outright controls and bans, or through a more intangible inculcation of a culture of self-censorship among those who research or teach China-related issues. While there has always been suspicion of what CIs are *really* there to do, this has intensified as investigations into other forms of Chinese political influence increased in the 2010s, particularly but not only in Australasia and North America.

The devil is partly in the detail, and partly in the presentation. The detail includes employment contracts that impose restrictions on who can be appointed—for example, not those who have a record of supporting the Falun Gong. In terms of presentation, former CCP propaganda chief Li Changchun's assertion in 2009 that CIs were "an important part of China's overseas propaganda set-up" has become the starting point for many appraisals of CIs and has been taken as an official statement of pernicious intent (even though, as we have already noted, propaganda has different connotations in China than in the West).[69] Moreover, the eagerness of Chinese leaders to visit and praise CIs when on overseas trips only serves to increase the sense of them being part of the political machinery directed from the very top.[70]

Certainly, there have been cases where CIs or the Hanban have acted in ways that have done harm to their reputation (in addition to controlling hiring criteria, as noted above). Interference in the European Association of Chinese Studies Conference in Portugal in 2014 is perhaps the most striking example of a direct intrusion into academic independence in a way that alienated large parts of the academic China studies community.[71] There is no way of knowing how widespread self-censorship has become. That said, the main concern about CIs seems to be not so much about what they have done to date as what they *might* do in the future. Most important of all, CIs feed into more general suspicions of China's global objectives—or, more correctly, this suspicion shapes the way that CIs are viewed. They are increasingly seen as forming part of a multifaceted "United Front" project through which the CCP forms relationships with political, economic, and societal elites and groups in other countries to "support and promote . . . foreign policy goals."[72] CIs have been identified as one of the tools of influence promotion, occupying the "gray areas" between licit and illegal forms of political interference,[73] and their impact on political debate has been the subject of inquiries in Australia, the United States, and the UK. They have become part of larger and sometimes unspecific concerns about the consequences of the rise of China for the functioning of politics within specific individual Western democracies, and also maybe for the future of the existing liberal global order.

# Conclusion

Separating out the impact of cultural interactions from other processes and instruments of international exchange is inherently difficult, probably impossible. These cultural projects do not exist in isolation, but coexist alongside a range of other forms of connectivity: economic, diplomatic, military, ideational, and so on. Opinions and perceptions of China, or any other country for that matter, are shaped by the totality of these engagements and not just one of them. One thing we can say with some certainty is that China's voices and Chinese views of China's rise are now more available than ever before, especially for those who don't speak or read Chinese. They are also more listened to and accessed then ever before.

In some parts of the world, there does seem to be some evidence that they have not just been listened to, but also embraced. In parts of Africa, for example, Madrid-Morales points to a "politically welcoming environment" for Chinese initiatives—though he also notes that what he calls the "foreign policy jargon" of "win-win relations and mutual benefit" with concrete economic and other projects does quite a lot to create a positive impression of China that cultural projects both feed into and benefit from.[74] It might be rather cynical to suggest that a culture is more attractive when it is accompanied by money—but maybe not totally incorrect. Nevertheless, it is important to recognize that there has been at least some success in getting the message across.

But as the example of CIs show, Chinese initiatives have been far from universally welcomed. This might partly be because the pre-existing perception of China can dictate the way that the interaction is perceived, rather than that interaction changing the perception. If, for example, there is a concern that China is trying to change the world, and that China's leaders maintain a commitment to, in the words of Xi Jinping, "give a good Chinese narrative, and better communicate China's messages to the world,"[75] then this looks very much like evidence of this transformative project, rather than a benign attempt to correct misunderstandings. So while China's leaders might use the term "soft power," the promotion of a preferred national image by a concerted effort coordinated and funded by the state can look somewhat less than "soft" among target audiences. As a result, what started out as a project to weaken the "China Threat Thesis" has in some places actually strengthened existing China threat perceptions.[76] It might turn out that the cultural promotion project does a better job of helping win supporters in the developing world than it does changing minds in the West.

The lukewarm (at best) reception might also be partly due to a perceived disjuncture between what the Chinese state promotes as a vision of China, and what it does on a daily basis. As argued in this chapter, there remains a clear emphasis on China's historical cultural roots as a source of attraction, backed up by China's contemporary economic weight. The way in which China has attained this economic growth and power in ways that don't conform to neoliberal prescriptions and expectations is also considered to be attractive too. But despite the new mantra of Chinese self-confidence in its own systems and paths, the way China's political system is structured and organized does not seem to have much magnetism. Many find China's growing military might less than attractive too—particularly, but not only, in China's own back yard. So, the key to how stories about China are told and understood in the future is likely to depend more on how the Chinese state utilizes its power at home and abroad than it does on the continuation of an expansive cultural promotion project.

# Notes

1. In 2013, the China National Tourism Agency even produced guidance on how to behave overseas in order to prevent tourists becoming a form of negative soft power.
2. Yuan Zhenjie, Guo Junwanguo, and Zhu Hong, "Confucius Institutes and the Limitations of China's Global Cultural Network," *China Information* 30, no. 3 (2016): 334–356.
3. I have explored what I believe to be these conceptual and definitional problems in more detail in Shaun Breslin, "The Soft Notion of China's 'Soft Power,'" Chatham House Asia Program Paper No. 3, February 2011, https://www.chathamhouse.org/sites/default/files/public/Research/Asia/0211pp_breslin.pdf.
4. For further studies of China's soft power see: Li Mingjiang, *Soft Power: China's Emerging Strategy in International Politics* (Lanham, MD: Lexington Books, 2009); Ingrid d'Hooghe, *China's Public Diplomacy* (Amsterdam: Brill, 2014); Sheng Ding, *The Dragon's Hidden Wings: How China Rises with Its Soft Power* (Lanham, MD: Lexington Books, 2008); Clive Hamilton, *Silent Invasion: China's Influence in Australia* (Sydney: Hardie Grant, 2018); Michael Barr, *Who's Afraid of China? The Challenge of Chinese Soft Power* (London: Zed Books, 2011); and Hongyi Lai and Yiyi Lu, eds., *China's Soft Power and International Relations* (London: Routledge, 2012).
5. It became the Chinese People's Association for Friendship with Foreign Countries in 1969 and is still in operation today.
6. Zhang Weihong, "China's Cultural Future: From Soft Power to Comprehensive National Power," *International Journal of Cultural Policy* 16, no. 4 (2010): 344.
7. To learn Chinese in order to then take degree courses in Chinese in medicine, science, and engineering and so on. Very small numbers of students had first traveled to China in the 1950s. See Hannane Ferdjani, "African Students in China: An Exploration of Increasing Numbers and Their Motivations in Beijing," Stellenbosch University Centre for Chinese Studies, September 2012, http://citeseerx.ist.psu.edu/viewdoc/download?doi=10.1.1.470.8611&rep=rep1&type=pdf.
8. Mayumi Ito, *The Origin of Ping-Pong Diplomacy: The Forgotten Architect of Sino-US Rapprochement* (Basingstoke: Palgrave, 2011).

9. For details of this origins period, see Anne-Marie Brady, *Marketing Dictatorship: Propaganda and Thought Work in Contemporary China* (Lanham, MD: Rowman and Littlefield, 2008); and David Shambaugh, "China's External Propaganda Work: Missions, Messengers, Mediums," in *Party Watch Annual Report 2018*, edited by Julie Bowie and David Glitter, 25–33 (Washington, DC: Center for Advanced China Research, 2018).

10. Rogier Creemers, "Never the Twain Shall Meet? Rethinking China's Public Diplomacy Policy," *Chinese Journal of Communication* 8, no. 3 (2015): 309.

11. Wang Hongying, "National Image Building and Chinese Foreign Policy," *China: An International Journal* 1, no. 1 (2003): 46–72.

12. Li Mingjiang, "Soft Power in Chinese Discourse: Popularity and Prospect," in *Soft Power: China's Emerging Strategy in International Politics*, edited by Li Mingjiang, 31 (Lanham, MD: Lexington, 2009).

13. David Shambaugh, *China Goes Global: The Partial Power* (Oxford: Oxford University Press, 2013): 210.

14. Zhang, "China's Cultural Future."

15. David Shambaugh, "China's Soft Power Push: The Search for Respect," *Foreign Affairs* (June–July 2015): 99.

16. Anne-Marie Brady, "Magic Weapons: China's Political Influence Activities under Xi Jinping," Woodrow Wilson Center Kissinger Institute on China and the United States, September 2017, https://www.wilsoncenter.org/sites/default/files/magicweaponsanne-mariebradyseptember162017.pdf, 9.

17. Elizabeth Perry, "Cultural Governance in Contemporary China: 'Reorienting' Party Propaganda," Harvard-Yenching Institute Working Paper, 2013, 4, http://nrs.harvard.edu/urn-3:HUL.InstRepos:11386987.

18. Yong Deng, *China's Struggle for Status: The Realignment of International Relations* (Cambridge: Cambridge University Press, 2008).

19. Shambaugh, "China's Soft Power Push."

20. Andrew Scobell, "Learning to Rise Peacefully? China and the Security Dilemma," *Journal of Contemporary China* 21, no. 76 (2012): 713–721.

21. Kingsley Edney, "Building National Cohesion and Domestic Legitimacy: A Regime Security Approach to Soft Power in China," *Politics* 35, no. 3–4 (2015): 259–272.

22. And it is probably worth repeating here the argument, captured in Shambaugh's *China Goes Global: The Partial Power*, that any view that does not coincide with the Chinese state's official stance is dismissed (or belittled) as being based on misunderstanding rather than being a genuinely held different opinion. Shambaugh, *Partial Power*, 263–264.

23. Yang Jiechi, "Working Together to Build a World of Lasting Peace and Universal Security and a Community with a Shared Future for Mankind," Address at the Opening Ceremony of the Seventh World Peace Forum, Tsinghua University, Beijing, 14 July 2018, https://www.fmprc.gov.cn/mfa_eng/zxxx_662805/t1577242.shtml.

24. Wu You, "The Rise of China with Cultural Soft Power in the Age of Globalization," *Journal of Literature and Art Studies* 8, no. 5 (2018): 766.

25. John Eperjesi, "Crouching Tiger, Hidden Dragon: Kung Fu Diplomacy and the Dream of Cultural China," *Asian Studies Review* 28, no. 1 (2004): 30.

26. Kingsley Edney, "Soft Power and the Chinese Propaganda System," *Journal of Contemporary China* 21, no. 78 (2012): 909.

27. Zhang Xiaoling, "How Ready Is China for a China-Style World Order? China's State Media Discourse under Construction," *Ecquid Novi: African Journalism Studies* 34, no. 3 (2013): 99.

28. Holly Aylett, "An International Instrument for International Cultural Policy: The Challenge of UNESCO's Convention on the Protection and Promotion of the Diversity of Cultural Expressions 2005," *International Journal of Cultural Studies* 13, no. 4 (2010): 355–373.

29. Antonios Vlassis, "Soft Power, Global Governance of Cultural Industries and Rising Powers: The Case of China," *International Journal of Cultural Policy* 22, no. 4 (2016): 485.

30. Chen Dongxiao, "China's 'Host Diplomacy': Opportunities, Challenges, and Undertakings," China Institute of International Studies, November 2014, http://www.ciis.org.cn/english/2014-11/14/content_7369348.htm.

31. Wang Hongying and Xue Yinghu, "The New Great Leap Forward: Think Tanks with Chinese Characteristics," CIGI Papers No. 142, September 2017, https://www.cigionline.org/sites/default/files/documents/Paper%20No.142.pdf.
32. Yuan Peng, "China's International Strategic Thought and Layout for a New Era," *Contemporary International Relations* 28, no. 1 (2018): 28.
33. For the evolution of Chinese think tank activity, see Silvia Menegazzi, *Rethinking Think Tanks in Contemporary China* (Basingstoke: Palgrave, 2017).
34. Tim Winter, "One Belt, One Road, One Heritage: Cultural Diplomacy and the Silk Road," *The Diplomat*, March 2016, https://thediplomat.com/2016/03/one-belt-one-road-one-heritage-cultural-diplomacy-and-the-silk-road/.
35. Daya Thussu, Hugo de Burgh, and Shi Anbin, "Introduction," in *China's Media Go Global*, edited by Daya Thussu, Hugo de Burgh, and Anbin Shi, 2 (New York: Routledge, 2018)..
36. Sun Wanning, "Mission Impossible? Soft Power, Communication Capacity, and the Globalization of Chinese Media," *International Journal of Communication* 4 (2010): 54–5.
37. Daya Thussu, "Globalization of Chinese Media: The Global Context," in *China's Media Go Global*, edited by Daya Thussu, Hugo de Burgh, and Shi Anbin, 19 (New York: Routledge, 2018). Details can be found on its website (http://chinaplus.cri.cn), which itself is available in forty-seven different languages as well as both simplified and traditional Chinese.
38. See Anne-Marie Brady, "China's Foreign Propaganda Machine," *Journal of Democracy* 26, no. 4 (2015): 51–59; and Shambaugh, "China's Soft Power Push."
39. Creemiers, "Never the Twain."
40. Zhou Qing'an and Wu Yanni, "The Three Patterns of Chinese International Communication," in *China's Media Go Global*, edited by Daya Thussu, Hugo de Burgh, and Shi Anbin, 249 (New York: Routledge, 2018).
41. Thussu, "Globalization of Chinese Media," 19.
42. Jukka Aukia, *The Disrespected State: China's Struggle for Recognition through "Soft Power,"* University of Turku PhD thesis, 2017, 83.
43. For details see Louisa Lim and Julia Bergin, "Inside China's Audacious Global Propaganda Campaign," *The Guardian*, December 7, 2018, https://www.theguardian.com/news/2018/dec/07/china-plan-for-global-media-dominance-propaganda-xi-jinping.
44. His tweet on the topic from September 26, 2018, is available at https://tinyurl.com/yacyk934.
45. Emily Feng, "China and the World: How Beijing Spreads the Message," *Financial Times*, July 12, 2018, https://www.ft.com/content/f5d00a86-3296-11e8-b5bf-23cb17fd1498.
46. Koh Gui Qing and John Shiffman, "Voice of China: China's Covert Radio Network Airs China-Friendly News across Washington and the World," Reuters, November 2, 2015, https://www.reuters.com/investigates/special-report/china-radio/.
47. See http://en.people.cn/n3/2018/0706/c90828-9478507.html.
48. See http://www.chinadaily.com.cn/static_e/printmedia.html.
49. Anton Harber, "China's Soft Diplomacy in Africa," *Ecquid Novi: African Journalism Studies* 34, no. 3 (2013): 150.
50. Hong Junhao, "From the World's Largest Propaganda Machine to a Multipurposed Global News Agency: Factors in and Implications of Xinhua's Transformation since 1978," *Political Communication* 28, no. 3 (2011): 377–393.
51. Examples include reciprocal years of each other with France from 2003–2005 and Russia in 2006–2007, and Chinese Cultural Years in Germany in 2012, the UK in 2015, and Mexico in 2017.
52. Robert Delaney, "How America's Embrace of Chinese Culture Boosts Beijing's Soft Power," *South China Morning Post*, September 28, 2017, https://www.scmp.com/news/world/united-states-canada/article/2113141/how-americas-embrace-chinese-culture-boosts-chinas.
53. Antonios Vlassis, "Soft Power, Global Governance," 490.
54. See Siu Leung Li, "Kung Fu: Negotiating Nationalism and Modernity," *Cultural Studies* 15, no. 3–4 (2001): 515–542.
55. Christina Klein, "Kung Fu Hustle: Transnational Production and the Global Chinese-Language Film," *Journal of Chinese Cinemas* 1, no. 3 (2007): 189–208.

56. Naomi Green, *From Fu Manchu to Kung Fu Panda: Images of China in American Film* (Hong Kong: Hong Kong University Press, 2014).
57. Thussu, "Globalization of Chinese Media," 22.
58. Shi, "China's Role in Remapping," 40.
59. Falk Hartig, "Confucius Institutes and the Rise of China," *Journal of Chinese Political Science* no. 17 (2012): 69.
60. Pan Su-Yan, "China's Approach to the International Market for Higher Education Studies: Strategies and Implications," *Journal of Higher Education Policy and Management* 35, no. 3 (2013): 252.
61. In order, South Korea, Thailand, Pakistan, Russia, Kazakhstan, India, and Vietnam
62. Lily Kuo, "Beijing Is Cultivating the Next Generation of African Elites by Training Them in China," *Quarz*, December 14, 2017, https://qz.com/1119447/china-is-training-africas-next-generation-of-leaders.
63. For example, the survey of returning Chinese students from Japan and Canada in Han Donglin and David Zweig, "Images of the World: Studying Abroad and Chinese Attitudes towards International Affairs," *The China Quarterly* 202 (2010): 290–306.
64. For example, Hong, "EU-China Education Diplomacy."
65. Seong-Hun Yun, "Do International Students' Direct Experiences with the Host Country Lead to Strong Attitude-Behavior Relations? Advancing Public Diplomacy Research and Beyond," *International Journal of Communication* 9, no. 8 (2014): 787–809.
66. Ane Bislev, "Student-to-Student Diplomacy: Chinese International Students as a Soft-Power Tool," *Journal of Current Chinese Affairs* 46, no. 2 (2017): 81–109.
67. Information taken from the Hanban website at http://english.hanban.org/node_10971.htm.
68. James Paradise, "China and International Harmony: The Role of Confucius Institutes in Bolstering Beijing's Soft Power," *Asian Survey* 49, no. 4 (2009): 647–669.
69. To the extent that it is quite hard to find the original source, which appears to be "A Message from Confucius: New Ways of Projecting Soft Power," *Economist Special Report*, October 22, 2009, https://www.economist.com/special-report/2009/10/22/a-message-from-confucius. The quote had been repeated 487 times according to Google on December 19, 2018. Li was Chair of the CCP Central Guidance Commission for Building Spiritual Civilization at the time.
70. Lo and Pan, "Confucius Institutes," 519.
71. The association's own report on the affair is available at http://chinesestudies.eu/?p=584.
72. Brady, "Magic Weapons."
73. June Teufel Dreyer, "A Weapon without War: China's United Front Strategy," Foreign Policy Research Institute Asia Program, February 6, 2018, 2 https://www.fpri.org/article/2018/02/weapon-without-war-chinas-united-front-strategy.
74. Dani Madrid-Morales, "China's Digital Public Diplomacy towards Africa: Actors, Messages, and Audiences," in *China-Africa Relations: Building Images through Cultural Co-operation, Media Representation, and Communication*, edited by Kathryn Batchelor and Zhang Xiaoling, 129 (London: Routledge, 2017).
75. Cited in Shambaugh, "China's Soft Power Push," 99.
76. Sun Wanning, "Slow Boat from China: Public Discourses Behind the 'Going Global' Media Policy," *International Journal of Cultural Policy* 21, no. 4 (2015): 400–418.

# 8

# China's Global
# Governance Interactions

KATHERINE MORTON

*The past cannot be changed, but the future can be shaped.*

Xi Jinping[1]

In recent years the Chinese approach toward global governance has shifted imperatively beyond a traditional defensive stance and toward active engagement. This new alignment in Chinese foreign policy suggests a growing confidence on the part of the CCP leadership in China's domestic governing arrangements as well as its capacity to lead by example in international affairs. New shifts in Chinese discourses, diplomacy, and responses to key global challenges seem to reflect a new global leadership ambition on the part of the Xi Jinping administration. China's deepening engagement in global governance is a reflection of its rising power and international status as well as a long-standing aspiration to contribute toward the making of international order on its own terms. In the words of President Xi in his report to the 19th Party Congress, "China will continue to play its part as a major and responsible country, take an active part in reforming and developing the global governance system, and keep contributing Chinese wisdom and strength to global governance."[2]

In practice the Chinese approach toward governing the world appears to be contradictory. China is now strengthening its status within global institutions, while simultaneously sponsoring alternative governing arrangements. It is playing a stronger role in global economic governance in particular, yet still supporting a traditional division of responsibility between developed and developing nations. Now as an active player in international rulemaking, China's normative stance is evolving in ways that reaffirm traditional notions of sovereignty while maintaining political flexibility over what constitutes legitimate rules of

Katherine Morton, *China's Global Governance Interactions* In: *China and the World.* Edited by: David Shambaugh, Oxford University Press (2020). © Oxford University Press
DOI: 10.1093/oso/9780190062316.003.0008

international conduct. In this sense, China's rule-making behavior is now more consciously aligned with its national development and security imperatives.

An important question thus arises: what is the scope of China's leadership ambition in global governance? Is it to govern the world on more equal terms? Or simply to change the rules of international conduct to suit its own national rejuvenation project?

The argument presented in this chapter is that a deeper strategic shift is now taking place concerning China's interactions within the evolving system of global governance.[3] Under Xi Jinping's leadership this shift is most visible in relation to China's stronger position in the United Nations; its more self-confident role in global policymaking; and the sponsorship of institutions at the regional level, spanning the Shanghai Cooperation Organization (SCO), Asian Infrastructural Development Bank (AIIB), and the Conference on Interaction and Confidence-Building Measures in Asia (CICA) together with a host of bilateral forums. The clearest signal of China's leadership ambition lies in the promotion of the Belt and Road Initiative (BRI) as a trans-continental mechanism for building an open world economy that promises to serve the many and not just the few, while also acting as a transmission belt for Chinese political interests and values. How this grandiose project intersects with existing liberal governing arrangements has yet to be clearly articulated by policymakers in Beijing, leading to suspicions over Chinese intentions and pushback from recipient states, even from those states that supposedly have the most to gain from Chinese economic largesse.

At this moment, Xi Jinping's ambition to shape the future trajectory of global governance has reached an inflection point at which China's growing political leverage in international affairs could tip the balance in favor of either a stronger global consensus or fragmentation based upon overlapping zones of influence. Current patterns of engagement suggest that Chinese normative influence is already affecting the global agenda in ways that reinforce a dual-track approach, especially in relatively ungoverned spaces such as cyberspace where the rules of international conduct are still in the making. Paradoxically, the US retreat from multilateralism under the Trump administration combined with its antagonistic policy toward China on trade and investment could conceivably nudge Chinese policy more in the direction of strengthening existing liberal rules of engagement. Either way, in transitioning toward global leadership, China will likely accrue multiple benefits in the short term, but encounter a number of political and strategic dilemmas over its longer-term commitment.

This chapter begins with a brief discussion of the relationship between power and responsibility in global governance in the contemporary era. It then presents an analysis of China's evolving approach toward global governance and the motivations behind its activist stance under Xi Jinping. Attention then turns to examining China's current role in shaping governing rules, norms, and institutions in relation to four areas of global policy: international trade and investment, foreign intervention and peacekeeping, global climate change, and cybersecurity. These cases represent key realms of global governance where the Chinese presence is most visible, where its interests intersect with global priorities, and where the boundaries of Chinese engagement have yet to be fully defined. Across all these cases the focus of analysis is upon identifying specific turning points in China's changing role in global governance, reflecting upon past practice for the purpose of highlighting ongoing developments under the Xi Jinping administration. In conclusion, the chapter discusses some of the major dilemmas confronting China in its transition toward global leadership.

## Power and Responsibility: Who Governs the World?

Simply put, global governance can be understood as the evolving realm of institutions, processes, and rules that seek to govern international affairs in the absence of a world government. Intellectual and policy debates on global governance reflect a wide spectrum of ideas ranging from the utopian ideal of a new world order, to concerns over the rights and responsibilities associated with the delivery of global public goods, and more skeptical theories that highlight the continuing problem of structural inequality within existing global institutions and the dominance of Western values.

In the current era, growing geopolitical competition, especially between the United States and China, fuels anxieties that international cooperation will gradually decline. It is also tempting to conclude that a leadership vacuum is likely to emerge in response to mounting global challenges. The imperative to rebalance interests and responsibilities between dominant and emerging powers has proven difficult to achieve in practice. Even more worrying is the breakdown in the liberal consensus underpinning collective action at the international level. Under the Trump administration, US withdrawal from the Paris Climate Agreement, Trans-Pacific Partnership (TPP), Human Rights Council (HRC), and Intermediate-Range Nuclear Forces Treaty (INF), together with the United Kingdom's troubled exit from the European Union, suggests a growing tension over the balance between national and international obligations on the part of liberal states and their political constituencies.

In response to these developments, many scholars now predict greater gridlock within the system of global governance, its eventual fragmentation into regions, or even the return to traditional spheres of influence. Others are more sanguine about the potential to reform the existing global system via new forms of plurilateralism and a genuinely global approach toward international rulemaking. Either way, we are likely to see harder bargains between states over the costs and benefits of international cooperation, reinforcing the need for strong global leadership.

For global governance theorists, political leadership is seen as a social process of bargaining, negotiation, and persuasion to achieve a common goal rather than a competition to dominate the global agenda. In the absence of leadership from above, collective action can still take place among a myriad of states, corporations, international organizations, or non-governmental organizations (NGOS). Many examples confirm that a bottom-up process can lead to effective collective action such as the ongoing plurilateral negotiations over an Environmental Goods Agreement under the World Trade Organization (WTO) currently supported by forty-six member states including China, or the Trade in Services Agreement relating to the digital economy facilitated by the European Union.

Power asymmetry is important, but not all-determining. This is not to suggest that the arena of global governance is devoid of strategic competition. The history of post–World War II institution building suggests that positive advances take place when strategic interests and normative persuasions come together to reinforce the benefits of international cooperation. How leading states negotiate interests and values, and on what basis, is what matters in determining institutional outcomes. A fundamental requirement on the part of powerful states is to uphold the principle of responsibility. As proposed by some scholars, the idea of custodial responsibility offers an additional means of achieving a vision beyond the immediacy of negotiations and short-term interests.[4] It requires a shared consensus over a common goal or mission on the basis of clearly divided roles and responsibilities. In this sense, global governance relies upon achieving a greater symmetry between power and responsibility among leading states, who may not all be great powers (often the quest for greatness can distract attention away from collective responsibility) but are willing to act in ways that reinforce an equilibrium between national interests and international obligations.

A recurring debate in the study of international relations (IR) is the relationship between great power and responsibility dating back to the work of historians, sociologists, and English School international IR scholars in the 1960s and 1970s.[5] Hedley Bull's conception of great power responsibility takes material preponderance as given, but equally places emphasis upon "special rights and duties" for the purpose of maintaining international order—a responsibility that is constitutive of power, endorsed by leaders, and recognized by other states and their peoples.[6] Since the late 1990s, scholars have turned their attention to China's rising power and international responsibility. In the edited book titled *Power and Responsibility in Chinese Foreign Policy* first published in 2001, Yongjin Zhang and Greg Austin outlined an alternative conceptual approach toward China's rising power that avoids a sharp dichotomy between responsible and irresponsible behavior. Rosemary Foot

has taken the argument further in suggesting that China does not share the dominant conception of what it means to be a responsible power. In her view, China
is caught between two opposing objectives: to build coalitions with ideologically
like-minded states, and to embrace the existing norms articulated within the international governing system.[7]

The scholarly literature in China is rich with ideas on how China can become
a more responsible player in international affairs with a number of dissenting
critiques.[8] Until recently the idea of global governance was not fully accepted
within scholarly and policy circles. Indeed, the traditional Chinese policy stance
is deeply skeptical. Chinese concerns over the dominance of power politics in
international relations have tended to overshadow its approach toward engaging with the global governance agenda. Understood as a Western invention to
constrain China's rising power, for many years debates over global governance
were seen as a distraction away from the more fundamental task of strengthening China's rightful position in an asymmetric world.

Above all, politics is central to the Chinese position. From Beijing's perspective, the growing importance of global governance in the post–Cold War era has
been inextricably linked to Western values of liberal democracy. As a consequence,
China has sought to defend against the notion that international responsibility is
based upon shared political values. More recently, a stronger emphasis upon globalization has started to shift the Chinese political discourse more in favor of dealing with global challenges. No longer seen as a Western Trojan horse to contain
China's rise, the global governance agenda is now seen as a useful mechanism for
projecting Chinese interests and values onto the international arena. Today, the
Chinese call for a genuinely global approach toward international rulemaking is
reflective of changing structural conditions, not least the shift in the material balance of power in China's favor, as well as the growing pressures from developing
and non-Western nations for a more inclusive international order.

The idea that China is simply acting opportunistically as a leading advocate of
global governance in stark contrast to the semi-retreat of the United States merits
further scrutiny. This assumption is misleading because it discounts the pattern
of China's integration into governing institutions over time, and grossly under-
estimates the strategic turn that has taken place under Xi Jinping to strengthen
China's role as a trendsetter in international affairs. This shift is apparent at both
the strategic and normative levels.

## China's Leadership Role in Global Governance

China's transition toward global leadership has taken place gradually over the past
decade or more. From the mid-2000s onwards, Chinese foreign policy discourses

began to reflect a growing interest in the importance of a Chinese voice in international affairs; Chinese representation in international institutions expanded more widely across economic, security, and legal realms of global policymaking; and participation in international regimes intensified. In particular, the Global Financial Crisis (GFC) provided an opportunity for China to assert its leadership credentials in the face of the declining legitimacy of Western-centric models of economic governance. "South-South cooperation" (南南合作) became the new mantra for China to showcase its contribution to the world, thus revitalizing its long-standing pledge to act on behalf of the developing world in bringing about a fairer, more just, and more equal governing system of international affairs.

## The Strategic Turn under Xi Jinping

Under the Xi Jinping leadership we have witnessed a significant strategic shift in the direction of shaping the system of global governance rather than simply navigating around it. The approach is aimed at bringing benefits to the many and not just the few in order to augment China's reformist credentials while simultaneously advocating Chinese interests and values. China's sponsorship of the global development agenda is indicative of its rising influence over one of the central pillars of the United Nations aimed at expanding prosperity across the globe. In his first speech to the UN General Assembly (UNGA) in September 2013, China's foreign minister Wang Yi set out a new framework for China's active engagement in global governance with a pledge "to voice Chinese views, offer Chinese wisdom, propose Chinese solutions, and support more global public goods."[9]

Speaking for the first time at the UNGA in September 2015, President Xi set out his vision of a "community of shared future for mankind" (构建人类命运共同体) based upon sovereign equality, inter-civilizational dialogue, win-win cooperation, and the peaceful resolution of disputes.[10] In reiterating Chinese support for the delivery of global public goods, he further announced the establishment of a UN peacekeeping standby force of 8,000 troops (full registration was completed in September 2017), a $100 million fund to support operations in Africa via the African Union, and a $1 billion ten-year China-UN Peace and Development Fund.[11] In reference to its role as a responsible major power, China has fully embraced the UN 2030 Agenda for Sustainable Development, building upon its positive track record as one of the only developing nations to achieve most of the targets set under the Millennium Development Goals (2000–2015).

The idea of a community of shared destiny can be traced back to the Bandung Asian-African Conference in April 1955 and the so-called "Bandung spirit" that resulted. It reflects a desire to order the world on the basis of the principle of peaceful coexistence that renders the idea of universality untenable and supports equality among politically diverse domestic regimes. The concept has also been employed to describe the relationship between mainland China and Taiwan as a means of mollifying political divisions and appealing to a common cultural heritage. In effect, it is an Asian-centric idea reinvented for a global audience.

First appearing in a report at the CCP 18th National Congress in November 2012, Xi Jinping expanded upon the idea of a "community of shared future for mankind" in a speech at the UN office in Geneva in January 2017. In his words: "All countries should jointly shape the future of the world, write international rules, manage global affairs, and ensure that development outcomes are shared by all."[12]

Internally, China's reformist approach toward global governance was first discussed at the CCP Central Committee Foreign Affairs Work Conference on work related to foreign affairs held in November 2014.[13] The meeting underscored the importance of working to reform the system of global governance by taking a leadership role in international rulemaking, especially in relation to the global economy. Two years later, Xi discussed China's role in global governance at a Politburo meeting with a particular focus upon shaping the rules of emerging issues—cyber, maritime, polar, anti-corruption, climate change, and outer space. At a second CCP Conference on foreign affairs held in June 2018 it was agreed that China should lead the reform of the global governance system based upon the principles of fairness and justice.[14] Under the new CCP mandate, Chinese elites are now confidently advocating the benefits of authoritarian statist norms for governing the world. Crossing this political threshold has been a major impetus behind Xi Jinping's strategic turn toward global governance.

## China-Sponsored Institutions and Norms

China's engagement in international institutions has been a long time in the making, dating back to earlier Republican influence in the immediate aftermath of World War II, and PRC participation following the announcement of the reform and opening policy under Deng Xiaoping in 1979. In general, China's track record in playing a leadership role has been minimal. It has been most prominent in relation to social, economic, and cultural affairs, with less influence over security and human rights. China has still not ratified the UN Convention on Political and Civil Rights.

Over the past decade, Chinese representation at the United Nations has become more prominent in economic and legal affairs: Zhang Tao, former deputy governor of the China's central bank, was appointed deputy managing director of the International Monetary Fund in 2016; Yi Xiaozhun, former deputy commerce minister, was reappointed for a second term as deputy director general of the WTO in 2017; and in 2014 Zhou Houlin was elected secretary-general of the International Telecommunication Union. Xue Hanqin's appointment as the first Asian woman to become the vice president of the International Court of Justice in 2011 also reflects China's growing influence in international legal affairs. Chinese representatives now sit on the International Tribunal for the Law on the Sea (Gao Zhiguo), the Appellate Body of the WTO (Hong Zhao), as well as the International Law Commission (Huang Huikang). China, like the United States, is not a party to the International Criminal Court.

The 2018 arrest in China of the president of INTERPOL, Meng Hongwei, on charges of bribery and corruption suggests that Chinese law under one-party rule takes precedent over the integrity of international institutions. This case pits China's Central Commission for Discipline Inspection against the world's leading law enforcement agency. It is also an indication internally that the newly formed CCP National Supervisory Commission sits above the Supreme People's Court.[15]

China's sponsorship of international institutions is most visible at the regional level. The establishment of the AIIB in 2016 under the chairmanship of Jin Liqun, ex-chairman of China International Capital Corporation, revealed a determination to influence trends in development financing commensurate with Chinese economic influence—in part a response to US resistance against China's voting status at the IMF, but also a reflection of a desire to leverage Chinese economic advantages on the basis of a "win-win" formula. Headquartered in Beijing, and with a paid-in capital of around $20 billion, the AIIB is currently targeting energy and transport projects with plans to expand into the water and ICT sectors. China's membership of the BRICS-led New Development Bank (NDB) is on the basis of equal voting shares. The NDB is headquartered in Shanghai with an initial subscribed capital of $50 billion and authorized capital of $100 billion. To date, project financing has largely focused upon renewable energy and infrastructure within BRICS states. In contrast, the $40 billion Silk Road Fund established at the end of 2014 is directly linked to the BRI and infrastructure projects in Russia, Central Asia, and Pakistan.

It is still an open question whether the BRI can offer a new direction in transcontinental governance that genuinely supports mutually beneficial governing arrangements. In many ways, this is the ultimate test of China's contribution toward governing the world. It is conceivable that the informality underpinning the BRI will allow for more spontaneous collective action. But this should not distract attention away from the lack of clarity over the rules of the silk roads both in relation to trade and investment and international peace and security.

In the security realm, China has become increasingly active in sponsoring the SCO as a platform for advocating common interests rather than collective security. China has also skillfully used its chairmanship of the Conference on Interaction and Confidence Building Measures in Asia (CICA) to advocate Asian solidarity and the need for a new approach toward international security that favors mutual benefits and common development. Above all, a strong preference for strategic partnerships prevails, attesting to the perceived importance of counterbalancing the US-led alliance based system.

## China's Leadership Role in the Making

Overall, current trends suggest that Xi Jinping's new ambition to play a leadership role in global governance is driven by three primary motivations:

1. To defend Chinese interests on a global scale.
2. To strengthen China's strategic role in institution building.
3. To broaden China's normative voice as a means of legitimating its role as a global power.

For a more detailed account of Chinese leadership let us now turn to an examination of key areas of global policy.

### International Trade and Investment

It is self-evident that China has a large stake in the global trading regime. In 2017 China became the world's largest trading nation by value (estimated at $4.1 trillion).[16] Following an extended period of negotiations it acceded to the WTO in 2001, agreeing to stringent accession protocols relative to its stage of development. Despite the fact that at the time of accession a condition was put in place to grant market economy status automatically following a fifteen-year period of membership, China's market economy status is still not recognized by the United States, European Union, Canada, Japan, and Mexico, among others. As a consequence, Chinese firms are disproportionately affected by anti-dumping complaints. In aggregate, China is on the receiving end of the third highest number of cases under the WTO dispute settlement system (43, compared to 152 cases against the United States and 85 against the EU).[17]

China's performance in the WTO has been fairly positive. It has an active track record as a third party in dispute settlement (total 164 cases), and it has also pushed salient concerns on behalf of developing nations. The dominant behavioral pattern is one of learning to defend its interests from within the system.

The greatest disruption to the global trading regime comes from the ongoing trade dispute between the United States and China orchestrated by President Trump in 2018—a salutary reminder of how quickly the regime can unravel in the absence of a strong consensus between the world's leading economic powers. Over the past decade, the bilateral trade deficit has increased from $268 billion in 2008 to $344 billion in 2018.[18] Tit-for-tat conflict over trade restrictions is merely a smokescreen for much deeper underlying tensions over China's techno-nationalist approach toward market competition. While many states have industrial policies in place that protect strategic industries, the Made in China 2025 agenda falls far short of meeting higher international standards of transparency and sustainability. The slow pace of domestic reforms, especially in relation to the protection of Intellectual Property Rights (IPRs), further raises concerns that the China model of development may over time serve to undermine the rules of the liberal market economy.

The flip side of this argument is that China's global economic dominance is exposing some of the many gaps and weaknesses within the international trade regime. Rules of the digital economy do not, as yet, exist. This is a particular problem given the blurred distinction between commerce and national security reinforced by the upward trend in cyber-enabled espionage, as will be discussed later. Under the WTO, national security concerns are left to the discretion of the member states. Hence, what constitutes the rules of the game is increasingly mediated by individual states in accordance with national legislation. A recent decision to join new talks over a digital trade accord, despite concerns over controlling the Internet, is a sign of China's commitment toward strengthening the multilateral trading regime in the face of rising strategic competition with the United States.

One of the most significant gaps in global economic governance today is the lack of a multilateral investment regime. The inherent difficulties involved in balancing investor protection with the right to national development have stymied international negotiations over investment liberalization dating back to the establishment of the Bretton Woods system in 1948.[19] Aligned with the necessity of attracting foreign investment, over the past two decades, developing countries have taken the lead in establishing reciprocal arrangements for foreign investment.[20] More recently, the pace of investment liberalization from below has gathered momentum. In 1999 the number of bilateral investment treaties totaled 1,857.[21] Twenty years later that number has risen to 2,363.[22] China now leads the world in BITs (128), followed by the Czech Republic (113).[23]

It is the qualitative dimension across the broad spectrum of bilateral and multilateral economic governing arrangements that matters. In this regard, the Trans-Pacific Partnership (TTP) is distinct from existing multilateral trade agreements in that it builds upon advanced Free Trade Agreements (FTAs) to address domestic regulations that affect trade and investment.[24] Following American withdrawal, the potential to combine regional economic integration with higher standards of economic cooperation is likely to remain more limited. As noted by Ling Shengli from the China Foreign Affairs University in Beijing, China has limited incentive to join the partnership, given its strategic concerns over status.[25] It is also the case that Chinese trade-related labor and environmental regulations do not conform to existing international standards.

China's leadership role has been more visible in relation to the pursuit of open regionalism in contrast to a more institutionalized approach toward binding rules and higher standards as promoted under the TPP. China has supported the ASEAN-led Regional Cooperation Economic Partnership (RCEP) initiative that offers an alternative lower-cost model of open regionalism. The Free Trade Area of the Asia Pacific (FTAAP) is also seen as a reliable mechanism for promoting trade liberalization and investment due to its broader geographical scope. Indeed, at the APEC Forum in 2014 President Xi Jinping announced support for pushing ahead with the FTAAP.[26]

As a trans-continental framework, the BRI constitutes a more systematic approach toward leveraging China's national strengths for the purpose of building an open global economy that promises to deliver multiple benefits beyond Chinese borders. The problem is that, to date, Chinese loans do not conform to minimum legal safeguards and regulatory standards as required under existing international law. Overall, Chinese-sponsored multilateral financial institutions, as discussed earlier, make an important financial contribution but have yet to prove their value in facilitating a shift toward genuine financial, economic, and environmental sustainability.

In building an open world economy via other means it would appear that China's primary motivation is to lessen its dependency upon foreign powers, in the form of either technology transfer or Western-dominated international institutions that place unacceptable demands upon China's slowing economy. It has been reluctant to sign up to binding agreements that reduce the political space for flexible accommodation. It is also the case that the Chinese approach toward outbound investment has been influenced by its experience of inward investment. For example, the idea that states are the final arbiters of their own national development is deeply embedded within the Chinese mindset. Self-reliance worked for China, and it is also expected to work for the world. In this regard, it is no surprise that growing complaints over China's contribution toward the rising debt problem in lesser-developed states are often dismissed.

Trade and investment is the one arena of global governance where China is most vulnerable to US coercion, and arguably where it has been the most complacent. The Global Financial Crisis in 2008–2009 helped to underscore the extent to which China benefits from a liberal rules-based system of governance. Whether the Chinese leadership can move in the direction of more responsible global economic leadership in the face of mounting pressures at home is a complex question to address. For ideological reasons, governing principles of disclosure and transparency are not fully accepted, thus making it difficult to gain recognition for the strengths as well as the weaknesses of China's so-called socialist market economy. Regardless of one's ideological standpoint, it is fair to say that China needs to take more responsibility within the realm of global economic governance—less on an equal footing, and more on the basis of a leading world economic power.

## Foreign Intervention and Peacekeeping

Within the governing realm of international peace and security, China has gained an international reputation for its role in UN peacekeeping. Once viewed as a weapon of imperialist ambition, Chinese participation in peacekeeping has increased exponentially over the past two decades. In 2018 it ranked second place among the top ten contributors to the UN's peacekeeping budget (10.25 percent, compared to 28.47 percent from the United States).[27] China first sent engineering troops to the UN Transitional Authority in Cambodia (UNTAC) in 1992. This was a significant symbolic act at the time, given that the PRC had provided foreign aid and military support to the genocidal Pol Pot regime.[28] Historically, geopolitical calculations have far outweighed humanitarian concerns on China's southern periphery. Today, evidence suggests that Chinese engineers and medical officers are helping to change local perceptions by taking a neutral stance, but this is likely to be a long-term process of trust building.[29]

Over the past decade, China has gradually expanded its participation in international peacekeeping—sending police officers to Haiti, and engineers to Sudan and the Democratic Republic of Congo. Crossing an important threshold in 2013, a force protection company of 170 Chinese troops participated in the UN stabilization mission (MINUSMA) in Mali. By the end of 2018, China had contributed a total of 2,515 troops and military experts, and 151 police to UN peacekeeping missions (ranking tenth in the world).[30] If the 8,000-standby force promised by Xi Jinping in 2015 is deployed, China will become the largest contributor to UN troops, surpassing Ethiopia, Bangladesh, and India. Many scholars have referred to China's increasing involvement in peacekeeping missions as a sign of normative change. Converging interests appear to be behind this shift, including the need to protect investments and workers abroad, maintain a peaceful international environment for development, facilitate the modernization of the military, and improve China's image as a responsible power.[31]

At a broader level, involvement in peacekeeping missions has provided useful political leverage over the trajectory of UN humanitarian interventions.[32] Humanitarian crises are now officially seen as a "legitimate concern of the international community."[33] However, new thinking on sovereignty that holds states accountable for alleged human rights violations is seen as a dangerous precedent. To date, in supporting some interventions to protect civilians subject to the approval of the UN Security Council (UNSC) and the consent of the host country, China has taken a minimalist stance based upon pragmatism rather than conviction. That said, confusion still exists over its responses to crises in Libya, Syria, Ukraine, and Yemen respectively, suggesting that deep divisions over the responsibility to protect norms remain intact.

What has changed is the new commitment to protect Chinese citizens abroad. In February 2011 when the Libyan authorities used force against protestors leading to an escalation in violence, China supported UNSC resolution 1970 invoking the Responsibility to Protect (R2P). At the time, the PRC government faced a serious dilemma when it discovered that an estimated total of 36,000 Chinese citizens were also in-country. Following an emergency evacuation, Beijing engaged diplomatically with both parties to the conflict to seek a peaceful resolution while also protecting its commercial interests. Patriotic campaigns to showcase the state as the great protector of the people are now embedded in popular culture. *Wolf Warrior II*, released in 2017, features Leng Feng (a modern-day version of Mao's exemplary soldier Lei Feng) as a special operative saving Chinese medical aid workers from foreign mercenaries in an African war zone. This film has achieved the highest box office success on record in China.

As a permanent member of the UNSC, China is in a unique position to shape the global humanitarian agenda. It has special responsibilities for maintaining international peace and security that set it apart from other emerging powers. Based upon the principle of "great power unanimity," its veto power in Security Council decision-making provides significant influence over international interventions.[34] China vetoed Security Council sanctions against Myanmar in 2007 and blocked draft resolutions condemning the Syrian government's violent suppression of opposition forces in October 2011, February 2012, and July 2012 respectively. Russia's annexation of Crimea in 2014 presented a genuine dilemma for Beijing: the Xi Jinping leadership was forced to adjudicate between traditional national sovereignty concerns in the face of secessionist movements and a desire to maintain a united front with Russia against regime transition in Ukraine. At the time, energy interests helped to tip the balance in favor of a strategic alignment with Russia.

For both ideological and economic reasons, China is likely to remain a conservative advocate of foreign intervention; however, the maintenance of a purely defensive posture is under strain and may well prove untenable over the longer term. The expansion of combat troops on the ground is already exposing a number of risks. For example, the UN stabilization campaign in Mali (MINUSMA) has a mandate "to deter threats and take active steps to prevent the return of armed elements" if necessary by force.[35] In May 2016 one Chinese peacekeeper was killed and five wounded in a mortar attack by Islamic extremists on the UN peacekeeping base at Gao in northeastern Mali. A couple of months later, two more Chinese peacekeepers were killed when their vehicle hit a rocket-propelled grenade in South Sudan. These fatalities are already increasing Chinese support for more robust UN mandates.

Over time, China's deeper involvement in complex humanitarian operations will likely enhance its legitimacy to play a leading role in peacekeeping reform, especially if President Trump acts upon his threat to reduce the US contribution to the UN peacekeeping budget. Where we are likely to see a much more visible Chinese presence is in relation to postwar reconstruction. China's current role in Yemen is instructive in this regard.[36] It has supported all UN resolutions on the Yemen conflict and participated in the UN-brokered peace process as well as the Gulf Cooperation Council political transition process bringing about the transfer of power from President Saleh to Abd-Rabbu Mansour Hadi. After the seizure of power by the Iranian-backed Houthis and the Saudi Arabia–led air strike campaign, China has continued to work behind the scenes to broker a peace agreement while offering emergency food aid. Recent efforts to link postwar reconstruction in Yemen to the BRI is evidence of the ways in which this new global platform is being integrated into the existing architecture of international peace and security.

## Global Climate Change

China's leadership role in climate change presents the ultimate test case for assessing its leadership ambition in global governance. Following the Trump administration's withdrawal from the Paris Agreement, attention is turning to China as the next in line to take up the leadership challenge in ensuring the implementation of the agreement, and the post-2020 climate action agenda. In reality, sustaining political momentum is most likely to occur on the basis of co-leadership rather than China single-handedly taking the lead. Notwithstanding references to China's willingness to sit in the driver's seat, China's active involvement in climate change negotiations is largely driven by national development imperatives. Failing to act upon a domestic sustainability agenda would be the equivalent of political suicide for the CCP. Yet the leadership still struggles to come to terms with its rising international obligations—both in relation to mitigating the negative effects of $CO_2$ emissions, and in responding to the global climate adaptation agenda.

The European Union has played a leadership role on climate change for decades, culminating in the Paris Agreement in 2015. On the Chinese side, taking action has been a much slower process on account of its stage of economic development and ideological persuasions. China ratified the UN Framework Convention on Climate Change (UNFCCC) in 1994, but remained cautious over making commitments. In foreign policy terms, climate change was primarily interpreted as a Western-inspired agenda that could undermine China's right to development space. In the 1990s, building upon the momentum in domestic environmental policymaking, climate change emerged on the policy agenda as a means of encouraging technological innovation and cleaner industrial practices. At the turn of the century, skepticism over the motives of richer nations still prevailed. China's international position was predicated upon making contributions to address climate change on the basis of the principle of common but differentiated responsibilities and respective capabilities.

By 2007 China had overtaken the United States (with 25 percent of the world's total $CO_2$ emissions) to become the world's biggest emitter. This rapid development presented an enormous challenge for both the Chinese government and global efforts to reduce carbon emissions, given that since the establishment of the UNFCCC in 1992 the North-South development divide had defined rights and responsibilities concerning climate action. As a rising economic power, caught between the North and the South, China's status was unique, thus exacerbating the problem of how to apportion responsibility among leading states.

Co-leadership between the United States and China played a significant role in breaking the impasse. In the lead-up to the UNFCCC Conference of the Parties (COP) meeting in Paris in December 2015, Presidents Obama and Xi reached a consensus: the United States would emit 26 percent to 28 percent less carbon in 2025 than it did in 2005. That is double the pace of reduction it targeted for the period from 2005 to 2020.[37] In return, China pledged to reach peak carbon emissions by 2030 by ensuring that clean energy sources such as solar power and wind made up at least 20 percent of China's total energy production. To resolve the issue of financial transfers from the North to the South, the United States pledged $3 billion to the UN Green Climate Fund and China promised to set up a South-South Climate Cooperation Fund with an initial endowment of 20 billion RMB ($3.1 billion).[38] In retrospect, this historic consensus represented the apogee of US-China great power responsibility.

The new bottom-up approach toward global climate governance based upon nonbinding nationally determined contributions now meshes more comfortably with China's domestic prerogatives. As the world's largest investor in renewable energy and the low-carbon economy, China stands to gain considerably from the global shift toward emissions reduction. More recently, it has used its international status effectively to promote new norms such as carbon intensity reduction, the low carbon economy, and ecological civilization (态明文核)as a means of forging a consensus among industrialized nations while offering leadership to support South-South cooperation, especially in Africa. At the 2018 UNFCCC (COP24) Conference, held in the Polish city of Katowice, China's chief climate change negotiator, Xie Zhenhua, played a constructive role in negotiating the so-called "rule book" for implementing the Paris Agreement. What remains unchanged is China's continuing resolve to retain its status as a developing country, thus lessening the burden of international responsibility.

From a global leadership perspective, the current Chinese position is unlikely to yield strong results in terms of lessening the climate burden, or bridging the responsibility gap between industrialized and developing nations. That would require recognition of China's unique status relative to its international obligations. Over the coming years, the broader impact of the Chinese model of development will likely face greater scrutiny. The internationalization of state-owned enterprises under the mandate of the government's "go global" strategy requires climate resilient safeguards; climate-proofing infrastructure development along the new Silk Roads presents a major challenge; and external pressures to engage at a deeper level will also likely arise from Chinese military peacekeeping operations in climate vulnerable regions of the world.

## Global Cybersecurity

The Chinese approach toward governing cyberspace is also predicated upon a domestically driven agenda, but with a much stronger emphasis upon national security concerns. When Xi Jinping took over as general-secretary of the CCP in 2012, China lagged far behind other leading states in developing a cyber strategy. It was still largely dependent upon foreign-made IT software and operating systems while also lacking a coordinated defense system against cyber attacks on critical infrastructure.[39] The consensus among leading scholars and policy analysts at the time was that China faced a major challenge in catching up. Those on the more hawkish side of the spectrum advocated adopting a cyber deterrence strategy.[40] Many viewed the potential militarization of cyberspace and the likely spillover effects on strategic competition in outer space and the maritime arena as posing an existential threat to international peace and stability.[41] Few disagreed with the proposition that China was a passive player in shaping the rules of international conduct in cyberspace. As expressed succinctly in the words of Li Hong: "The future international cyber system will to a large extent depend upon related cyber standards, and international legal frameworks. Whoever is involved in the formation of these legal frameworks and rules from the outset can seize an advantageous position."[42]

Within a very short time frame China has fulfilled its mission to become a strategic player in cybersecurity governance, building upon a solid foundation at the domestic level. China is now home to some of the largest tech firms in the world on the basis of market capitalization (as of March 2018)—Tencent ($511 billion), Alibaba ($477 billion), and Baidu ($88 billion) respectively.[43] It has made major advances in science and technology, and its domestic capacity to innovate in the field of ICT technologies has risen sharply in recent years. With over 800 million Internet users, the domestic market provides a major advantage in boosting innovative capacity. A fundamental incentive behind China's emerging leadership in global cyber governance is thus the need to protect its own critical infrastructure as well as ensure that fair standards are in place to support the expansion of ICT networks at home and abroad.

What makes the Chinese position particularly significant is the fact that it is operating with other states in a relatively ungoverned space. A global consensus over what constitutes cybersecurity and how best to build a framework of rules, norms, and institutions to govern cyberspace does not as yet exist.[44] The closest approximation to a universal treaty is the European Convention on Cybercrime (known as the Budapest Convention), which came into force in 2001 (currently involving sixty-two parties). China alongside Russia and India has refused to sign the Convention on the grounds that it embodies European values and lacks global reach. Instead, Beijing has participated in the global cybercrime experts group launched by the ITU in 2007 that addresses legal, technical, and procedural measures as well as capacity building and international cooperation.[45]

In essence, information security aims to control the flow of information, expand the censorship of online content, as well as defend networks and computers from exploitation. In contrast, the idea of cybersecurity is more narrowly focused upon cyberattacks on critical infrastructure, offensive military operations in cyberspace, electronic espionage, and bulk data interception.[46] At the Fourth Meeting of the GGE (Group of Governmental Experts on Developments in the Field of Information and Telecommunications in the Context of International Security, otherwise known as the GGE process) in 2015, the parties agreed upon a common code of conduct in cyberspace drawing upon existing international law and the UN Charter in promoting an open, secure, peaceful, and accessible ICT environment while recognizing the principle of state sovereignty and the international obligations upon states concerning wrongful acts attributable to them. On account of growing political divisions, the GGE process has now separated into two groups composed of those seeking further clarification of the application of international law to cyberspace as agreed in 2015 and those states preferring the establishment of a new cybersecurity treaty, including China.

For its part, China has also participated in a parallel process through the SCO culminating in a separate international code of conduct on information security sponsored by China and Russia at the UNGA in 2011 and 2015.[47] The draft code also appeared in the GGE 2015 agreement cosponsored by Tajikistan, Uzbekistan, Kazakhstan, and Kyrgyzstan.[48] The code seeks to strengthen the role of the state in countering cybersecurity threats, with a strong emphasis upon combating terrorism, secessionism, and extremism.[49] In contrast to the liberal cyberspace agenda, state responsibility for wrongful acts and support for freedom of expression in cyberspace are omitted from the text.

The Chinese normative contribution is focused upon extending the principle of sovereignty to cyberspace and building a system of cyber governance based upon peace, shared governance, and shared benefits.[50] According to China's International Strategy for Cooperation in Cyberspace released in 2017, cyber sovereignty is defined as follows:

> Countries should respect each other's right to choose their own path of cyber development, model of cyber regulation and Internet public policies, and participate in international cyberspace governance on an equal footing. No country should pursue cyber hegemony, interfere in other countries' internal affairs, or engage in, condone or support cyber activities that undermine other countries' national security.[51]

In contrast to the US-led multi-stakeholder approach, China has set up an alternative platform for international dialogue under the rubric of the Wuzhen Conference held in Zhejiang province near the headquarters of Alibaba.[52] Hailed by Xi Jinping as "one of China's most important contributions to the world, marking a major step in the forward march of transforming the global order of cyberspace governance," the Wuzhen process has attracted the participation of governments and private firms.[53] In combination these trends suggest that China's policy toward the global governance of cyberspace is focused primarily upon (1) the preservation of domestic controls over information and data; (2) the standardization of ICT to reap the economic benefits of outbound investment and; (3) the prevention of malicious activity conducted by states and non-state actors as well as dangerous military operations in cyberspace.

Building China into a strong Internet power (网络强国) goes hand in hand with stringent controls. China's cyberspace is protected against foreign competition from Facebook, Google, and Twitter, and all social media content is heavily censored. Tencent's private messaging platform WeChat allows the state to monitor information more easily than the public Weibo platform provided by Sina.com.[54] It has, therefore, become the preferred social media app currently in use in China today. New facial recognition technology provided by SenseTime further reinforces the reach of the state and empowers law enforcement agencies to detect dissent within crowded public spaces.[55] In the words of Rogier

Creemers, the "Chinese leadership has sought to reposition technology within its architecture of public power."[56] In effect, the CCP has harnessed technology for the purpose of ideological dominance.

Given that over 50 percent of the Chinese population own a smartphone, and censors are now ubiquitous, a dual incentive exists for Chinese tech firms to both benefit from the innovative potential of the huge domestic market while simultaneously working with the state to strengthen internal controls. China's cybersecurity law of June 1, 2017, claims to protect private data and safeguard cyber sovereignty and national security.[57] Sensitive data relating to Chinese citizens and/or national security must be stored on domestic servers. Data localization practices allow law enforcement agencies to access personal data even when hosted by foreign firms. Ambiguity over what constitutes sensitive data means that these firms are potentially exposed to charges of industrial espionage.[58]

A central question for global cyber governance is the extent to which domestic preferences are shaping global regulatory standards. Xi Jinping has extended his concept of a community of shared destiny to cyberspace; Chinese ICT systems increasingly dominate cross-border communications networks; and under the ITU, Chinese policymakers are actively engaged in rulemaking on technical standards. Furthermore, as part of the BRI agenda, China has promoted an "information silk road" as a twenty-first-century version of the information superhighway advocated by former US vice president Al Gore in the 1990s, focused upon the free flow of information, cultural exchange, and narrowing the digital gap over access rather than spreading democracy and freedom. This virtual BRI is composed of cross-border optical cables on land and undersea, trans-continental networks, and satellite communications. It has the potential to tip the fragile global consensus in favor of surveillance over freedom of information.

On a number of levels, the relationship between national security and commerce is becoming more fraught, especially between the United States and China over cyber-enabled espionage. In September 2015, during Xi Jinping's first official visit to the United States, President Obama and President Xi agreed to refrain from undertaking cyberespionage for commercial gain. Prior to the visit, the Treasury Department was preparing to evoke Executive Order 13694 authorizing the sanction of Chinese companies and officials involved in stealing IP and trade secrets from US entities.[59] At the time, the US Justice Department had already indicted five PLA officers for stealing secrets from Westinghouse Steel and other US companies in May 2014.

On the US side, accusations against China have ratcheted up in recent years, leading to the banning of US technology exports in some cases, and in others the blocking of US firms from buying foreign technology equipment that is deemed to pose a risk to national security. A Pentagon order issued in August 2018 banned the US government from using equipment produced by world-leading telecoms companies Huawei and ZTE. The former's monopoly over 5G wireless networks is testing commitment on all sides toward maintaining the integrity of ICT systems, especially in democratic liberal states where surveillance is a major political concern.

In regard to the prevention of malicious activity in cyberspace, China is both a target and a potential aggressor. For example, it was badly affected by the May 2017 Wannacry ransomware attacks on account of its dependency upon the Windows XP operating system.[60] China has tended to take a low-profile approach over the thorny issue of attribution, avoiding taking sides in the dispute over the alleged North Korean cyberattack on Sony Pictures in 2014.[61] It has also refrained from joining coalitions. In the absence of an international sanctions regime for cyberspace, coalitions of states are increasingly involved in conferring attribution on the basis of sharing intelligence across borders. For example, in February 2018 seven nations attributed the NotPetya cyberattacks to Russia (United States, Australia, Canada, Denmark, Estonia, Lithuania, UK).

In stark contrast, the Chinese position on lethal autonomous weapons is more aligned with the global consensus. China is a party to the UN Convention on Prohibitions or Restrictions on the Use of Certain Conventional Weapons that may be deemed to be excessively injurious or to have indiscriminate effects (ratified in 1982). It is also a member of the Group of Governmental Experts (GGE) on emerging technologies in the area of lethal autonomous weapons systems (LAWS).[62] Beijing supports the applicability of existing humanitarian law to LAWS while recognizing special characteristics such as full autonomy, indiscriminate effect, and the issue of evolution through learning.[63] Together with twenty-six other states, China has supported a prohibition on the use of fully autonomous weapons.[64] Both the United States and Russia have opposed the ban.

## Is China a Responsible Leader in Global Governance?

To conclude, the departure point for this chapter was a conceptual focus upon the relationship between power and responsibility as a means of framing the debate over China's expanding global governance interactions. It is clear that China is now in the process of substantially shaping the global agenda by pushing forward its preferred ideas, interests, and values. China's structural power alone does not translate easily into shaping the rules of international conduct. And the Chinese preference for flexible accommodation in international rulemaking makes it difficult to gauge the degree to which it is abiding by the principle of international responsibility. The Chinese position on global governance is primarily driven by the need to defend its "core interests" (核心利益) and the security of the CCP regime, strengthen China's status within international institutions, and promote a pluralistic vision of shared international responsibility. In essence, it is a form of national self-strengthening with global characteristics.

Under Xi Jinping the shift toward taking a leadership role in reforming global governance is directly linked to counterbalancing the dominance of a liberal-based international order. At least on the basis of the cases presented, it would seem that China's adoption of a dual-track approach may lead to a convergence of interests in specific areas such as peacekeeping, post-conflict reconstruction, the de-carbonization of the economy, or lethal autonomous weapons. But it is unlikely that the desired community of shared common destiny will assuage rising concerns over China's global economic ambition in the absence of higher international standards. Most worrying for liberal states is the development of alternative arrangements that do not appear to converge with existing governing arrangements such as the Wuzhen process. The CCP leadership does not accept the universality of liberal norms. As a consequence, a central motivation behind the push for cultural and political diversity is the legitimization of Chinese statist and authoritarian norms. The BRI remains the ultimate test case of whether it is possible to modify current practice to confirm with a more liberal global consensus.

At this moment in time, China is on track to substantially influence the future trajectory of global governance. But along the way it is likely to face a number of dilemmas. First and foremost, is the issue of its unique status as an emerging global power. China has outgrown its traditional role as *primus inter pares* among developing nations. Likewise, as a peer competitor with the United States, it faces limited options for establishing a *modus vivendi* in the absence of substantive domestic reforms. Where China fits as a leading power in the world will remain a contentious issue, especially if the endgame is to reform global governance in accordance with a particular power hierarchy. Second, performance legitimacy concerns are likely to increase as China shifts from a declaratory leadership position on global governance to actual implementation. This is already evident in the cases presented, revealing a significant gap between Beijing's rhetorical stance and its capacity to implement policies. Third, leadership once sought needs to be maintained. For China, as in the case of other powerful states, meeting growing expectations over responsible leadership is likely to become an ever more demanding task.

# Notes

1. Statement by HE Xi Jinping President of the People's Republic of China at the General Debate of the 70th Session of the UN General Assembly, "Working Together to Form a New Partnership of Win-Win Cooperation and Create a Community of Shared Future for Mankind," New York, September 28, 2015.

2. Full text of Xi Jinping's Report at the 19th CPC National Congress Xinhua, March 11, 2017, available at http://www.xinhuanet.com/english/special/2017-11/03/c_136725942.htm.

3. The argument draws upon my forthcoming book *China Re-Orients the World: The Legitimacy Paradox in Global Governance*, to be published by Oxford University Press.

4. This idea is similar to that of great custodial responsibility, as discussed in Simon Reich and Richard Ned Lebow, *Good-Bye Hegemony: Power and Influence in the Global System* (Princeton: Princeton University Press, 2014).

5. See Talcott Parsons, "On the Concept of Political Power," *American Philosophy Society* 107, no. 3 (June 1963): 232–262; Leonard Krieger, "Power and Responsibility: Historical Assumptions," in *The Responsibility of Power: Historical Essays*, edited by Leonard Krieger and Fritz Stern (London: Macmillan, 1967); and Hedley Bull, *The Anarchical Society: A Study of Order in World Politics* (London: Macmillan, 1977).

6. Bull, *The Anarchical Society*, 200–229.

7. Rosemary Foot, "Chinese Power and the Idea of a Responsible State," *The China Journal* 45 (January 2001): 1–19.

8. See Ren Xiao, "Yanjiu he lijie Zhongguo de guoji zeren" [Studying and understanding China's international responsibility], *Shehui Kexue* (Journal of Social Science) 12 (2007): 24–27; and Zhu Liqun and Zhao Guangcheng, "Zhongguo guoji guannian de bianhua yu gonggu: gongli yu qushi" [The Change and Consolidation of China's International Ideas: Dynamics and Trends], *Waijiao Pinglun* (Foreign Affairs Review) 1 (2008): 18–26. For a dissenting voice see Li Limin, "Lixing bianxi Zhongguo zerenlun" [Rationally Discuss China's Responsibility Theory], *Renmin Luntan* (People's Tribune) 6 (2007).

9. Statement by Wang Yi at the General Debate of the 68th Session of the United Nations General Assembly, New York, September 27, 2013, available at https://gadebate.un.org/sites/default/files/gastatements/68/CN_en.pdf.

10. For a broader discussion see Ruan Zongze, "Goujian renlei mingyun gongtongti zhuli zhong-guo zhanlüe jiyu qi" [To construct a community of destiny for mankind to facilitate China's period of strategic opportunity], *Guoji Wenti Yanjiu* 1 (2018).

11. The United Nations Peace and Development Trust Fund is divided into the Secretary-General's Peace and Security Sub-Fund and the 2030 Agenda for Sustainable Development Sub-Fund under the Department of Economic and Social Affairs. See http://www.un.org/en/unpdf/index.shtml.

12. Speech by Xi Jinping at the UN Office in Geneva January 23, 2017, available at http://iq.chineseembassy.org/eng/zygx/t1432869.htm.

13. Ministry of Foreign Affairs of the People's Republic of China, "The Central Conference on Work Relating to Foreign Affairs Was Held in Beijing," November 29, 2014, http://www.fmprc.gov.cn/mfa_eng/zxxx_662805/t1215680.shtml.

14. Ministry of Foreign Affairs of the People's Republic of China, "Xi Jinping Urges Breaking New Ground in Major Country Diplomacy with Chinese Characteristics," June 23, 2018, available at https://www.fmprc.gov.cn/mfa_eng/wjdt_665385/wshd_665389/t1571296.shtml.

15. Julian Ku, "Why China's Disappearance of Interpol Chief Matters," *Lawfare* blog, October 9, 2018, available at https://www.lawfareblog.com/why-chinas-disappearance-interpols-chief-matters. The new National Supervisory Commission set up after the National People's Congress in March 2018 can now detain a person up to six months without charge or access to a lawyer. See https://www.nytimes.com/2018/10/07/world/asia/china-interpol-men-hongwei.html.

16. China was an original signatory to the General Agreement on Tariffs and Trade (GATT) in 1948 just prior to the establishment of the PRC; it reapplied in 1986 and eventually joined the WTO in 2001.

17. https://www.wto.org/english/tratop_e/dispu_e/dispu_by_country_e.htm.
18. https://www.census.gov/foreign-trade/balance/c5700.html.
19. Ryaz Dattu, "A Journey from Havana to Paris: The Fifty-Year Quest for the Elusive Multilateral Agreement on Investment," *Fordham International Law Journal* 24 (2000): 274–314.
20. Ibid.
21. UNCTAD/ITE/IIA/2 Bilateral Investment Treaties 1959–1999, available at http://unctad.org/en/Docs/poiteiiad2.en.pdf.
22. See http://investmentpolicyhub.unctad.org/IIA.
23. Ibid.
24. Ann Capling and John Ravenhill, "Multilateralizing Regionalism: What Role for the Trans-Pacific Partnership Agreement?" *The Pacific Review* 24, no. 5 (2011): 553–575.
25. Ling Shengli, "Will China Join TPP Is Not the Question," *China Daily*, 20 March 2017.
26. Donald Lewis "China Ushers In New FTAAP Era," *China Daily*, November 22, 2016, available at: http://www.chinadaily.com.cn/opinion/2016-11/22/content_27456948.htm.
27. See https://peacekeeping.un.org/en/how-we-are-funded.
28. Andrew C. Mertha, *Brothers in Arms: Chinese Aid to the Khmer Rouge 1975–1979* (Ithaca, NY: Cornell University Press, 2014).
29. Miwa Hirono, "China's Charm Offensive and Peacekeeping: The Lessons of Cambodia—What Now for Sudan," *International Peacekeeping* 18, no. 3 (2011): 328–343.
30. See https://peacekeeping.un.org/en/troop-and-police-contributors.
31. For an extended discussion of motivations behind China's growing peacekeeping presence see Shogo Suzuki, "Seeking Legitimate 'Great Power Status' in Post–Cold War International Society: China and Japan's Participation in UNPKO," *International Relations* 1 (2008): 45–63; and Wu Zhengyu and Ian Taylor, "From Refusal to Engagement: Chinese Contributions to Peacekeeping in Africa," *Journal of Contemporary African Studies* 29, no. 2 (2011).
32. Zhao Lei, "Two Pillars of China's Global Peace Engagement Strategy: United Nations Peacekeeping Operations and International Peacebuilding Operations," *International Peacekeeping* 18, no. 3 (2011): 387.
33. Position Paper of the People's Republic of China on the United Nations Reforms, June 7, 2005, http://www.china-un.org/eng/chinaandun/zzhgg/t199101.htm.
34. Decisions in the Security Council are made by affirmative vote of nine out of the fifteen members. including the permanent five.
35. Security Council unanimously approves new UN Peacekeeping Mission in Mali, April 26, 2013, https://www.unric.org/en/latest-un-buzz/28406-security-council-unanimously-approves-new-un-peacekeeping-mission-in-mali.
36. I-Wei Jennifer Chang, *China and Yemen's Forgotten War* (Washington, DC: United States Institute of Peace, January 2018).
37. Coral Davenport, "Obama and President Xi of China Vow to Sign Paris Climate Accord Promptly," *New York Times*, March 1, 2014.
38. See https://www.greenclimate.fund/how-we-work/resource-mobilization.
39. See Liu Zengliang, "Zenyang goujian zhongguo wangluo bianfang" [How to establish China's Cyber Defences] *Renmin Luntan* 8 (2008): 38–39; and Li Hong, "Conglin faze jiaju wangluo zhanzheng fengxian" [A legal jungle increases the danger of cyber war] *Renmin Luntan* 8 (2011): 22–23.
40. See Qiao Liang, "Zhongguo de xin junshi biange quanmian qibu" [China's new military revolution steps forward], *Tongzhou Gongjin* 11 (2009): 11–12. For a more moderate position see Dong Qingling and Dai Chengzheng, "Wangluo kongjian weishe baofu shi-fou kexing?" [Cyber deterrence: is retaliatory strategy possible?] *Shijie Jingji yu Zhengzhi* 7 (2012): 99–116.
41. Cheng Chun, "Wangluo junbei kongzhi de kunjing yu chulu xiandai guoji guanxi" [The dilemma of network arms control in contemporary international relations] *Xiandai guoji-guanxi*, February 2012, 16.
42. Li Hong, "Conglin faze jiaju wangluo zhanzheng fengxian" [A legal jungle increases the danger of cyber war] *Renmin Luntan* 8 (2011): 23.
43. See https://www.afr.com/personal-finance/shares/what-investors-need-to-know-about-chinas-big-trio-baidu-alibaba-and-tencent-20180306-h0x3f9.

44. Elena Chernenko, Oleg Demidov, and Fyodor Lukyanov, "Increasing International Cooperation in Cybersecurity and Adapting Cyber Norms" (New York: Council on Foreign Relations, February 23, 2018). The UK definition of cybersecurity denotes efforts aimed at "the preservation of confidentiality, availability and integrity of information in cyberspace, including the internet and other networks and forms of digital communication" (Foreign and Commonwealth Office, July 2017).

45. Joyce Hakmeh, *Building a Stronger International Legal Framework on Cybercrime* (London: Chatham House June 2017), available at https://www.itu.int/en/action/cyberse-curity/Pages/gca.aspx. Out of 96 members, two participated from PRC—Chen Yin and Du Yuejin from the Ministry of Information and Industry.

46. Adam Segal, "Chinese Cyber Diplomacy in a New Era of Uncertainty" (Stanford, CA: Hoover Institution, Aegis Paper Series, No. 1703, June 2, 2017).

47. The SCO Code of Conduct on Information Security discourages the use of information and communications technologies or networks to "interfere in the internal affairs of other States" and seeks to curb information that "incites terrorism, separatism or extremism."

48. The Group noted document A/66/359, circulated by the Secretary-General at the request of the Permanent Representatives of China. See http://www.unidir.org/files/medias/pdfs/developments-in-the-field-of-information-and-telecommunications-in-the-context-of-international-security-2012-2013-a-68-98-eng-0-518.pdf. Also see "China, Russia, Tajikistan, Uzbekistan International Code of Conduct on Information Security," http://undocs.org/A/66/359.

49. See https://ccdcoe.org/updated-draft-code-conduct-distributed-united-nations-whats-new.html.

50. See China's International Strategy of Cooperation in Cyberspace issued by MOFA and CAC on 2 March 2017—State Council Information Office, People's Republic of China, available at www.scio.gov.cn/32618/Document/1543874/1543874.htm.

51. Ibid.

52. Xi Jinping speech available at http://www.chinadaily.com.cn/world/2015wic/2015-12/16/content_22724841.htm. The idea of that "the internet sovereignty of China should be respected and protected" was first put forward at the official level in China in the 2010 Internet White Paper. See State Council Information Office, People's Republic of China, *The Internet in China, Xinhua*, June 8, 2010, http://news.xinhuanet.com/english2010/china/2010-06/08/c_13339232.htm.

53. Sarah McKune and Shazeda Ahmed, "The Contestation and Shaping of Cyber Norms through China's Internet Sovereignty Agenda," *International Journal of Communication* 12 (2018): 3835–3855.

54. Rogier Creemers, "Cyber China: Upgrading Propaganda, Public Opinion Work, and Social Management for the Twenty-First Century," *Journal of Contemporary China* 26, no. 103 (2017): 85–100.

55. Raymond Zhong, "How China Walled Off the Internet," *New York Times*, November 18, 2018.

56. Rogier Creemers, "Cyber China."

57. See http://cn.chinadaily.com.cn/2017-05/31/content_29558817.htm.

58. Yuan Yang, "China's Cybersecurity Law Rattles Multinationals," *Financial Times*, May 30, 2017.

59. Lorand Laski and Adam Segal, "A New Old Threat Countering the Return of Chinese Industrial Cyber Espionage" (New York: Council on Foreign Affairs, December 2018).

60. In a ransomware attack, malware is used to encrypt a user's data and demand payment to unlock it; see Julia Carrie Wong and Olivia Solon, "Massive Ransomware Cyberattack Hits Nearly 100 Countries around the World," *The Guardian*, May 12, 2017, available at: https://www.theguardian.com/technology/2017/may/12/global-cyber-attack-ransomware-nsa-uk-nhs.

61. White House Press briefing on the attribution of the Wannacry malware attack to North Korea, December 19, 2017, https://www.whitehouse.gov/briefings-statements/press-briefing-on-the-attribution-of-the-wannacry-malware-attack-to-north-korea-121917/.

62. 2018 Group of Governmental Experts on Lethal Autonomous Weapons, https://www.unog.ch/__80256ee600585943.nsf/(httpPages)/7c335e71dfcb29d1c1258243003e8724?OpenDocument&ExpandSection=3.

63. China Position Paper, *Group of Governmental Experts of the High Contracting Parties to the Convention on Prohibitions or Restrictions on the Use of Certain Weapons Which May Be Deemed to Be Excessively Injurious or to Have Indiscriminate Effects*, Geneva, April 9–13, 2018, GGE.1/2018/WP.7, 11 April 2018. Available at https://www.unog.ch/80256EDD006B8954/(httpAssets)/E42AE83BDB3525D0C125826C0040B262/$file/CCW_GGE.1_2018_WP.7.pdf.

64. No author, "Use of 'Killer Robots' in War Would Breach Law, Say Campaigners," https://www.theguardian.com/science/2018/aug/21/use-of-killer-robots-in-wars-would-breach-law-say-campaigners.

# 9

# China's Global Military-Security Interactions

PHILLIP C. SAUNDERS[*]

As with other dimensions of foreign relations and international interactions assessed in this volume, China's national security calculations have become increasingly global in nature. The expansion of Beijing's international military-security footprint has paralleled its diplomatic, economic, and cultural ties (as described in the three previous and six subsequent chapters).[1] This includes a range of military and security cooperation programs with other countries, involvement in multilateral security organizations, and unilateral developments undertaken by China's military, the People's Liberation Army (PLA).

China's military modernization is a principal driver of its expanding and multifaceted global security presence. Over the past three decades the PLA has transformed itself from a large ground force–dominated organization into a modern military with naval and air forces capable of operating outside China's borders. Improvements in capabilities and expanding Chinese national interests have turned the PLA from an insular force that was devoted to protecting China's territorial homeland and that rarely interacted with foreigners or deployed overseas, into a military that interacts regularly with foreign counterparts, is deeply involved in international peacekeeping, has deployed a counter-piracy task force 5,000 miles away to the Gulf of Aden for a decade, and has become a more effective instrument for advancing Chinese foreign policy objectives.

The PLA has not fought a major war since its invasion of Vietnam in early 1979 or employed significant lethal force against a foreign military since its border skirmishes with Vietnam ended in the late 1980s. Major improvements in PLA military capabilities have been matched by relative restraint in using those capabilities in combat. But militaries do more than fight wars. Chinese Communist Party (CCP) leaders regularly use the PLA as an instrument for both domestic and international missions. Some of these objectives persist from

Phillip C. Saunders, *China's Global Military- Security Interactions* In: *China and the World*. Edited by: David Shambaugh, Oxford University Press (2020). © Oxford University Press
DOI: 10.1093/oso/9780190062316.003.0009

the revolutionary era, and some have been added as China's overseas interests have expanded along with its modernization and integration into the global economy.

This chapter reviews China's overseas security interests and the military missions the PLA has been tasked to perform by CCP leaders. It then discusses the PLA's organization and capabilities, with an emphasis on those relevant for operating beyond China's borders. China's military and security interactions include traditional military missions (mostly focused on Asia), military diplomacy efforts to support Chinese foreign policy objectives by engaging foreign military counterparts and providing public goods, and a new emphasis on protecting China's expanding overseas economic and security interests. The chapter briefly explores each of these dimensions, highlights the tensions and synergies between these competing objectives, and considers how China's global military and security interactions are likely to evolve in the future.

## Protecting China's Overseas Interests

China's remarkable economic growth in the reform era has been facilitated by increased integration into the regional and global economy. China opened itself to foreign trade, investment, technology, management and quality-control practices, and education in order to stimulate domestic economic growth, a strategy that has proved remarkably successful in building China's comprehensive national power and in generating a new basis of legitimacy for the CCP by raising living standards. Rapid growth increased Chinese demand for imported components, oil and natural gas, and food and tied the employment of millions of Chinese workers to exports to global markets. China's integration with the global economy received a further boost when former presidents Jiang Zemin and Hu Jintao urged Chinese companies to "go out" into the world by investing abroad to acquire natural resources and technology and to compete for foreign construction contracts.[2]

The growing importance of trade and increased PRC investment and citizen presence overseas, often in politically unstable places, have prompted Beijing to take measures to secure its new interests. In 2004, Hu Jintao gave the PLA the "New Historic Missions," which include defending China's expanding international interests.[3] The PLA has responded with naval counter-piracy patrols in the Gulf of Aden and evacuations of PRC citizens during unrest in Libya and Yemen. Social media and press coverage of PRC citizens caught in dangerous situations have produced growing calls by the Chinese public for the government to protect PRC citizens abroad.[4] China's overseas presence has deepened further with the Belt and Road Initiative (BRI), an ambitious plan to fund infrastructure construction to increase China's connectivity with Eurasia and the rest of the world.[5]

The result is that the PRC now has a significant diplomatic, economic, and human presence in almost every country. In addition to diplomatic facilities, China now has some 30,000 enterprises located overseas, and more than 100 million Chinese travel overseas every year.[6] The cumulative value of China's overseas investment and construction combined since 2005 is now approaching $2 trillion.[7] The PRC presence in any particular country is a function of its natural resources; Chinese investments in factories, mines, and infrastructure; Chinese commercial and BRI construction projects; and Chinese companies and individuals pursuing economic opportunities. The total number of PRC citizens living and working overseas may be as high as five million.[8]

Given that part of China's comparative advantage in making infrastructure loans and commercial investments is a greater tolerance for risk, it is not surprising that China often has significant investments and citizens in politically unstable parts of the world. Parello-Plesner and Duchâtel cite more than thirty mass attacks on PRC citizens abroad from 2004 to 2015, and at least sixteen cases where PRC citizens had to be evacuated due to natural disasters or political unrest.[9] As the BRI continues to expand the PRC presence in volatile regions such as Africa, the Middle East, Central Asia, and South Asia, this presence (and the resulting risk of attacks on PRC investments and citizens) will continue to grow.

Chinese analysts, scholars, and officials have engaged in active debates about the best means of protecting Chinese overseas interests.[10] The PLA has been tasked to protect China's overseas interests as part of its "New Historic Missions," and the PLA Navy and Air Force have used the need to evacuate PRC citizens as a rationale for increased investments in power projection capabilities. The PLA Navy's presence in the Gulf of Aden and logistics base in Djibouti provide both expeditionary capabilities and a base in a strategic location that could be used to support a variety of evacuation and other operations to support Chinese overseas interests. Moreover, the PLA has reportedly expressed interest in bases in other countries, such as Pakistan, and Chinese companies have investments or contracts to operate port facilities in a number of other countries that might eventually translate into direct naval access arrangements.

However, discussions with Chinese analysts and PLA officers indicate reluctance to rely too heavily on military forces to secure Chinese overseas interests. They argue that a larger PLA overseas presence would create frictions with host country populations, involve Chinese soldiers in local political disputes, and potentially entail long-lasting and costly overseas commitments to maintain stability.[11] While some PLA officers are eager to use overseas interests as a means to justify power projection capabilities and overseas bases, most analysts advocate a more cautious approach that places greater emphasis on private security forces and efforts to improve the capacity of host governments to maintain stability and protect Chinese interests.[12] This is the approach China has taken to protect its interests in the China-Pakistan Economic Corridor, which runs through the volatile Balochistan province.

The one set of Chinese overseas interests likely to produce a greater PLA role in the future is the need to protect China's sea lines of communication (SLOCs), especially those that carry oil and natural gas from the Middle East and Africa through the Indian Ocean and the Malacca Strait to China. Despite efforts to build pipelines and diversify supplies, Chinese political leaders are aware that China's dependence on imported energy is a strategic vulnerability, and worry that the US or the Indian Navy could cut off the flow of energy and natural resources in the event of a military conflict. PLA Navy (PLAN) officers have used this contingency to argue for the need for China to invest heavily in blue water navy capabilities that could help protect SLOCs from interdiction by a hostile navy.[13] However, the high costs of building a large blue water navy capable of deploying thousands of miles from China and engaging in major combat operations suggest that decades will be required to build this kind of capability.

## Chinese National Security Interests and PLA Military Missions

China's 2015 Defense White Paper provides a useful overview of how the PLA and its military strategy support broader national security objectives,[14] and it lists eight military tasks for the PLA:

1) To deal with a wide range of emergencies and military threats, and effectively safeguard the sovereignty and security of China's territorial land, air, and sea;
2) to resolutely safeguard the unification of the motherland;
3) to safeguard China's security and interests in new domains [space and cyberspace];
4) to safeguard the security of China's overseas interests;
5) to maintain strategic deterrence and carry out nuclear counterattack;
6) to participate in regional and international security cooperation and maintain regional and world peace;
7) to strengthen efforts in operations against infiltration, separatism, and terrorism so as to maintain China's political security and social stability; and

8) to perform such tasks as emergency rescue and disaster relief, protection of rights and interests, guard duties, and support for national economic and social development.

As a Party-Army whose loyalty is to the CCP rather than to the Chinese state, the PLA is responsible for defending the Party against any internal or external political challenges. Strengthening party control is an important objective of the ongoing anti-corruption campaign and the military reforms that were instituted in 2015.[15]

The PLA's mandate includes domestic missions such as maintaining political security and social stability, traditional military missions such as nuclear deterrence and protecting China's sovereignty and security, new missions such as protecting China's economic development and China's interests in space and cyberspace, and nontraditional security missions such as emergency rescue, disaster relief, and regional and international security cooperation.

These missions require a range of advanced military capabilities, including a "lean and effective" nuclear deterrent force[16] and the ability to conduct offensive and defensive operations in the space and cyber domains, which PLA strategists view as critical to success in modern warfare.[17] They also require the ability to project power beyond China's borders by deploying military forces to protect Chinese overseas interests and to conduct military diplomacy.

## The Path to a Modern PLA

China's road to a modern military has been long.[18] The foundations of today's PLA date from the heyday of Sino-Soviet security cooperation from 1950 to 1960. The Soviet Union provided weapons, production technology, technical assistance, doctrine, and training that helped China build a basic defense industry and a military focused on conducting ground force combined arms (infantry, tank, artillery) operations. However, the 1960 Sino-Soviet split led to the withdrawal of Soviet advisers and technical assistance and forced the Chinese defense industry and the PLA to proceed on their own. By the start of the reform era in 1978, the defense industry was still struggling to produce slightly modernized versions of 1950s Soviet designs, and the 1979 Sino-Vietnamese war laid bare numerous shortcomings in the performance of PLA ground forces.

Deng Xiaoping included military modernization as one of the "four modernizations," but China's pressing need to build overall economic and technological capacity meant that military modernization was given the lowest priority. Improved relations with the Soviet Union in the late 1980s allowed China to regain access to Soviet weapons, and the PLA was able to procure modern Su-27 fighters, advanced Kilo class diesel submarines, and Soveremenny destroyers equipped with advanced anti-ship cruise missiles in order to gain experience operating and maintaining modern weapons systems. These systems were procured in relatively small quantities, with the hope that the Chinese defense industry could use access to these systems to improve its own design and production capabilities and eventually eliminate dependence on imported weapons.

Several developments led CCP leaders to accelerate the measured pace of PLA modernization. First, US military success in the 1991 Gulf war shocked PLA leaders. The United States and its coalition allies were able to use precision-guided munitions and advanced intelligence, surveillance, and reconnaissance (ISR) capabilities to take apart the Iraqi military (the fourth largest in the world) and its air defenses in a matter of weeks, while suffering few casualties. The US success demonstrated the critical role information plays in modern war, and that China's military—much less well equipped than Iraq's—was equally vulnerable.[19] Second, the March 1996 Taiwan Strait crisis—during which the United States sent two carriers toward Taiwan following PRC exercises and missile launches intended to influence the Taiwan presidential elections—convinced PRC leaders that the threat of Taiwan independence was growing, and that the US military might intervene on Taiwan's behalf. In response, Chinese leaders increased military budgets and accelerated modernization efforts, while PLA planners began studying how to deter, delay, or defeat US military forces that might intervene in a future crisis. Third, the accidental US bombing of China's embassy in Belgrade in the midst of the 1999 Kosovo conflict was interpreted by Chinese civilian and military leaders as a deliberate US action intended to intimidate China. Although Chinese leaders ultimately decided to seek to stabilize relations with Washington (a task facilitated by al-Qaeda's September 11, 2001, attacks on the United States), the bombing reinforced Chinese suspicions about US hostile intentions and led to additional funding for PLA modernization.[20]

The PLA's broad modernization program continued, but PLA leaders also increased efforts to acquire or develop specific capabilities that might deter, delay, or defeat US military forces attempting to intervene in a conflict near China. The PLA would benefit from home field advantage, while US forces would have to deploy from bases farther away in Japan, Guam, Hawaii, or the continental United States. Accordingly, the PLA invested in an array of "anti-access/area denial" (A2/AD) capabilities that would raise the costs and risks for US forces operating in or near China. These included advanced diesel submarines (which could attack US naval forces deploying into the Western Pacific) and advanced surface-to-air missile systems such as the Russian S-300, which could target US fighter and bomber aircraft, anti-ship cruise missiles optimized to attack US aircraft carrier battle groups, long-range missiles that can strike US bases as far as Guam, and even an innovative anti-ship ballistic missile that could attack US carriers.[21] China also sought to exploit US military dependence on space systems by developing a range of anti-satellite (ASAT) capabilities that could degrade, interfere with, or directly attack US satellites and their associated ground stations. Collectively, these investments represented an asymmetric effort to degrade US military advantages in order to give a less capable PLA force a chance of success in a conflict. PLA strategists hoped that the ability to inflict significant casualties on US forces would deter US policymakers from intervening.

PLA modernization is about more than just modern weapons. Chinese strategists also seek to harness the advantages of US and Russia–style joint operations, which integrate the capabilities and actions of multiple services to achieve synergistic effects. This was a major shift for the ground force–dominated PLA, which had previously viewed naval and air forces in terms of their role in supporting ground force operations. In 1993, the PLA promulgated a new military strategy that prioritized the need to prepare for high-tech regional conflicts and described joint operations as the "main form" of future operations.[22] A 2004 doctrinal revision placed even more emphasis on what became known as "integrated joint operations," which highlighted the need for deeper cooperation between units from different services.[23] These high-level efforts to define the nature of future warfare were matched by efforts to develop operational campaign doctrine detailing *how* the services would work together to accomplish specific tasks, and a series of joint exercises that tested the ability of the different services to work together.[24]

At the same time, PLA theorists increasingly emphasized the importance of information in advanced warfighting and sought to emulate the US emphasis on information encapsulated in "network-centric warfare." If accurate information about enemy forces could be passed quickly to commanders and down to operational units, military forces could gain the initiative and reap operational synergies that would dramatically increase their effectiveness. Conversely, attacks on adversary intelligence, communications, and command-and-control systems could produce paralysis and force individual units to fight in isolation, at a huge disadvantage.[25] In 2004, PLA doctrine shifted to a stress on the need to fight and win "local wars under conditions of informationization," subsequently changed in 2015 to winning "informationized local wars" (信息化局部战争).[26]

This doctrinal shift implied a shift from an emphasis on asymmetrical means to give a weaker PLA a chance to prevail against a more capable US military toward a more symmetrical approach where the PLA would attempt to replicate important aspects of US military concepts, systems, and organization in order to beat the United States at its own game. This required the ability to compete effectively in the traditional warfighting domains of land, sea, and air as well as the nuclear, space, cyber, and electromagnetic domains. These efforts were hindered by army's dominance of key PLA leadership positions and the lack of a joint command-and-control system that could make forces from all services could work together.

China's early 2016 military reforms, launched by Xi Jinping, involved an extensive and unprecedented reorganization of the PLA intended to enhance its political reliability and improve its ability to conduct integrated joint operations.[27] The reforms jettisoned the old Soviet military organizational template— which had guided the PLA for seven decades—in favor of an American-style joint command-and-control system. The reforms abolished the powerful general departments in favor of an expanded Central Military Commission (CMC) staff under Xi Jinping's direct supervision and moved from seven army-dominated military regions to five joint theater commands with control over all ground, naval, air, and conventional missile forces within their area of responsibility. Each theater has responsibility for a specific set of cross-border or maritime contingencies. The post-reform role of the military services has shifted from operational command to "force building" (e.g., "plan, train, and equip" functions). Each service headquarters is now responsible for developing military equipment, recruiting and training personnel, setting training requirements, and providing trained and equipped forces to the joint theater commands. See Table 9.1 for a summary of the impact of reform and modernization on the PLA services and forces.

With these reforms in the protracted process of implementation, the PLA is well on the way to becoming a modern military of world-class standards. This does not mean, however, that the reorganization will be either immediate or easy. Such bureaucratic reforms break many "iron rice bowls" and infringe on entrenched institutional interests. They take a long time to implement and can be anticipated to encounter pushback. Nonetheless, this is exactly the organizational overhaul that the PLA has long needed.

## China's Security Environment

Xi Jinping's repeated emphasis on the need for the PLA to be able to "fight and win wars" highlights the priority the CCP places on traditional military missions such as protecting China's sovereignty and security. Most of China's potential security threats and all of its unresolved land and maritime territorial disputes are in Asia. Unlike Russia, which has sought to destabilize its neighbors to maintain its regional influence, China has sought to promote stability and enlist the support of neighboring countries in managing domestic threats such as terrorism and separatism. From 1998 to 2008, China achieved remarkable success in improving relations with its neighbors by employing a range of diplomatic,

*Table 9.1* **Post-Reform PLA Services and Forces**

| Service/Force | Impact of Reform and Modernization |
| --- | --- |
| Army (PLAA) | Established new Army headquarters; downsized army by 300,000; reorganized most forces into thirteen group armies with a standardized group army-brigade-battalion structure with modular, deployable brigades and battalions. |
| Navy (PLAN) | Upgrading and expanding number of major combat platforms (ships, submarines, aircraft); building second and third aircraft carriers; developing air defense and replenishment capabilities to project power into the Western Pacific and Indian Ocean for "far seas protection"; four operational nuclear ballistic missile submarines. |
| Air Force (PLAAF) | Operating fourth-generation fighters; developing next-generation stealth fighter and new strategic bomber; reorganized paratrooper corps, fighter aircraft, and attack aircraft into brigades; deploying new strategic transport aircraft to improve power projection; increasing focus on offensive operations and training over water. |
| Rocket Force (PLARF) | Upgraded to independent service; deploying second-generation nuclear missiles that are mostly mobile (and more survivable), more accurate, longer-range, and in some cases equipped with multiple warheads; conventional missile bases and brigades now under operational control of joint theater commands. |
| Strategic Support Force (SSF) | Consolidates PLA space, counter-space, cyberspace, electronic warfare, and psychological warfare capabilities in one organization to support Central Military Commission and theater commands. |
| Joint Logistics Support Force (JLSF) | Provides logistics support for joint operations at the theater command level and below; primarily focused on contingency operations within China or on borders, but will likely develop expeditionary logistics capabilities. |
| People's Armed Police (PAP) | Downsized paramilitary force refocused on domestic stability and supporting military operations in wartime and crisis; reforms centralized control of PAP under the Central Military Commission; China Coast Guard now reports directly to the PAP. |

*Source*: Phillip C. Saunders et al., eds., *Chairman Xi Remakes the PLA: Assessing Chinese Military Reforms* (Washington, DC: National Defense University Press, 2019).

military, and economic assurance measures. During this period, China's rapid growth and increasing integration into the regional and global economy made it the largest export market for almost all countries in Asia. This approach was predicated on a patient approach to territorial disputes and restraint in the employment of Chinese military forces (even as PLA budgets grew and military modernization efforts accelerated).[28]

However, in 2009 a more assertive Chinese posture emerged on a range of bilateral, regional, and global issues.[29] Chinese diplomatic bullying, assertive military and paramilitary actions, and disregard for foreign reactions undid many of the gains from Beijing's charm offensive. In particular, the aggressive means used to advance Chinese maritime sovereignty claims in the South China Sea and East China Sea did considerable damage to Beijing's efforts to persuade others that China's rise would be peaceful.[30]

China's strategic dilemma is finding a way to reconcile the rest of Asia to a dominant Chinese regional role without precipitating a conflict with the United States or destabilizing the region. Chinese diplomacy emphasizes Beijing's peaceful intentions and efforts to promote mutually beneficial "win-win" solutions, but China's claims to land and maritime territories it does not currently control complicate its efforts to reassure its neighbors. These include land border disputes with India and Bhutan; claims to land features and waters in the South China Sea that are also claimed by Taiwan, Vietnam, Malaysia, Brunei, and the Philippines; disputes over the Senkaku/Diaoyu Islands with Japan; and the unresolved issue of Taiwan's status, which the PRC regards as an inalienable part of Chinese territory.

The need to preserve a peaceful regional environment for economic development—a necessity for internal stability—is in tension with the desire to use China's power to achieve nationalist territorial goals at the expense of its neighbors. What China sees as defensive actions to "safeguard sovereignty and territorial integrity" are viewed by neighboring states as intimidation and threats to advance Chinese territorial claims. Even those countries that do not have territorial disputes with Beijing are wary of how a powerful, unrestrained China might behave.

Taiwan is the most difficult of these issues because it relates directly to the CCP's nationalist credentials and because the CCP has defined unification with Taiwan as an essential element of the "great rejuvenation of the Chinese people" by 2049. Beijing would strongly prefer to resolve the Taiwan issue peacefully, but has refused to rule out the use of force and is developing military capabilities to coerce Taiwan (including advanced systems to deter and raise the costs of US military intervention). The mix of persuasion, coercion, and united front tactics in China's policy toward Taiwan varies depending on circumstances.

When Ma Ying-jeou was president of the Republic of China (2008–2016), his Kuomintang (KMT) party accepted the "1992 consensus," which they defined as "one China, separate interpretations." Under this political framework, the two sides signed a range of economic and administrative agreements strengthening cross-strait ties, even as Ma resisted PRC pressure to engage in political talks. Democratic Progressive Party (DPP) candidate Tsai Ing-wen, who became president in May 2016, has refused to accept the "1992 consensus" and its core connotation that Taiwan is part of China, a condition unacceptable to most members of her nominally pro-independence party. Beijing has responded by increased diplomatic and military pressure, including wooing away several countries that had formally recognized Taiwan, military exercises, and a series of air and naval deployments around the island. The KMT's success in local elections in November 2018 suggests that it has more resilience than many observers expected. Nevertheless, growing PLA capabilities and China's willingness to use them overtly to pressure Taiwan are likely to undercut PRC efforts to persuade Taiwan voters that unification is a desirable choice.

Taiwan remains the main driver of PLA modernization, but the military reforms are also intended to improve the PLA's ability to respond to contingencies along its borders and maritime territory, including collapse or instability on the Korean peninsula, a territorial conflict with India, terrorist threats in Central Asia, or a maritime conflict in the South China Sea or East China Sea. PLA modernization and military reforms have significantly improved the PLA's ability to deploy joint forces in response to a contingency; employ national-level assets like paratroopers, counter-space systems, and offensive cyber capabilities; deploy reinforcements from other theaters; and have the logistics and other support necessary for sustained operations. Moreover, the theater commands plan for all these contingencies and train to execute their plans, which both improves their capabilities and exercises a deterrent effect on potential adversaries.

China resolved almost all of its land border disputes in the aftermath of the breakup of the Soviet Union in 1991.[31] The two exceptions are its border disputes with India and a much smaller boundary dispute with Bhutan. The Sino-Indian dispute was the proximate cause of the 1962 Sino-Indian war, and is tangled up in Indian domestic politics and India's complicated relationship with Pakistan. Periodic Chinese intrusions across the border foment anti-China suspicion within the Indian military, government, and political class; the most recent was a June 2017 standoff caused when China began constructing a road into Doklam, territory claimed by both China and Bhutan. India deployed forces across the border in response, a standoff ensued, and both India and China subsequently withdrew their forces. Although China and India have worked to improve bilateral relations in the aftermath of the confrontation, this illustrates how China's efforts to strengthen its territorial claims can aggravate regional tensions.[32]

A similar shift toward a more assertive Chinese policy on maritime territorial claims became evident in late 2008 and 2009, partly in response to actions by other claimants to submit specific territorial claims under the UN Convention on the Law of the Sea (UNCLOS). China responded with a range of diplomatic, military, paramilitary, and legal measures to assert its sovereignty over the disputed territory. China's approach to maritime disputes has evolved over time, from viewing challenges by others as opportunities to expand effective control of disputed territories (as in the April 2012 Scarborough Shoal and September 2012 Senkaku/Diaoyu Islands incidents) to proactive efforts to strengthen Chinese claims (such as the unilateral November 2013 declaration of an Air Defense Identification Zone [ADIZ] in the East China Sea and the May 2014 deployment of an oil exploration platform in waters claimed by Vietnam). In 2014, China began massive land reclamation operations in the South China Sea to build seven small land features into large artificial islands with ports, airfields, radars, and barracks. In a September 2015 meeting at the White House, President Xi Jinping stated that China had "no intention to militarize these features," but China subsequently installed missiles and radars on many of the sites.[33]

These efforts to use growing naval and paramilitary capabilities to assert China's maritime territorial claims have not involved the use of lethal force. China has relied primarily on the China Coast Guard and maritime militia to enforce its claims, putting a law enforcement face on its coercive actions. The coast guard is often backed up by PLA Navy (PLAN) forces, and some operations such as the May 2014 Haiyang Shiyou 981 oil drilling rig incident involve a well-coordinated mix of assets from state-owned enterprises, the PLA Navy, the China Coast Guard, and the maritime militia.

The tactics China employs to manage the tensions between pursuing its territorial and maritime claims and maintaining good ties with its neighbors include:

1) Employing economic inducements and punishments;
2) dividing opposition in ASEAN by differentiating between claimants and non-claimants;
3) employing incremental "salami tactics" to expand China's effective control of disputed maritime territories without military confrontation;
4) emphasizing paramilitary forces rather than military forces;
5) portraying China's actions as defensive responses to challenges by others;
6) citing actions by rival claimants to justify actions that strengthen Chinese control;
7) using China's overall military power advantage to intimidate rival claimants; and
8) negotiating crisis management mechanisms to reduce the risk of escalation.

China's use of "gray zone" coercive tactics short of war has made it difficult for its adversaries to respond. China has improved its strategic position in the South China Sea and East China Sea, but is unlikely to be able to persuade other claimants to give up occupied land features without using force. Most claimants do not want to pay the domestic political costs of abandoning their claims, but are equally unwilling to fight to defend them against a superior Chinese military. The result is a new equilibrium, where China has strengthened its position but cannot fully resolve the territorial disputes without using force.

This new status quo comes with some costs for China. Many of the countries in the Asia-Pacific region have strengthened their security ties with the United States and other countries in the region to balance against Chinese pressure. Many are also increasing their defense budgets and acquisition of advanced weapons to improve their maritime domain awareness and ability to respond to Chinese military actions.[34] China's rejection of adverse legal rulings, such as the UN Permanent Court of Arbitration in The Hague ruling in the Philippines case against China's South China Sea claims, has also damaged China's reputation as a country that respects international law.

Chinese officials are aware of these costs and have taken some steps to move toward a less aggressive posture. These include diplomatic efforts to engage ASEAN on negotiations for a Code of Conduct on the South China Sea, efforts to improve relations with countries that have territorial disputes with China (including Japan, India, the Philippines, Vietnam, and Malaysia), use of economic investment and loans to help fund infrastructure investments in the Asia-Pacific, and efforts to articulate a positive vision for regional security. Not surprisingly, China's vision for the region is long on principles and calls for cooperation, while making no mention of China's assertive actions and the changing regional balance of power.

## Military Diplomacy and Security Cooperation

China's 2017 White Paper on Asia-Pacific Security Cooperation calls for intensified "military exchanges and cooperation to offer more guarantees for peace and stability in the Asia-Pacific region" and cites "positive contributions to the maintenance of world peace and regional stability" by China's armed forces. It argues that China has "promoted dialogue and cooperation on maritime security, participated in United Nations peacekeeping missions, international counterterrorism cooperation, escort missions and disaster-relief operations, and conducted relevant joint exercises and training with other countries."[35] The White Paper makes clear that Beijing sees military diplomacy and security

cooperation as tools for assuaging concerns about how China will use its growing military power.

Chinese military writings over the last decade highlight the growing
importance of military diplomacy. Stated objectives include supporting overall national foreign policy, protecting national sovereignty, advancing national
interests, and shaping the international security environment.[36] Xi Jinping
cited several specific goals for Chinese military diplomacy in a January 2015
speech to the All-Military Diplomatic Work Conference, including supporting overall national foreign policy, protecting national security, and promoting military construction (e.g., military force-building). Xi also highlighted
the goals of protecting China's sovereignty, security, and development interests.[37] In addition to these openly acknowledged objectives, the PLA uses
military diplomacy to gather intelligence, learn new skills, benchmark PLA
capabilities against those of other nations, and build interoperability with
foreign partners.

Much of the PLA's current military diplomatic activity is focused on protecting and advancing specific Chinese strategic interests and managing areas of
concern. Chinese military diplomacy emphasizes interactions with the United
States, Russia, and countries in Asia.[38] Given these priorities, China's military
has stepped up its out-of-area interactions.[39] China is increasingly dependent
on oil and natural gas imported from the Middle East and Africa; the PLA
Navy's counter-piracy presence in the Gulf of Aden facilitates strategic ties in
the Middle East and Africa, helps guarantee China's energy security, and provides operational experience in protecting China's sea lines of communication
(SLOCs). Xi Jinping's signature foreign policy contribution is the Belt and Road
Initiative; PLA interactions with militaries in Europe, Africa, and Asia reinforce
this effort.[40]

The following description of these diverse activities relies on a National
Defense University open-source database to analyze the expansion of PLA
diplomatic activities, with an emphasis on senior-level visits, exercises with
foreign militaries, and port calls. Figure 9.1 shows trends in Chinese military
diplomacy. The data show that military diplomatic interactions expanded from
a relatively low base through 2010 and have remained relatively constant since
then. Senior-level visits have fallen from their 2010 peak, but visits and meetings
still make up the overwhelming majority of Chinese military diplomatic interactions. The data show a steady increase in the number of military exercises and
port calls beginning in 2009. The PLA also has robust academic and functional
exchange programs with various countries. It is also actively engaged in nontraditional security cooperation, especially UN peacekeeping and counter-piracy
operations.

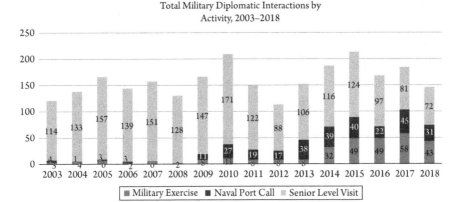

*Figure 9.1* Total Military Diplomatic Interactions by Activity, 2003–2018

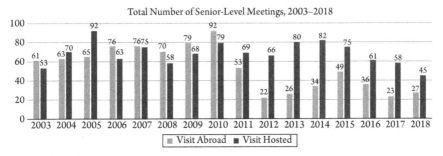

*Figure 9.2* Total Number of Senior-Level Meetings, 2003–2018

## Senior-Level Visits

Senior-level visits mostly involve PLA officers who are Central Military Commission (CMC) members or theater commander grade and above. The minister of defense takes the lead in engaging foreign military leaders, but the CMC vice chairs, service commanders, commanders of the CMC Joint Staff Department (JSD) and the CMC Political Work Department (PWD), and the JSD deputy commander with the foreign affairs and intelligence portfolio also meet regularly with foreign counterparts.[41] Figure 9.2 shows PLA senior-level interactions with foreign militaries.

The data show several interesting patterns. The first is that PLA senior-level visits abroad peaked in 2010, and are down significantly since then. Second is that before 2010, there was rough parity between visits abroad by PLA officers and visits hosted in China, in keeping with the expectation of reciprocity. Since then, senior PLA officers have been less willing to travel overseas to visit foreign counterparts, and foreign military officers and defense officials have become more willing to visit China without a reciprocal visit. This likely reflects tighter travel restrictions as part of the anti-corruption campaign and greater demands on senior PLA officers due to military reforms.[42] The data also reveal a pattern that corresponds to the five-year Chinese political cycle—that is, overseas visits by senior PLA officers dipped significantly in years with a Party congress (2007, 2012, 2017) and peaked during their third full year in office (in 2005, 2010, and 2015).[43] The data reflect increased senior PLA officer participation in multilateral meetings such as the Shanghai Cooperation Organization (SCO) Defense Ministers' Meeting, the ASEAN Region Forum (ARF) Defense Ministers' Meeting Plus (ADMM+), the Shangri-La Defense Dialogue in Singapore, and the Xiangshan Forum in Beijing. Senior PLA officers attending these meetings often schedule multiple bilateral counterpart meetings in conjunction with these multilateral meetings.

## Military Exercises

Jettisoning Mao's longtime directive that the PLA would never exercise with foreign militaries, would not build military bases abroad, and would not enter into military alliances, the PLA abandoned the first of these prohibitions by conducting bilateral and multilateral "combined exercises" (联合演习) with other countries beginning in 2002. The PLA often refers to combined exercises with other militaries as "joint exercises" even if they only involve a single service (this chapter uses US terminology, which considers these "combined exercises"). Joint exercises involve multiple services; exercises with multiple branches of a single service are combined arms exercises. Exercises are further categorized by function.[44] Combat exercises emphasize combat skills on the high end of the conventional spectrum of conflict, including live-fire drills and combat simulations; combat support activities include communications, engineering, resupply, logistics, survival skills, and fleet navigation and maneuvers. Military Operations Other Than War (MOOTW) include search and rescue, humanitarian assistance/disaster relief (HA/DR), and medical exercises. Antiterrorism exercises are lower-intensity, small-unit activities that may include conventional combat operations on the lower end of the spectrum.

Figure 9.3 shows a major increase in the volume of PLA participation in combined exercises with foreign partners, including a significant increase in participation in multilateral exercises. The PLA Navy (43.6 percent) and PLA Army (41.3 percent) are most involved in exercises with foreign counterparts; the PLA Air Force conducts 8.7 percent of exercises and the PLA Rocket Force is not known to have exercised with foreign militaries. Only 6.5 percent of PLA exercises with foreign militaries are joint exercises.

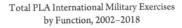
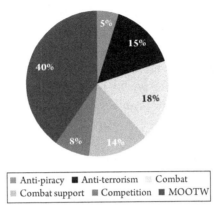

*Figure 9.3* Total PLA International Military Exercises by Function, 2002–2018

*Figure 9.4* Total PLA Military Exercises by Type, 2002–2018

Figure 9.4 shows the breakout of exercise type by function.

Most of the exercises the PLA conducts involve military operations other than war (MOOTW) or are anti-piracy or anti-terrorism exercises aimed against non-state threats. This makes them politically inoffensive, since they involve common interests and are not aimed against third countries. These types of exercises typically do not involve extensive operational interactions or reveal advanced military capabilities.

The exceptions include the SCO Peace Mission exercise series (since 2007), various bilateral exercises with close security partners such as Pakistan and Thailand, and the Sino-Russian Naval Cooperation and Joint Sea naval exercises. The SCO Peace Mission exercises are described as counterterrorism exercises but often involve the participation of large units conducting conventional combat operations (including air defense and strike operations). The Naval Cooperation exercise series has sometimes been held in sensitive waters (include the Baltic Sea, the Mediterranean Sea, and the South China Sea) and has evolved to include more combined arms operations (including combined anti-submarine warfare training and amphibious assaults).[45] Such combat-related exercises may help the PLA improve its operational capabilities by learning from advanced militaries, create a degree of interoperability with foreign counterparts, and send a political signal of China's willingness and ability to cooperate militarily with other countries.

## Port Calls and Counter-Piracy Operations

From 1985 to 2008, the PLA Navy typically conducted only a handful of port calls per year, most of which were "friendly visits" without much operational interaction with the host nation's navy (see Figure 9.5). The PLA Navy's participation in counter-piracy deployments in the Gulf of Aden since December 2008 generated new requirements for replenishment port calls and provided new opportunities for friendly visits to foreign ports.[46] As of January 2019, the PLA Navy had deployed thirty-one three-ship escort task forces (ETFs) to the Gulf of Aden. The operational requirements of deploying and sustaining ETFs crowded out port calls by PLA Navy ships other than the Peace Ark hospital ship from 2009 to 2012. Since 2013, the PLA Navy has been able to balance the operational requirements of maintaining a continuous counter-piracy presence in the Gulf of Aden while resuming a more robust program of non-ETF port calls.

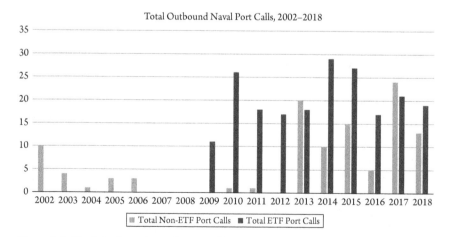

*Figure 9.5* Total Outbound Naval Port Calls, 2002–2018

PLA Navy ETFs conduct two types of port calls. Replenishment visits usually last two to five days, during which the vessels receive fuel, fresh water, vegetables, and fruits. Crews are usually met by the Chinese ambassador and military attachés, but the vessels are not open for public display and the crew does not interact with the host country's navy. Friendly visits generally last two to four days, with the crew usually met by the Chinese ambassador and military attachés, as well as host country government and naval officials.

PLA Navy counter-piracy ETFs have some opportunities to visit and interact with foreign escort task forces and personnel. On May 4, 2013, Rear Admiral Yuan Yubai, commander of ETF-14, hosted the commander of the multinational counter-piracy Combined Task Force 151 on the *Harbin* destroyer.[47] Although China has declined to participate in the multinational task force, some Chinese ETFs have conducted combined maritime exercises with other navies.

Since the area of operations for ETFs is focused on Somalia and the Gulf of Aden, where the piracy threat is greatest, replenishment port calls have generally been in the Middle East and North Africa, especially in Oman and Djibouti. The establishment of China's first overseas logistics base in Djibouti in 2017 abandoned Chairman Mao's prohibition against overseas bases. It has reduced the need for replenishment at other facilities, but PLA Navy ETFs have continued to conduct four to six friendly port calls in Europe, the Middle East, Africa, South Asia, and Southeast Asia once their four-month operational patrol is complete.

The PLA has used non-ETF port calls to engage foreign militaries in other parts of the world. This has included port calls in conjunction with multilateral exercises such as the 2016 Rim of the Pacific (RIMPAC) exercise, deployments by independent PLA Navy task forces, visits by cadet training ships, and deployments of the *Peace Ark* hospital ship to other regions. For example, in 2018 the *Peace Ark* conducted a long deployment that included port calls and humanitarian work in four South Pacific countries and seven countries in South America and Latin America.[48]

## Educational and Functional Exchanges

PLA education and academic exchanges (院校交流) include military educational institution leader visits, cadet and professional military education student delegation visits, training foreign military personnel at PLA military educational institutions, and individual PLA officers studying abroad. The PLA also conducts functional exchanges with foreign militaries on specific subjects, including operations, logistics, management, and military medicine. Functional exchanges usually involve visiting expert delegations, and often are conducted by individual PLA services under the direction of the CMC Office of International Military Cooperation.[49]

Although the PLA has published some aggregate data in its defense white papers, finding specific information on educational and functional exchanges is difficult. The white papers indicate a steady increase in Chinese military personnel studying abroad, from "more than 200 Chinese military personnel" in Russia, Germany, France, Great Britain, Pakistan, Bangladesh, Thailand, and Kuwait in 1999–2000 to "over 900 military students" studying in more than thirty countries in 2007–2008. The 2008 defense white paper also notes that "twenty military educational institutions in China have established and maintained inter-collegiate exchange relations with their counterparts in over 20 countries, including the United States, Russia, Japan, and Pakistan. Meanwhile, some 4,000 military personnel from more than 130 countries have come to China to study at Chinese military educational institutions." The lack of comparable data makes it difficult to observe any change in trends since the 18th Party Congress.[50]

## Security Dialogues

China also maintains "defense dialogues" or "strategic dialogues" with twenty-six countries and regional organizations,[51] including the United States, Russia, Japan, India, Great Britain, France, Germany, Australia, Brazil, Egypt, European Union, Indonesia, Israel, Jordan, African Union, Gulf Cooperation Council, Mexico, Nigeria, Pakistan, Peru, Portugal, South Africa, South Korea, Syria, Turkey, and the United Arab Emirates. These began in 2005 and are now viewed by China as important venues of confidence building.[52] These usually (but do not always) include PLA personnel. Their content varies by partner country, but they are generally surveys of regional and global security and foreign policy trends.

## Arms Sales

China's arms sales are conducted to generate profits for the defense industry and to support broader Chinese foreign policy objectives. China has long had a niche as a supplier of medium-capability, medium-cost weapons systems sold to countries with limited defense budgets or unable to purchase more-advanced weapons from Western suppliers. As the quality of the weapons produced by China's defense industry has improved, sales have increased. China was the fifth largest international arms exporter over the period from 2013 to 2017, selling arms to forty-eight countries over this period. Pakistan accounted for 35 percent of Chinese exports, followed by Bangladesh (19 percent) and Algeria (10 percent).[53] One area where China is competitive is in armed Unmanned Aerial

Vehicles (UAVs), which it has sold to several states in the Middle East and North Africa, including Iraq, Saudi Arabia, Egypt, and the United Arab Emirates.[54]

## Peacekeeping Operations

The PLA first became involved in UN peacekeeping operations (UNPKO) in 1990, when it sent five military observers to the UN Truce Supervision Organization. By the end of September 2014, China had deployed more than 27,000 military personnel around the globe to twenty-three UN peacekeeping missions.[55] Eighteen PLA soldiers have been killed performing peacekeeping duties. China is one of the top ten contributors of troops and police, and the biggest contributor among the five permanent members of the UN Security Council. China also pays the second largest share of UN peacekeeping costs. As of December 2018, a total of 2,517 PLA personnel were implementing peace-keeping tasks in nine UN mission areas, with the largest contributions to the UN missions in Mali, Sudan, Congo, Central African Republic, and Darfur.[56]

Most PLA peacekeeping troops are military observers, engineers, transporta-tion soldiers, and medical officers, but the PLA sent its first security forces to the UN mission in Mali in June 2013 and deployed its first UNPKO infantry battalion abroad to South Sudan in December 2014. The 700-member battalion was equipped with drones, armored infantry carriers, antitank missiles, mortars, light self-defense weapons, and bulletproof uniforms and helmets, among other weapons that were "completely for self-defense purposes."[57]

In addition to deployed troops, China has also established a standing peace-keeping force of 8,000 that is available for UN peacekeeping missions. The force includes six infantry battalions, along with supporting engineering, transport, medical, security, and helicopter units, as well as other air and naval transport assets. China has also established a training center for police and military peace-keepers, which has reportedly trained about 500 peacekeepers from sixty-nine countries.[58] China derives considerable prestige from its contributions of troops, money, and training expertise to UN peacekeeping operations, which comport with its preferred UN-centric model for global governance and support its claim that a stronger PLA is a force for peace.[59]

## Partners for Military Diplomacy

The previous section discussed what the PLA does with its foreign partners; this one describes who those partners are. PLA military diplomacy places heavy emphasis on great powers; Russia and the United States are the PLA's two most frequent military diplomatic partners. Both nations participate in a full range of

*Table 9.2* **The PLA's Top 10 Partners, 2003–2018**

| Rank | Country | Region | Exercises | Port Calls | Senior Meetings | Grand Total |
|------|---------|--------|-----------|------------|-----------------|-------------|
| 1 | Russia | Russia | 42 | 1 | 68 | 111 |
| 2 | Pakistan | Asia | 36 | 10 | 57 | 103 |
| 3 | United States | North America | 15 | 6 | 82 | 103 |
| 4 | Thailand | Asia | 20 | 7 | 49 | 76 |
| 5 | Australia | Asia | 19 | 8 | 45 | 72 |
| 6 | Singapore | Asia | 9 | 8 | 40 | 57 |
| 7 | Vietnam | Asia | 2 | 4 | 45 | 51 |
| 8 | New Zealand | Asia | 5 | 6 | 37 | 48 |
| 9 | India | Asia | 13 | 4 | 29 | 46 |
| 10 | Indonesia | Asia | 8 | 5 | 30 | 43 |

military diplomatic activities with the PLA, including military operations other than war and various functional exchanges not captured in the quantitative data. Table 9.2 lists the PLA's top ten partners over the period 2003–2018.

Beyond the United States and Russia, the pattern of the PLA's military diplomatic interactions over the last sixteen years exhibits a clear geographic focus on Asia. Eight of the PLA's top ten partners are in Asia, and 40.5 percent of the PLA's military diplomatic interactions from 2003 to 2018 were conducted with countries in Asia, nearly twice as many as Europe, the next most common region.[60] Many of China's top partners are also US treaty allies (Thailand, Australia, and New Zealand) or security partners (Singapore, Vietnam, India, and Indonesia).

Figure 9.6 shows travel by PLA leaders to different parts of the world from 2003 to 2018. The data show the high priority placed on Asia, the United States, and Russia. Europe is also a regular destination for PLA leaders, with South America, Africa, and the Middle East less frequent destinations. The country and regional priorities in China's military diplomatic interactions appear to correspond closely with Chinese foreign policy priorities.

The PLA is also using military diplomacy to shape China's security environment. For instance, most non-ETF port calls are friendly port visits in Asia, highlighting Chinese attempts to assuage neighbors concerned about its new naval might. The *Peace Ark* routinely stops at multiple Asian ports in order to cultivate China's image as a benign power that can make positive contributions to regional security. Since 2010, shaping efforts have increasingly displayed

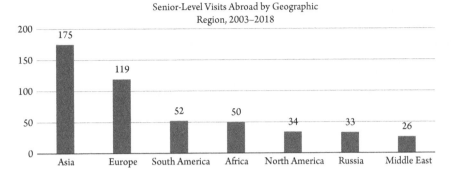

*Figure 9.6* Senior Level Visits Abroad by Geographic Region, 2003–2018

Chinese military capabilities rather than downplaying them. Military exercises have become more combat-oriented and sometimes appear designed to deter or discourage potential opponents. For example, China partnered with Russia to carry out a missile defense exercise in May 2016, shortly after a row over US deployment of the THAAD missile defense system in South Korea.[61]

Increased volume of PLA military diplomatic activities does not necessarily translate into influence. The PLA's foreign military relations are subject to a number of constraints. PLA military diplomacy is constrained by what activities foreign counterparts are willing and able to do with the PLA. China's increasingly assertive behavior on the international stage could reduce the willingness of some militaries to interact with the PLA. Resource limitations, including the small staff of the CMC Office of International Military Cooperation and the demands placed on senior PLA officers by ongoing military reforms, are likely to reduce the number of PLA military engagements for the next several years.

Other constraints stem from the nature of the Chinese system and the desire of the CCP to exert tight control over the military. Chinese culture emphasizes form over substance, and China's strategic culture makes it averse to binding security agreements. PLA officers are subject to top-down directives, tight control of political messaging, and the need to protect information about PLA capabilities, which inhibits candid conversations with foreign counterparts.[62] Most PLA interlocutors are not empowered to negotiate or share their real views, which makes it difficult to build strong personal or institutional ties with foreign counterparts.[63] As a result, much of China's military diplomatic activity consists of formal exchanges of scripted talking points during senior-level meetings, occasional naval port calls, and simple scripted military exercises focused on nontraditional security issues. These activities support existing relationships but are unlikely to build much strategic trust or support deeper military cooperation.

# Conclusion

This chapter has documented a dramatic expansion in the volume and geographic scope of China's military-security interactions with other countries. The PLA has moved from being an insular military confined within China's land borders to a military with a regular presence throughout the Asia-Pacific region and a periodic presence in most regions of the world. While Chinese leaders like to argue that China's growing military power and expanding power projection capabilities make a positive contribution to global and regional security, many of China's neighbors view the PLA as a potential threat, especially countries that have land or maritime territorial disputes with China or who worry that China seeks regional hegemony.

China has actively embraced military diplomacy and nontraditional security cooperation as a means of supporting Chinese foreign policy and assuaging concerns about its growing military power. However, the growing volume of senior-level meetings, friendly port calls, and bilateral and multilateral exercises has not succeeded in easing regional concerns. Nevertheless, most countries have embraced military-to-military engagement with the PLA as part of their broader efforts to manage their relationship with China and to moderate Chinese external behavior.

The biggest future unknown is the extent to which China's growing overseas interests will stimulate a larger PLA military presence outside of Asia, and the development and deployment of a blue water navy, additional overseas bases, and expeditionary PLA capabilities. While some in the PLA hope to leverage the need to protect overseas interests to justify increased military spending and power projection capabilities, the prevailing opinion among Chinese analysts is that overreliance on military capabilities to protect Chinese interests would be costly and potentially counterproductive.

Instead, China is likely to place greater emphasis on expanding its training, intelligence sharing, and security assistance programs to help host countries strengthen their capacity to maintain stability and protect Chinese interests. In cases where there are direct threats to China's internal security and host country internal security capabilities provide inadequate, China may wind up deploying military or paramilitary troops to protect its interests.[64] Some host countries may view such a Chinese presence as enhancing their security; others may resent it as a violation of their sovereignty. The expansion of Chinese overseas interests, and the close connection of these interests with China's domestic stability, will force Chinese civilian leaders to make difficult choices. This is part of the cost of China's new role as a great power with global interests.

# Notes

\* The views expressed are those of the author and do not necessarily reflect those of the National Defense University, the Department of Defense, or the US government.

1. See Ashley J. Tellis et al., *China's Expanding Strategic Ambitions* (Seattle: National Bureau of Asian Research, 2019); and David Shambaugh, *China Goes Global: The Partial Power* (New York: Oxford University Press, 2013).

2. See Elizabeth C. Economy and Michael Levy, *By All Means Necessary: How China's Resource Quest Is Changing the World* (New York: Oxford University Press, 2014).

3. Daniel M. Hartnett, *The PLA's Domestic and Foreign Activities and Orientation* (Washington, DC: US-China Economic and Security Review Commission, March 4, 2009).

4. Jonas Parello-Plesner and Mathieu Duchâtel, *China's Strong Arm: Protecting Citizens and Assets Abroad* (New York: Routledge, 2015), 37–41.

5. For up-to-date overviews of BRI scope and projects, see Mercator Institute for China Studies, "Mapping the Belt and RoadI: This Is Where We Stand," July 6, 2018, https://www.merics. org/en/bri-tracker/mapping-the-belt-and-road-initiative; the associated MERICS BRI database; and the Center for Strategic and International Studies "Reconnecting Asia" database and interactive map, https://reconnectingasia.csis.org/map/.

6. Foreign Ministry figures cited in Timothy R. Heath, *China's Pursuit of Overseas Security* (Arlington, VA: RAND, 2018), ix.

7. Given the problems in tracking the ultimate destinations of Chinese overseas investment in official Chinese data, the American Enterprise Institute–Heritage Foundation "China Global Investment Tracker" is the best source for data on Chinese investment and construction projects in particular countries and regions. See http://www.aei.org/china-global-investment-tracker/.

8. See Parello-Plesner and Mathieu Duchâtel, *China's Strong Arm*, 24–31.

9. Ibid., 28–29.

10. See Mathieu Duchâtel, Oliver Bräuner, and Zhou Hang, "Protecting China's Overseas Interests: The Slow Shift from Non-Interference," SIPRI Policy Paper 41 (June 2014); Wuthnow, *Chinese Perspectives on the Belt and Road Initiative*; and Kristen Gunness and Oriana Skylar Mastro, "A Global People's Liberation Army: Possibilities, Challenges, and Opportunities," *Asia Policy* 22 (July 2016): 131–155.

11. Author's interviews, Beijing, December 2017.

12. See Heath, *China's Pursuit of Overseas Security*.

13. See M. Taylor Fravel and Alexander Liebman, "Beyond the Moat: The PLAN's Evolving Interests and Potential Influence," in *The Chinese Navy: Expanding Capabilities, Evolving Roles*, edited by Phillip C. Saunders et al., 41–80 (Washington, DC: National Defense University Press, 2011).

14. State Council Information Office, *China's Military Strategy* (May 2015).

15. See Joel Wuthnow and Phillip C. Saunders, *Chinese Military Reforms in the Age of Xi Jinping: Drivers, Challenges, and Implications*, China Strategic Perspectives 10 (Washington, DC: National Defense University Press, March 2017); and Defense Intelligence Agency, *China Military Power: Modernizing a Force to Fight and Win* (Washington, DC: Defense Intelligence Agency, 2019).

16. See M. Taylor Fravel and Evan S. Medeiros, "China's Search for Assured Retaliation: Explaining the Evolution of China's Nuclear Strategy," *International Security* 35, no. 2 (Fall 2010): 48–87.

17. See *China's Military Strategy*; and Junshi Kexueyuan Junshi Zhanlüe Yanjiu Bu [Academy of Military Science Strategic Research Department], *Zhanlüexue 2013 Nianban* [The Science of Military Strategy, 2013 Edition] (Beijing: Academy of Military Science Press, 2013).

18. For earlier assessments see Ellis Joffe, *The Chinese Army after Mao* (Cambridge, MA: Harvard University Press, 1987); David Shambaugh, *Modernizing China's Military: Progress, Problems, and Prospects* (Berkeley: University of California Press, 2002); David Shambaugh, ed., *China's Military in Transition* (Oxford: Clarendon Press, 1997); James R. Lilley and David Shambaugh, eds., *China's Military Faces the Future* (Armonk, NY: M. E. Sharpe, 1999); and Srikanth Kondapalli, *China's Military: The PLA in Transition* (New Delhi: Knowledge World

Press, 1999). For more recent surveys see Dennis J. Blasko, *The Chinese Army Today: Tradition and Transformation for the 21st Century*, 2nd ed. (London: Routledge, 2015); Roger Cliff, *China's Military Power: Assessing Current and Future Capabilities* (Cambridge: Cambridge University Press, 2015); and You Ji, *China's Military Transformation* (Cambridge: Polity Press, 2016).

19. Dean Cheng, "Chinese Lessons from the Gulf Wars," in *Chinese Lessons from Other Peoples' Wars*, edited by Andrew Scobell, David Lai, and Roy Kamphausen, 153–200 (Carlisle, PA: Strategic Studies Institute, 2011).

20. David M. Finkelstein, *China Reconsiders Its National Security: "The Great Peace and Development Debate of 1999"* (Alexandria, VA: CNA Corporation, 2000).

21. *Military and Security Developments Involving the People's Republic of China 2018* (Washington, DC: Office of the Secretary of Defense, 2018), 59–80.

22. M. Taylor Fravel, "Shifts in Warfare and Party Unity," *International Security* 42, no. 3 (Winter 2017/2018): 73–74.

23. Fravel, "Shifts in Warfare and Party Unity," 79–80.

24. James Mulvenon and David Finkelstein, eds., *China's Revolution in Doctrinal Affairs: Emerging Trends in the Operational Art of the Chinese People's Liberation Army* (Alexandria, VA: CNA Corporation, 2005).

25. The PLA calls this "systems attack" or "systems confrontation." See Jeff Engstrom, *Systems Confrontation and System Destruction Warfare: How the Chinese People's Liberation Army Seeks to Wage Modern Warfare* (Arlington, VA: RAND, 2018).

26. Fravel, "Shifts in Warfare and Party Unity," 79–80.

27. See Phillip C. Saunders, Arthur S. Ding, Andrew Scobell, Andrew N. D. Yang, and Joel Wuthnow, eds., *Chairman Xi Remakes the PLA: Inside Chinese Military Reforms* (Washington, DC: National Defense University Press, 2019).

28. See Phillip C. Saunders, "China's Role in Asia: Attractive or Assertive?" in *International Relations of Asia*, edited by David Shambaugh and Michael Yahuda, 2nd ed., 147–172 (Lanham, MD: Roman and Littlefield, 2014).

29. See Jeffrey A. Bader, *Obama and China's Rise: An Insider's Account of America's Asia Strategy* (Washington, DC: Brookings Institution Press, 2012), chapter seven; and the discussion in Michael D. Swaine, "Perceptions of an Assertive China," *China Leadership Monitor* 32 (2010).

30. Michael D. Swaine and M. Taylor Fravel, "China's Assertive Behavior—Part Two: The Maritime Periphery," *China Leadership Monitor* 35 (2011).

31. M. Taylor Fravel, *Strong Borders, Secure Nation: Cooperation and Conflict in China's Territorial Disputes* (Princeton: Princeton University Press, 2008).

32. Joel Wuthnow, Satu Limaye, and Nilanthi Samaranayake, "Doklam, One Year Later: China's Long Game in the Himalayas," *War on the Rocks*, June 7, 2018.

33. David Brunnstrom and Michael Martina, "Xi Denies China Turning Artificial Islands into Military Bases," Reuters, September 25, 2015. For up-to-date analysis of the South China Sea disputes, see the CSIS Asian Maritime Transparency Initiative website at https://amti.csis.org/.

34. See Stockholm International Peace Research Institute (SIPRI) arms transfer and defense expenditure databases: https://www.sipri.org/research/armament-and-disarmament/arms-transfers-and-military-spending.

35. State Council Information Office, *China's Policies on Asia-Pacific Security Cooperation* (January 2017).

36. See Kenneth Allen, Phillip C. Saunders, and John Chen, *Chinese Military Diplomacy, 2003–2016: Trends and Implications*, China Strategic Perspectives 11 (Washington, DC: National Defense University Press, July 2017), 7–11.

37. Yang Lina and Chang Xuemei, eds., "Xi Jinping: Jinyibu kaichuang junshi waijiao xin jumian" [Xi Jinping: Start a New Phase of Military Diplomacy], Xinhua, January 29, 2015.

38. China's Asia-Pacific white paper provides numerous examples of the role of military diplomacy in advancing China's regional policy and relations with the United States and Russia. See State Council Information Office, *China's Policies on Asia-Pacific Security Cooperation*, January 11, 2017.

39. See Larry M. Wortzel, *The Dragon Extends Its Reach: China's Military Power Goes Global* (Potomac, MD: Potomac Books, 2013).

40. Peter Cai, *Understanding China's Belt and Road Initiative* (Sydney: Lowy Institute, 2017); and Joel Wuthnow, *Chinese Perspectives on the Belt and Road Initiative: Strategic Rationales, Risks, and Implications*, China Strategic Perspectives 12 (Washington, DC: National Defense University Press, October 2017).

41. These are post-reform positions; for the pre-reform equivalents see Allen, Saunders, and Chen, *Chinese Military Diplomacy*, 16–17.

42. Detailed planning for the reforms began in 2013, and execution of the reforms started in late 2015 and will continue through 2020.

43. 2007 was a partial exception, but it was an unusual Party Congress year where the CCP general-secretary, premier, and the two CMC vice chairmen all kept their positions and were more able to travel.

44. The term *joint* is used in PRC English-language media. Chinese media use 联合, which can mean *combined, combined arms*, or *joint* in US military parlance.

45. Allen, Saunders, and Chen, *Chinese Military Diplomacy*, 27–29.

46. Andrew S. Erickson and Austin M. Strange, *No Substitute for Experience: Chinese Antipiracy Operations in the Gulf of Aden* (Newport, RI: US Naval War College, 2013).

47. Yan Meng and Yao Chun, "CTF 151 Commander Visits 14th Chinese Naval Escort Taskforce," *People's Daily*, May 8, 2013.

48. Atmakuri Lakshmi Archana and Mingjiang Li, "Geopolitical Objectives Fuel China's *Peace Ark*," *East Asia Forum*, October 13, 2018; "China's Naval Hospital Ship Concludes 205-Day Overseas Mission," Xinhua, January 19, 2019.

49. Eric Hagt, "The Rise of PLA Diplomacy," in *PLA Influence on China's National Security Policymaking*, edited by Phillip C. Saunders and Andrew Scobell, 218–248 (Stanford, CA: Stanford University Press, 2015).

50. See Allen, Saunders, and Chen, *Chinese Military Diplomacy*, 38–40.

51. This paragraph is drawn, with permission, from David Shambaugh, *China Goes Global*, 300.

52. See Chen Xulong, "Understanding China's Strategic Dialogues," *China International Studies* (November/December 2010): 16–36.

53. Pieter D. Wezeman, Aude Fleurant, Alexandra Kuimova, Nan Tian, and Siemon T. Wezeman, *Trends in International Arms Transfers, 2017* (Stockholm: Stockholm International Peace Research Institute, March 2018).

54. US Department of Defense, *Assessment on US Defense Implications of China's Expanding Global Access* (Washington, DC: Department of Defense, December 2018), 5.

55. Zhang Tao, "China Sends First Infantry Battalion for UN Peacekeeping," Xinhua, December 22, 2014.

56. See United Nations Peacekeeping, "Troop and Police Contributors," https://peacekeeping. un.org/en/troop-and-police-contributors.

57. Zhang Tao, "China Sends First Infantry Battalion for UN Peacekeeping"; Yao Jianing, "China to Send First Infantry Battalion for UN Peacekeeping," *China Daily*, December 23, 2014.

58. Christoph Zürcher, *30 Years of Chinese Peacekeeping* (Ottawa: University of Ottawa Centre for International Policy Studies, January 2019).

59. See Courtney J. Fung, *China's Troop Contributions to UN Peacekeeping*, United States Institute of Peace Peacebrief 212, July 26, 2016.

60. The Europe data do not include Russia, which was counted separately to show its relative importance.

61. Franz Stefan-Gady, "China and Russia to Hold First Computer-Enabled Missile Defense Exercise in May," *The Diplomat*, May 2, 2016.

62. Wan Fayang, *Zhongguo junshi waijiao lilun yu shijian* [Chinese Military Diplomacy—Theory and Practice] (Beijing: Current Affairs Press, 2015).

63. James P. Nolan, "Why Can't We Be Friends? Assessing the Operational Value of Engaging PLA Leadership," *Asia Policy* 20 (July 2015): 65.

64. This appears to be the explanation for a secret Chinese PAP base inside Tajikistan. See Gerry Shih, "In Central Asia's Forbidding Highlands, A Quiet Newcomer: Chinese Troops," *Washington Post*, February 18, 2019.

# CHINA'S BILATERAL AND REGIONAL RELATIONSHIPS

# 10

# China's Relations with the
# United States

ROBERT SUTTER

This chapter reviews Chinese Communist Party (CCP) and People's Republic of China (PRC) interactions with the United States since the 1940s, and it reveals a general pattern of the United States at the very top of China's foreign priorities. Among those few instances where China seemed to give less attention to the United States was the post-2010 period, which saw an ever more powerful China advancing at US expense (with seeming disregard of US reaction). That trend has changed since 2017, as the Trump administration's whole-of-government hardening against China has compelled Beijing to curb some of its assertiveness and adopt a defensive stance. Though a strongman ruler in many respects, Xi Jinping has been personally solicitous of his American counterpart, relying on cordial diplomacy to move America away from confrontation and toward negotiations sought by China.

In contrast, for many decades America's attention to China, though often strong, usually was subservient to overriding American concern with the Soviet Union. Thus, President Nixon and later presidents gave high priority to use improved relations with China to US advantage in the broader global contest with the USSR. Once the Soviet Union collapsed, this rationale ended and relations drifted; Washington and Beijing have yet to come up with an enduring framework for cooperation. However, China's rapid advance in economic, military, and diplomatic power has progressively alarmed the US government, which now sees China as its main international danger.

Looking forward into the future, deteriorating US-China relations have enormous consequences for both countries, the Asia-Pacific region, and the world. The United States remains the world's leading power, with only China coming close to matching America's influence. China's economy is forecast to surpass the size of America's within the next several years. It already is the world's

Robert Sutter, *China's Relations with the United States* In: *China and the World*. Edited by: David Shambaugh, Oxford University Press (2020). © Oxford University Press
DOI: 10.1093/oso/9780190062316.003.0010

largest trader, as a leading trader with all its neighbors, largest manufacturer, largest holder of foreign exchange reserves, and an increasingly important source of investment, loans, and assistance. China accounts for 25 percent of global industrial output. Its production of goods is half again greater than that of the United States. China in 2017 contributed one third of the growth in the global economy.[1]

With this economic strength, China's ambitious and expanding Belt and Road Initiative (BRI) undermines US economic influence in Asia and the world, increasingly placing Beijing at the center of international economic trade, finance, and investment networks. Meanwhile, China's neighbors and businesses throughout the world, including the United States, rely heavily for their prosperity on the China market and even more on the complicated production chains that center on China, which exports a large share of such production to the United States as well as other Western countries. The value of US-China trade was $635.4 billion in 2017, with a US deficit of $335.4 billion—far surpassing any other pair of countries.[2]

China's military budget and capacity have grown rapidly, with a focus on the rim of China where Beijing faces American forces on the north, east, and south. Notably, China's naval shipbuilding has already produced a surface force larger in numbers than the US Navy—which, unlike China, has global responsibilities.[3] China's ability to concentrate its naval deployments in the western Pacific provides it a substantial potential strategic advantage.

To explore these and other issues, this chapter first reviews the history of Chinese Communist Party (CCP) and People's Republic of China (PRC) relations with the United States to discern interests and issues of relevance today. It then examines developments over the past decade to provide a lead-in for discussion of contemporary developments. It concludes by assessing key variables determining the relationship's dynamic going forward.

# Historical Patterns of Interaction
## Initial Contacts and Cold War "Containment"
## (1941–1968)

The crucible of Chinese Communist-American relations began with the American entry into the war with Japan in 1941. The following thirty years saw failed efforts at engagement followed by armed conflict and protracted confrontation over fundamental differences, with many still relevant today.

World War II solidified American policy priorities in China and the Asia-Pacific region. First, the United States worked to maintain a balance of power in Asia favorable to American interests and opposed to domination of the region by hostile powers. Second, US economic interests required unimpeded access to the region's economies. Third, Americans values mandated fostering human rights, democracy, and America's view of good governance.[4]

Mao Zedong and the Chinese Communist Party (CCP) had strong and well-developed ideological and policy priorities of their own, many opposed to the above US interests. However, in the 1940s, impressive US power in China led to CCP pragmatism in seeking to avoid confrontation with American power. But CCP efforts to improve relations failed, as the United States backed the CCP's opponent Chiang Kai-shek. Mediation efforts in 1944 and 1945 by US envoy Patrick Hurley strengthened this bias in favor of Chiang, and it was not reversed in US envoy George Marshall's further mediation efforts during the years 1945–1947. Enormous loss of American influence came as the Communists defeated Chiang's armies on mainland China in 1949 and aligned with the Soviet Union in early 1950s,[5] thus catalyzing a cathartic "who lost China?" debate and McCarthyite witch hunt.

Strongly opposed to continued American influence around China's rim, Mao joined Soviet strongman Joseph Stalin in supporting Kim Il-sung's attack on South Korea in June 1950. Their calculation that the United States would not intervene proved wrong. Entering the war with full force, the United States also undertook the defense of Chiang Kai-shek's remnant regime on Taiwan. However, the US-led rollback of the North Korean invaders prompted US miscalculation in militarily invading North Korea, seeking reunification of the peninsula under American auspices. In response, China launched massive infantry attacks driving back MacArthur's and allied forces, fighting them to a stalemate over the next two and a half years.[6]

Mao used the profound crisis of the Korean War to remove American influence in China as mass campaigns consolidated CCP rule. He solidified alignment with Stalin and in return received much-needed assistance. Once the armistice ended the Korean fighting, China began to provide substantial military supplies and guidance to Communist Viet Minh fighting US-backed French forces in Indochina.

For its part, the United States established a full economic and diplomatic embargo on China. Its containment policy involved bases around China with hundreds of thousands of US troops and large-scale US military support and economic assistance to US alliance partners in Japan, South Korea, the Philippines, Taiwan (Republic of China), and Thailand. Australia and New Zealand also aligned with the United States against China. Domestically, US officials favoring pragmatism in dealings with Beijing often were removed or silenced.

During the 1950s and 1960s, American and Chinese leaders paid close attention to one another for negative reasons. US military force around China's rim was perceived as a direct threat that Beijing was determined to oppose. China launched substantial armed attacks in 1954–1955 and 1958 against US-backed Nationalist forces occupying islands close to the Chinese mainland. To end both crises, the United States strongly supported Taiwan and again threatened China with nuclear attack. In response, with Soviet assistance, Beijing began its own program to develop nuclear weapons to counter such "nuclear blackmail."

A thaw in US-China tensions during the period 1955–1957 coincided with China and the Soviet Union both pursuing "peaceful coexistence" with non-communist states. China adopted a widely welcomed moderate foreign policy stance at the summit of Asian and African leaders at Bandung, Indonesia, in April 1955. It followed with an agreement starting US-China ambassadorial talks in Geneva in August 1955. Beijing sought to show progress, but the United States was wary of undermining Taiwan and containment of China. The talks resulted in acrimony and were suspended in 1957, coincident with more radical Chinese domestic and foreign policies during the Great Leap Forward mass campaign (1958–1961) and the Taiwan Straits crisis of 1958.

At the turn of the decade, Maoist China broke with the Soviet Union and launched high-profile international efforts to oppose both the United States and the Soviet Union (the "dual adversary" strategy). China continued strong support for Vietnamese Communists fighting US-backed South Vietnam. As a counter to US military presence in Vietnam and Southeast Asia, China trained and provided support for tens of thousands of Communist-led insurgents in Burma, Cambodia, Thailand, Malaysia, Indonesia, and the Philippines. China had become a bellicose and provocative challenge to American interests in Asia.

President John Kennedy (1961–1963) tried to find common ground with the USSR to thwart China's nuclear program, a driver for the Limited Test Ban Treaty with the Soviet Union in 1963 that China strongly condemned. Perhaps no US president was more preoccupied with the immediate military threat posed by China than Lyndon Johnson (1963–1969). Vietnam dominated US foreign policy. During that long war, American forces also faced hundreds of thousands of Chinese anti-aircraft, railway, construction, and support troops sent to Vietnam and nearby Laos. Johnson was particularly anxious to avoid prompting full-scale Chinese military intervention. US diplomats signaled these US intentions in the otherwise moribund US-China ambassadorial talks in Warsaw.

## Rapprochement (1969–1989)

The contemporary, closely intertwined Sino-American relationship began 1968 in very adverse circumstances. With the start of the Cultural Revolution (1966–1976), Maoist China became severely isolated and ideologically rigid, virulently opposing both the United States and the Soviet Union. The US government was committed to its massive war effort in Vietnam and overall strong containment of China. US political isolation and economic embargo against Beijing continued. Nevertheless, the two sides would overcome deep animosity and profound differences to move toward rapprochement. The main reason was their respective serious weakness in the face of advancing Soviet power challenging US and Chinese core interests.[7]

For China, escalating tensions with Moscow involved the threat of direct military attack that China was unprepared to counter. Border clashes were followed by explicit Soviet threats in 1969 to use their markedly superior military forces along the border to invade China and destroy its nuclear weapons production facilities. US intelligence believed that attacking Soviet forces could readily conquer Beijing.

Advancing Soviet military power also reached parity with and, in some critical areas, surpassed that of the United States. The concurrent Vietnam quagmire massively drained American resources, with Moscow increasing support for Hanoi, seeking to further weaken America. The sense of crisis showed in searing American experiences during 1968. In January, the Tet Offensive in South Vietnam graphically showed the failure of the war effort. Antiwar pressure compelled Lyndon Johnson to end his re-election bid in February. Martin Luther King's assassination in April saw two weeks of burning and rioting in Washington. In June, antiwar candidate Robert Kennedy won enough delegates to gain the Democratic nomination, only to be assassinated. The Democratic convention saw unprecedented antiwar demonstrations that were violently suppressed by club-wielding police, shocking Americans watching on television.

Republicans nominated Richard Nixon, who claimed to have a plan to deal with the Vietnam morass. He did not speak much about China, although in a 1967 article in the magazine *Foreign Affairs*, Nixon obliquely signaled his desire to bring China into the "family of nations."[8] Nixon moved quickly to begin what would turn out to be the gradual withdrawal of over 600,000 US troops from around China's periphery in Asia. This change effectively ended US military containment of China. Nixon also pursued vigorous efforts to develop secret communications channels with China.

China's response to the new US president remained erratic until 1971. Intense Soviet pressure threatening military attack in 1969 inclined Chinese decision-making to seek cooperation with Washington against Moscow. However, Defense Minister Lin Biao, supporting top generals, and influential radical civilian leaders later designated as the "Gang of Four" seemed opposed. The struggle for power among contending Chinese leaders in 1971 resulted in the death of Lin Biao and the arrest of China's top military leaders. The Gang of Four were not removed until after Mao's death in 1976. Mao's endorsement of the US opening came in meeting National Security Adviser Henry Kissinger during his secret visit to Beijing in July 1971, paving the way for Nixon's successful visit in 1972.

Meanwhile, President Nixon feared US leadership and popular opposition to an opening to China that required meeting China's demand to sacrifice US official relations with Taiwan. He managed this problem through secrecy, keeping Congress and the public in the dark.

Over the next decade, progress in establishing diplomatic and economic relations was impressive. However, it stalled at times, notably because of recurring differences over Taiwan and approaches to the Soviet Union. China pushed President Jimmy Carter (1977–1981) to take a harder line against Soviet expansion. It objected strongly to the congressionally written Taiwan Relations Act in April 1979 that was very much at odds with US administration commitments in breaking relations with Taiwan. Beijing approved strong American reaction to the Soviet military invasion of Afghanistan in December 1979 and cooperated with the United States in clandestinely supporting Afghan resistance forces.

President Ronald Reagan (1981–1989) signaled greater support for Taiwan, including arms sales. Beijing doubled down on diplomatic pressure and reached a vague compromise in the communiqué of August 1982. The Reagan administration then re-evaluated its China policy, seeing Beijing as less important than in the past against the Soviet Union, especially when Mikhail Gorbachev (1985–1991) sought to reach accords with Washington. Meanwhile, US-China economic relations began to grow now that China was increasingly open to foreign interchange under Deng Xiaoping's reform agenda. To a degree, commercial ties replaced the declining of the Soviet threat as a driver of US-China cooperation.

## Post–Cold War:
## Recurring Tension, Weak Strategic Frameworks

China's violent crackdown in June 1989 against demonstrators at Tiananmen Square in Beijing and other cities, together with the concurrent ending of the Cold War and demise of the USSR, shattered US-China cooperation. Ideological differences re-emerged strongly. For several years, China remained on the defensive. President George H. W. Bush (1989–1993) endeavored to preserve communications with top Chinese leaders and US "Most Favored Nation" trade status for China, but his administration also dismantled military ties and criticized China's authoritarian regime. Meanwhile, Taiwan's rapid democratization led to more US initiatives toward Taipei. In 1992 President Bush undermined the August 1982 communiqué's vague limit on US arms sales to Taiwan with the sale to Taiwan of 150 advanced US F-16 fighter aircraft worth over $5 billion, and he sent the first US Cabinet member to visit the island since the United States broke official ties in 1979.[9]

Beijing now increasingly perceived the United States as a direct threat to continued Communist Party rule. It shored up patriotic indoctrination of public and elite opinion that continues up to the present day. This effort reinforces deep suspicion of, and strong opposition to, American policies and practices. For many years, Chinese official commentary and media widely criticized US policies in Asia and the world as "hegemonism" designed to contain and counter China's rise and preserve US leadership (seen at odds with China's preferences for a multipolar world order), but now Beijing began to see the United States as an existential threat to its political longevity.

Under these circumstances, attempts to establish a lasting framework for US-China cooperation failed during the Clinton, George W. Bush, and Obama administrations. Clinton's disregard for Chinese concerns in granting the Taiwan president a visa to visit the United States in 1995 led to a protracted Chinese show of force with live fire military exercises including ballistic missiles targeting Taiwan over the course of nine months. Clinton eventually decided to send two US aircraft carrier battle groups to the waters east of Taiwan in order to deter Chinese aggression. At the same time, he held summit meetings with Chinese leaders under the rubric of an emerging US-China "strategic partnership." US-China engagement at this time included deliberations on China's entry into the World Trade Organization in 2001 and passing of a US law granting permanent "normal" (previously known as Most Favored Nation) trade status to China. But the progress was offset by major crises, notably over the US accidental bombing of the Chinese embassy in Belgrade in 1999, and the following vandalism of US diplomatic properties in China by Chinese government-organized demonstrators.

The George W. Bush administration (2001–2009) thought Clinton was weak in dealing with China. The president scrapped the strategic partnership framework and in his first year stressed a tougher policy toward China and more explicit support for Taiwan. In April 2001 Bush publicly pledged that the United States would do "whatever it takes" to support Taiwan if it were attacked by China. But the terrorist attack on America in September 2001 was followed by a recalibration of administration priorities, with China emerging more as a partner than an opponent. Meanwhile, Taiwan president Chen Shui-bian (2000–2008) alienated the American government with pro-Taiwan independence maneuvers that risked China-US military conflict.

In 2005 the Bush government came up with a proposed framework for relations in which China would be encouraged through engagement with the United States to develop as a "responsible stakeholder" with the United States and other powers in managing global issues. With Chinese commentary voicing wariness about alleged US efforts to get China to commit to onerous international responsibilities, Beijing demurred.

Coming into office in the midst of a massive economic crisis and recession in 2009, the Barack Obama government (2009–2017) sought to preserve the stability of the China-US relationship, evident in the later years of the Bush administration, through enhanced engagement and deepened cooperation. At the time, some prominent Americans called for the United States and China to act as a "G-2"—two world leading powers managing global affairs. Again, China was wary of unwanted costly international commitments and demurred.

## Barack Obama, Donald Trump, and Xi Jinping: Rivalry Supersedes Pragmatism

As seen in the moderation of George W. Bush administration's policy toward China, a general pattern emerged in first decade of the twenty-first century wherein both the United States, under Bush and Obama, and China, under CCP leader and president Hu Jintao (2002–2012), emphasized pragmatism and positive engagement for three main reasons. First, both governments benefited from positive engagement in supporting stability in the Asia-Pacific, peace on the Korean Peninsula and in the Taiwan Strait, and cooperation on global economics and governance, climate change, terrorism, and nuclear nonproliferation. Second, both governments saw that the two powers had become so interdependent that emphasizing negatives would hurt the other side, but also would hurt them. And third, both leaderships were preoccupied with a long list of urgent domestic and foreign priorities, and sought to avoid serious additional problems with one another.[10]

However, long-standing differences between the two countries were not significantly changed as a result of pragmatic engagement. They began to worsen as China took steps beginning in 2009 that tested the resolve of the new Obama administration. In reaction came only a measured US response in a broader policy of American engagement (so-called rebalance or pivot) with the Asia-Pacific. Again China reacted negatively. Chinese assertiveness and differences with Washington only grew with the rise to power of Xi Jinping (2012–).

Four categories of Chinese differences with the United States have deep roots, with many going back to ideological and strategic issues of the Maoist period. They are: (1) opposition to US support for Taiwan and involvement with other sensitive sovereignty issues, including Tibet and disputed islands and maritime rights along China's rim; (2) opposition to perceived US efforts to change China's political system; (3) opposition to the United States playing the dominant role along China's periphery in Asia; and (4) opposition to many aspects of US leadership in world affairs.

US differences with China (reviewed in the following section) involve clusters of often-contentious economic, security, political, sovereignty, foreign policy, and other issues. Most have become more important for the United States as China has grown recently to be seen as a "peer competitor" with the United States, with the possibility of overtaking and dominating America. As in the past, areas of friction developed in tandem with a wide range of cooperation between the two governments and societies developed notably during the period of pragmatic cooperation in the previous decade. However, the Trump administration, more than any other US government since normalization of relations over forty years ago, signaled a radical course change in US policy toward China, viewing Beijing more as a malign competitor than a promising partner.

## Xi Jinping Challenges America

President Xi repeatedly placed other foreign and domestic priorities above his avowed—but increasingly hollow—claims to seek a positive relationship with the United States. Xi's preferred framework for US-China relations, which called for a "new type of great power relationship" (新型大国关系) that would respect China's "core interests" (核心利益) was viewed warily by the United States, partly because Chinese core interests seemed to come at the expense of China's neighbors and other US interests. The framework marked the most recent in the list of proposals noted earlier that have failed to create a structure to bridge differences and create lasting cooperation in the post–Cold War period.

Xi Jinping began the process of changing China's policies with major negative implications for the United States as he prepared to take control of Communist Party and state power in 2012. The caution and low profile of the previous Hu Jintao leadership were viewed with disfavor. The string of Chinese actions and initiatives were truly impressive in seven different areas.

First, the government orchestrated the largest mass demonstration against a foreign target ever seen in Chinese history (against US ally Japan over disputed islands in September 2012). It followed with diplomatic, military, and economic pressure against Japan not seen since World War II. Second, China used coercive and intimidating means to extend control of disputed territory at neighbors' expense, notably in rapidly building island military outposts in the disputed South China Sea. Third, rapidly expanding advanced Chinese military capabilities were aimed at American forces in the Asian Pacific region. Fourth, Chinese cooperation with Russia grew steadily closer as each power endeavored to undermine US influence in their respective spheres of influence. Fifth, unfair

Chinese restrictions on access to China's market, demands that foreign enterprises share sensitive manufacturing and production data, industrial espionage and cyber theft for economic gain, gross infringements on international property rights, and reluctance to contribute regional and global common goods all advanced as China's economy grew. Sixth, China used its large foreign exchange reserves, massive excess construction capacity, and strong trading advantages to develop international banks and to support often grandiose Chinese plans for Asian and global infrastructure construction, investments, loans, and trade areas that excluded the United States and countered American initiatives and support for existing international economic institutions. Finally, Xi Jinping tightened political control domestically in ways grossly offensive to Americans seeking political liberalization and better human rights conditions in China.[11]

President Obama proved to be less than effective in dealing with the various challenges posed by Xi Jinping's actions. His administration gave top priority to supporting an overall positive US approach to engagement with China, and the president was reticent to confront China. Differences usually were dealt with in private consultations. Even if they seemed important, they were kept within carefully crafted channels and were not allowed to spill over and impact other elements in the relationship. Thus, the Obama government followed a deliberative and transparent approach to China policy that was predictable and eschewed "linkage," that is, the seeking of US leverage to get China to stop behavior offensive to the United States by linking the offensive Chinese behavior to another policy area where the United States would threaten actions adverse to important Chinese interests. It was easy for China to determine how the US president was likely to act in the face of Chinese challenges; unpredictable uses of power against China seemed unlikely, allowing China to continue its advances at American expense.

## US Whole-of-Government Opposition to China's Challenges

Chinese officials responsible for US-China relations were aware that President Donald Trump was the opposite of President Obama as far as the above noted features of deliberation, transparency, predictability, linkage, and use of power were concerned. Nonetheless, they were confident that whatever differences President Trump had with China could be dealt with readily through negotiations and making what the US president called "deals" that perhaps would involve some economic or other comparatively minor concessions from China.

In its first year, 2017, the Trump administration devoted top priority in Asia to pressing North Korea to halt its development of nuclear weapons. This effort involved unprecedented US pressure on China to get North Korea to denuclearize. Beijing accommodated the United States and applied much more pressure than in the past on North Korea. The year 2017 also saw President Trump make China a centerpiece of his personal efforts to build friendships with Asian leaders in summit meetings in Washington and the Trump Mar-a-Lago resort in Florida and during the president's lengthy trip to Asia in November.

In contrast, the Trump government's National Security Strategy of December 2017 and its National Defense Strategy of January 2018 employed harsh words about China as a predatory strategic rival.[12] The strategies represented the beginning of a strong and public US government pushback against Chinese challenges regarding a broad array of issues. In these documents, China was the top danger to US national security. Added to China's military power and assertive actions in the Asia-Pacific was the danger China posed to the United States if it carried out its plan to be the leading country in various high-technology industries seen as essential for sustaining US international leadership and national security.

In communications with Congress, administration officials repeatedly highlighted the latter danger, which represented a newly prominent and important issue in 2018 added to long-standing American grievances against China. US Trade Representative Robert Lighthizer issued a dire warning against the many covert and overt ways China unfairly took advantage of the United States. Using language that in the past had been reserved for describing the danger posed by thousands of Soviet nuclear weapons pointed at the United States, Lighthizer in March 2018 said Chinese practices represented "an existential threat" to the United States.[13]

Meanwhile, FBI director Christopher Wray highlighted for Congress another newly prominent issue: Chinese overt and covert influence operations, including espionage in the United States. He warned repeatedly that America needed a "whole of society" effort to counter Beijing's perceived nefarious actions.[14]

Congressional members of both parties saw the wisdom in the administration's warnings and began to take action, making 2018 the most assertive period of congressional work on China since the tumultuous decade after the Tiananmen crackdown. The most important foreign policy legislation of the year, the National Defense Authorization Act, passed the Congress and was signed into law in August. On China, it stressed "whole of government" American counter-efforts that hit China hard on so-called influence operations and the high-technology industrial threat to the United States, and also pushed back against China regarding the South China Sea and Taiwan. The law echoed those administration officials viewing China as the primary threat.

The tone of the legislation and discourse by officials in the administration and on Capitol Hill showed a new urgency. China was now viewed as a peer competitor undertaking predatory actions against US interests. Without US countermeasures, China was now seen as likely to dominate high-technology industries essential to US leadership in economy and overall national security.

Around this same time, punitive tariffs against China began to pile up. In June, President Trump announced 25 percent tariffs on $50 billion worth of Chinese goods. In July, the administration threatened to place 10 percent tariffs on another $200 billion of Chinese imports; in August that rate was determined to rise later to 25 percent. By September the 10 percent tariffs were imposed on the $200 billion of Chinese imports, and they were scheduled to rise to 25 percent at the end of the year. Also in September, tariffs on $267 billion worth of other China imports were being considered. China responded with tariffs on almost all of the much smaller amount of US exports to China.

Throughout the fall, administration officials continued to turn up the rhetorical heat on China. Trump, in the world spotlight at the UN General Assembly, condemned China for influence operations seeking to undermine the Republican Party in US midterm elections. Echoing the tough rhetoric on China coming from National Security Advisor John Bolton and Secretary of State Mike Pompeo, Vice President Mike Pence in October strongly laid out the administration's case against China's challenges countering the United States, promising protracted US counterefforts. That was followed by a series of actions undertaken notably by the US departments with responsibility for domestic and international security and espionage, diplomacy, and commerce, and was summed up again by Pence during his hardline remarks about China in international summits in Asia in November. A result was a negative atmosphere for the Trump-Xi summit of December, which called a temporary halt to escalating US punitive trade tariffs against China, pending agreement involving extensive US demands by March 2019.

While Trump remained friendly and respectful with President Xi, the administration made progress in getting allies and partners to work together to thwart Chinese influence operations and acquisition of foreign high technology, and to counter Chinese adverse trade, industrial espionage, and other economic practices. US military and economic challenges to China's advances in what the US government now called the Indo-Pacific region included the steady increase in US military capacity along with allied preparations and economic and investment plans in competition with China's wide-ranging Belt and Road Initiative (BRI). In unprecedented behavior since the normalization of US-China relations four decades ago, the US government has publicized repeated transits of US warships in the Taiwan Strait. Allies Australia, Japan, France, and Great Britain joined the United States in supporting the 2016 UNCLOS tribunal verdict against China's South China Sea claims and in carrying out naval activities in the region that China opposes.

## Current Issues and Arenas of Interaction

China and the United States differ on a wide variety of issues of importance and arenas of interaction in their relationship. China usually gives higher priority to sovereignty issues regarding Taiwan and other areas claimed by Beijing. And it is highly sensitive to matters involving regime policies controlling individual or political rights that are criticized by the American government. The United States sometimes takes a strong stance on human rights and political rights in China, but at other times (including in the Trump administration) it gives these issues lower priority. The American government has remained very sensitive to the threat China's growing advanced military capacity poses for US forces in the region and for regional allies and partners. As noted above, the United States has growing concerns about Chinese illegal and nefarious methods in achieving prominence in high-technology industries, and heightened concerns about Chinese "influence operations" and espionage in the United States and American allies and partner countries.

As noted above, such differences did not appear to be particularly problematic in the period of pragmatic cooperation emphasizing positive engagement in the decade prior to the ascendance of Xi Jinping. Part of the reason was the establishment and use of consultative mechanisms—often known as strategic dialogues—as means to allow for private discussion of US-China differences in ways that did not impact negatively the overall relationship. China favored these dialogues. For thirty years, the Chinese government has relied on such dialogues to deal with sensitive issues that if publicized could cause more friction than sought by Beijing, embarrassment over compromises or unpopular commitments China made, or disapproval by Chinese elite and public opinion. Though more open than China in publicly informing the Congress, media, and the public about private discussions with Chinese officials, American leaders also often favored keeping secret the findings of dialogue discussion with China, notably when the current policy was being criticized by the Congress, the media, and public opinion.[15]

Presumably reflecting China's preferences, President Trump agreed with President Xi at their first meeting at the Mar-a-Lago resort in April 2017 to establish four high-level mechanisms for senior leaders to discuss issues. They are known as the Diplomatic and Security Dialogue, the Comprehensive Economic Dialogue, the People-to-People Dialogue, and the Law Enforcement and Cyber Security Dialogue. Other important dialogues took place between the two militaries. While the various dialogues have met, they have not achieved much.

The United States, especially with the 2018 pushback against China's challenges, has changed how differences are addressed in US-China relations. For now, the American side is setting the agenda for issues to be discussed, notably by being much more public than past American administrations in registering US concerns over major differences with China through words and actions that often embarrass and upset Chinese government counterparts. China has remained on the defensive, seeking to protect its rights and interests—but avoiding initiatives that might worsen the situation. The US priority moved from pressing North Korea, the top priority of US-China relations in 2017, to punitive tariffs and other disputes in 2018.

## Korean Peninsula

President Trump, Secretary of State Pompeo, and other senior US leaders remain optimistic that the unprecedented pressure applied by the United States against North Korea's nuclear weapons and ballistic missile development in 2017 resulted in agreements reached in the June 2018 US summit with North Korea leader Kim Jong-un that will lead to the US goal of denuclearization of North Korea. Many others are not optimistic, predicting that Kim will delay for the foreseeable future making significant compromises on North Korean nuclear weapons and ballistic missiles until his regime security is fully guaranteed. Chinese pressure including cutting trade and investment links with North Korea was deemed important in getting Kim to stop testing and make agreements with President Trump. China has relaxed its pressure after the Trump-Kim summit, and is urging the United States to make concessions in order to prompt Kim to respond with steps along what appears to be a long process leading to denuclearization.[16]

South Korean president Moon Jae-in also favors US concessions to the North in line with South Korea's active positive engagement with North Korea, seeking to ease tensions and promote engagement between the two Koreas despite the lack of substantial progress on denuclearization. China has put aside at least for now the high-pressure tactics it used against South Korea in an unsuccessful effort to stop the deployment of the advanced US ballistic missile defense system known as Terminal High Altitude Area Defense (THAAD) in South Korea to protect against a North Korean attack. Whether China and South Korea will now seek common ground on dealing with North Korea in ways that undermine US efforts to denuclearize North Korea remains to be seen.

## Restrict China on Advanced High Technology; Employ Punitive Trade Tariffs

The National Defense Authorization Act of August 2018 has provisions that expand the size and power of the Committee on Foreign Investment (CFIUS) and other legal measures to protect high technology from acquisition by China in its headlong and often illegal and nefarious ways to achieve dominance in high-technology industries essential to US international leadership. US administration and congressional leaders have urged much greater vigilance against Chinese theft and espionage in the high-technology areas. The US government has made strong public efforts with allies and partners to condemn Chinese cyber theft and espionage to steal high technology.[17]

Such practices added to long-standing US complaints about unfair Chinese trade and investment practices, leading to a massive American trade deficit with China and other impediments to US economic growth. Together, they provided the reasons for the US government's imposing punitive tariffs in July and August against $50 billion of Chinese goods entering the United States. China for its part denied wrongdoing and retaliated against US punitive tariffs. The Information Office of China's State Council issued a seventy-one-page white paper in September 2018 that dismissed the US Special Trade Representative (USTR)'s March 2018 report of investigation findings justifying the punitive tariffs. It denounced US actions as "trade bullyism." Nevertheless, because of the various negative Chinese trade and investment practices, under direction of the president, USTR imposed additional tariffs on approximately $200 billion of imports from China on September 24, 2018.[18]

## China's Influence Operations

Since 2018 the leaders of the FBI, other units of the Department of Justice, and other US government officials responsible for American domestic security have been joined by prominent congressional members from both parties urging greater investigation and remedial actions against what are depicted as Chinese "influence" operations that go beyond normal public diplomacy. The issue is addressed in the National Defense Authorization Act, among other legislation. According to an authoritative recent report,[19] Chinese operations are seen as covert and corrupting efforts designed to influence policy decisions of interest to China. As seen by the exposure of such Chinese behavior in places such as Taiwan, Australia, Singapore, New Zealand, and Europe, the Chinese Communist party-state leverages a broad range of Party, state, and non-state actors to advance its influence-seeking objectives, and in recent years it has significantly accelerated both its investment in and the intensity of these efforts. The main agencies responsible for foreign influence operations include the CCP's United Front Work Department, the Central Propaganda Department, the International Liaison Department, the State Council Information Office, the All-China Federation of Overseas Chinese, and the Chinese People's Association for Friendship with Foreign Countries. These organizations and others are bolstered by various state agencies such as the Ministry of Foreign Affairs and the Overseas Chinese Affairs Office of the State Council, which in March 2018 was merged into the United Front Work Department, reflecting that department's increasing power.[20]

Related to the above concern in protecting American high technology from illicit Chinese acquisition in the technology sector, China is engaged in a multifaceted effort to misappropriate technologies it deems critical to its economic and military success. Beyond economic espionage, theft, and the forced technology transfers that are required of many joint venture partnerships, China also captures much valuable new technology through its investments in US high-tech companies and through its exploitation of the openness of American university labs. This goes well beyond influence-seeking to a deeper and more disabling form of penetration. The economic and strategic losses for the United States are viewed as threatening not only to help China gain global dominance of a number of the leading technologies of the future, but also to undermine America's commercial and military advantages.

As it does in cases of exposure of operations in Taiwan, Australia, and elsewhere, China denies the charges of covert and malign influence operations in the United States. It sees the charges as prejudiced against China and designed to thwart China's legitimate advance to international leadership.

## The Taiwan Issue

President-elect Donald Trump sharply broke with past practice in December 2016 by accepting a congratulatory phone call from Taiwan president Tsai Ing-wen, publicly questioning US government support for the policy that "one China" includes Taiwan, and reacting promptly to Chinese criticisms with blunt public complaints about unfair Chinese economic policies and military expansion in the disputed South China Sea. President Trump subsequently was persuaded to publicly reaffirm support for the American One China policy during the new US president's first phone conversation with President Xi Jinping on February 9. Xi reportedly refused to speak with President Trump until he did so. The two leaders had an amicable meeting at the Mar-a-Lago resort in April, with Trump averring that he would not talk with the Taiwan president again without approval of the Chinese president.

Nevertheless, Chinese officials and commentators have reacted with growing concern to significant advances in US support for Taiwan over often strenuous Chinese objections, including the president's signing of legislation unanimously passed by Congress in March 2018 calling for higher-level US official visits to Taiwan, strong affirmations of US support for Taiwan in the

National Defense Authorization Act of August 2018, US publicity to repeated American warship patrols in the Taiwan Strait, higher-level treatment of the Taiwan president in transit stops in the United States, and substantial US arms sales to Taiwan.

Against this background, the Taiwan issue has again become a top priority for Beijing in its interactions with Americans. This follows a period of less prominence of the issue during the years of amicable cross-strait relations initiated by Taiwan president Ma Ying-jeou (2008–2016) that was strongly supported by the Bush and Obama governments with a strictly implemented One China policy avoiding actions that would upset the cross-strait thaw.

The future outlook is clouded. Potential Chinese retaliation heads the list of reasons for the United States to avoid seriously upsetting Beijing over Taiwan. Nonetheless, President Trump remains unpredictable, several high-level officials have a long record of strong support for Taiwan against China, and there is broader disregard for China's sensitivities seen in various US initiatives in the broad US pushback against China on other sensitive issues in the relationship.[21]

## Power Shift in Asia and the World

American strategic documents and statements of the current administration and Congress view—with increasing concern—broad-ranging Chinese efforts under President Xi Jinping to undermine American leadership in Asian and world affairs. China's rapid buildup of military capacity seems on track to seriously challenge and displace the US position as the leading power in the Asia-Pacific. Heading the list of potential flashpoints of armed conflict with US forces are Taiwan, the South China Sea, North Korea, and Japan. Even though the US Navy shipbuilding plan aims for 308 warships for America's global responsibilities, and the current administration has what many deem an unrealistic goal of 355 warships, China is the largest ship-producing country in the world and at current production rates will soon reach 400 Navy warships focused on dealing with American power in one area of the world, the Asia-Pacific. The naval buildup comes in tandem with a rapid increase of other Chinese security forces, including coast guard and maritime militia, very useful in controlling disputed territory in the South China Sea in ways that the United States seems ill-equipped to counter. [22]

China marries its security challenges with economic initiatives building on China's unmatched strengths in key areas. As noted, China is on track to become the world's largest economy. The most important trader for all its neighbors, China provides international loans and financing much larger than that of existing international finance organizations like the World Bank and the Asian Development Bank. And Chinese construction firms have an enormous capacity with decades of experience. Against this background, President Xi's grandiose Chinese economic plan, the Belt and Road Initiative (BRI), proposes massive Chinese investment, infrastructure development, and other economic interactions throughout China's periphery and spreading to all corners of the world with China as the center.[23]

US strategy sees these impressive Chinese efforts endangering America's long-standing objective to support and preserve a balance of power in Asia favorable to US interests. The Chinese efforts also are seen to threaten the long-standing American economic objective of unimpeded access to the markets of Asia. Meanwhile, Beijing cooperates more closely with Russia and thereby diverts American strategic attention as the two powers work together to weaken America as they advance themselves at the expense of US interests in their respective spheres of influence (China in Asia and Russia in Europe and the Middle East).[24]

The still-emerging American response involves increases in US military capacity in Asia; efforts to solidify relations with allies and partners in what the US government now calls the Indo-Pacific region (the focus is on growing ties with Japan, India, and Australia, the strategically most important powers willing to cooperate closely against Chinese expansionism); and new American economic initiatives designed notably to engage the powerful American private sector to compete with China's state-directed BRI program. Secretary Pompeo in August 2018 promised US security assistance to Asia worth $300 million and a "down payment" for economic efforts to mobilize the private sector in the region worth $133 million. Much more significant was the passage of the BUILD Act in October 2018 committing $60 billion in US investment financing for projects abroad, widely seen as in direct competition with China's BRI. Meanwhile, Japan, Australia, and India have joined with the American efforts or have parallel measures of their own that work against China's BRI ambitions.[25]

## Counter-Narcotics Cooperation

Given the priority of the current US government to check serious Chinese challenges to American interests, US government support for various elements of positive cooperation in past administrations' interaction with China has waned. Some active dialogues continue, notably between the US and Chinese military leaders, but the previous administrations' high-level government interchange over climate change and global governance seems past.

An exception is the increasingly active cooperation in counter-narcotics efforts linked to the so-called fentanyl epidemic in the United States. In 2017, about 29,000 Americans died from overdosing on synthetic drugs, mostly in the fentanyl class. The vast majority of fentanyl used in the United States is manufactured and shipped from China. President Trump in August 2018 tweeted that: "It is outrageous that Poisonous Synthetic Heroin Fentanyl comes pouring into the US Postal System from China. We can and must END THIS NOW." Presidents Trump and Xi agreed to take stronger cooperative actions on this matter during their December 1, 2018, meeting in Argentina that otherwise focused on trade and economic issues. In practice, US and Chinese counter-narcotics officials have cooperated closely for years and recently have scrambled to deal with this new epidemic. US ambassador to China Terry Branstad in June 2018 called US-China cooperation to stem opioid trafficking "one of the true bright spots in the US-China relationship."[26]

## Looking to the Future—Key Variables

The main driver of contemporary US-China relations—the wide-ranging hardening of US policy toward China—was not well foreseen in China or the United States. The hardening has momentum within the administration and the Congress. The opposition of leading US critics of this policy seems weak as those critics were supporters of previous US government emphasis on close engagement with China, which now appears negligent in dealing with the major negative challenges American faces from China today. Further examination of negatives regarding China's approach to the United States also could easily focus on previously neglected issues like the bad impact on US interests posed by ever increasing alignment between Xi Jinping's China and Vladimir Putin's Russia. This axis of authoritarian rulers presents serious and broad challenges for key interests of the United States that thus far have been rarely publicly addressed in the administration or the Congress.

However, the situation in US-China relations is fluid and remains subject to change not easy to foresee. Notably, the current US policy does not show overwhelming support from American public opinion, which largely continues to show wariness of the Chinese government and its practices at home and abroad, but registers nothing like the sense of danger depicted in US executive and legislative branch discourse over the past year.[27] And the costs of such an across-the-board policy have not yet been felt in the form of increased government outlays to pay for stronger international and domestic security, lost opportunities for American businesses, and increased prices for goods from China paid by American consumers. Such costs are sure to have an increasing impact on the Congress, perhaps reducing the current support for the current tough policy toward China. Meanwhile, President Trump remains unpredictable and very ambivalent about China. He rarely speaks in terms of the harsh indictment of negative intent of Chinese policies seen in the administration and congressional discourse. He values close relations with President Xi, even accommodating him to reduce US sanctions imposed on a leading Chinese firm caught undermining US sanctions against Iran by transferring US technology products to Iran.

The effectiveness of tough US policy toward China will depend heavily on whether American allies and partners are willing to support US security, economic, and diplomatic measures against Beijing or seek advantage in US-China friction to improve their economic and other relations with China. Several allies and partners have demonstrated support for the US-backed positions against China on the disputed South China Sea and against Chinese illegal and grossly unfair economic practices, notably tactics to acquire high technology from foreign firms. But these governments are wary of what some in the West perceive as US efforts to use punitive tariffs to "decouple" China from international production chains that would come at great expense to the firms of US allies and partners that rely on these production chains. Most of these states also have been on the receiving end of US punitive tariffs, generally to a much less degree than China, but the impact reduces their support for such unilateral and disruptive US measures.

At bottom, the main determinant of how large a cost America and its allies and partners will bear depends on the reaction of the strongman leader Xi Jinping. If and when China puts aside its current defensive posture in dealing with US pressures, and adopts a much tougher policy against the United States and its allies and partners (Chas Freeman's chapter in this volume outlines such potential steps that Beijing could take), it will have a big impact on the direction of China-American relations. For now, Beijing appears to see its interests best served by avoiding a major confrontation, allowing the costs of its trade retaliation to US punitive tariffs to impact American companies and consumers. Observers in the West foresee a likelihood that China will sustain the defensive posture seen recently and endeavor to wait until the 2020 election and a possible new American government more amenable to Beijing. At the same time, others warn of much stronger Chinese measures, with some recalling the Taiwan Straits crisis of 1995–1996, forcing America to choose between backing down and risking war with China. The costs and risks for China of such a dramatic move are great, but few are fully confident that Beijing will avoid them in a situation of protracted tension caused by the hard shift in American policy.

# Notes

1. Wayne Morrison, *China's Economic Rise*, Congressional Research Service Report RL33534, ) February 5, 2018 (Washington DC: Library of Congress.
2. Larry Diamond and Orville Schell, *China's Influence and American Interests* (Stanford, CA: Hoover Institution Press, 2019), 6.
3. Robert Ross, "The End of US Naval Dominance in Asia," *Lawfare*, November 18, 2018.
4. Michael Green, *By More Than Providence* (New York: Columbia University Press, 2017).
5. Tang Tsou, *America's Failure in China* (Chicago: University of Chicago Press, 1963).
6. After the Chinese intervention, MacArthur further advocated the use of nuclear weapons and a possible invasion of China; he was soon replaced by President Truman. For overviews of developments see Warren Cohen, *America's Response to China* (New York: Columbia University Press, 2010); and Michael Schaller, *The United States and China* (New York: Oxford University Press, 2015).
7. For overviews of developments see William Kirby, Robert Ross, and Gong Li, *Normalization of US-China Relations* (Cambridge, MA: Harvard University Press, 2005); and Robert Sutter, *US-China Relations* (Lanham, MD: Rowman & Littlefield, 2018), 61–90.
8. Richard Nixon, "After Viet Nam," *Foreign Affairs* 46, no. 1 (Oct. 1967): 111–125.
9. For overviews of developments see David M. Lampton, *Same Bed, Different Dreams* (Berkeley: University of California Press, 2001); and David Shambaugh, ed., *Tangled Titans* (Lanham, MD: Rowman & Littlefield, 2013).
10. For coverage of developments, see Shambaugh, *Tangled Titans*; Jeffrey Bader, *Obama and China's Rise* (Washington, DC: Brookings Institution, 2012); Michael Swaine, *America's Challenge* (Washington DC: Carnegie Endowment for International Peace, 2011); and Sutter, *US-China Relations*, 145–164.
11. Orville Schell and Susan Shirk, *US Policy Toward China* (New York: The Asia Society, 2017).
12. White House, *National Security Strategy of the United States*, December 2017, accessed January 4, 2018, https://www.whitehouse.gov/wp-content/uploads/2017/12/NSS-Final-12-18-2017-0905.pdf; and US Department of Defense, *Summary of the National Defense Strategy of the United States*, January 2018, accessed March 1, 2018, https://www.defense.gov/Portals/1/Documents/pubs/2018-National-Defense-Strategy-Summary.pdf.
13. David Lynch, "Trump's Raise the Stakes Strategy," *Washington Post*, July 21, 2018, A14.
14. For an overview of developments, see Robert Sutter, "Pushback: America's New China Strategy," *The Diplomat*, November 2, 2018.
15. Bonnie Glaser, "The Diplomatic Relationship," in *Tangled Titans*, edited by David Shambaugh, 172–176.
16. Scott Snyder, "China's Multiple Roles in the Korea Drama," *Comparative Connections* 20, no. 2 (2018): 83–92.
17. Addie Cliffe, Alan W. H. Gourley, Paul Rosenand, and Jana del-Cerro, "US National Security Review of Foreign Investment: Revisions to CFIUS Legislation Signed into Law," Crowell & Moring, August 21, 2018, accessed January 10, 2019, https://www.cmtradelaw.com/2018/08/u-s-national-security-review-of-foreign-investment-revisions-to-cfius-legislation-signed-into-law/.
18. US Special Trade Representative, *Update Concerning China's Acts, Policies, and Practices*, November 20, 2018, accessed January 10, 2019, https://ustr.gov/sites/default/files/enforcement/301Investigations/301%20Report%20Update.pdf; and "China Releases White Paper on Facts and Its Position on Trade Friction with US," *Xinhua*, September 24, 2018, accessed January 10, 2019, http://www.xinhuanet.com/english/2018-09/24/c_137490176.htm.
19. Diamond and Schell, *China's Influence and American Interests*.
20. Diamond and Schell, *China's Influence*, 159-160.
21. Prashanth Parameswaran, "Where Will US-Taiwan Relations Under Trump End Up?" *The Diplomat*, September 27, 2018.
22. Ross, "The End of US Naval Dominance."

23. Morrison, *China's Economic Rise*, 45–47.
24. Robert Sutter, *China-Russia Relations: Strategic Implications and US Policy Options*, National Bureau of Asian Research, NBR Special Report No. 73, September 2018.
25. Sutter, "Pushback: America's New China Strategy."
26. Bryce Pardo, "Evolution of the US Overdose Crisis: Understanding China's Role in the Production and Supply of Synthetic Opioids," Testimony before the House Foreign Affairs Committee Subcommittee on Africa, Global Health, and Global Human Rights, September 6, 2018.
27. Chicago Council on Global Affairs, "China Not Yet Seen as a Threat by the American Public," October 19, 2018.

# 11

# China's Relations with Russia

ALEXEI D. VOSKRESSENSKI

Russia's relations with China (and vice versa) have evolved steadily during the post-Soviet period. Leaders on both sides have proclaimed, for a number of years now, that their bilateral relations are at their best point in history. How did the China-Russia relationship reach such a stage, especially given their long (and largely discordant) history? And what does it mean for the future?

## The Logic of Normalization

Initially, during the first years of the post-Soviet epoch, Russia's foreign policy elites were divided over how to approach China in the aftermath of the breakup of the USSR.[1] One group bemoaned the breakup of the USSR, while the majority embraced the changes in foreign policy as well as Russia's transformation into a market democracy. This majority group expected Russia to become fully integrated into "the European home" and believed that other foreign policy actors and areas would be objectively relegated to the background. This perspective was a challenge to China.

However, soon after coming to power, the Yeltsin government confirmed that it prioritized normalizing relations with China, Russia's most important eastern neighbor, thus pursuing continuity in the course begun under Gorbachev. The Yeltsin government was keen to build good-neighborly and pragmatic relations that would yield specific rewards, such as strategic stability along the Russia-China border, large-scale trade, and development of small businesses and joint ventures—while simultaneously pursuing the opportunity to dynamically build ties with Western countries.

The lack of Western determination to fairly integrate Russia stood in contrast to the actions of the experienced Chinese diplomats, who, disregarding the many stumbling blocks in China's relations with the new, democratic Russia at

Alexei D. Voskressenski, *China's Relations with Russia* In: *China and the World*. Edited by: David Shambaugh, Oxford University Press (2020). © Oxford University Press
DOI: 10.1093/oso/9780190062316.003.0011

the early stage (in particular, China's support for the State Committee on the State of Emergency) and the challenging legacy of the past (political disagreements and the border disputes), adopted a highly pragmatic stance. The Chinese side was prepared to consider a mutually acceptable solution to the territorial dispute, and to develop economic contacts without linking them to political or ideological issues. So, as early as the autumn of 1992 the Chinese-Russian relationship acquired what might be called a new dimension, mainly because of the start of dynamic growth of bilateral economic and military cooperation. In the mid-1990s, Russia's internal political situation changed as well: the nation's political elite were beginning to feel bitter not only about the country's growing geopolitical weakness, conditioned by the half-hearted, compromised reforms, but also about the "told you so" attitude with which the West and Japan were beginning to look at that weakness and which stood in sharp contrast to China's amiable patience and readiness to consistently forge ties with Russia.

The expansion of Western economic and political interests across Eurasia following the collapse of the USSR helped to fuel the China-Russia entente. The evolving economic mercantilism, political populism and authoritarianism, as well as the world economic crisis, were strengthening perceptions of political elites in China and Russia forging further bilateral cooperation was in both nation's national interests. A byproduct of this growing connectivity is their increasing anti-Western stance.

It is partially because of this that China and Russia are on the verge of increasing their interdependence in politics, economics, science, education, and culture through restructuring their economic and political domains to better conform to developing the transregional economic space by connecting the space of the Eurasian Economic Union (EEU) with Chinese transregional "Belt and Road" (BRI) projects.[2]

## The First Structural Stage in Chinese-Russian Cooperation

The establishment of a common security space between China and the USSR through the normalization of their relations eliminated the military threat, enhanced the semblance of a common security space across Eurasia, and created hopes for an expanded common economic space notwithstanding the differences in political regimes. Though China (like the USSR) in the past attempted to recreate its special relationship with the United States, there were stark disagreements within the upper echelons of the Chinese government over what kind of a relationship the West and China should have. By improving relations with Russia, China hoped to counterbalance Russia's moving closer to the West and the United States. Thus, the first structural stage in Sino-Russian cooperation began.

Notwithstanding the past bloody clashes on the Sino-Soviet border near Damansky Island in 1969, the Russian military also discovered an advantage to developing economic and political ties with China.[3] The quickly modernizing China obtained enough resources to launch the military modernization program that had been hindered by the Western embargo on Chinese arms purchases after the crackdown in the Tiananmen Square. Strengthening political and economic ties with China to include huge weapons and later energy sales enabled the new Russian Federation to re-establish its position in the international system by arguing that its period of economic difficulties had ended.

Chinese-Russian cooperation initially took off from a very low base, inherited from the period of confrontation in the 1960s–1980s, but already by the second half of the 2000s they evolved into close multidimensional strategic cooperation.[4] The progress was grounded in agreements reached during the last phase of the Soviet Union's history. During Mikhail Gorbachev's landmark visit to Beijing in May 1989, the parties reached a preliminary agreement concerning demarcation of most of the Sino-Soviet border, and two years later, when General-Secretary of the Communist Party of China (CCP) Jiang Zemin came to Moscow, the agreement was signed. After a brief lull in the relations caused by the aftermath of the failed coup in Moscow (which Beijing supported) and the Chinese government's caution in relation to the first foreign policy steps of the new Russian leadership, relations were put on a stable track. As early as December 1992, President Yeltsin made an official visit to China, where leaders of the two countries adopted a joint statement on the basics of mutual relations. In the same year China and Russia began to actively expand their military cooperation. In 1994, when Jiang Zemin made a return visit, he called Chinese-Russian relations "a constructive partnership." Following these developments Jiang Zemin again visited Moscow in 1995 to participate in a celebration marking the end of World War II in Europe and said to his Russian counterpart that "there are no problems in our bilateral relations."

The biggest breakthrough, however, happened in 1996, during yet another summit in Beijing, when the two sides issued a joint statement on their willingness to build "a strategic partnership" based on equality and trust. Its main achievement was that the parties arrived at a practical solution for border disputes that used to cause much strain in the relationship. Equally important was an accord reached by the parties over the main issues of international politics.[5] China and Russia adopted identical or similar positions on all major international issues, including the Kosovo crisis in 1999, declaring that they shared the conviction that the world was moving to a "multipolar" model and that dictatorship or hegemonic domination by any single power were unacceptable.

During the late-1990s Sino-Russian relations shifted even further from a previous ideological bias to pragmatism.[6] Experts in both China and Russia felt generally positive about this shift, albeit for different reasons. In both countries the prevailing opinion in the late 1990s was that the West had not lived up to the expectations as a strategic partner: it did not continue to provide economic assistance and pursue strategic cooperation with Russia, ignoring external manifestations of the Russian political elites' changed economic and political views and national interests; it did not stop NATO's eastward expansion; it increased its political and strategic pressure on both countries and was ever more often placing political considerations at the center of its decision-making regarding the character and intensity of its economic interaction with Russia. This was gradually producing more and more points of disagreement between the Russian (and later also between the Chinese) and Western mainstream political elites. Against this backdrop, Chinese political elites, whose depth of disagreement with the West Russia did not understand, used to tell their Russian counterparts that they would stick with the principles of normalization agreed upon by Gorbachev and Deng Xiaoping and later confirmed by Yeltsin and Jiang Zemin.

Both countries' efforts to elaborate and put into practice mutual trust-building measures gradually bore fruit in the form of the so-called "Shanghai process," which originated from the Chinese-Soviet negotiations about specific measures to build mutual trust and about practical demilitarization of the border, as well as the talks about demarcation of the border. The talks of the Shanghai Five countries (China, Russia, Kazakhstan, Kyrgyzstan, and Tajikistan) led to further strengthening of mutual trust in military matters and to the signing of the relevant agreements in 1996, as well as the mutual border demilitarization agreement in 1997. At the same time the Shanghai Five countries continued to discuss the remaining border issues, gradually working out demarcation agreements that were signed by China and the other Shanghai Five countries. When these issues were more or less resolved, members of this informal group of Shanghai Five decided to re-establish themselves as a "real" regional alliance with an expanded agenda. This organization was called the Shanghai Cooperation Organization (SCO). The Declaration on the Establishment of the Shanghai Cooperation Organization was signed at a meeting of the heads of six states (the Shanghai Five plus Uzbekistan) on June 15, 2001, and on June 7, 2002, the parties approved the Charter of the Shanghai Cooperation Organization—a foundational document defining goals, objectives, principles, structure, and main focuses of activity of this new regional body. The charter makes the SCO responsible for developing multifaceted cooperation for the purpose of strengthening and maintaining peace. The organization was (and is) gradually expanding, joined lately by states with observer status (Afghanistan, Belarus, Iran, and Mongolia) and the Dialogue Partner status (Azerbaijan, Armenia, Cambodia, Nepal, Turkey, and Sri Lanka).

The SCO's main area of activity is cooperation in security matters, counteracting separatist movements and international fundamentalist organizations, fighting extremism and terrorism (in Central Asia), and strengthening military cooperation. Sustained efforts to build trust, in particular in military matters and in the area of security, little by little strengthened Chinese-Russian economic cooperation, which by the 1990s was making slow progress on account of the general weakness of Russia's economy. In the course of that decade, however, Russian companies were gradually strengthening their foothold in the Chinese market and the volume of trade between the two countries was beginning to grow. Late 1997 to early 1998 saw what essentially amounted to a breakthrough in China-Russia economic relations: the two countries signed a contract worth $3.3 billion as partners in the construction of a nuclear power plant in Lianyungang, Jiangsu province. Whereas the structure of China-Russia economic cooperation was initially dominated by subcontracting labor, it later extended into other fields—construction subcontracting, trade in technologies, and even, little by little, joint investment. By the end of the first decade of China-Russia cooperation, Russia already had about 400 firms with Chinese investment, mostly in agriculture, the timber industry, public catering, and retail. During the late 1990s, the volume of trade with China grew dramatically. The volume of Russian exports, meanwhile, constantly exceeded the volume of Chinese exports, and Russia's positive trade balance in the period 1992–2001 amounted to more than $26 billion, which boded well for the decade to come. Chinese investment in Russia's economy at that period did not exceed $300 million, lagging behind Japanese investment.

Little by little under the new bilateral contracts, Russia began to assist China in its nuclear power projects (such as the construction of the nuclear power plant in Jiangsu province), uranium mining, and its electric power industry. The most promising joint projects have been oil and gas production in Siberia and the Russian Far East and the construction of pipelines to deliver fuel to China's northeastern provinces. Despite the geopolitical and communicative difficulties, cooperation in the power sector began to gain speed: the construction of the Sino-Russian oil pipeline was launched, whereas Gazprom (together with Royal Dutch Shell) won a tender to build a gas pipeline from eastern Siberia to Shanghai.

In the area of military cooperation, exchanges were looking better than in the energy sector. In the 1990s, military exports accounted for at least 20 percent of the overall volume of Russian exports to China. The logic of Sino-Russian cooperation in this area in the 1990s was quite simple: China needed military know-how and military hardware and software, access to which was banned due to Western sanctions in the aftermath of the Tiananmen Square incident in 1989, whereas the Russian government needed money to pay wages to hundreds of thousands of workers employed in its military-industrial complex. According to an account of Aleksey Kotelkin (then the head of Rosvooruzhenie, Russia's state-run arms export company), revenues from weapons shipments covered at least 50 percent of the weapons production costs, and the bulk of the profits was generated by the sales of weapons and technologies to China. As a result, China was provided with the opportunity to upgrade the second postwar generation of armaments to the fourth, and even "fourth plus" generation of military hardware—whereas Russia was able to preserve its military-industrial complex following the disintegration of the Soviet Union.

In the 1990s (at least during the first half of the decade and partially in the second as well), to some extent these developments suited Russia too—they provided it with resources to modernize its arms production facilities and enabled it to preserve and develop friendly relations with China, making China its main partner in military-industrial cooperation for nearly a decade. Diplomatic experts (such as Igor Rogachev and Alexander Losyukov) meanwhile assured the international community and international experts that as Russia proceeded, it was taking measures not to upset the existing military balance in East Asia and not to undermine international stability. China thus became the key buyer of Russian weapons. When Russia's economy was in a bad shape during the transition period (1992–1997), Beijing bought approximately $6 billion worth of arms, spending about $1 billion on Russian military hardware and software annually. These included Sukhoi-24, -27, -30, and -35 fighter jets, Sovremenny-class destroyers, Kilo-class submarines, S-300 and S-400 surface-to-air missile systems, Kamov multirole helicopters, a variety of turbofan jet engines, and assistance with rocket programs.[7]

Thus, in the first decade after the breakup of the USSR, Sino-Russian cooperation was gradually gaining in stability and becoming mutually beneficial, owing mainly to military and energy-sector cooperation. Intergovernmental and interregional commissions were set up to handle practically every area of cooperation—by the late 1990s the two countries had already signed more than 120 country-to-country intergovernmental agreements and hundreds of interdepartmental agreements, and Chinese-Russian relations were becoming stable and mutually beneficial. At the same time, the political component of Chinese-Russian cooperation became much stronger than the economic one (whereas the latter lacked stability, real dynamism, and strategic quality).

## The Second and Third Stages
## of Chinese-Russian Cooperation

Concerning Russian-Chinese cooperation, Russian analysts of China have fallen into three main camps: optimists, pessimists, and pragmatists. The divisions hold to this day although the arguments of each group have varied over time.[8] For all three groups, the major question to answer has been whether Russia could trust China as a reliable ally capable of helping Russia not only overcome its economic difficulties, but also to construct a world and regional order beneficial to Russia's improved position in international affairs. All Russian analysts believed that a Russian-Chinese partnership at that time would help Russia rise without being subordinated to the United States in an American-led world, while at the same time not becoming dependent on China. The question of congruence/incongruence of Russian and Chinese interests was put aside and the view that Russia could find its own solution to its economic problems triumphed. The possible problems of China's emergence as a new economic superpower on a border with Russia were considered minor compared to the alleged unfair treatment of Russia by the West. Russian experts essentially viewed China's rise to be a smooth and non-conflictual process.

For the Russian authorities the most important issue was—and still is—the consolidation of Russian and Chinese domestic political regimes and the benefits of this for stabilizing and counterbalancing Western influence. For the purposes of building up strong anti-Westernism and anti-Americanism, certain segments of the Russian political elite agree even to subsume Russian great power status in the international arena by making Russia subordinate to Chinese strategic, political, and economic interests.[9] This was contrary to the aspirations of the majority of the Russian elite who, regardless of their political beliefs, want to see their country strong, free, and independent in both its internal development and its foreign policy, but it suited well China's interests.

At this stage of the relationship, liberally minded Russian optimists argued that helping the economic rise of China would mean a less authoritarian China. The Russian pessimists stressed that Russia's relative economic inefficiency coupled with increased political authoritarianism indirectly (or even directly) supported by China could lead to problems on both Russia's western and eastern diplomatic and political "fronts." For pragmatists in Russia, the most important issue was, and still is, China's military modernization and where the direction of this force projection would be: north, south, or both?

So, putting aside the sharp internal discussions on their future character, Chinese-Russian bilateral relations were generally driven by predominantly pragmatic calculations to help each other's advances in internal economic development and also in the international arena, and by providing ad hoc diplomatic support, with more and more distinct shared authoritarian political aims with a strengthening anti-Western orientation. There has also been a growing congruence of Sino-Russian interests on a global level and more bilateral regional cooperation based on a certain economic complementarity during the second and third structural stages of their cooperation. In the second stage, closer cooperation in all fields (international, economic, political, and cultural) was established.[10] The third stage of Chinese-Russian cooperation was marked more by concerns about its implications for international rather than internal politics—it emerged at the beginning of Putin's second term as president of Russia. The third stage began during the end of Dmitry Medvedev's presidential term and coincided with the onset of the global financial crisis. This triggered the emergence of an indecisive interim period that is still going on. During this third stage, the Russian political elite decided that, with the help of China, it was possible to further stabilize Russia's Asian "underbelly" (especially in Central Asia) and, moreover, to strengthen it in a space where China and Russia enjoyed generally close strategic understanding. This outcome was seen as welcome even if, for Russia, it meant a strengthened China in Central Asia. During this third stage, ties have become closer than ever, causing one notable American study to label them the "axis of authoritarians."[11]

The growing bilateral cooperation during the second stage was streamlined after Putin came to power—who identified the duality of Russia as a European and Asian state and, accordingly, the presence of two equal vectors, European and Asian, in Russia's foreign policy was formulated in his landmark essay "Russia: The New Eastern Perspectives."[12] The Russian president confirmed that China was to remain Russia's strategic partner, as it was during Yeltsin's presidency. However, Putin was careful to mention some new features of the partnership: the emphasis on preserving and strengthening the multipolar world and the need for Russia's and China's joint efforts to maintain the strategic equilibrium. During Putin's second visit to Beijing he signed the Beijing Declaration, and he and his Chinese counterpart issued a joint Sino-Russian statement on anti-missile defense. This declaration and the statement on further rapprochement emphasized the new opportunities for strengthening multifaceted cooperation in other areas, previously more or less neglected or underfunded: education, culture, health care, and so forth. Simultaneously it took some time for experts to awaken to the fact that the joint statement on anti-missile defense marked a serious shift in the Russian political elite's views on the international situation compared to the previous decade, and that the Russian military-industrial complex, buttressed with the revenues from arms sales to China, was exercising an ever-greater influence over the country's policies in general.

Jiang Zemin's visit to Moscow in July 2001 brought new impressive results. This time the parties went further than just signing declarations—they decided to cement their relations with a full-blown twenty-year Treaty of Good-Neighborliness and Friendly Cooperation (valid through 2021). They also agreed to continue consultations for the purpose of finding a mutually acceptable final solution for the disputed islands at Russia-China border that remained under Russia's jurisdiction.

The signing of the new Sino-Russian treaty, the signatories believed, closed the book on the past difficult history of Sino-Russian relations and opened up an avenue for cooperation on a solid and law-based foundation—the absence of the treaty was an obstacle to finalizing negotiations regarding the remaining unresolved border issues and to tangibly increasing the trade volume. Importantly, both sides stressed, the 2001 Sino-Russian Treaty did not unite the two countries into a formal military or political alliance, nor did it stipulate any obligations to jointly respond to aggression (other than to "consult" if either side felt threatened); what it did was very pragmatically spell out the parties' intent to cooperate more closely on a regular basis, without specifying the main forms of this cooperation.

It was further stated that the document was not directed against third countries, but on the other hand, both China and Russia were against the undermining of sovereignty caused by the acceleration of globalization. These provisions were reflected first of all in the strengthening of Chinese-Russian cooperation under the United Nations' aegis, and their joint desire to uphold the role of this organization as an international organ adopting consensual decisions while respecting individual nation-states' sovereignty. The treaty de facto echoed the evasive concept of "multipolar world" and became what might be called the conservative anchor standing in the way of the rapid unilateral changes in the twenty-first-century world. As for the bilateral relationship, the treaty set forth the norms of bilateral stability that the Chinese and Russian political elites had long been waiting for: the refusal to discuss pros and cons of political development and specific political systems, as well as adopting a conservative approach to the issue of human rights, which guarantees against interference with internal affairs. The treaty further prohibited third countries from using the territory of China or Russia in a fashion infringing on Russia's or China's sovereignty, security, and territorial integrity—in other words, the document described mutual obligations that would prevent separatist movements, including ethnic minorities and any separatist actions on their part, as well as international terrorist organizations from operating from Russia or China. Article Six of the treaty recognizes the existing state borders between China and Russia.

Generally, the Treaty reflects the two countries' national priorities in a particular historical period and lays the groundwork for solving the main problems, such as achieving stability and political equilibrium in their relations. That is, the treaty reflects the real dismantlement of the "Cold War mentality" (in Jiang Zemin's words) among the Chinese and Russian political elites while also mapping out the course of development for the relations between two countries that were neither allies nor foes. While these are called in the treaty "relations of a new type," it does not specify the features of these relations that would make it impossible to reactivate an ideological component when the political environment changes. However, the treaty lays a real political and legal foundation for stable, predictable, multifaceted relations (as Foreign Minister Sergei Lavrov put it) between the two countries.

However, the international situation soon began to change dramatically. The terrorist attack on the United States on September 11, 2001, was followed by the coalition combat operations in Afghanistan—that is very close to China's conflict-prone ethnic enclaves in Xinjiang that previously had an experience of existing independently from China. The operations in Afghanistan were met with apprehension by the Chinese authorities but supported by the Russian leadership, which unequivocally condemned the acts of terror against the United States. In view of all this, and especially anxious after the American invasion of Iraq in 2003, China developed a fear of possible Russian-American anti-ballistic missile defense agreements and NATO's expansion in disregard of Beijing's interests.

The American invasion of Iraq, undertaken in defiance of the opinion of China's and Russia's leaders, who believed that UN Security Council Resolution 1441 obligated Iraq to cooperate with the international inspectors but did not authorize an armed invasion of the country, strengthened even more the Chinese and Russian leaders' solidarity. In fact, the period saw growing disagreement between Russia and the United States, and between China and the United States, over the question of sovereignty, with Russia adopting a more active and conservative position than China, with the latter's absolute approval. The invasion of Iraq, along with the almost concurrent crisis on the Korean peninsula (2003), strengthened Russia's and China's diplomatic interaction in the efforts to peacefully settle these problems.

In 2002, the most tangible changes in the relationship were taking place in trade, economic interaction, and military cooperation. When China's new leader Hu Jintao came to Russia in May 2003, the parties signed yet another declaration, which made a special mention of the North Korean problem and emphasized the need to ensure that Korea remain non-nuclear or, in other words, essentially neutral in the strategic power balance in Northeast Asia. In 2004 China's and Russia's foreign ministers additionally signed the complementary agreement concerning the eastern portion of Chinese-Russian border—this document, according to China's leader Hu Jintao, amounted to a final settlement of the two countries' border issues.

The border deals made the parties ever more eager to establish closer economic ties bilaterally and under the SCO's aegis. On September 14, 2001, the heads of the SCO member states met for the first time in Almaty, and signed a memorandum on the main directions of regional economic cooperation to create a suitable environment for trade and investment. In October 2002, in Beijing, the SCO held its first forum on investment and development in the power sector, followed by a new meeting of the Council of Heads of Government who approved a program of multilateral economic cooperation of the SCO member states, outlining the main objectives of economic integration up to 2020. As new financial resources were becoming available, the SCO member states, in addition to handling security issues, decided to expand their cultural/humanitarian cooperation in education, science, and health care.

With this in mind, it was decided to establish and develop a network of existing universities in the SCO member and observer states, which began to gain momentum by the end of the second decade of Chinese-Russian cooperation. The SCO member states set out on an ambitious objective of ensuring international quality of education under the SCO aegis while also keeping the Soviet educational achievements in the post-Soviet sovereign states. In the area of technologies, the cooperation is aimed at increasing the pool of jointly developed technologies and forging the future Russian–Chinese–Central Asian technology space.

In addition to the SCO, by the mid-2000s another unofficial regional organization was created—RIC (Russia, India, China), later expanded into BRICS (Russia, India, China, Brazil, South Africa). The BRICS has yet to become an alliance or formalize itself into a regional organization. Unlike the SCO, with its focus on security issues, which require the coordinated work of law-enforcement and security organs, the BRICS has prioritized the problems of development of international financial institutions, favoring the member states' quickly growing markets, whose combined economic power make them players to reckon with in global financial/economic operations.

The border deals between China and Russia strengthened, in particular, cooperation and coordination between their armed forces: already in August 2005 China and Russia began a joint military drill "Peace Mission—2005" (with Mongolia joining in 2018), which emblematized the shared eagerness to enhance the capacity for response to the new challenges and threats facing both China and Russia.

To help bring China and Russia ever closer, 2006 and 2007 were proclaimed as the Year of China in Russia and the Year of Russia in China, respectively, and at least 600 cultural, science- and technology-related, and political-economic events were carried out under the auspices of these programs. Both occasions were inaugurated by the respective country's top leaders, which was an important official signal of the deepening cooperation between the two countries' political elites.

In 2008, after a series of talks, China and Russia finalized legal aspects of the demarcation of the last two disputed areas of the border located in its eastern section, and on July 21, 2008, during the Russian foreign minister Sergei Lavrov's visit to China, the parties signed the final protocol demarcating the

China-Russia border, which came into force on October 14, 2008. This deal was very important for Russia, since the demarcation of its border with China had been an old problem, which the parties were finally able to settle by finding a mutually acceptable diplomatic solution.

The frequency of meetings of the two countries' leaders continued—in 2009 alone Hu Jintao and then Russian president Medvedev met six times—testimony to their close relationship. As the result of all these meetings, in 2010, during Medvedev's maiden visit to China, the parties signed a series of new documents and agreements, the most important among them being the joint statement on deepening Chinese-Russian partnership and strategic interaction. Besides, the parties signed a bilateral agreement on cooperation in the fight against terrorism, separatism, and extremism; a contract for oil deliveries to China via the Skovorodino-Daqing pipeline; and several agreements concerning expansion of cooperation in gas industry. Thus, the parties formalized their bilateral cooperation in the power industry, confirmed their positions vis-à-vis extremism and separatism, and chalked out steps to promote cooperation in using nuclear energy for peaceful purposes.

The "color revolutions," and then the "Arab spring," further strengthened China's and Russia's common political resolve: Russia was mostly worried about the international impact of the "color revolutions" and their possible repercussions for the situation in Russia, whereas China was anxious not only about its general domestic political situation. Beijing was determined to prevent the wave of protests in the Muslim world from spreading to Xinjiang and other regions populated by Muslim or primarily Chinese ethnic minorities. This new political unity of Chinese and Russian diplomats produced a statement of support for UN resolution 1970/2011 which introduced sanctions against Libya; a vote of abstention on UN resolution 1973/2011 introducing a no-fly zone over Libya; and condemnation of the NATO bombing of Libya as violating this resolution.

## Further Expansion of Ties Amid Some New Problems

The second post-Soviet decade of Chinese-Russian relations, while witnessing a significant expansion of trade ties, was marked by an imbalance in economic relations that showed no sign of abating. The volume of Chinese-Russian trade grew annually by 30 percent during the period 2000–2008; in 2008 it amounted to nearly $68 billion (see Figure 11.1). Although in 2009 the global financial crisis caused the volume to decline, by the end of the decade it again reached the pre-crisis level. At the same time the economic relations showed a new trend toward instability: the share of imports from China grew significantly (up to 69 percent) and China became Russia's leading trade partner. By then China's share of Russia's foreign trade was 10.2 percent, while Russia's share of China's

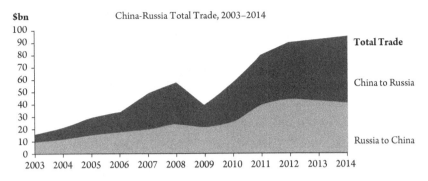

*Figure 11.1* China-Russia Total Trade, 2003–2014

was slightly over 2 percent. During that period the share of machine tools and equipment in Russian exports to China declined dramatically (to less than 2 percent). Russia was now supplying China mostly with raw materials (fuels, felled trees, sawn wood products, wood pulp, ores and iron concentrates, fertilizers, fish, etc.), whereas the focus of Chinese imports in Russia began to shift toward machine tools, equipment, transportation vehicles, industrial chemicals, household electronic appliances, and consumer goods. Thus, compared to the Soviet period, China and Russia swapped places in their economic cooperation: Russia became for China a provider of raw materials (some experts and political analysts in Russia go so far as to call Russia "China's raw material appendage"), while China became a supplier of finished goods, including machine tools and petrochemicals.

At the same time, by the end of the second decade the two sides were apparently beginning to show more interest in mutual investment: on January 13, 2009, Chinese leaders and Putin met for talks in China, signing over twenty agreements on specific areas of cooperation, which, when realized, increased Chinese direct investment in Russia's economy twofold in the years 2008–2009 alone. This investment was mostly concentrated in such fields as the processing of minerals for export, the timber and power industries, light industry and textiles, construction, and freighting.

In the second decade (2000–2010), Chinese-Russian military cooperation showed signs of decline, however, because of Russia's efforts to diversify military cooperation and expand its pool of international markets and partners. At the same time, Chinese-Russian cooperation in the energy industry was proceeding throughout the second decade more dynamically than in the first. In 2001, Russia and China reached a deal to build a pipeline from Russia to China. A big impetus to this project was given by China's loans to Rosneft and Transneft in the amount of $25 billion in exchange for deliveries of 15 million tons of Russian oil to China during the following twenty years. By the start of the third post-Soviet decade of Chinese-Russian relations, Russia was ranked, variously, fourth or fifth among China's energy providers and became one of China's most important partners in this sector, which is pivotal for the development of the Chinese economy. In addition to the hydrocarbon sector, Chinese-Russian cooperation was focused on gas, nuclear, and electric power.

In the third stage of Chinese-Russian cooperation, Russia was beginning to consider China an attractive prospective market for industrial, high–technology (including military) production and resources, and their bilateral trade started to flourish because of the massive Russian sales of hydrocarbons that was considered a strategic asset to both countries—in Russia because it tied China to Russia, in China because it made China less vulnerable in terms of energy needs.

For China, partnership with Russia at this stage evolved to be the major factor bolstering its efforts to transform itself into a global power, since Russia provided it with political, military, diplomatic, and technological support. Without the active role of Russia, and Russia's anti-Western (either soft or rigid) policies, it would hardly have been possible to hinder the formation of an international coalition that could prevent China's progression to the status of a first-tier power. With the help of Russia, China has made significant advances in modernizing its armed forces and gained access to energy markets not controlled by the Western states. This situation further helped China improve its economic status at a time when the whole world was thrown into a recession. To further develop their strategic partnership, China and Russia signed a universal treaty that put an end to the border question and broadly opened Chinese markets to Russian industrial products and financial activity.

## The Praxis of Chinese-Russian Pragmatism and Future Scenarios.

The Ukrainian/Crimean crises and Russia's involvement in Syria shifted the Russian ideological balance in favor of rising nationalism, anti-Americanism, and anti-Westernism, which paved the way for heated discussions on the need to improve Russian-Chinese cooperation. Sanctions and anti-sanctions politics, ideological provocations, and hybrid conflicts flourished; however, they did not evolve into the full-fledged Cold War between the West and Russia. The United States and the EU, being under economic and political strains themselves, were compelled to closely observe the tactical coordination of Russia's and China's international policies—especially concerning Iran, Iraq, NATO, North Korea, Libya, Syria, and in the UN Security Council; Chinese-Russian military-technical cooperation, energy and transport structures, and the developing sub-regional security system in Eurasia; as well as the demographic shifts on both sides of the border.[13]

Chinese-Russian relations in the third decade of the post-Soviet era are officially characterized as "trustful constructive partnership to promote comprehensive strategic interaction in the 21st century." Under the Sino-Russian Treaty of
2001, Chinese-Russian strategic interaction and partnership in certain circumstances (both domestic and international) can even transform into an alliance.[14]
Experts already announced that if hostility in the American attitude toward both
China and Russia rise, both countries may use a form of a military alliance as an
instrument to counterbalance negative military trends. It is also clear that rejuvenation of the Russia-India-China (RIC) mechanism signifies moves in the same
direction. In 2017, Pakistan and India joined the SCO as full members. The SCO
thus became an international regional organization—the first one created by
China in partnership with Russia and other countries of the Eurasian region. So
all necessary mechanisms to ensure security in the Eurasian space between the
EU, Russia and China, and Pakistan and India were created with a possibility of
a Chinese-Russian military alliance being a necessary backbone and the "fuse"
against the most malign external developments for both countries.

At the same time, neither China nor Russia stands to gain from this sort of
exigency, although the balance in relations in the partnership can vary to a certain degree depending on the international environment and domestic political
situation in each country.[15] Some Russian analysts, meanwhile, argue that China
uses the China-Russian strategic partnership in China's favor to modernize its
armed forces, whereas many of the hundreds of Sino-Russian economic agreements are not fully operative and the economic partnership still has to realize
its full potential. However, bilateral trade reached approximately $100 billion in
2018, and cooperation in the spheres of science, culture, and education between
the two countries is developing at a greater pace.

In Russia, there is an influential school considering China as its sole most
promising partner.[16] According to this line of thinking, intensification of
Chinese-Russian economic relations in the future can also lead to intensification
of relations with countries of Southeast Asia, especially those that have an economically active Chinese diaspora. The region's industrial profile, too, indicates
a strong possibility of this sort of intensification of economic cooperation with
China: heavy industry, knowledge-based sectors, and extractive industries in
Russia, and agriculture, light industry, and a surplus of labor in China; the investment potential of south China and overseas Chinese, and Russian Far East's
need for investment; and comparable levels of scientific and technological development in China's northeast and the industrial base in Russia's Far East. Besides,
mutual penetration of the economies of the southern area of Russia's Far East
and China's northeast may give additional impetus and political motivation for
further cooperation. In both countries the most radical left-wing view within
this stream of thought consists of hailing China ideologically with arguments

that further bringing Russia closer to China will inevitably lead to Russia's more intensively copying China's authoritarian model with certain characteristics of China's political system.

The counter-arguments against, are also fairly weighty.[17] They include non-Chinese territories that are claimed by China as its "historic lands," the problem of China's demographic pressure on Russia's thinly populated Far East, and China's "sea claims" that exacerbate the already complicated security situation in East Asia—all of which objectively reduces the window of opportunity for economic projects in the region in general and in Russia's Far East in particular. Some segments of Russia's foreign policy and military elite believe that China is one of the few states that can pose a genuine threat to Russia's national interests. At the same time, it is clear that the present offers no alternative to the development of Chinese-Russian economic relations. This means that in the near future China is to remain an important—and maybe *the most important*—trade and economic partner for Russia in the region because the persistent structural problems of the Russian economy are still getting in the way of economic relations with other partners (Japan, ASEAN, EU), and the relations with the United States have entered a critical stage unprecedented in their history, resulting in a nearly complete termination of economic, social, and political ties.

However, with respect to this line of thinking in Russia, there are also several contravening arguments, including the necessity to search for a regional geopolitical counterweight. Japan, which is geographically very close to Russia, has the capital and the technologies that, under certain circumstances, can become a catalyst for economic development of Russia's Far East—something that has been impossible to achieve for at least the last century. As for the arguments against this scenario, there is mostly just one: Japan's strategic decision to massively invest in Russia is tied in with the demand to solve the territorial dispute between Japan and Russia. Potential access to America's financial and technological resources, with a real "reset" of the relations with Washington, is another factor. A combination of Russia's oil and gas with the pipelines and railroads criss-crossing China, Mongolia, two Koreas, and Japan in principle create the needed critical mass to kick-start Northeast Asia's stunted regionalism through Russian involvement.

## Conclusion and Outlook

The main result of the nearly three decades of China-Russia cooperation that passed through three distinctive structural stages following the breakup of the Soviet Union is that in terms of their structure (but not the volume) Chinese-Russian economic relations have not quite become a strategic partnership as announced. In other words, the declared formula of Chinese-Russian strategic partnership remains still mostly political, amounting to mutual support of ruling elites. Russia is trying to offer such political and economic conditions for Russian and international (including Chinese) businesses in Russia's eastern regions, and to come up with such political and economic deterrents and incentives for Russian-Chinese and other types of regional economic interaction with international partners that would guarantee a stable development for Russia's Far East for the first time in history. By 2018, Russia formulated the concept of "territories of priority development" with its system of priorities and cumulative modernization incentives, as well as deterrents to negative economic tendencies to foster development of Russia's Asian border regions. However, a political shift of Russia prioritizing Chinese economic interests to ensure the further fostered development of the Russian Far East cannot be completely excluded.

In June 2019 Moscow and Beijing adjusted the terminology of their relationship yet again—proclaiming a "comprehensive strategic partnership of coordination in the new era."[18] The key term here is "coordination," suggesting that the two nations have entered the fourth structural stage in their bilateral relations.

# Notes

1.  See Alexei D. Voskressenski, "The Perception of China by Russia's Foreign Policy Elite," *Issues and Studies* 33, no. 3 (1997): 1–20.
2.  See Xing Li and Alexei D. Voskressenski, eds., *Ya-Ou zhongxin kuaquyu fazhan tizhi jizhi yanjiu* (Mechanisms of Transregional Development in Central Eurasia: Analysis and Prognostications) (Beijing: Jiuzhou Press, 2016); Isabelle Facon, "Les fondements inédits du partneriat sino-russe au 21e siècle," *Annuare français de relations internationales* (Université Panthéon-Assas—Centre Thucydide) 18 (2017): 693–707.
3.  See Sherman Garnett, ed., *Rapprochement or Rivalry? Russia-China Relations in a Changing Asia* (Washington, DC: Carnegie Endowment for International Peace, 2000).
4.  For further on Russia-China relations, see James Bellaqua, ed., *The Future of China-Russia Relations* (Lexington: The University Press of Kentucky, 2010); Bobo Lo, *Axis of Convenience: Moscow, Beijing, and the New Geopolitics* (Washington, DC: Brookings Institution Press, 2008); Alexander Lukin, *China and Russia: A New Rapprochement* (Cambridge: Polity, 2018); and Richard Ellings and Robert Sutter, eds., *Axis of Authoritarians: Implications of China-Russia Cooperation* (Seattle: National Bureau of Asian Research, 2018).
5.  Alexei D. Voskressenski, *Russia and China. A Theory of Inter-State Relations* (London and New York: Routledge Curzon, 2003).
6.  See Garnett, *Rapprochement or Rivalry?*
7.  See, e.g., "What Russian Weapons Are Being Bought by China?" *South China Morning Post*, September 21, 2018, https://www.scmp.com/news/china/military/article/2165182/what-weapons-china-buying-russia.
8.  See Voskressenski, "The Perception of China."
9.  See James Bellaqua, ed., *The Future of China-Russia Relations*.
10. See Garnett, *Rapprochement or Rivalry?*
11. See Richard Ellings and Robert Sutter, eds., *Axis of Authoritarians: Implications of China-Russia Cooperation*.

12. Vladimir Putin, "Russia: New Eastern Perspectives," available at http://en.kremlin.ru/events/president/transcripts/21132.

13. See James Bellaqua, ed., *The Future of China-Russia Relations*.

14. See Huasheng Zhao, "Lun Zhong E Mei xin sanjiao guanxi (On the New China-Russia-USA Triangular Relationship)," *Eluosi Dong'ou Zhongya Yanjiu* (Russian, East European, and Central Asian Studies) 6 (2019): 1–25.

15. See Li and Voskressenski, eds., *Ya ou zhongxin kuaquyu fazhan tizhi jizhi yanjiu*.

16. *Sovremenniye Rossiisko-Kitaiskiye Otnosheniya* (Current Russian-Chinese Relations) (Moscow: Deli-Plus Publishers, 2017).

17. Yuri Galenovich, *Za kulisami amerikano-kitaiskikh otnoshenii* (Behind the scenes of American-Chinese relations) (Moscow: Russkaya Panorama, 2019).

18. "China, Russia Agree to Upgrade Relations for a New Era," *Xinhua*, June 6, 2019, http://www.xinhuanet.com/english/2019-06/06/c_138119879.htm.

# 12

# China's Relations with Europe

FRANÇOIS GODEMENT

China's relations with Europe are extensive and still growing. They include intensive state-to-state diplomacy, public diplomacy, and "influence operations" that increasingly involve lobbying of European elites, an outsize trade relationship as well as an investment strategy leading to increasing friction, people-to-people exchanges that consist primarily of tourist and student flows from China to Europe, and cultural influences or soft power.

In these contexts, the relationship is "comprehensive," as characterized in official statements by both sides. But it is not "strategic," the other adjective frequently used in joint statements, nor is it the "partnership" claimed by both sides, unless one defines these terms differently. China also has a "strategic partnership" with ASEAN (the Association of Southeast Asian Nations), a regional grouping that claims neutrality in international affairs. The Chinese meaning of the adjective "strategic" is that there are no major conflicts in the relationship: in his 2004 Brussels speech, then premier Wen Jiabao said that the adjective "strategic" means that the relationship "transcends the differences in ideology and social system and is not subjected to the impacts of individual events that occur from time to time."[1] Yet the existence of an arms embargo by the European Union on China since 1989, the divergences of interpretation of international law regarding territorial issues, and the disputes over values that repeatedly crop up in the relationship and in international institutions are limiting the "strategic partnership" to a negative reassurance regarding open conflict.

The relationship also does not occur in a vacuum. Europeans would prefer to conduct interest-based relations with China in a way that is not subject to their truly strategic partnership—that with the United States. Yet the ups and downs of the China-US relationship have their influence. In good times, because the United States takes little heed of European interests; in less good times, because the overall alliance dictates restraint on Europeans, or simply because they share common values across the Atlantic. Since 2017, new gaps have appeared inside

François Godement, *China's Relations with Europe* In: *China and the World*. Edited by: David Shambaugh, Oxford University Press (2020). © Oxford University Press
DOI: 10.1093/oso/9780190062316.003.0012

the transatlantic alliance that would seem to encourage more independent conduct by Europeans of their China policies. Yet this occurs against the backdrop of China's rise turning into the strongest totalitarian revival since the death of Mao. While there remains much space for sectoral cooperation between China and the European Union, there remains a gnawing question: to whose benefit? There is much less space for larger compromises between political and economic systems that are diverging instead of converging. Europe-wide policies are now increasingly based on coldly realist views of China, while member states retain some competitive deal-making with China.

The European realist approach is matched with skeptical views by China of Europe. This is neither new nor uniform. The PRC's attention to Europe started from the Sino-Soviet split, expanded during the latter part of the Cultural Revolution, and accelerated with the reform era under Deng Xiaoping. But Europe has long been seen by China as the "second" or "intermediate" world, and a potential pole in a multipolar world. But decades of low growth, the Euro crisis, the specter of fragmentation illustrated by Brexit and the rise of populism, and the sheer difficulty for an integrated grouping that is not a federation to match China's Leninist and centralized party-state's negotiating ability are having an effect on Chinese perceptions. As a result, China's policies have focused much more on the European Union. The European Union and its member states have to work hard in order to demonstrate that they can stay the course—irrespective of what that course may be.

## The EU and China: A Historical See-saw

The relationship between China and European nations has been rewritten and largely turned around over the last four decades.[2] From Europe's presence and influence in China, the main issues have shifted and now revolve around China's presence and influence in and near Europe. Crucially, Chinese investment in Europe has now overtaken European investment in China.

Europeans were, with Japan, the main perpetrators of the "carving up" of China according to what official PRC history calls the "semi-colonial" era. But they also formed the institutional backbone of modern China—for example, the customs administration was adopted from Britain, the organization of the military from Germany, many vestiges of European culture penetrated urban China (Shanghai became known as the "Paris of the East"), and European political liberalism served as a model for many Chinese intellectuals.

After the departure of Westerners in 1949, Soviet Russia became the imagined path to Chinese modernity. The PRC's European experience in its first decade was largely confined to relations with Eastern European fraternal parties and countries and their Soviet mentor. There again, influence flowed largely one way, with the 1956 Eastern European dissent echoing inside the Chinese Communist Party (CCP) before Mao decided to become the guardian of Marxist-Leninist orthodoxy following the death of Stalin. In the other direction, Maoism made very few inroads into Europe, confined largely to splinter groups on the left and to the lonely Albanian exception. When Mao cited France as a partner in 1964, it was as an alternative source to the Soviet Union for imports, certainly not as a market for which China had simply nothing suitable to offer.

It is therefore no wonder that, after Mao's death in 1976, the first decades of an intensified Europe-China relationship would be marked by European self-confidence in its own model and its ability to influence China on the path of reform and opening up. One of the first European Economic Community (EEC) programs in China, in 1984, was actually designed to help China improve business management and export more of its goods: in the next year, the EEC signed a Trade and Cooperation Agreement that holds to this day.[3] Aid from member states and from the EU focused on goals that were as much developmental as commercial, at a time when the United States did not provide such assistance. The negotiations during the 1980s for the return of Hong Kong to Chinese sovereignty resulted in a system that was supposed to preserve British-created institutions until 2047.

Following the political comeback of Deng Xiaoping in 1977, China also found a growing but limited geopolitical use for Europe. Europe was termed the "second world" (along with Japan), and as such became terrain for China to expand its influence beyond "third world" allies and in resisting the "first world's" two superpowers. There were growing economic and trade relations, and an increasingly well-staffed PRC embassy to Belgium that simultaneously served in relations with the European institutions. Meanwhile, in the first decade of increased Chinese military budgets after 1979 and the conflict with Vietnam, Beijing was able to source European—as well as some American—weaponry and dual technologies.

The Tiananmen demonstrations in 1989 and the ensuing repression soured the atmosphere between the PRC and Europeans. Europe put in place sanctions—including an end to commercial loans—and a declarative arms embargo that required European Council unanimity and could only be reversed by another unanimous vote. European aid was to be confined to cases of poverty alleviation. The arms embargo, human rights, the Taiwan issue after the 1995–1996 missile crises in the Taiwan Straits, and Tibet all became contentious issues in Europe-China relations. European arms sales to Taiwan—and especially French jetfighters and frigates—created open crises. From 1990 to 1997, European members of the UN Human Rights Commission tabled annually (with the United States) a resolution on human rights violations in China. Scandinavian governments,

Germany, and the "new Europe" liberated from Soviet domination were fairly consistent with these policies.

Yet China came back in full focus in 1997–1998, thanks to the Asian financial crisis. During that decade, the epicenter of Asian growth moved twice, first from crisis-struck Japan to Southeast Asia in 1991, and again to China after the Asian financial crisis of 1997. Europeans had developed, under the influence of Singapore, a more diverse set of relations with Asia in 1995 through the Asia-Europe Meeting (ASEM). As Southeast Asia went into an economic eclipse the relationship with China became both paramount and focused around trade and direct investment by European firms inside China. From the relaunch of China's opening by Deng in 1991 during his "Southern Tour," to the successful conclusion in 2001 of thirteen years of negotiation for China to enter the WTO, a positive climate reappeared where the China market played a central role. Intra-European competition was also a factor. While one German firm, Siemens, sold as much to China as all French firms combined, France's publicly backed lending to China exceeded that to all countries except neighboring Algeria. Tied by its deal for the return of Hong Kong to China in 1997, Britain made the best of it by achieving as much influence as it could in China's banking and insurance business. All three linked business with politics, as heads of government brought to China imposing business delegations (which were cautious in any criticism of China). Italy, itself a dual economy not unlike the two-tiered Chinese system, managed quite a bit of trade without much of an intergovernmental relationship, but this exception was ignored. Europeans, often armed with very little knowledge of the workings of the Chinese party-state bureaucracy, generally believed that with China, business followed diplomacy. EU-level annual summits started in 1998, with an increasing web of sectoral consultations (including human rights) established and agreements concluded.

It was then that China entered what it termed a "honeymoon" with the European Union. In 1998, the EU and United States did not table a resolution on China at the UN Human Rights Commission in Geneva. When the United States resumed the practice in 1999, Europeans did not follow suit.[4] The criticisms by Chancellor Gerhard Schröder of Germany and President Jacques Chirac of France of the US-led Iraq war may also have encouraged China. Both leaders came out in early 2004 in favor of lifting the EU arms embargo, and China began a diplomatic campaign with all other European governments for the same purpose. The EU was meant to adopt a Code of Conduct on arms exports that would be more precise. The terse wording of the 1989 arms embargo,[5] a statement without legal enforcement, had indeed left many loopholes—starting with "dual use" sales (of civilian technologies with military applications), in which the United Kingdom excelled above others.[6] In fact, export control regulations at the EU and national levels now matter more than the symbolic arms embargo.

But if the opposition of the United States and Japan to lifting the arms embargo was predictable, it is more surprising that China did not put forward any concession on its part that might have helped to justify its removal.

In December 2004 the EU finally agreed with China to "continue to work toward lifting the embargo," which actually meant it deferred a decision that has never arisen since. The whole episode confirmed to China that whatever the different ideologies and interests within the European Union, and the neutralist temptations of distancing Europe from the United States, the transatlantic alliance—including American requests for support—remained the anchor of Europe's foreign policy.

In 2003, both sides had embarked on setting up a "comprehensive strategic relationship." In the same year, China's State Council published its first policy paper on Europe. The paper stated that there was "no fundamental conflict of interest between China and the EU and neither side poses a threat to the other." It was heavily predicated on China's needs and interests, requiring the EU to strictly abide by the "One China Principle," and raising other issues such as Tibet, arms sales, and human rights. In sum, the "strategic" nature of the relationship was based on negative reassurances and continued support for China's development. Meanwhile, the EU worked on its fourth China strategy paper, which was released in 2006 under the title *Closer Partners, Growing Responsibilities*. It explained that engagement was an obligation, proposed to strengthen the strategic partnership, and set as a goal the conclusion of a Partnership and Cooperation Agreement (PCA) that would replace the 1985 Trade and Cooperation Agreement with a much wider and more ambitious text. To this day, no PCA has been concluded, in part because in EU external diplomacy this type of agreement requires common views on values from both signatories, but also because China believes the 1984 trade and cooperation agreement cannot be beaten in terms of relative advantage to itself.

In less than two years, relations darkened again in 2008 with the Sudan, Tibet, and Olympic crises coming one after another. Germany, France, and the United Kingdom have incurred (over an increasing length of time from one case to the other) the wrath and practical sanctions by Beijing for what it considered to be official receptions of the Dalai Lama. So did Denmark. A correlation between these events and curtailed exports to China is evident.[7]

This carrot-and-stick approach by China constituted a role reversal with Europe, helped by two trends over the same period of time. First, Chinese tourist spending in Europe vastly increased, and there was a marked growth of Chinese direct or financial investment after the global financial crisis broke out in late 2008 and as it turned into the Euro Crisis in 2010. At the European Council meeting of October 24, 2010, it was decided to seek out China and other emerging countries to enlarge the resources of the European Financial

Stability Facility (EFSF), the rescue fund established earlier. In a number of European economies, public assets were up for sale—and some could say this was a "fire sale." China stepped up its bilateral or sub-regional efforts within Europe.[8] It skillfully managed to appear as a lender of last resort in the case of Greece, in fact taking substantial losses on its lending. China also became a much more demanding and difficult partner to the European Union as a whole. And these tactics paid off. European government members no longer received the Dalai Lama and became much less outspoken on other human right issues. The award of the Nobel Peace Prize to the jailed dissident Liu Xiaobo created another test in 2010—one which China would win after six years with a pledge by Norway that it "fully respects China's sovereignty and territorial integrity, attaches high importance to China's core interests and major concerns, will not support actions that undermine them, and will do its best to avoid any future damage to the bilateral relations."[9]

China's broader external policy shift—with strident nationalism, assertiveness, or territorial creep toward neighbors, and the vastly increased footprint of the PLA—constitute the wider background that has shaped the present relationship. China decisively entered a crisis-ridden Europe with prospects of investment and lending, while its assertiveness in foreign policy, its hard stance on human rights, and related issues are at increasing variance with European public opinion.

The list of changes is long. China's "going out" policy for its companies, a tourist outflow that has become a political tool in itself, the growing presence of Chinese actors in central and southern Europe, and convergence with Putin's Russia on many international issues have all made Europeans sit up and take notice of China's expanding footprint. Last but not least, from 2013 onwards, China's new Belt and Road Initiative (BRI) has captured the minds of European business leaders and many political leaders as well. By resurrecting a nineteenth-century European myth, Xi Jinping's China created a perfect echo chamber for Europe's dream of relations with China.

Since 2016, EU-China relations have again entered a new phase. A continually widening EU trade deficit, Chinese overcapacities being exported, aggressive investment strategies, the realities of European division, and stalling dialogues with Beijing have resulted in more defensive EU policies. Europe has thus decided against granting "market economy status" to China, launched new trade defense measures in 2017, and passed an investment screening regulation mechanism in 2018. In the last year of the present commission's mandate, its president Jean-Claude Juncker is calling for a further curb on the requirement for unanimous voting—and that is also the result of China's successful lobbying campaigns with a few member states.

# Coping with China's Drive into Europe

Overall, China's presence and influence in Europe have vastly increased. In spite of multiple sectoral dialogues and meetings,[10] this has taken place more at the level of bilateral relations with member states, and through local initiatives by China's firms and its public diplomacy and propaganda arms, rather than through a top-down process with the European Union. This is not for a lack of attention or realism by the bureaucracies in Brussels. A new EU strategy adopted in 2016 calls on China to make substantial progress in several areas: domestic reform, reciprocity, an investment agreement, rules-based connectivity, contributions to public goods including security, rule of law and human rights, and sustainable development.[11]

But China's delivery on its commitments has been slow, and sometimes non-existent. The annual EU-China High-Level Economic and Trade Dialogue (HED) did not take place in 2011, 2012, and 2014. The sectoral exchanges were to follow the *EU-China 2020 Strategic Agenda for Cooperation* adopted in November 2013.[12] This was indeed a genuine pledge to widen cooperation, putting peace and security as the first "pillar" of the relationship. Overall, it prescribed no fewer than 94 "key initiatives" in areas covering peace and security, prosperity, sustainable development, and people-to-people exchanges. Many of these have not been fulfilled. Those that have led to concrete developments are usually based on strong Chinese interests: among these, scientific innovation and cooperation, fusion energy research (albeit at member state level), 5G broadband networks, visas for diplomats, police cooperation with Europol, and food safety. Space, where cooperation on the Galileo GPS project has stopped because of European concerns, remains an area where China is pushing for more with EU member states. "Connectivity" deserves a special mention because it is the focus of a long and difficult dialogue between the EU and China and has come to be associated with the Belt and Road Initiative. Talks and common projects have been hampered by the lack of agreement on common rules for public projects and financing, whether in Europe or in third countries. While China has reportedly reached a compromise in principle with Japan to implement BRI projects in Southeast Asia, according to OECD rules, the three yearly meetings for the EU-China connectivity platform have to date produced only a vague commitment to "international standards."[13] By contrast, no results have been achieved on a Comprehensive Investment Agreement, save an inconclusive exchange of offers in July 2018 on fisheries and on civil aviation.

Meanwhile, China has expanded its reach into Europe in at least three different areas: (1) investment consisting largely of mergers and acquisitions (M&A) activity; (2) "influence" activities carried out by a wide range of Chinese state and semi-state actors; and (3) outright military presence through China's naval deployments into European waters, sometimes in cooperation with the Russian navy.

China's direct investment in Europe skyrocketed in 2016 to €35 billion (excluding Norway and Switzerland). These figures abated in 2017 and 2018, in part because Beijing prevented "hot money" outflows under the pretext of investment, in part because of the fear of a backlash abroad regarding Chinese purchases. The falloff is not equivalent to the nearly complete stop of Chinese direct investment in the United States. Overall, China has bought or invested in European assets amounting to at least $318 billion from 2008 to the end of 2017. The continent saw roughly 45 percent more China-related activity than did the United States during this period (in dollar terms).[14] More than the total amounts, it is the choices of investment that matter. Among Chinese acquisitions in the EU from 2005 to 2017, 117 cases out of 336 were directly related to "Made in China 2025" targets. Of these, 63 relate to the 2014–2017 period, among which 42 were for 2016 and the first half of 2017.[15] Although 2016 purchases of high-tech German companies, including the widely reported Kuka case, have dominated the news, there is a geographical dispersion of these purchases. The pattern of these high-technology purchases continues, as well as scientific cooperation projects in the sensitive areas. The other area for investment has been in critical infrastructure, from energy distribution and telecom networks to ports. In the last instance, no complete picture exists as yet, because one must add ports that have come under direct management by Chinese companies, those where terminals have been acquired, major acquisitions by Hong Kong companies with obvious common interests with the PRC, and multiple offers of similar acquisition or management control made literally around the whole of Europe, including the Arctic Circle, Iceland, and the Azores. A Chinese company is also the operator of Haifa and a future Ashdod port (Israel), and China's support to the Syrian regime creates the possibility of a Chinese operation in Latakia or Tartus.

These activities continue. In June 2018, a Chinese company bought Linxens, a French chipmaker specializing in security and identity products.[16] In November 2018, Portugal signed a memorandum of understanding with China on BRI that coincides with a promise to develop Sines—the closest European port to Panama, but one that is fairly remote from European economic nodes. Sweden, a member state that had not made up its mind in 2017 regarding an EU investment screening process, has seen all three possibilities outlined above unfolding: three Swedish semiconductor companies were acquired by China in 2018,[17] while in February 2018, negative publicity in the Swedish media caused China to stop the acquisition of Lysekil. In this deep water harbor, proposed mega developments were to be coupled with a new high-speed train line linking Sweden with Norway. It has also turned out that China's earth observation satellite station at Kiruna on the Arctic Circle, inaugurated in late 2016, is in fact a project run by PLA-affiliated personnel. A similar project has been launched in 2017 in Greenland, a Danish dependent territory, and China has signed an agreement with Portugal in late 2018 to create a satellite launch base in the Azores. These moves, along with the issue of 5G and Huawei, are creating a pushback on potential technology phishing and spying activities in a growing number of EU member states.

China's diplomacy of influence at the bilateral and sub-regional levels have also increased. The 16 + 1 process with Central and Eastern Europe (with the exception of Moldavia and Belarus, the latter having been invited by China to one annual summit) has been the most notable.[18] Unquestionably, China has sought to create a regional organization that would provide an alternative to the EU in the region—but it has failed so far in that venture because EU tendering requirements, the attraction of the single market, and residual anti-communism are strong factors. China has not invested that much in these countries (as opposed to commercial loans). In reality, the 16 + 1 process is run along lines that resemble the Shanghai Cooperation Forum (SCO) or the Forum on China-Africa Cooperation (FOCAC)—but with less financial clout. Stung by hardly veiled criticism from some Central and East European think tanks, Beijing has apparently thought of downgrading the forum,[19] but so far Beijing is sticking to its plans. The 16 + 1—created in 2012—predates Xi Jinping's BRI, but both narratives tend to merge, so that a pullback from the 16 + 1 would also reflect on the BRI. China seems to have learned the lesson. After hyping up a potential 5 + 1 format with Nordic Europe, and starting a forum with six southern Europe member states in 2013 and 2015 (ostensibly on maritime cooperation), Beijing now seems to pull back and deal at the bilateral level.

Beyond these official efforts, China's united front, propaganda, and media affiliates are expanding their influence channels into Europe. As of the end of 2018, there are around 173 Confucius Institutes operating in Europe—more than in the Americas (161) or Asia (118).[20] Chinese news outlets pay to provide content to local media. In Western Europe, this involves paid supplements. For example, the *China Daily*, the official English-language newspaper, gets its "China Watch" inserts placed in newspapers all over the world. Such publications in Europe include *Le Soir* and *De Standaard* in Belgium, *Zemia* in Bulgaria, *Le Figaro* and *Le Monde* in France, *Handelsblatt* in Germany, *El País* in Spain, and the *Daily Telegraph* and *Guardian* in the UK. In other agreements, the official Xinhua News Agency acts as a news content provider—as other press agencies would do—and these are more confusing because the origin of the content is less visible, if it is visible at all. In France, China Radio International (CRI) now provides content on China's economy to BFM, the 24-hour news channel that is increasingly emerging as the French version of Fox News.[21] In Greece, the Athens Press Agency has a content agreement with Xinhua, while the Maltese National Broadcaster has one with CGTN (the successor name to CCTV). At a Silk Road Forum hosted by the Athens-Macedonian News Agency, a number of news agencies and press outlets from CEE and Mediterranean counties, as well as Turkey and Russia, pledged mutual cooperation including news coverage and staff exchanges.[22]

China's influence activities also include a good deal of outreach to political figures. Contentious cases involving acting heads of government include Viktor Orbán, prime minister of Hungary, and Miloš Zeman, president of the Czech Republic. But just as impressive is the invitation process and courtship of former prime ministers or chancellors in France, Germany, and the UK, and the enlisting of former high civil servants on boards of Chinese companies (which is impossible in the other direction). The practice is not unique to China, but it is leading to interrogations about conflicts of interest and rules for avoidance at the EU and member states levels.

China's advance into Europe also has a hard power edge. There is growing involvement between China and Russia on joint naval exercises and increased military cooperation in European waters. "Joint Sea" maneuvers occurred in the eastern Mediterranean in 2015. After the ruling from The Hague's Maritime Arbitration Panel went against China in July 2016, the two countries held their second "Joint Sea" maneuvers in the South China Sea. And in July 2017, they conducted the same exercises in the Baltic Sea. China placed this in a wider context of ship visits to EU member states: three Chinese ships undertook a long circumnavigation of Europe that year. In the Mediterranean, they conducted live fire exercises, a joint exercise with the Italian navy in the Tyrrhenian Sea, and they visited the Greek port of Piraeus, as well as a Romanian port in the Black Sea. The flotilla went on through the Atlantic to join the Russian Navy in the Baltic, later making port calls in Finland, Latvia, and the UK. In October 2018, the PLAN and the EU Naval Force in the Gulf of Aden (set up to counter piracy) together staged a rescue-at-sea exercise from China's military base in Djibouti.

## Coordinating European Responses

Strikingly, the four types of increased presence by China described above mostly happen at the level of relations with, and inside, member states—as opposed to EU-wide developments. By late 2016, China's multifaceted advances into European hearts and wallets began to face new obstacles. China's leaders had essentially snubbed those avenues of discussion with the European Union that might be disadvantageous to them—such as the High-Level Macroeconomic

Dialogue, and several sessions of the annual EU-China Dialogue on Human Rights. Talks for a bilateral investment treaty were stalling. From 2012, the EU was particularly aware that a new initiative by China—the 16 + 1 summit format with Central and East European countries, of which five were not EU member states—might be a Trojan horse to defeat European unity. Most of all, the deadline for the transition in China's accession to the WTO was looming at the end of 2016. The EU, unlike some other partners that dealt with these issues by an administrative regulatory process, had cornered itself with a legal framework: it had to make a legal determination, one way or another.

To this one should add more recent distractions: Brexit, the illiberal drift of two and perhaps more EU member states away from common founding principles of the European Union, and the election of an American president who challenges several international institutions and threatens to break away from rules for free trade. These three trends make it more difficult for Europe to be sure of full support for any long-term strategy toward China. The climate of rising competition and confrontation in China-US relations since 2018 has opened some speculation of a potential "triangle," where China and Europe would identify converging views to "rescue" multilateral institutions. Climate and environmental issues are the main global issues on which the European Union seeks to find areas of convergence, with attempts at joint discussion of needed WTO reforms coming more recently. China itself is now quietly encouraging these views, without providing much fuel for them.

In this context, it may seem miraculous that the European Union has increased its cohesion on essential issues it faces with China: the trade balance and dumping of goods on European markets, reciprocity on public procurement, investment screening as a mean to protect technology phishing, and sovereignty over critical infrastructures.

That same cohesion is much less evident on geopolitical issues and values in the relationship. Europe has splintered over the South China Sea, and again over human rights in China. It is no accident that the former geo-economic issues are dealt with by qualified majority voting in the European Union, while many issues of Common Foreign and Security Policy (CFSP) require unanimity voting, resulting in lowest-common-denominator decisions. It does not have to be that way. In fact, the Lisbon Treaty included a "bridging clause" that allows the Council to decide on qualified majority voting (QMV) in any CFSP matter.[23]

That China-related issues have come closer to the top of the European agenda is a tribute to China's far-reaching economic and political projection abroad. It is that projection which explains the greater efforts by many member states to reach common views and achieve a coordinated approach to China.

Conflicting trends are therefore shaping Europe-China relations. China's trade surplus with the EU had exceeded €180 billion in 2015,[24] and the steel production glut from China provided a graphic and socially meaningful illustration of this (see Figure 12.1).

China's 2016 corporate acquisition drive in Germany, often involving key technologies, turned around the government and part of the business community of Europe's leading economy. For its part, China decided to hang on to its claim that "market economy status" was a foregone conclusion, to which the EU was legally bound by China's accession protocol to the WTO. Instead, Europe changed course and circumvented the issue with new criteria for anti-dumping applying to non-market economies and more efficient implementation of trade remedies. The issue of reciprocity entered the EU lexicon on Chinese public markets and economic sectors before it became American policy. The EU also set about to create an EU-wide investment screening process. An earlier attempt had failed in 2013, but this time the Commission's proposal was finally adopted in December 2018.

China's response so far has been underwhelming. It has resorted to WTO arbitration against the EU on the issue of market economy status, narrowed down to anti-dumping criteria. For two years in a row—2016 and 2017—there were no joint resolutions at the annual EU-China Summit. But China's leaders have also been caught unprepared for the policy shift toward China by Donald Trump and his administration. At the June 2017 EU-China Summit, China's refusal to sign long-prepared joint statements was motivated on the surface by

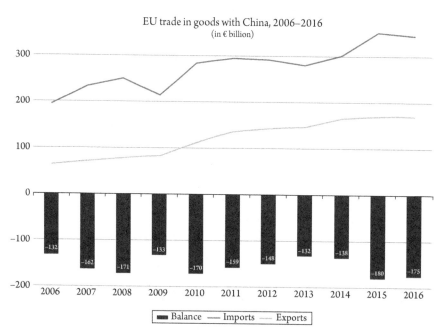

*Figure 12.1* EU Trade in Goods with China, 2006–2016

the EU's request that China withdraw its legal recourse to the WTO on market economy status. But by taking this position, China also refused to take a common stance with Europe on climate issues—thus staying neutral to the Trump administration's rejection of the Paris COP-21 agreement.

In that time span, China's leadership was hoping to reach a compromise with the Trump administration over trade. That hope for a quick fix to the US-China relationship has disappeared since. China simultaneously faces a hardening of America's China policy on several fronts, and increasingly common views among the EU, Japan, and the United States on the transfer of critical technologies and Chinese investment in sensitive sectors. Simultaneously, China has largely lost the benefit of the United Kingdom's frequent support on trade and investment issues inside the EU. The Brexit vote has abridged the "golden era" of relations and brought a government that is, as of now, more reactive to the security challenges from China.

The European doubts over further withdrawals of the Trump administration from international commitments and institutions, and the very real Chinese anxiety over the new US trade policy and sanctions, have brought more conciliatory words from both China and the EU. The July 2018 EU-China summit ended with a joint statement that lists convergences: among these, "commitment to multilateralism," "commitment to the continued, full and effective implementation of the JCPOA," support for a two-state solution concerning the Palestinian problem, "resisting protectionism and unilateralism," and an annual plan to further promote infrastructure connectivity between the EU and China—all of which could also be read as criticism of current American positions. This is even more pronounced on climate and energy issues, where there is recognition of the Paris Agreement as an "historic achievement." The EU not only recommitted to support funding of $100 billion per year from developed to developing economies for climate finance, but also promised to push for an increase in the size of the transfer by 2025. The joint statement appeared to make important European concessions, while China made commitments for the future in several areas. The word "reciprocity," for instance, was absent from the statement. In a very bland fashion, the text recognized both China's and the EU's "respect for the maritime order and international law."[25] The summit also reconfirmed cooperation in research and innovation, an important issue since the EU's Horizon program has been described as being utilized primarily by China to access European scientific development.

China, for its part, committed once more to working toward joining the General Procurement Agreement, and to conclude, possibly by the end of the year, an agreement on geographical indications of origin. It also converged on support for "the stabilization of Libya." In a later speech to the European Parliament, the EU's High Representative/Vice President Federica Mogherini went very far in acknowledging renewed engagement by China with the EU: "I have seen in these last six, seven months a very strong engagement from the Chinese side, and also from the European side *that I have been able to channel* [emphasis added] in working more and more in the multilateral framework, in the multilateral system on global issues, in general terms."[26]

The question is, do these words portend real and significant concessions by China, justifying a change of strategy by the EU on the important trade and economic issues? The EU appears to be working simultaneously on two fronts. Only days after the July EU-China summit, Jean-Claude Juncker and Donald Trump met and issued a joint statement that aimed, inter alia, at reciprocal and fairer trade, at working on WTO reform with like-minded partners, and addressing "unfair trading practices, including intellectual property theft, forced technology transfer, industrial subsidies, distortions created by state owned enterprises, and overcapacity."[27]

As the year 2018 drew to a close, there was, once more, no tangible delivery by China on its earlier and, in some cases, often repeated commitments. Instead, China has made an unexpected opening to foreign companies, and this has benefited some European firms. Thus, it announced that the insurance and automotive sector would be open, within three to five years, to 100 percent ownership of China-based subsidiaries by foreign firms. Whatever the actual value of this opening—said by some to be targeted at sectors where Chinese companies have already gained the upper hand on the domestic market—some European firms, predominantly German or French, seem to have been the beneficiaries: BMW, BASF, Allianz, Axa, and BNPP have been able to avail themselves of this opening (as well as Exxon). Significant as they are for individual firms, these openings are largely taken as deal-making rather than a more structured opening. At the end of the year, China's NDRC made good on an old promise—it finally issued a "negative list" for foreign investment, a development sought both by American and European partners.

Meanwhile, China's Ministry of Foreign Affairs issued a third policy paper on the European Union (previous documents were published in 2003 and 2014). The text contained some changes in content and form. Europe's "strong overall strength" was not placed in the context of its economy. The policy paper also cited the dialogue with Central and Eastern European countries (CEE) as an example of "win-win cooperation" and promised to deal with the EU and UK "in parallel" after Brexit. Further, "mutual respect" now preceded "equality" in the list of overriding principles for the relationship. Beyond the reiteration of the One China principle, the Tibet issue, and even more precise limits on relations with Taiwan, it added Hong Kong and East Turkestan as no-go zones for European diplomacy. It no longer placed human rights issues as differences in values. It hoped that member states would protect Chinese nationals, asking also these to play a role as a bridge. It listed think tank exchanges as a factor in deepening cooperation, as well as media exchanges in the context of a Belt and Road News Network. Finally, it did not repeat some commitments that had been made in the July 2018 EU-China summit, such as joining the GPA and signing an agreement on indications of geographic origin. The text remained surprisingly unconcerned with issues of high technology, whether on investment or transfer, by noting casually that "the EU should ease its high-tech export control on China" (export controls at present exist at the EU level only for weapons). More broadly, the text expressed "hopes that the EU will keep its investment market open, reduce and eliminate investment hurdles and discriminatory barriers." But the real answer to the new EU investment screening regulation lies in Article 37 of the newly planned Foreign Investment Law, "where any country or region takes discriminatory prohibitive, restrictive, or other similar measures against the People's Republic of China with respect to investment, the People's Republic of China may take corresponding measures against such country or region based on the actual circumstances."[28] China does not recognize reciprocity in the negotiating process but knows well how to practice it outside of that process. The use of the term "region" can only apply to the European Union and matches its use in China's policy paper on Europe.

A provisional conclusion is therefore that China—and in fact both sides—are making efforts to find common language, especially on global issues and multilateral processes where they can converge in principle. This is in no small way dictated by the uneasiness on the European side with the Trump administration retreats from liberal internationalism and multilateralism. But, for China, it is even more a side-effect of being confronted by trade reprisals from the United States and the risk of seeing a united front form against China on issues of investment and technology transfer. It remains very hard to identify new policies from China that would match its more engaging approach to the European Union— so much so that the most important accusation from Europeans is about the gap between China's words and deeds.

## Contradictory Visions of Europe

The above findings lead to two possible conclusions. One is that, in classic united front rhetoric, China's party-state and its foreign affairs mouthpiece dissemble on their views of Europe: they pay token respect to European integration (a term that is preferred to that of unity) but they play upon the diverse interests of member states. There is of course ample justification for holding this view. Yet the insistence of China's experts of European affairs, and its official policy papers, that China values European integration, coupled with the obvious attraction of a single market that is the largest in the world to this day, rings true, as reflected in the redirection of China's direct investment toward Europe in recent years. China's leaders like to remind their counterparts that their many visits to Europe—including by Xi Jinping to the European Commission and Council in 2014, the first ever by a Chinese head of state—are an indication of their prioritizing Europe.

There may be therefore another conclusion. Although China has invested quite a bit in the knowledge of European affairs, including at universities and think tanks, this is a very small subset of China's expert community, and only a small sliver of its wider society. There were very dark views from China's economic press during the Euro crisis, some of it merely echoing Euroscepticism. Europe was in trouble—sometimes, said by the world's top financial newspapers, to be on the verge of disintegration. If China's EU experts, a very small subset of China's elites, mostly maintained the view that market integration and EU institutions retained their strength, China's business circles did not hold the same view, as demonstrated by reporting from leading financial newspapers.[29] Similarly, a study based on a 2010 opinion poll found that the more educated business elites were also more skeptical about EU-China relations.[30]

While Europe is China's No. 1 tourist destination, the weight that Chinese opinion gives to Europe is far more limited. A recent opinion poll of the global views from Chinese youth, as reported by the *Global Times*, finds that the bilateral relationship with the greatest import to China is with the United States, chosen by 63.5 percent of respondents, followed by Russia, with 37.6 percent, and Europe with only 12.7 percent. This is a marked difference with a reliable 2010 survey that had consistently shown the EU ahead of Russia in terms of influence on global affairs.[31] Even more tellingly, among thirteen global events that "left the greatest impression" in 2018, Europe came last with 13.3 percent.[32] In a way, this is not surprising, because Europe is not, and has never been, viewed as a fully fledged strategic actor in PRC political culture. It was always an intermediary in a world between superpowers.

A recent study of Chinese views on Europe reinforces this conclusion,[33] but with unexpected policy conclusions. The authors quite rightly point out that the source of European strength and unity can only be found internally—essentially China, as other major partners, considers Europe from a realist perspective. But this soon veers into Europessimist conclusions, and a catalogue from China's wish list about Europe. Europe should adopt only policies that are "considered constructive by the Chinese leadership." It argues that the 2017 rejection by Greece of a European statement criticizing China's human rights record "is not bereft of reason." To propose curtailing criticism of China's human rights practices is to ignore that European democracy is the area that gets the highest support from Chinese public opinion: in 2010, 66 percent of elites polled, 55 percent of "ordinary people" answered that they liked "European ideas about democracy," with only 5.8 percent and 12.2 percent expressing a dislike.[34] Reducing the promotion of democratic and human rights values amounts to downgrading a long-term asset for Europe. More to the point, the authors explain—again, quite rightly—that reciprocity is more a process than a principle; but the story of the past years' engagement with China precisely demonstrates that China has often eluded or stymied this process.

# Conclusion

After forty years of "reform and opening up" by China, and its rise as the world's second economy, the terms for the relationship between Europe and China have been turned around. This is in spite of some facts that relativize China's actual might. The integrated European economy is the largest in the world, and it will remain the second largest after Brexit. It maintains a current account surplus and an overall positive trade balance—but this may also be at the expense of faster growth. The EU firms' invested capital in China still exceeds China's FDI into Europe—but this is true of total stocks, not current flows, and does not take into account "gray" Chinese capital creeping into Europe. Europe has weathered the Euro crisis, and China's filibustering tactics in negotiations have, in fact, brought a realist backlash in the EU institutions and many of the member states. Strikingly, the moderation or abstention by many member states on the issue of human rights after the 2008–2010 standoffs on Tibet and Liu Xiaobo's Nobel Prize have not resulted in more flexibility by China on other issues. Nor has the 16 + 1 summit process brought more investment to Central and Eastern Europe.

What the relationship has come to is a *crisis of mutual expectations*. Europeans, and especially the European Union as a negotiating bloc, expected increasing reforms as China's economy rose, and in fact Europe has repeatedly been promised major changes (from monetary policies to agreements on issues ranging from investment to public procurement). These changes have not come, nor has China been forthcoming so far on rules and norms for third-party cooperation, even in the EU's closest neighborhood, the Balkan accession candidates to the EU. Instead, China has been mounting a strategy of aggressive investment into Europe's high technology and infrastructure sectors, which are mostly open. Since China's divergent practices and advocacy on values such as human rights have also intensified, the main areas of attraction remaining are the China market and financial flows into Europe—M&A activity, real estate, tourism, and even so-called "golden visas." This is significant for some Europeans, hardly so for a bloc with a unified policy.

Official Chinese disappointments also exist, of course. The arms embargo and what China calls resulting restrictions to high-technology transfers have long been sore points, as is Europe's refusal to accept China in the WTO as a full "market economy." To this one should add complaints about European interference over human rights and increasing concerns about Europe's future openness to Chinese investment. But China's pattern of negotiation with the EU is not based on mutual compromise. It is rather a push-and-shove strategy: get what you can and claim the rest, in the belief that the other side will give in, sooner or later. In addition, the list of topics on which China requires acquiescence or silence is huge: from Taiwan and Tibet to Xinjiang, Chinese Islam, human rights, Hong Kong, South China Sea, and increasingly obstacles in the way of its economy's international expansion. If a requirement one hears from high-placed Chinese sources is "to accept the fact you are dealing with the Chinese Communist Party,"[35] the intensified and broadened range of its ambitions make compromise a hard goal to reach on both sides.

# Notes

1. Wen Jiabao, Speech at the EU-China Trade and Investment Forum, Brussels, May 6, 2004, http://www.chinamission.be/eng/zt/t101949.htm.
2. For a surveys of the relationship see Harish Kapur, *Distant Neighbors: China and Europe* (Geneva: Pinter Publishers, 1990); David Shambaugh, *China and Europe: 1949–1995* (London: SOAS Contemporary China Institute, 1996); David Shambaugh, Eberhard Sandschneider, and Zhou Hong, eds., *China-Europe Relations: Perceptions, Policies, and Prospects* (London: Routledge, 2008); and Nicola Casarini, *Remaking Global Order: The Evolution of Europe-China Relations and Its Implications for East Asia and the United States* (Oxford: Oxford University Press, 2009).
3. For an EEC internal account of relations in the early years, see Memo to the EEC-China Joint Committee, January 9, 2017, unsigned, available at http://aei.pitt.edu/66105/1/EEC-CHINA_JOINT_COMMITTEE.pdf.
4. Permanent Mission of the PRC to the UN office at Geneva, "China and the Human Rights Mechanism," April 23, 2004, available at http://www.china-un.ch/eng/rqrd/jblc/t85088.htm.
5. Contained in Annex II of Presidency Conclusions, European Council, Madrid, June 26 and 27, 1989, 25, available at https://www.iss.europa.eu/sites/default/files/EUISSFiles/CP_149_Asia.pdf.
6. For an up-to-date assessment of EU arms sales and dual use transfers to China, see Mathieu Duchatel, "Intangible Technology Transfers in EU-China Relations," in *Guns, Engines, and Turbines: The EU's Hard Power in Asia*, edited by Eva Pejsova, EUISS, Chaillot Paper no. 149 (November 2018), 33–42.
7. Andreas Fuchs and Nils-Hendrik Klan, "Paying a Visit: The Effect of the Dalai-Lama on International Trade," *Journal of International Economics* 91 (2013): 164–177.
8. See Philippe Le Corre and Alain Sepulchre, *China's Offensive in Europe* (Washington, DC: Brookings Institution Press, 2016).
9. Statement of China and Norway on Normalization of Bilateral Relations, December 19, 2016, available at http://www.xinhuanet.com/english/2016-12/19/c_135917147.htm.
10. For an organizational chart of these dialogues, as of November 2015, see: https://eeas.europa.eu/sites/eeas/files/2015_november_eu-china_dialogue_architecture.jpg.

11. *Elements for a New EU Strategy on China*, JOIN (2016) 30 final, European Commission, 22 June 2016, available at http://eeas.europa.eu/archives/docs/china/docs/joint_ communication_to_the_european_parliament_and_the_council_-_elements_for_a_ new_eu_strategy_on_china.pdf.

12. European External Action Service, "EU-China 2020 Strategic Agenda for Cooperation," available at http://eeas.europa.eu/archives/docs/china/docs/eu-china_2020_strategic_ agenda_en.pdf.

13. See the minutes for the third meeting, July 1617, 2018, available at https://ec.europa.eu/ transport/sites/transport/files/2018-07-13-chairs-meeting.pdf.

14. Bloomberg, "How China Is Buying Its Way into Europe," April 23, 2018, available at https://www.bloomberg.com/graphics/2018-china-business-in-europe/?utm_ medium=email&utm_source=newsletter&utm_term=181222&utm_campaign=bop.

15. ECFR EU-China Power Audit Key Deals, 2005–2017, available at https://www.ecfr.eu/ page/-/Key_deals_1.pdf.

16. "China's Unigroup Buys French Chipmaker Linxens for \$2.6bn.," *Financial Times*, June 25, 2018, https://www.ft.com/content/f919b032-8fe5-11e8-b639-7680cedcc421.

17. https://www.svd.se/staten-salde-spjutspetsbolag-till-kina--trots-militara-kopplingar.

18. See Weiqing Song, ed., *China's Relations with Central and Eastern Europe: From "Old Comrades" to New Partners* (London: Routledge, 2017).

19. Author interviews in Beijing, September 2017.

20. "Confucius Institutes and Confucius Classrooms," Confucius Institutes headquarters (Hanban), available at: http://english.hanban.org.

21. http://www.lettreaudiovisuel.com/partenariat-entre-radio-chine-internationale-et-bfm-business/.

22. François Godement and Abigael Vasselier, *China at the Gates—A New EU-China Power Audit*, European Council on Foreign Relations (2017), available at https://www.ecfr.eu/page/-/ China_Power_Audit.pdf.

23. See Wanda Troszczynska-Van Gederen, The Lisbon Treaty's provisions on CFSP/CSDP— State of Implementation, 9–10, Directorate General for External Policies Policy Department, DG EXPO/B/PolDep/Note/2015_263 EN, October 2015, European Parliament, available at http://www.europarl.europa.eu/RegData/etudes/IDAN/2015/570446/EXPO_ IDA(2015)570446_EN.pdf.

24. Or \$200 billion in 2015 average annual exchange rate.

25. Joint Statement of the 20th EU-China Summit, Brussels, July 17, 2018, available at https:// eeas.europa.eu/delegations/china_en/48424/Joint%20statement%20of%20the%20 20th%20EU-China%20Summit.

26. Speech by Federica Mogherini, Strasbourg, September 11, 2018, available at https://eeas. europa.eu/headquarters/headquarters-homepage/50337/speech-hrvp-mogherini-plenary-session-european-parliament-state-eu-china-relations_en.

27. July 25, 2018, EU-US Joint Statement on Trade, available at https://www.marketwatch.com/ story/text-of-joint-us-eu-statement-on-trade-2018-07-25.

28. Unofficial translation of Foreign Investment Law of the People's Republic of China (Draft), China Law Translate, December 26, 2018, available at: http://www.fdi.gov.cn/1800000121_ 39_4872_0_7.html.

29. François Godement, "La presse chinoise est euro-pessimiste," China Analysis no. 28, March– April 2010, 14–17, available at https://centreasia.hypotheses.org/files/2017/05/China_ Analysis_no_28.pdf.

30. Lisheng Dong, "Chinese Perceptions of the European Union," *Journal of Contemporary China* 23, no. 88 (2014): 756–779.

31. Ibid., 766.

32. *Huangqiu Shibao* (Global Times), December 28, 2018, available at http://world.huanqiu. com/exclusive/2018-12/13915204.html.

33. V. K. L. Chang and F. N. Pieke, "Europe's Engagement with China: Shifting Chinese Views of the EU and the EU-China relationship," *Asia Europe Journal* 16 (2018): 317.

34. Dong, "Chinese Perceptions of the European Union," 764.

35. Comment by a former Chinese government official, Beijing, December 2018.

# 13

# China's Relations with Asia

MICHAEL YAHUDA

China's relations with the countries of Asia are of crucial importance in shaping the development of the country as well as in determining much of the character of China's relationship with the world.

The chapter will first consider China's relationships with Asia as a whole since the end of the Cold War, when China replaced the United States and Japan as the main trading partner of nearly all the Asian countries and when it became a maritime power of major significance in the region and beyond. Second, the analysis will focus more closely on developments during the period since Xi Jinping came to power in 2012. Third, the chapter will assess the significance of China's relations with each of the Asian sub-regions in turn.

## An Overview

There is no part of Asia today that is not under the influence of China. China is not only the most important trading partner of nearly all Asian countries, but Asian economies are also tied to China in complex production chains involving multinational companies and state-owned industries. In fact, most of them are caught up in asymmetrical economic interdependencies with their huge neighboring country. The gap in spending on the military is so significant that China's expenditure in 2017 of $228 billion exceeded the total of *all* the other Asian countries *combined*. From a Chinese perspective, account must also be taken of the military spending of its strategic competitor, the United States, which amounted to $610 billion the same year.[1] The question of how China has used its military preponderance over its neighbors, some of whom are allies and partners of the United States, will be considered later.

The Chinese, however, do not have a tradition of thinking about Asia as a coherent geopolitical concept. Traditionally, they have thought in terms of the

Michael Yahuda, *China's Relations with Asia* In: *China and the World.* Edited by: David Shambaugh, Oxford University Press (2020). © Oxford University Press
DOI: 10.1093/oso/9780190062316.003.0013

world around them as "all under Heaven" under the authority of their emperor, "the Son of Heaven," to whom all other rulers were subordinate. The Chinese also claimed that their dealings with others were based on a morality of peace and benevolence. However, using Chinese dynastic sources, scholars in the West have exposed these claims to be self-serving myths.[2] Yet contemporary Chinese scholars and leaders continually repeat the assertion that the Chinese have never invaded others. In an address to the United Nations, Xi Jinping claimed: "For several millennia, peace has been in the blood of us Chinese and a part of our DNA."[3] Not surprisingly, such claims have not gone down well with many of China's neighbors in the current era, who can point to many historical examples of attacks and invasions by their overbearing giant neighbor.

These conflicting images of China have tended to undermine the trust of neighboring countries. Moreover, the recent revival of the concept of "all under Heaven" (天下) as a vision of harmonious global unity in contrast to the Westphalian system of separate states has not found much support in Asia because of the implication that it would require Chinese centrality.

China's relations in Asia are also influenced by the legacy of the Cold War. On the positive side is China's adherence to the "Five Principles of Peaceful Coexistence" (especially, with their emphasis on the legitimacy of different systems of state governance and the opposition to interference in the domestic affairs of other states).[4] On the negative side is China's history in the Mao era of supporting revolutionary insurgencies against some of its neighboring governments. Although that aspect of interference in other states has receded, it has been replaced in recent years by attempts to promote leaders and regimes judged to be friendly. There also continues to be active materiel support for rebellious forces in Myanmar and in Northeast India.[5]

The main breakthrough in relations with Asian countries followed the Nixon opening to China in 1972. Not only did Japan and most of the ASEAN states open diplomatic relations, but they and the Overseas Chinese contributed greatly to the beginnings of the modernization of the Chinese economy in the late 1970s and continued to do so through the 1980s. Moreover, the ASEAN countries and especially Thailand played a crucial role in opposing Vietnam's invasion of Cambodia in 1989 and in supporting the subsequent Chinese attack on Vietnam, which demonstrated support for China's strategic goal of constraining Vietnam.[6]

## Since the End of the Cold War

After the dissolution of the Soviet Union in December 1991, China no longer faced even the prospect of an attack from the north and it had the strategic dispensation to shift the focus of its economic and military attention to its maritime periphery, where the prospects for its modernization lay. In addition, the Chinese now had the opportunity to cultivate relations with the entire Asian region, which held the key to their long-held aspiration to emerge as the major power in the region, to which their history and size made them feel entitled. However, China's rulers were to find that the opportunities of cultivating Asian countries were to clash with the nationalist aims of gaining control of what they claimed were sovereign territories, which were also claimed by other states. Additionally, China would find difficulties in promoting their own interests in ways that were congruent with those of their neighbors.

At first, the main focus of China's leaders, especially under the leadership of Deng Xiaoping, was maintaining Communist Party rule and the promotion of rapid economic development. Given the need to focus on developing the economy with the assistance of the outside world, Deng Xiaoping advised the other leaders and his successors to "keep a low profile and bide your time, while also getting something accomplished" (*taoguang yanghui yousuo zuowei*, 韬光养晦有所作为; literally to "hide one's brightness but do some things").

This was generally understood to avoid seeking prominence, while quietly improving China's position. But events intervened that threatened to throw the invitation to quietism off course. However, the ramifications of these events tended raise the strategic value of Asia in Chinese estimations. It was only the repercussions of the Tiananmen massacre of June 4, 1989, that alerted China's leaders to the crucial role that the Asian countries as a whole could play in averting the international isolation of China. Apart from Japan, Australia, and New Zealand, Asian countries did not join the West's condemnation, and it was Japan that pressed the others to scale down the sanctions. The significance of the Asian neighbors continued to be apparent after the collapse of the Eastern European states later that year, when Indonesia and Singapore recognized the PRC in 1990. Then, after the dissolution of the Soviet Union in December 1991, the emperor of Japan paid a first-ever visit to China in 1992.

China then found that the countries of Southeast Asia could be diplomatically useful to China in the wake of its failure to intimidate Taiwan in the lead-up to the island's first presidential elections in 1996. It was at that point that the Chinese found that the Asian countries to the south could be useful as a diplomatic counter to what was seen as the exercise of US soft and hard power. Beijing then put a stop to the nationalist policy of occupying islets in the South China Sea, as shown in 1988 by forcefully displacing the Vietnamese from several outcrops and in 1995 by stealthily occupying Mischief Reef in the Exclusive Economic Zone of the Philippines. Instead, in 1996 and 1997 it promoted its "New Security Policy" of peaceful consultation and cooperation. The Asian financial crisis later that year provided China with an opportunity to present itself as a responsible and benevolent power by refusing to devalue its currency, as others in the sub-region had done. China's diplomatic achievement can be seen from the extensive praise it received from its southern neighbors and President Clinton, even though China had acted very much in accordance with its financial and trade interests and had contributed at best $4 billion to the recovery as compared with Japan's $40 billion.[7]

Building on that, China went on what has been called a "charm offensive" for the following decade (1997–2008).[8] Its then premier, Zhu Rongji, declared at an ASEAN meeting in November 1999, "China cannot develop without East Asia, neither can East Asia develop without China." The following year he initiated an FTA with ASEAN (the first country to do so), which came into effect in 2002. Trade grew rapidly from $43 billion in 2002 to $231 billion in 2008 and then to $515 billion in 2017 (according to Chinese Customs statistics), despite the souring of political relations beginning in 2008.

The cumulative effect of America's prolonged wars in the greater Middle East and the global financial crisis of 2008 convinced the Chinese that America was in real decline. The Chinese economy, by contrast, had prospered and its military had modernized to the extent that it could prevail against its neighbors in the "near seas" (近海). Imbued with a strong sense of national entitlement to the islets and their associated maritime areas within the well-known "nine-dashed line" in the South China Sea (SCS), the Chinese became far more assertive in advancing their claims from 2008 onwards. Backed by militarily superior coast guard ships, Chinese fishing fleets operated in waters claimed by other littoral states and used low-scale force to ward off local challenges. Matters came to a head at an ASEAN meeting in Hanoi in July 2010. In response to the urgent requests of ASEAN governments, the US secretary of state, Hillary Clinton, claimed an American national interest in the SCS, demanded that the dispute be settled peacefully, and offered her services to help reach a multilateral agreement. Although the Chinese had agreed in 2002 to a Declaration of Conduct in the SCS between itself and ASEAN as a whole, times had changed and China now insisted that matters of sovereignty and questions of joint production had to be settled only on a bilateral basis between China and the separate other claimant states. In fact, the Chinese side was furious with Clinton, accusing her of interference, and an angry Chinese foreign minister, looking directly at his Singaporean equivalent, declared "China is a big country and other countries are small. And that is a fact."[9]

China began to use its superior weight to exploit divisions within ASEAN in order to prevent the body from making statements it regarded as objectionable. In 2012, Cambodia, at China's behest, prevented ASEAN for the first time from issuing an annual statement. In that year China also reneged on an agreement with the Philippines to withdraw its military vessels from Scarborough Shoal (within the Filipino Economic Exclusion Zone) that had been brokered by the United States. The Obama administration refrained from imposing any cost on the Chinese side. Meanwhile, China had used its economic heft to "punish" Japan and the Philippines for displeasing it by denying the former supplies of scarce rare earth minerals and the latter by causing imported bananas to rot in port on spurious grounds.

China had increasingly come to be seen in the region in a negative light, using its economic and military power to pursue its own narrow interests and paying no attention to environmental and local concerns, despite espousing mellifluous words

## The Impact of Xi Jinping

Xi Jinping's assumption of leadership in 2012 took place amid the purge of a major aspirant to the leadership (Bo Xilai). Xi immediately launched a prolonged campaign against corruption in the Party, which strengthened his personal leadership by purging potential opponents and increasing his popularity. He expanded the number of the Party Leading Small Groups (领导小组), which set the full range of policy agendas for the Politburo—and Xi chaired all of them, giving rise to the quip that he was "Chairman of Everything." He elevated the governing role of the Party by enhancing the leadership roles of Party cells in organizations throughout China, including all enterprises (whether state-owned, private, or even foreign-owned). Western influence was drastically reduced, especially from educational institutions. Lawyers and advocates of human rights were harassed and persecuted even more than before. The armed forces were also brought under his tight control, with numerous senior generals, high-ranking officers, and commanders purged on the grounds of corruption.

From the outset Xi Jinping assumed command of all the dimensions of China's foreign relations—including strategy, policymaking, diplomacy, economics, trade, military, ideology, propaganda, and so on. Arguably, many of these matters needed more centralization and better coordination as a dispersal of authority had taken place under the collective leadership of the previous leader, Hu Jintao. For example, operations in the SCS were conducted by five separate regional and functional organizations, each pursuing its own interests. Yet it was becoming increasingly important that policy and actions be subject to a single authority. At stake was coordinating various competing agendas such as satisfying China's nationalist goal of consolidating its sovereignty over its claims in the SCS, while preventing a united resistance by the other claimants.

## "The Chinese Dream"

One of Xi Jinping's first acts on becoming leader was to take his fellow members of the Politburo Standing Committee to the newly refurbished National Museum in Beijing, to see an exhibition that started with illustrations of China's past greatness as a civilization and a global power that was then brought down and humiliated by outside powers for a hundred years until, under the leadership of Mao Zedong and the Chinese Communist Party, the Chinese state was established anew in 1949. Since then, the exhibit showed how through many tribulations the Chinese people had rebuilt the economy and China's international standing. On November 29, 2012, he announced to his colleagues the goal of realizing "the Chinese Dream" of the "great rejuvenation of the Chinese nation"—the slogan used by Chinese nationalists including previous communist leaders for more than 100 years. Despite the abstract character of the "dream," Xi developed more specific content over the next five years. Xi pointed to the "twin centenaries" (2021 of the founding of the Party and 2049 of the founding of the PRC) as targets for achieving particular levels of economic and social success. By May 2017, Xi Jinping summarized his (or what he presented as China's) aspirations for a new international order: "We should foster a new type of international relations featuring 'win-win cooperation,' and we should forge a partnership of dialogue with no confrontation, and a partnership of friendship rather than alliance. All countries should respect each other's sovereignty, dignity and territorial integrity; respect each other's development path and its social systems, and respect each other's core interests and major concerns. . . . What we hope to create is a big family of harmonious coexistence."[10]

It should be noted that Xi's presentation constituted, in effect, a rejection of the basis for the American strategic position in Asia. He explicitly rejected alliances, which have been central to the American provision of the public goods of security, trade, and other economic exchanges in the Asia-Pacific, and from which all member states have benefited (none more than China). By demanding "respect" for "core interests," Xi also required all other states contesting China's claims to sovereignty to cede to China's asserted sovereign control. To be sure, the government's official position is that such disputes should be settled by bilateral negotiations, but given that China asserts that its claims in the SCS, for example, are "indisputable," and given the huge disparity between China's economic and military power and those of its Southeast Asian neighbors, it is not difficult to envision whose "core interest" would be likely to prevail.

## Belt and Road Conundrums

Perhaps the most significant of Xi Jinping's innovation in foreign relations has been his project of "One Belt, One Road" (一带一路), or as it has come to be called, his "Belt and Road Initiative" (BRI), first announced in 2013. It has been presented as the "New Silk Road" and it is designed to establish extensive connections between China and the rest of the world by a series of road, rail, and sea links across Asia to Europe, including the Middle East and Africa. These various linkages are expected to have industrial zones at suitable locations en route. Chinese commentators have also explained that the BRI will help China to develop its disadvantaged frontier areas in the country's west and southwest regions. It should also help dispose of its domestic problems of overproduction, by the building abroad of infrastructure, including road, rail, ports, power plants, electricity grids, pipelines, mineral, gas and oil extraction installations, and so on.

In the five years since the BRI came into operation it has had mixed success. China established the Asian Infrastructure and Investment Bank (AIIB), with current membership of about sixty states. Many projects have been started and built, but their costs and their operations often are undisclosed. Some of the less developed and smaller countries have found themselves over-indebted to China for projects that have turned out to be unviable economically, leaving the countries in "debt traps." Sri Lanka became the best-known example when it was forced to lease land and port facilities to China for ninety-nine years to pay for a $1 billion debt and yet more unpayable debts remain. Corruption has been a major and abiding problem. The prime minister of Malaysia, the veteran Mahathir Mohammed, visited Beijing in August 2018 and canceled two rail projects valued at $20 billion, warning the Chinese government against a "new form of colonialism."[11] It is only fair to note that BRI has enjoyed more success in landlocked Central Asia, where its infrastructure capabilities have no competition and projects completed such as the railroads in Uzbekistan and another linking Kazakhstan, Uzbekistan, and Iran, in addition to the Khorgos dry port on the China-Kazakh border have been well regarded. Nevertheless, questions have arisen about the economic viability of projects elsewhere.[12]

The BRI has tarnished China's reputation as a reliable partner due to the opaqueness of the negotiations for the various projects, the constant suspicion of corruption surrounding them, the concern that they are primarily focused on serving Chinese interests (some of which are regarded as strategic and lacking in economic merit), and, finally, that a good number of them result in debt traps for the recipient country. An emerging problem is that they can implicate China in rivalries and complex regional problems that threaten the Chinese capacity to handle them.

Pakistan, "the all-weather friend," is a prime example. The China-Pakistan Economic Corridor originally valued at $62 billion has been hailed as one of the most important and successful projects of the BRI. But the election of a new prime minister, Imran Khan, brought to the fore the seriousness of Pakistan's low foreign reserves. The new government reached agreement with the IMF for a loan subject to onerous conditions. Khan also secured a $6 billion loan from Saudi Arabia and although the Chinese agreed to extend a loan in principle, they insisted on further negotiations. China had great expectations for the rebuilt Gwadar Port near the entrance to the Persian Gulf, to which they had constructed a road link from Xinjiang. But in 2018, as their Gwadar project neared completion, China's leaders found that they were in danger of becoming caught up in the great Middle East divide between Saudi Arabia and Iran. Xi Jinping was finding that his BRI was leading new foreign policy conundrums he could not have envisioned.

If the BRI is to emerge as a success it will first have to navigate the many difficulties and obstacles that lie in its ways through both continental and maritime Asia. Meanwhile the major powers of Asia, Japan, India, and Australia regard the whole enterprise with suspicion as designed to establish China's dominance of the trade of the Asian region and beyond. Even though Japan's prime minister, Shinzo Abe, agreed in his path-breaking visit to Beijing in October 2018 to participate in some BRI projects, it remains to be seen whether and how such joint activities would take place. Japan's key ally, the United States, has been opposed to the BRI since its inception an opposition that has intensified under the Trump's administration, which perceives the BRI as designed to establish Chinese control over Asian countries and to gain strategic dominance over the vast Eurasian landmass and beyond from which America would be excluded. It is increasingly regarded in Washington as part of a broader Chinese design, to undermine democracies and to establish an international order more to the liking of its own and other dictatorships.

## New Challenges in the South China Sea

In September 2013, China began dredging huge amounts of soil, sand, and coral from the seabed around the seven islets it had occupied in the SCS. By 2017, the land reclamations had reached a coverage of 3,200 acres. The Chinese side pointed out that other claimants including Vietnam, the Philippines, Malaysia, and Taiwan had reclaimed land and built fortifications in earlier years without incurring American wrath. In fact, Vietnam, which occupied twenty-nine islets, the Philippines eight, and Malaysia five, had each constructed an airfield on the land of one of their islands.

The American response was that their land reclamations were paltry compared to China's. Besides which, as the most powerful regional power, the ramifications of China's island building were of major strategic significance for the region and beyond. China had gained considerable control over a sea passageway (the Malacca Strait) through which cargo valued at $5 trillion passed every year. The SCS was the main link between the Pacific and Indian Oceans, and from the perspective of the Southeast Asians, China had suddenly thrust itself into the heart of Southeast Asia, leaving them no option but to rely on the United States as a hedge or a balancer against China's overwhelming military power. Using officially sponsored scholars, China pointed out that they were their permanent near neighbors, whereas the United States was located across the Pacific and that its policy interests and commitments may change or be diluted.[13]

Although China's island military bases were vulnerable to annihilation in the event of war, the Chinese had been careful to use incremental tactics, which they called a "cabbage strategy" by which different layered maritime numerous forces were used to overwhelm an adversary and which the Americans had called the tactics of "salami slicing." The Americans presented no effective answer, as the Obama administration was anxious to avoid military conflict that might lead to war, especially as Obama sought China's cooperation in dealing with North Korea and with global issues such as climate change. In the end the Obama administration was unable to impose sufficient costs upon the Xi Jinping government that would have caused it to back down. However, Obama did initiate a policy by which the US Navy and Air Force carried out occasional freedom of navigation patrols (FONOPs) in the SCS, which traversed maritime domains claimed by China that the Americans regarded as illegal. The Chinese response was to harass the American vessels and planes by sending their own to deny the Americans access through close encounters of a dangerous kind. The practice has been followed more vigorously by the Trump administration.

It was left to the Philippines to challenge the legality of China's actions and its maritime claims in the International Tribunal in the Hague. It received formal support from Vietnam and encouragement from the Obama administration on the grounds of American adherence to international law and associated legal norms. In the event, in July 2016 the Tribunal dismissed China's actions as illegal and stated that its various claims had no legal foundation. China refused to accept the ruling. The Obama administration in effect changed tack and urged its ally to seek a diplomatic solution. Coming after Obama had done nothing to cause the Chinese to pay a price for their reneging on the deal his administration mediated between the Philippines and China to have the naval vessels of both the Philippines and China withdraw from the disputed Scarborough Shoal in 2012, it is hardly surprising that Southeast Asians put little faith in Obama's statements of support.[14]

However, Obama had much to say about the way in which President Rodrigo Duterte of the Philippines was elected in June 2016 encouraged the police and vigilantes to kill suspected drug dealers and users without trial. The antagonized Duterte then turned to China, which offered him support and attractive economic projects, as he reduced still further the American military presence in the Philippines. Obama was also openly critical of the military coup in Thailand, which also turned to China. This left a general impression in the region, rightly or wrongly, that American relative power had declined, at least to the extent that it was unwilling to confront China and that the Southeast Asians had to deal with the menacing shadow of China as best they could.

# China and Asia's Sub-Regions

## Northeast Asia

Northeast Asia has been China's most important point of geopolitical vulnerability in China's modern history. Mao's armies were able to push back the American-led UN forces from the border with North Korea (otherwise known as the Democratic People's Republic of Korea—DPRK) in 1950 in a war that ended in an armistice in 1953 that still keeps the protagonists apart. The Korean War was the first time that Chinese forces were able to hold their own against technologically superior Western armies in contemporary history.

The northeast Asian neighborhood has continued to be the main strategic source of threat to China. From a long-term point of view, Japan and its alliance with the United States constrain China's naval access to the Pacific and its ability to take over Taiwan in order to complete the nationalist goal of unifying China. America's alliance with South Korea (the Republic of Korea—ROK) also contributes to the pressure on China and has had the effect of allowing the DPRK to sustain the unusual position of being dependent upon China while simultaneously defying it.

The Stalinist dictatorship of the Kim family regime consistently resisted Chinese pressure to reform and open its economy to the outside world, fearing that the regime would lose power. Its ideology, *Juche* (translated as "self-reliance"), really emphasizes a fierce independence and racial purity and a refusal to defer to stronger powers. After the end of the Cold War, China developed a policy toward the DPRK that favored maintaining the status quo, which was to characterize its policy ever since. In Beijing's view, the alternative could lead to Korean unification under the auspices of the South and its American ally, which would be strategically highly disadvantageous to China, or result in the collapse of the North and the destabilization of the entire Korean peninsula. That would create social and economic problems for China's adjoining northeastern provinces and damage China's economy as a whole, threatening the survival of the Chinese regime too.

By 1993 the isolated Kim regime had begun to reactivate its nuclear weapons program in the hope that it would become a guarantor of its survival. The reactivation led to a crisis with the United States, which could have led to war. Beijing, however, lent its "good offices" to help reach a settlement, called "the framework agreement," whereby in return for freezing its nuclear development the United States together with its allies would supply the North with heavy oil to meet its drastic shortage of fuel and help construct a nuclear reactor capable of producing only energy. By the time the agreement broke down several years later, China had taken the lead in convening meetings of the six regional states ("the Six Party Talks"), for which it was much praised, especially by the United States. China's policy did not change even after North Korea first tested a nuclear device in 2006 and continued to develop its nuclear and missiles program. In fact, the Chinese side surreptitiously supported the program and prevented UN sanctions from undermining the Northern economy. Obviously, China's successive leaders calculated that it was more in their interest to maintain stability on the Korean peninsula, even if they had to tolerate the acquisition of a powerful nuclear capability by their recalcitrant neighbor.

Xi Jinping was so angered by the hostile attitude and brutality of Kim Jong-un, who became leader in his late twenties in December 2011 on the death of his father, that the two did not meet until just before Kim was to meet President Trump in June 2018. The advent of Trump changed the dynamics of Northeast Asia, first with his policies on trade (see below) and, second, with his approach to North Korea. In response to Kim's nuclear and missile-enhanced testing Trump spent 2017 ratcheting up the rhetoric and the bellicose threats of war until he abruptly changed course when Kim claimed to have reached the point where he could stop all testing because he now had the capability of sending nuclear armed missiles to the continental United States. Trump then unprecedentedly agreed to hold a summit meeting with Kim in Singapore in June 2018. Prior to that meeting Kim visited China twice to meet with Xi, indicating that regardless of their previous hostility and Kim's fierce independence, Kim still needed China's backing before he could risk the possible consequences of a summit with the American leader, even though a bilateral meeting with the American president would be a huge boost to Kim's standing at home and abroad. For good measure Kim met Xi again following the summit, presumably to debrief him.

China's role on the peninsula was further enhanced by the leftist leader of South Korea, President Moon Jae-in, who sought better relations with the North by enhancing economic relations, reducing the scale of their military confrontation, and increasing the dialogue with Kim. These were all measures favored by China as designed to reach a negotiated end to the hostile divide, even though Washington held to the old view that the denuclearization of the North had to precede ending sanctions and reaching an accommodation with the Kim regime.[15]

China's relations with Japan have long been mixed. The end of the Cold War resulted in both an intensification of economic relations and increasing hostility in the political, nationalist, and strategic dimensions of the relationship. Japan had played a key role in helping the modernization of the Chinese economy in the 1980s and as China's leading trader. It was also instrumental in reducing and eliminating most of the Western sanctions after Tiananmen. But Japan became the key target in the subsequent rise and dissemination of state-sponsored Chinese nationalism. Attitudes on both sides hardened and China intensified its maritime pressure on the Senkaku/Diaoyu islands, which were administered by Japan and claimed by China.

Japan, however, was a major Asian power in its own right and, unlike the Southeast Asian states, Japan had the maritime and aerial forces to resist China's maneuvers.

The advent of Xi Jinping's leadership in 2012 resulted in the restriction of anti-Japanese riots, which had characterized the previous twenty years. But that did not signify a reduction in the hostility toward Japan displayed by the assertive new leader, who was characterized by his assertiveness at home and abroad. The two major Asian countries, whose economies ranked second and third in the world, have different fundamental interests and values. Above all, Japan is a crucial ally of the United States, which is pledged to treat the Senkakus as the rest of Japan, which it is pledged to protect. Under the premiership of Shinzo Abe, Japan has become more militarily active within the region and has increased its military spending to better defend its outer islands.

Japan has also become a major force in resisting Chinese attempts to dominate regional multilateral trade arrangements. Following Trump's immediate withdrawal from the Trans-Pacific Partnership (TPP), Japan picked up the leadership of it and promised to set up an Asia-Pacific FTA, which would go beyond reducing tariffs to include regulation of labor, safety, state-owned enterprises, environmental issues, and other concerns. Now called the Comprehensive and Progressive Agreement for Trans-Pacific Partnership, its remaining eleven members began to put it into practice in 2019. Japan also signed an FTA with the EU on similar lines that entered into effect in February 2019.

Japanese enterprises, like their European and American counterparts, have objected increasingly to China's trade practices, as inconsistent with international norms and as damaging to the international trade system. In particular, they protest Chinese insistence that foreign companies transfer their technological and trade secrets as a condition for operating in China and to the preference given to SOEs in government procurement and by hidden subsidies. They also object to Chinese theft of their intellectual property through undeclared cyber warfare. Japanese also point out that Chinese trade practices damage less-developed countries even more.[16]

However, the advent of Trump and his neo-mercantilist policy of "America First" and the resulting trade wars with allies as well as competitors have brought Japan and China somewhat closer together. President Xi and Prime Minister Abe held their first bilateral meeting on Chinese soil in October 2018 and agreed to "cooperate" more than "compete." Whatever improvement in relations may result from the summit, it is likely that their fundamental conflicts of interest and values will not be settled in the near future.

Those differences also extend to Taiwan, where the memory of Japan's colonization in the first half of the twentieth century is on the whole positive, especially when compared to the wartime memories of Korea and of China. Moreover, since Taiwan became a democracy, the relationship with Japan has been strengthened by their sharing of common values. The modernization and the strengthening of China's modern forces has had the effect of increasing the strategic significance of Taiwan for Japan. Taiwan, with Japan, is an important barrier (together with the Philippines) in being able to deny Chinese naval forces access to the Pacific Ocean in the event of a major military conflict involving China and the United States. Additionally, Japan would face the perils of encirclement by China were its giant neighbor to succeed in its long-established goal of unifying with Taiwan.

From Beijing's perspective, the Taiwan issue since the Cold War has evolved from being less a continuation of the civil war and an issue relating to the two superpowers into an issue relating to the United States and the domestic politics in Taiwan. From Beijing's point of view, America has reneged on the promises made in the three joint communiqués and it has come to use its vague military commitment to stop Beijing from forcing unification, thereby preventing the PRC from achieving the status to which it is entitled, having become a fully fledged global power. Meanwhile, as the island has become a democracy, China has found that the prospect for a peaceful route to unification is slipping away. Although the PRC is using its international power and standing in international organizations to isolate the island, the constraints on using force are increasing. China's difficulties with Taiwan are clearly growing.[17]

## Central Asia

The dissolution of the Soviet Union opened China's door to the newly established states of Central Asia. Early on, China reached a tacit agreement with the new states that it would help consolidate their sovereignty and territorial integrity against possible Soviet revanchism, while they would not assist disaffected fellow ethnic peoples in Xinjiang to resist Chinese rule. The next stage was China's economic engagement in a region rich in energy and other mineral resources. China built roads, rails, and pipelines linking the Central Asians with China. These were well received on the whole, especially by the local elites, particularly as Russia was in relative economic decline in contrast with China.

In 1996 the cooperation between China, Russia, Kazakhstan, Kyrgyzstan, and Tajikistan was formalized by what was called the Shanghai Five group, which in 2001 became the Shanghai Cooperation Organization (SCO), enlarged by the admission of Uzbekistan. Its mode of operation was similar to that of ASEAN, in operating by consensus, non-interference, and non-binding resolutions. It was deliberately non-Western and it expressed opposition to intervention in the domestic affairs of member states in the name of "humanitarianism" or "human rights." From the outset, at China's insistence, it was agreed to oppose the "three evils" of "terrorism, separatism and Islamic extremism." Member states also engaged in joint military exercises, notably, China with Russia, but there was no overall military grouping for the SCO as a whole.

From a Chinese perspective, the SCO became a useful framework for increasing its economic significance in Central Asia, without offending Russia, whose influence it was displacing. As noted, the Central Asian countries were also important for the development of the BRI. In 2016 the Chinese began to pay much attention to extirpating what was officially regarded as the terrorist threat from the Muslim people in Xinjiang and especially the Uighur people, hundreds of thousands of whom have been rounded up and detained in detention centers. Around that time, China's focus in Afghanistan and in Central Asia, more generally, began to shift from extracting economic gain to what China's leaders regarded as the growing terrorist threat connected with the rise of the influence of Islamic extremists returning from the former strongholds of ISIS in the Middle East. Consequently, Beijing has begun to balance its cultivation of Central Asia as a region for the expansion of economic opportunities with the concern about the region as the source of terrorist threats that need to be countered before they endanger Chinese domestic security.[18]

## South Asia

This used to be a region in which Pakistan in particular, and other neighbors of lesser importance, were cultivated by China in order to constrain India. India itself was regarded with disdain as an ineffective strategic challenger that nonetheless constituted a threat because of its interest in Tibet and its provision of an exiled home for the Chinese regime's foe, the Dalai Lama and his fellow Tibetans. Since the dissolution of the Soviet Union, India's main external supporter and arms supplier, India has become a partner of the United States and it has become more of a market economy. After initial opposition to the Indian testing of nuclear weapons in 1998, the United States became a supporter and enabled it to join three of the four main nuclear non-proliferation groups. China has opposed Indian membership in the fourth and most important: the Nuclear Suppliers Group. The other opponents have modified their positions, and China may follow suit as it would probably not wish to be seen as the only opponent.

Following its emergence as a maritime power in the first decade of the twenty-first century, China has been keen to be able to defend its trade routes, especially as the country's economy has become increasingly dependent on importing energy and raw materials. That, in turn, has fueled the urge to strengthen China's long-term strategic aim of becoming a respected global power, in addition to having become a major global trader. To this end, it has begun to establish or reconfigure ports in Sri Lanka, the Maldive Islands, Gwadar Port in Pakistan, and a military base in Djibouti in East Africa (China's first abroad). At the same time, China has become a significant player in the economies of India's other neighbors—including Nepal, Bhutan, Bangladesh, and beyond. As far as India is concerned, China has emerged as its main trading partner and a competitor with Japan and South Korea for the construction projects for much-needed infrastructure. India is the one major country with which border disputes remain to be settled and from time to time major incidents arise, such as the standoff in Doklam involving Bhutan in the summer of 2017. Although China still enjoys a geographical advantage of having the Tibetan plateau on which to build military infrastructure, in contrast to India, which faces the steep Himalayas, nevertheless the Indian armed forces have developed airfields, military installations, and other needed infrastructure that ensure that Chinese would no longer be able to command the easy victories of the 1962 War, which still rankles in India.

China's principal means of pressuring India continues to be its close relations with Pakistan, its "all-weather friend." It was China that helped Pakistan acquire nuclear weapons after it lost East Pakistan (now Bangladesh) in the 1971 War. Pakistan has benefited from China's much-needed economic assistance, perhaps no more than in the present vast series of projects called the China-Pakistan Economic Corridor (CPEC), discussed above. But, as previously noted, like other BRI projects this too has run into problems of causing excessive indebtedness, the suspicion of fraud and corruption, and arousing local opposition. More recently, there are signs too of Chinese impatience about the Pakistani use of terror even as a tactic against the stronger India. The Chinese concern is that terrorism might spread northwards.[19]

China's relations with India remain complex, incorporating both cooperation and competition. They are vast countries between whom a major war is inconceivable, of either the nuclear or the conventional kind. Yet skirmishes occur from time to time amid nationalist clamor on both sides and it is not inconceivable that these could escalate; but so far that has not happened and for the good reason that neither side can allow that to happen lest it arouse nationalist passions threatening either government's loss of control.[20]

## Southeast Asia

Despite what may appear as opposition and setbacks, China has not been made to pay a cost that is too much for it to bear for its assertive policies in Southeast Asia. This is also true for its policies of building dams on the upper reaches of the Mekong River, which are changing the river flows downstream to the detriment of the countries of Thailand, Laos, Cambodia, and Vietnam. Meanwhile, geostrategic competition between China and the United States is increasing in the region. Yet, many in the region regard China's dominance of Southeast Asia as inevitable and irreversible.

That narrative overlooks many problems, sources of resistance, and developments that stand in China's way. Chinese conduct in implementing its various projects, as we have seen, tend to be overwhelmingly self-serving, so that even countries that are openly subservient, such as Laos and Cambodia, find that they may be beneficial to China, but they cannot deliver sufficient economic returns for recipients and leave them with debts they cannot repay. No wonder a senior Cambodia minister told the author in 2014, "We are dependent on China, but we don't want to be dependent only on China." In fact, Japan has played such a role, allowing the dictatorial Hun Sen to play off the two great players against each other, while leaning more closely to fellow dictatorial China. Elsewhere in continental Southeast Asia, China's contemporary relations were mixed.

Thailand, unlike its fellow Southeast Asian countries, has traditionally assimilated ethnic Chinese. It has maneuvered successfully in the modern era between the major external powers to retain its independence. For most of the Cold War it maintained surreptitious relations with China, and since then China has cultivated the rulers of Thailand, whether of the Bangkok establishment or former prime minister Thaksin (who is himself of ethnic Chinese origin) or other groups. Ostensibly, China was the beneficiary of Obama's critical reaction to the military coup of May 2014, but in fact ties with Washington at lower levels including joint military exercises have continued. A deeper problem is the lack of attention by senior politicians in Washington, including Donald Trump. But even more than Cambodia, Thailand has been receptive to Japanese economic ties and also of South Korea and increasingly India.

Myanmar, however, is more closely tied to China, in part because of cross-border ethnic ties in the north and in part due to Western opposition to the role of the military. But as noted in the earlier discussion of China's BRI, Myanmar has put a halt to some of China's projects on grounds of cost and increasing indebtedness.

China has long found Vietnam a difficult neighbor, despite close trade relations and political commonality. Vietnam maintains a fierce independence in conjunction with the United States, Japan, India, and Australia. Even though both countries are ruled by communist parties, which pursue similar policies of economic reform and openness to the international economy, their relations are characterized by distrust. If the Vietnamese at elite and popular levels regard China as a bully that denies them their sovereign rights in the South China Sea, China's rulers regard Vietnam as an ingrate for not acknowledging the crucial assistance of China in its wars against France and the United States and they accuse their fraternal Communist Party of siding first with their main adversary, the Soviet Union in the 1970s and 1980s, and then in the twenty-first century with the United States and Japan. Yet despite the underlying enmity, each side recognizes the need to maintain effective working relations.

The Philippines, a long-standing ally of America, has varied between pursuing cold and warm relations with China according to the predilections of successive governments. The previous government of Benigno Aquino opposed China on the SCS, but the current president Duterte initially turned to China when he was criticized by Obama and was promised major economic assistance, which has yet to materialize. Since then, Duterte has shifted to a more balanced position, especially as American assistance was vital in enabling him to defeat the ISIS challenge in Mindanao.

Indonesia has always seen itself as the leading power in ASEAN, and has resisted China's efforts to impose its will on ASEAN. For example, in 2012 Indonesia issued a statement of six principles to fill in the vacuum caused by Cambodia's veto of an ASEAN joint statement (at the behest of China). More recently, Indonesia has resisted Chinese claims of the right to fish in waters near the Natuna Islands not far from the Straits of Malacca. Indonesia has blown up scores of foreign fishing vessels, including Chinese ones for penetrating into its Natuna EEZ, and now even the Chinese have drastically reduced the number of offending fishing boats. The Chinese government has quietly acquiesced, as may be seen from the BRI projects it has begun in Indonesia.

Singapore has long been a puzzle for Chinese rulers. It is a city-state with a mainly ethnic Chinese population that yet identifies itself as a multiethnic state that fiercely refuses to identify with China. The city-state is China's main economic partner in the region, but it is close strategically to the United States. Beijing does not appear to understand that one of the most important reasons for Singapore's resistance to accepting an identity as a Chinese outpost is due to its geographic vulnerability as a tiny irritant to the Muslim-majority states of Indonesia and Malaysia.

In sum, contrary to many reports, China does *not* dominate Southeast Asia. Resident countries have skillfully found means of retaining independence by seeking support elsewhere, notably from Japan, but also from the United States.[21]

## Australasia

China's relations with Australia, New Zealand, and the South Pacific Islands have moved from being highly welcomed and appreciated to become more contentious since 2015–2016. Up to that point the Chinese demand for Australian mineral and other resources, combined with massive Chinese investments and the substantial number of Chinese tourists and high fees-paying students, had enabled Australia alone in the Western world to benefit economically on a continuous basis for over twenty years without a downturn. The Australian economy continued to benefit even as the growth of the Chinese economy slowed from the double digits to just over half that rate. In 2017, for example, it registered a trade surplus of $50 billion with China. By that year, however, evidence emerged of Chinese penetration into the local associations, newspapers, educational institutions, the Australian ethnic Chinese, and even members of Parliament, who had to some extent come under the control of the Chinese Communist Party. Further, through bribery, intimidation, and coercion, agents of the CCP had penetrated all kinds of Australian institutions and suborned Australian politicians at state and federal levels, so that they served Chinese rather than Australian interests. The Australian government has since rejected Chinese high-tech companies' bids to invest in Australian telecommunications on the grounds of national security. With China in mind, the Australian government in July 2018 passed sweeping new laws to prevent interference by foreign governments.

The official Chinese response to all this was to deny all such claims and to regard the reports as signs of racist Sinophobia. The nationalist *Global Times* in Beijing found new terms to denigrate Australia, claiming that "Australia is not even a 'paper tiger,' it's only a 'paper cat' at best." The paper berated Australia in a way that reflected Chinese views toward many of its neighbors: "Australia calls itself a principled country, while its utilitarianism has been sizzling. It lauds Sino-Australian relations when China's economic support is needed, but when it needs to please Washington, it demonstrates willingness of doing anything in a show of allegiance."[22]

Chinese treatment of New Zealand has been similar and perhaps even worse. China had long been New Zealand's largest goods trading partner, a major source of students, migrants, and tourists, and has become very important as a multilateral and bilateral partner. Arguably, New Zealand was late to appreciate the extent of interference and penetration by the CCP into the country's politics and society. It had taken control of nearly all the local ethnic Chinese community's groups and Chinese-language media and all the ethnic Chinese student associations. One of its legislators has been revealed to be a CCP member who had worked for one of China's top military intelligence organizations. The New Zealand government responded to the increase of China's military activities in the South Pacific by announcing new defense spending followed by issuing a Defense Ministry Strategic Policy Statement in July 2018 that used uncharacteristically critical language about China. It was more a change in tone, as the statement included positive references to China's role in the Asia-Pacific, but the government stated that henceforth it would no longer be "pulling our punches and doing nothing about things we don't agree with."[23] New Zealand moved closer to Australia and the United States, its main strategic partners, announcing later that month that it would buy four submarine hunting vessels from Boeing, which, inter alia, facilitate operation in joint missions with its major Western allies.[24]

Both Australia and New Zealand have traditionally exercised a paternalistic oversight for the welfare of the fourteen Pacific Small Island Developing States (PSIDS), most of which have small populations and less-developed economies located in island groupings stretched over hundreds and thousands of miles of ocean, and which have become highly vulnerable to the effects of climate change. They have limited educational facilities and until recently have tended to send their students to the higher education institutions of Australia and New Zealand. However, in recent years their international relations have extended beyond the two aforementioned countries.

China has several interests in the PSIDS. First, it has long been engaged in diplomatic struggles with Taiwan to gain diplomatic recognition by the island states. These struggles have been carried out by so-called checkbook diplomacy. At present seven of the fourteen recognize Taiwan (i.e., the Republic of China), amounting to nearly half of the eighteen states in the world that still do so. Second, China is keen to cultivate the loyalty of the ethnic Chinese residents in the islands as they play important roles in the island economies and, from Beijing's perspective, they are an inherent part of the Chinese nation. Third, the Pacific islands have become important for China's fisheries as they command a collective EEZ of over 1.6 million square miles of ocean. Fourth, now that China has become a maritime nation, this vast area, which the Chinese foreign ministry calls "Oceana," has acquired increasing strategic significance.

Given the increasing attention paid to Chinese activities in the broad area, it should be noted that the amount of aid given to the Pacific islands since 2011 has actually declined. The total for donor countries has gone from $2.36 billion to $1.9 billion in 2016. In 2016 China ranked only fifth (i.e., even after Japan), but its total donations in the period 2011–2016 placed it tied for second with New Zealand at $1.2 billion (a sixth of Australian aid level). But China's aid was for "big ticket" items such as the International Convention Centre in Port Moresby, Papua New Guinea, and it was increasingly in the form of soft loans, which could lead to the creation of over-indebtedness. China, which is suspected of seeking to construct a military base on one of the islands, has since increased its infrastructure investments, but so have Australia and New Zealand.[25]

# Conclusion

China is clearly continuing to rise economically and strategically in Asia, but it still faces many problems and signs of pushback in several countries. It is therefore premature to claim that it has become—or is on the verge of becoming—*the* dominant power in Asia. The Trump administration has replaced the concept of "engagement" with that of "competition" with China and it has used tariffs as a weapon in order to change China's unfair trade practices, which have been central to its broader economic strategy. Much will depend on how China's leaders will adapt to the new confrontational American approach at a time, when the current economic model is under stress and needs to change toward a more open and consumer-led system.[26] Such a change would transform China's relations with its Asian neighbors as well as with the United States and the other developed economies.

# Notes

1. Stockholm International Peace Research Institute (SIPRI), "Military Expenditure by Country" (SIPRI, 2018), https://www.sipri.org/sites/default/files/1_Data for all countries from 1988-2017 in constant (2016) USD.pdf.
2. Alastair Iain Johnston, *Cultural Realism* (Princeton, NJ: Princeton University Press, 1995); and Yuan-Kang Wang, *Harmony and War* (New York: Columbia University Press, 2011).
3. Xi Jinping at UN meeting on climate change (Xinhua, January 19, 2017).
4. The "Five Principles of Peaceful Coexistence" were formulated in the Indian and Chinese joint statement of April 29, 1954. They are (1) mutual respect for each other's territorial integrity and sovereignty; (2) non-aggression; (3) non-interference in each other's internal affairs; (4) equality and mutual benefit; and (5) peaceful coexistence.
5. Thant Myint-U, *Where China Meets India* (New York: Farrar, Straus & Giroux, 2011).
6. Nayan Chanda, *Brother Enemy* (New York: Collier Books, 1986).
7. François Godement, *The Downsizing of Asia* (London and New York: Routledge, 1999).
8. David Shambaugh, "China Engages Asia: Reshaping the Regional Order?" *International Security* 29, no. 3 (Winter 2004/2005): 64–99.
9. Tom Mitchell, "China Struggles to Win Friends over South China Sea," *Financial Times*, July 13, 2010.
10. "Full Text of President Xi's Speech at Opening of Belt and Road Forum," Xinhuanet, May 14, 2017.

11. Lucy Hornby, "Mahathir Mohamad Warns against 'New Colonialism' during China Visit," *Financial Times*, August 20, 2018.

12. Marlène Laruelle and Sébastien Peyrouse, *The Chinese Question in Central Asia* (New York: Columbia University Press, 2012). See also Umida Hashimova, "Why Central Asia Is Betting on China's Belt and Road," *The Diplomat*, August 13, 2018.

13. Hou Songling and Chi Diantang, "PRC Scholars on China's Geostrategic Options Regarding Southeast Asia and Central Asia," *Ya-Tai Yanjiu* (Journal of the Chinese Academy of Social Sciences, Institute of Asia-Pacific Studies, April 25, 2003) (as translated by Foreign Broadcast Information Service, FBIS).

14. On China and the SCS see Bill Hayton, *The South China Sea* (New Haven, CT: Yale University Press, 2014).

15. On China and the two Koreas see Scott Snyder, *China's Rise and the Two Koreas* (Boulder, CO: Lynne Rienner Publishers, 2009).

16. On China and Japan see Ryosei Kokubun et al., *Japan and China Relations in the Modern Era* (London and New York: Routledge, 2017); Richard McGregor, *Asia's Reckoning: China, Japan, and the Fate of US Power in the Pacific Century* (New York: Viking, 2017); and Michael Yahuda, *Sino-Japanese Relations after the Cold War: Two Tigers Sharing a Mountain* (London and New York: Routledge, 2016)

17. On Taiwan see Richard Bush, *Uncharted Strait: The Future of China-Taiwan Relations* (Washington, DC: Brookings Institution, 2013); Alan M. Wachman, *Why Taiwan?* (Stanford, CA: Stanford University Press, 2007); and Shelley Rigger, *Why Taiwan Matters* (Lanham, MD: Rowan and Littlefield, 2011).

18. On China and Central Asia see Laruelle and Peyrouse, *The China Question in Central Asia*; and "China Says Terrorism Tops Meeting of Central Asian States," AP, April 24, 2018.

19. On Pakistan see Andrew Small, *The China-Pakistan Axis: Asia's New Geopolitics* (Oxford: Oxford University Press, 2015).

20. On the background to relations between China and India see Francine R. Frankel and Harry Harding, eds., *The India-China Relationship* (New York: Columbia University Press, 2004). For a more recent account see T. V. Paul, ed., *The China-India Rivalry in the Globalization Era* (Washington, DC: Georgetown University Press, 2018).

21. The literature on China's relations with Southeast Asia and its various countries is huge. A useful starting point is Ian Storey, *China and Southeast Asia* (London and New York: Routledge, 2011); see also Lowell Dittmer and Ngeow Chow Bing, eds., *Southeast Asia and China* (Singapore: World Scientific Publishing Co., 2017).

22. "Paper Cat Australia Will Learn its Lesson," *Global Times*, July 30, 2016, http://www.global-times.cn/content/997320.shtml.

23. Acting Prime Minister Winston Peters, cited in *New Zealand Herald*, July 10, 2018.

24. For a critical account of Chinese penetration into Australia see Clive Hamilton, *Silent Invasion* (Melbourne: Hardie Grant Books, 2018); and for an account of China's political activities in New Zealand see Anne-Marie Brady, "China in Xi's New Era: New Zealand and the CCP's 'Magic Weapons,'" *Journal of Democracy* 29, no. 2 (April 2018): 68–75.

25. On China and the South Pacific islands see Philippa Brant, "Mapping Chinese Aid in the Pacific" (Sydney: The Lowy Institute, 2015). For an account of China's recent upgrade of attention see Jason Scott, "China's Pacific Push Has the US Worried," *Bloomberg*, June 17, 2018.

26. Mike Pence, "Remarks Delivered on the Administration's Policy towards China" (Washington, DC: The Hudson Institute, October 4, 2018).

# 14

# China's Relations with Africa, Latin America, and the Middle East

JOSHUA EISENMAN AND ERIC HEGINBOTHAM

Over the last two decades, developing countries have become central to China's increasingly ambitious foreign policy makers. This trend accelerated after the 2009 global financial crisis, when China's leaders concluded that US "hegemony" was declining and that developing states were becoming ever more important partners in an increasingly multipolar world. In June 2018, China's "core" leader, Xi Jinping, reaffirmed this point in a speech to the Central Foreign Affairs Work Conference (FAWC) in which he said developing states are "naturally allied" with China, and China should deepen relations with "newly emerging powers" and "advance pragmatic cooperation and strategic coordination with the BRICS."[1]

China's prioritization of the developing world has taken place amid an evolution in the country's own sense of identity and place in the world. China now paints itself as both a developing country and a major power, a self-portrait that identifies a broad swath of potential partner countries while insulating Beijing from international leadership on tough issues, like the Syrian refugee crisis, that are unrelated to China's core interests. As Foreign Minister Wang Yi stated in 2016: "Although China is the world's second-biggest economy, in per capita terms we are behind over 80 other countries. This is why we say we remain a developing country, and we still must focus our efforts on development, not just at present, but for a very long time to come."[2]

This chapter begins by explaining China's conceptualization of the developing world and its position in Beijing's geostrategy. After describing the three characteristics of China's approach—asymmetry, comprehensiveness, and its interlocking structure—we then explain the various economic, political, and security policy tools that comprise it. China works to bring the separate strands of its foreign policy together in a comprehensive whole and to build synergies

Joshua Eisenman and Eric Heginbotham, *China's Relations with Africa, Latin America, and the Middle East* In: *China and the World*. Edited by: David Shambaugh, Oxford University Press (2020). © Oxford University Press
DOI: 10.1093/oso/9780190062316.003.0014

between component parts. Ultimately, we conclude that Beijing's primary objectives—regime survival and advancing China's position in an increasingly multipolar world—are probably insufficient to engender widespread political support among developing countries for a China-led world order.

## Developing Countries in China's Strategic Thought

Under Mao Zedong, China supported revolutionary and anti-colonial movements around the developing world.[3] After Deng Xiaoping became China's pre-eminent leader in 1978, political goals (with the exception of Taiwan) were subordinated in favor of economic ones. Today, while China's political efforts often serve its economic ends, economic means are increasingly employed to achieve political ends.

China's foreign policy practice has long based its interactions on partner states' characteristics: major powers (大国), peripheral states (周边国家), developing countries (发展中国家), and, since the 18th Party Congress in 2012, multilateral (多边) international forums.[4] The boundaries between these categories are ambiguous, and states may traverse two or more of them. Major powers are large, economically developed states—including the United States, Russia, Japan, Germany, Britain, and the European countries. Peripheral states include an array of both developing states and major powers in East Asia, Central Asia, South Asia, Russia, and Southeast Asia. Former president Hu Jintao declared, "Major powers are the key, surrounding (peripheral) areas are the first priority, developing countries are the foundation, and multilateral forums are the important stage."[5]

Under Xi Jinping, the sequence of discussions in major policy speeches suggests relations with major powers remain Beijing's top priority, but they have been joined on that level by a new class of developing states. Chinese strategists have gradually adopted an increasingly nuanced view of the developing world, differentiating "major developing states" (发展中大国) or "newly emerging powers" (新兴大国) from "other" developing states.[6] While there is no definitive list of major developing states, they appear to include several large, rapidly developing and politically influential states such as the developing members of the G-20—Argentina, Brazil, Mexico, South Africa, India, Indonesia, Saudi Arabia, Turkey, Iran, and Thailand.[7] By discussing these "newly emerging powers" in the same section (indeed, the same sentence) of his June 2018 FAWC speech, Xi Jinping placed them on par with "traditional major powers."[8]

China sees itself as both a major power and the leader of the developing states working to "democratize" key international institutions to give them greater representation.[9] Official statements depict the international system as evolving toward multipolarity and developing states as driving that process.[10] In 2016, He Yafei, former vice minister of foreign affairs, recognized the importance of building partnerships with countries that also seek a "multipolar world and democratic international relations." As these are primarily developing states, He argued that they should remain "the bedrock and strategic focus of China's major-country diplomacy."[11] To advance common political interests, Beijing has concluded bilateral "strategic partnership" agreements with major developing states and has collectively engaged subsets of them, most famously the BRICS to help balance Western dominance.[12] Established in 2009, the BRICS organization, which includes Brazil, Russia, India, China, and South Africa, seeks to coordinate political-economic positions and public statements among those nations.

Part of the developing world falls within China's "periphery" (周边), sometimes translated as "strategic periphery," which constitutes a geographic belt around China that is of particular strategic importance for Beijing. Some in China argue that the periphery's scope should be adjusted in accordance with Beijing's growing power and influence. Previously, the periphery was limited to Northeast Asia, Southeast Asia, South Asia, and Central Asia, but under the Xi administration the "greater periphery" (大周边) has been expanded to include West Asia, the South Pacific, and, by some definitions, East Africa.[13] In 2015 and 2016, China released official White Papers on Africa, Latin America, and the Middle East, thus underscoring the importance it attaches to those regions.[14]

This growing emphasis on the greater periphery reflects China's expanding global interests vis-à-vis the Belt and Road Initiative (BRI), and its increasingly tense relations with the United States, Japan, and Southeast Asian countries. Chen Xiangyang argues that to protect Chinese interests Beijing must promote unifying narratives among developing countries and expand its leadership in existing regional structures.[15] Still, regime survival remains Beijing's foremost priority and the primary determinant of its policies toward developing countries. The influence of domestic politics is reflected in the content and character of China's diplomacy, party-to-party relations, defense of sovereignty norms in international politics, and its near single-minded emphasis on economic development.[16]

The developing world is also important for Beijing's efforts to defend its "territorial integrity." After a "diplomatic truce" from 2008 to 2016, the competition for diplomatic recognition between Taipei and Beijing resumed with the election of Tsai Ing-wen in Taiwan. As of February 2019, the number of UN member states recognizing Taiwan had fallen to sixteen (plus the Holy See). To contain separatism in Tibet, China periodically uses rhetorical intimidation and sanctions against countries that host the Dalai Lama.[17] In addition to China's hard-power measures in the South China Sea, Beijing has solicited support from at least sixty-six mostly developing countries for recognition of its maritime claims.[18]

China has made common cause with developing states across a range of political-economic issues including environmental priorities and trade-offs, trade policy, technology standards, and the form and function of international institutions. From the most liberal democratic government to the harshest dictatorship, developing countries around the world regularly find their international positions match China's on numerous questions of common concern. New Delhi's UN General Assembly votes, for example, are more closely aligned with those of Beijing than Washington.[19] For China, state sovereignty and non-intervention are motivated by a desire to ward off international condemnation, sanctions, and intervention related to its human rights abuses and harsh policies toward dissidents and minorities in Tibet and Xinjiang.

## Three Characteristics of China's Relations with Developing Countries

China's relations with the developing world are characterized by asymmetry, its comprehensive approach, and the interlocking nature of its global, regional, and bilateral engagement. *Asymmetry* is the first and most enduring characteristic of China's relations with developing countries, and Beijing's calls for "brotherhood" and "equality" are merely attempts to downplay it.[20] Indeed, China's nominal GDP ($12.0 trillion in 2017) is almost double the total GDP of the other BRICS combined: India ($2.6 trillion), Brazil ($2.1 trillion), Russia ($1.5 trillion), and South Africa ($349 billion).[21] Beijing-created regional institutions like the Forum on China-Africa Cooperation (FOCAC) and the China–Community of Latin American and Caribbean States Relations Forum (China-CELAC Forum) alternate locations between China and different partner countries in these and other regions. Symbolically, this places China on par with entire regions and practically it enhances Beijing's already disproportionate agenda-setting power.

The second characteristic of Beijing's approach is *comprehensiveness*. Beijing combines the various methods explained below in ways that create synergies and maximize its leverage. China's policy banks, most notably the China Development Bank (CDB) and China Export-Import Bank (China Ex-Im), have become go-to lenders in the developing world, and its infrastructure and telecoms firms are building railroads, dams, airports, highways, and fiber optic networks in dozens of developing countries (see Barry Naughton's chapter in this volume). Taken together, China's package of incentives is often irresistible to capital-scarce developing countries.

Beijing's political and economic goals are inseparable, and officials regularly help arrange and close deals. While financial incentives are generally the most persuasive in Beijing's toolkit, China's comprehensive engagement goes beyond economics, and aims to build a stable, multifaceted, and mutually beneficial bilateral relationships. China's leaders claim that these relationships must be "high-quality" and include "a sense of justice and interests" (义益观).[22] Still, large amounts of Chinese business activity in Africa, Latin America, and the Middle East are conducted by independent profit-seeking small and mid-sized private firms that generally seek to avoid government entanglements.[23]

A third characteristic of China's engagement is its *interlocking structure*. As former vice foreign minister He Yafei explained, China's foreign policy involves "multi-centric, multi-layered and multi-pivotal sub-networks of regional and international cooperation that are interconnected and interwoven."[24] While all major states conduct diplomatic activities at the bilateral, regional, and global levels, China's engagement consists of a particularly tight latticework of overlapping institutionalized relationships. By building a dense network of interlocking relationships, Beijing works to create a stable and mutually reinforcing structure upon which to further its interests.

Multilateral forums boost legitimacy and showcase Beijing's benevolence, but the basis of China's relations with developing countries remains bilateral. Across the developing world, China has deepened its bilateral relationships and maintains "strategic partnerships" with some sixty-seven states.[25] Beijing's bilateral engagement is pursued in private and specifically tailored to its interests in that country. China's relations with nearby states are generally deeper and more complex, with a mix of political, economic, and sometimes territorial interests at play. China's relations with more distant developing countries have generally prioritized economics, yet in those countries too, political and security elements are becoming increasingly important. In particular, China's relations with emerging major developing powers (including the BRICS countries and G-20 members) cut across regional lines and have overlapping political, economic, and security components.

Within each region, Beijing places considerable emphasis on its relations with large and important anchor or "hub" states where circumstances of geography, politics, or economics make relations with China particularly propitious. These relationships tend to receive more attention in Beijing and be relatively stable over time. In East Asia, they include Indonesia and Thailand; in South Asia, Pakistan and India; in Central Asia, Kazakhstan; in

Africa, South Africa, Egypt, and Ethiopia; in the Middle East, Iran; and in Latin America, Brazil and Argentina. This list is not definitive and will continue to evolve over time.

As Srikanth Kondapalli's subsequent chapter explores in more detail, China's creation of regional organizations to coordinate its relations with developing regions is among the most distinctive features of its approach. In Africa, China initiated and funded the FOCAC, which convened for the first time in Beijing in 2000 and holds meetings every three years alternating between China and an African country. The leaders of fifty-one African countries attended the 2018 FOCAC in Beijing, roughly twice as many as attended the 73rd UN General Assembly.[26] Similarly, China initiated the China-Arab States Cooperation Forum in 2004, and the most recent gathering was held in Beijing in 2018.[27] Beijing has also used the China–Gulf Cooperation Council strategic dialogue established in 2010 to build relationships with the Sunni-dominated Gulf States, even while maintaining close ties with Tehran.[28] China was admitted as a permanent observer to both the Organization of American States (OAS) and Latin American Parliament in 2004, but the CELAC forum proved more attractive because, unlike the OAS, the United States is not a member. At the inaugural China-CELAC Forum in 2015, President Xi said Chinese financing into Latin America would reach $250 billion over ten years.[29]

## Methods of China's Engagement with the Developing World

### Economics

#### Trade

Trade growth is not purely, or even primarily, a function of state-led promotion activities, but whenever possible Beijing works to tip the balance in favor of Chinese interests. State-owned enterprises (SOEs), semi-private firms, private firms, and entrepreneurs all regularly work with state bankers, diplomats, and Party officials who help them ink deals and promote exports. China's commercial service attachés working in its African embassies reportedly outnumber US Foreign Commercial Service officers working in the region by some fifteen to one.[30]

Trade both contributes to and reflects GDP growth. China's GDP grew by a real compound annual growth rate (CAGR) of 8.9 percent between 1978 and 2017, while trade increased an average of 11.5 percent per year. Since 2015, however, both GDP and trade growth have slowed considerably.[31] China's trade grew by a real 0.9 percent in 2014, *shrank* by 9.9 percent in 2015, and shrank again by 5.4 percent in 2016, before recovering 8.2 percent in 2017. Private firms accounted for 38.1 percent of trade in 2016.[32]

Developing countries provide important raw materials for Chinese producers and growing markets for Chinese exports. In 1990, developing countries represented only 15 percent of China's total trade, but by 2000 they accounted for 19 percent, and by 2010, they had reached 31 percent of total trade. After peaking around 34 percent in 2012, the percentage has plateaued due to weakening Chinese demand for raw materials coupled with historically low oil and metals prices. The value of China's trade with the developing world was $29.4 billion in 1990 (measured in constant 2017 US dollars) and rose to $1.4 trillion in 2017 (about 34 percent of China's total foreign trade)—a real CAGR of 15.4 percent—compared to a 11.5 percent CAGR for China's total trade over that period. In 2017, China's trade percentages by region were: Southeast Asia and Western Pacific, 12.8 percent; Middle East, 5.6 percent; Latin America, 6.2 percent; Africa, 3.7 percent; South Asia, 3.1 percent; and Central Asia, 0.9 percent.[33]

## Investment

Developing countries, which offer both greater risks and returns, have been central to China's "going out" foreign investment strategy. As early as 1999, China had amassed about $155 billion in foreign reserves and was looking to gain higher yields and generate economic opportunities for SOEs in extractive and construction industries.[34] That year, at the Fourth Plenum of the 15th National Party Congress, Jiang Zemin launched the so-called going-out strategy (走出去战略), which encouraged firms to "establish branches overseas" and "explore international markets."[35] Subsequent decisions during the 2000s created funding mechanisms and banking services to facilitate trade and investment. In 2007, for instance, China's biggest lender ICBC bought a 20 percent stake in South Africa's Standard Bank for $5.6 billion, and in 2011 began onshore Chinese yuan accounts for African companies "to facilitate fast and effective trade relations with Chinese suppliers, buyers and related global customers."[36]

China's "going out" gathered momentum after 2010. Non-financial FDI flows increased from $3.8 billion (in 2018 US dollars) in 2003 to $204 billion in 2015—a real CAGR of 36 percent.[37] Outward FDI fell by 20 percent in 2017, to $162 billion, before rallying somewhat in 2018 ($169 billion)—despite a major contraction in FDI to the United States. The real CAGR for the entire period from 2003 to 2018 was 28 percent. According to official figures, emerging and developing states (excluding investment in offshore financial centers) comprised about 36 percent of China's total outbound FDI flow in 2017, with

14.9 percent going to developing Southeast Asia and Western Pacific, 7.3 percent to Africa, 4.0 percent to Central Asia, 2.5 percent to Latin America, and 2.0 percent to South Asia.[38]

While China's investment in developing countries has increased rapidly, it is not often the dominant player it is portrayed to be. In 2016, China's was the fourth largest investor in Africa, behind the United States, United Kingdom, and France; in 2017, it had the fourth largest number of projects in Africa behind the aforementioned three countries.[39] Simply put, Chinese investment does not dominate, but it has emerged over the last decade as a leader alongside other major actors.

### Debt Financing

Beijing has sought to expand its role in international financial institutions and has long pushed to change quotas and vote shares in the World Bank, International Monetary Fund (IMF), and Asian Development Bank (ADB).[40] In the World Bank, China has called for an end to Western dominance and advocated greater transparency in the president's selection.[41] Impatient with the pace of IMF reform, in 2014 Beijing helped established the Shanghai-based New Development Bank (NDB) (aka the BRICS bank) with $100 billion in initial funding.[42] In December 2014, Beijing also established the $55 billion Silk Road Fund, which is backed by China's sovereign wealth fund but open to private investors.

The Beijing-based Asian Infrastructure Investment Bank (AIIB) opened in December 2015 with fifty-seven founding member states, including thirty-seven from Asia.[43] Initial capital was $100 billion or about two-thirds the capitalization of the ADB and about half that of the World Bank.[44] Beijing's influence is mitigated since the AIIB president Jin Liqun reports to an international governing board, and while China holds the largest voting bloc (26 percent) it remains a minority stakeholder. In its first two years, the AIIB loaned out only $4.4 billion, far below its expected $10–15 billion per year.[45] In February 2019, Jin said "to improve its asset quality" the bank would push the cap on lending for infrastructure projects in China up from 3 percent to 10 percent of the bank's total loan portfolio.[46] Yet, given the already extensive investments in China's infrastructure compared with the urgent needs in other Asian countries, expanding AIIB lending to China may face pushback from other member countries.

Financing for Chinese-built projects in developing countries comes primarily from China's policy banks, the China Development Bank (CDB) and China Export-Import Bank, which were established in 1994 to finance projects that increase economic growth.[47] They provide large volumes of soft loans to developing countries under the condition that they hire Chinese SOEs to complete the projects. Once terms are reached, funds are transferred into the Beijing-based bank accounts of the host country, which then wires them to the SOE that is preselected to execute the project, often using Chinese materials and labor. By 2016, the loan portfolio of CDB and China Ex-Im Bank exceeded the $700 billion in outstanding loans from all six Western-backed multilateral banks combined.[48]

When the BRI (originally "One Belt, One Road") was announced in 2013, it created a political narrative and policy architecture to support China's policy banks to expand financing projects in developing countries on an unprecedented scale. BRI takes China's finance and infrastructure construction efforts to a new, and far riskier, level. Beijing is projected to allocate at least $1 trillion, and scores of multinational corporations, both Chinese and international, are angling to take advantage.[49] Internationally, the initiative spans over sixty countries and includes virtually every type of transportation infrastructure—rail, roads, ports, airports, electricity transmission, telecommunications, etc.[50] The Silk Road Economic Belt runs through Central Asia, West Asia, the Middle East, and Europe, while the Maritime Silk Road connects China to countries in Southeast Asia, Oceania, and parts of North and East Africa. BRI has subsumed many projects that were being considered long before it was launched, but the implicit political backing associated with the BRI imprimatur has spurred countless rebrandings of both foreign and domestic projects.

The AIIB's slow start and the Silk Road Fund's limited scale means the CDB and China Ex-Im are likely to continue financing the lion's share of BRI projects.[51] Some Chinese analysts are pessimistic about the prospects for BRI-related investments. They warn that BRI will saddle the country's already deeply indebted banking sector with large quantities of unserviceable foreign loans and fear Beijing's overreach has engendered pushback among policymakers in developing countries and in Western capitals. For instance, Renmin University professor Shi Yinhong warned in 2015 that "China should be mentally cautious, politically cautious, and strategically cautious when adopting BRI."[52] Indeed, it seems likely Beijing will have to reschedule or write off significant portions of debt in the coming years, as massive loans to politically friendly countries like Zimbabwe, Sri Lanka, and Venezuela show few prospects for principal repayment, let alone profits.

### Foreign Aid

China's approach to foreign aid differs in important ways from the members of the OECD's Development Assistance Committee, private Western donors like the Gates Foundation, and multilateral institutions like the World Bank. Rather than poverty alleviation, China's assistance, particularly its concessionary loan aid, is primarily focused on infrastructure development, tied to business contracts, and distributed on a state-to-state basis. Unlike Western countries and institutions, which often place conditions on aid, China's aid does not require audits and comes with "no political strings attached." The predictable result is that Chinese aid is easier for corrupt foreign leaders to "capture."[53]

China provided substantial economic assistance to developing states during the Mao era (1949–1976) but cut its foreign aid expenditures between 1978 and 2000. Since then, foreign aid has re-emerged as an important policy tool, and Beijing released White Papers on the topic in 2011 and 2014.[54] The budget for foreign assistance has grown rapidly over the last decade, with an average annual increase of 29.4 percent between 2004 and 2009. Between 2009 and 2012, China's aid disbursements totaled $14.4 billion, or about a third of the value of Beijing's total aid from 1950 to 2008.[55] China's aid comes in three varieties: grant aid (36 percent of the 2009–2012 total), interest-free loans (8 percent), and concessional loans (56 percent).[56] Over this period, roughly 52 percent of China's aid went to Africa, 31 percent went to Asia, and 8 percent went to Latin America to support various programs including emergency and medical assistance, technical and educational instruction, low-cost housing, and infrastructure.[57]

Until recently, the Ministry of Commerce and the Ministry of Foreign Affairs jointly handled foreign aid in a somewhat piecemeal fashion that did not provide year-on-year tracking, effectively prohibiting systematic evaluation. In 2018, however, as part of a sweeping overhaul of State Council and Central Committee organs, Beijing created an "international development cooperation agency" to oversee and coordinate foreign aid disbursements. According to State Councilor Wang Yong the new system "will give full play to foreign aid as a key means of major-country diplomacy, enhance strategic planning and coordination of foreign aid, and better serve the country's overall diplomatic layout and BRI."[58]

## Politics

### Economic Diplomacy

Bilateral "MoU diplomacy" is the most visible aspect of China's external engagement, and stories of trade promotion, foreign direct investment, and infrastructure financing are commonplace in China's official media. When China's leaders hold meetings overseas, they often travel with large business delegations and sign memoranda of understanding (MoUs) worth hundreds of millions, if not billions, of dollars. Although most deals never reach fruition, high dollar values are tantalizing for cash-strapped developing countries. In 2015, Xi Jinping and Pakistan's president Nawaz Shari signed fifty-one MoUs worth nearly $28 billion, the first phase of the more than $60 billion China-Pakistan Economic Corridor—a critical part of BRI.[59] Such deals, which are not legally binding, remain an important part of Beijing's comprehensive approach.

China also uses multilateral meetings as an occasion to ink deals. China had had a tradition of doubling pledges at FOCAC meetings: from $5 billion in 2006 to $10 billion in 2009, to $20 billion in 2012, and to $60 billion in 2015. At the 2018 FOCAC in Beijing, China maintained, but did not increase, its $60 billion commitment to Africa.[60] The first China-CELAC Forum announced the 2015–2019 Cooperation Plan, in which China pledged to invest $250 billion in Latin America over the next decade.[61]

### Non-Interference

At the most basic level, non-interference refers to Beijing's policy of near universal engagement. China continues to reference the decades-old mantra of the Five Principles of Peaceful Coexistence, emphasize state sovereignty and non-interference in its relations with developing states, and has vetoed UN resolutions that it feels violate the principle of state sovereignty.[62] This approach is attractive to many small and developing states, which warily guard their autonomy.

If a political change occurs in a partner state, as long as the new leaders do not recognize Taipei, Beijing will establish relations with them regardless of their ideology or human rights record. Faced with the problems of governing, new leaders in developing countries—especially those that capture power by force—generally overlook China's previous support for their political rivals. Yet, Beijing's approach aims to mitigate political risk in turbulent developing countries has not always worked. In Libya, South Sudan, and Venezuela, for instance, Chinese investors lost billions of dollars in contracts and capital during violent, long-lasting political transitions.

It is noteworthy that Beijing's interpretation of sovereignty norms is evolving as its relations with particular regimes deepen. During elections in Sierra Leone, Zambia, and Zimbabwe, China publicly supported and provided largesse to friendly African leaders and political parties.[63]

### Foreign Focused Propaganda

As China seeks to be a "cultural major power" (文化大国) it has stepped up its external propaganda (对外宣传) programs to that end.[64] A conceptual framework was adopted in 2004 under the formulation "China's peaceful rise," and became a national priority following Hu Jintao's speech to the 17th Party

Congress in 2007.[65] Since Xi Jinping's accession to power in 2012, Beijing's engagement with the developing world has become increasingly political. Xi has spoken repeatedly on the need to increase China's "soft power" (软实力) by, among other things, creating a compelling Chinese narrative and strengthening Beijing's capacity to convey its message overseas.[66] According to Xi's speeches, the Chinese people's unique history endows their nation with great natural advantages allowing it to become a global cultural power.[67]

As part of its "people-to-people" exchanges, every year Beijing sponsors tens of thousands of foreign youths training at China's universities and vocational schools. According to the Ministry of Education, there were 489,200 international students studying in China in 2017, up from about 290,000 in 2011.[68] In 2016, more than 264,976 foreign students in China hailed from Asia, but thousands of students are from other developing regions, with the greatest increase over the last three years coming from Africa.[69]

In 2004, the Confucius Institute program, run by the Ministry of Education's Hanban, was created ostensibly to promote the study of Chinese language and culture abroad. According to the Hanban headquarters website, in early 2019 there were 525 institutes around the world. Although most are in developed countries, 105 in the United States alone, 227 of 548 (or 41 percent) are in developing countries.[70] Confucius Institutes have faced growing scrutiny in the United States and other Western countries, as questions have been raised about foreign influence and the impact of these institutes on academic objectivity. Yet, such concerns have been muted in developing countries, where education funding is generally scarce.[71]

Outreach by the International Department of the Central Committee of the Communist Party of China (ID-CPC) is a historical and ongoing feature of China's foreign policy and supplements the diplomacy conducted by state organs (e.g., the MFA) and top leaders.[72] The Party's political outreach generally seeks to avoid the appearance of intervention in domestic affairs. In autocracies the ID-CPC generally does not interact with the opposition, while in democracies, it maintains ties with both ruling and opposition parties. In July 2018, ID-CPC chief Song Tao hosted a multilateral meeting in Tanzania that included forty African political parties from over thirty-six countries.[73]

The CPC has expanded its host diplomacy, cadre training, and outreach to political parties throughout the developing world.[74] Party cadre training is organized by the ID-CPC and conducted by academies, party schools, and other relevant training institutions.[75] These programs are explicitly political and are intended to improve foreign perceptions of China and legitimize CPC rule. Ethiopia was perhaps the earliest and most eager student of Chinese cadre training, and has dispatched delegations regularly to China since 1994.[76] As of 2015, the CPC has trained some 2,000 officials of the South Africa's African National

Congress (ANC).[77] In the summer of 2018, another 300 ANC cadres arrived to study "party building" (党建) in China.[78] In July 2018, Chinese construction firms broke ground on the Julius Nyerere Leadership School. Built with Beijing's support, the new training academy is for the ruling parties of Tanzania, South Africa, Mozambique, Angola, Namibia, and Zimbabwe.[79]

Beijing wants to improve younger generations' perceptions of its political system and gain elite support to counter what it sees as Western efforts to portray China in an unfavorable light. Since 2005, the official Xinhua News Agency has emphasized cooperation, content sharing, and media training programs with dozens of news outlets throughout the developing world.[80] To enhance China's influence and international image, Xinhua and CCTV have developed a training initiative for media professionals from developing countries.[81] In 2017, Renmin University hosted a ten-month media training program for forty-eight students from Africa, South Asia, and Southeast Asia on China's political, cultural, media, and economic studies.[82]

## Security

### Military Diplomacy and Peacekeeping

Until the 1990s, China paid scant attention to military diplomacy.[83] The PLA Navy's first fleet visit to a foreign port occurred in 1990, and it did not conduct its first combined exercise with a foreign military until 2002. The policy origins of China's expanded military engagement can be found in the 1998 National Defense White Paper, which presented China's comprehensive "new security concept" and contained the first official use of the term "military diplomacy."[84] Since then the scope and scale of China's military diplomacy has greatly expanded and now encompasses a wide range of activities.

China's most institutionalized security relationships, those including Defense and Security Consultation mechanisms, are with Southeast Asian states and South Asian states, although Beijing does conduct regular, albeit less established, dialogues with more distant major developing states such as South Africa, Egypt, and Turkey. The PLA Navy and Air Force now hold regular combined exercises with foreign militaries. In 2015, China committed $100 million in military assistance to the African Union, and in 2018 the first China-Africa Defense and Security Forum was held in Beijing, including senior military leaders from fifty African states.[85]

China is now among the top contributors of UN peacekeeping personnel and the largest among the permanent Security Council members. Until 2013, it dispatched only support forces, but that year sent its first combat troops to Mali, and in 2014 deployed a battalion to South Sudan. By 2019, China had committed more than 8,000 troops to the UN peacekeeping standby force, roughly 20 percent of the total, and as of January 2019, 2,508 Chinese peacekeeping personnel were serving in UN peacekeeping operations.[86] UN operations give PLA forces real-world experience in hostile foreign environments while enhancing China's image as the benevolent protector of peace and security in developing countries and an active contributor to the international system.

### Power Projection

China's security footprint in the developing world remains small relative to its economic heft but—as Phillip Saunders's chapter in this volume explains—it has grown over the last decade apace with Chinese interests and PLA capabilities (e.g., amphibious lift and at-sea replenishment). PLA warships and large cargo aircraft are increasingly being deployed and heavy bombers and aerial refueling tankers are likely to follow, suggesting that PLA power will continue to grow for the foreseeable future.

In 2004, Hu Jintao directed the PLA to prepare for "New Historic Missions" other than war, including the protection of China's growing national interests abroad.[87] Beijing's 2008 White Paper on China's National Defense identified a "diversified" mission set, including "counter-terrorism, stability maintenance, and emergency rescue and international peacekeeping."[88] The 2013 Defense White Paper discussed "protecting overseas interests," which stipulated that "vessel protection at sea, evacuation of Chinese nationals overseas, and emergency rescue have become important ways and means for the PLA to safeguard national interests."[89]

There are now calls both within the PLA and among the public to strengthen the military's capability to rescue Chinese nationals under threat abroad.[90] In 2011, the PLA helped evacuate thousands of Chinese from Libya, and did so again from Yemen in 2015. In the Libyan case, the PLA diverted a destroyer from the Gulf of Aden to Libya and flew forty sorties using Il-76 transport aircraft to evacuate more than 1,600 Chinese nationals.[91] China dispatched its first anti-piracy detachment to the Gulf of Aden in 2008 and by January 2019 had sent a total of thirty-one task forces, each usually consisting of two warships, helicopters, and a resupply vessel.[92] The PLA is currently building a nineteen-hectare logistics support facility to support the Southern African Development Community Standby Force in Botswana.[93]

Although China long eschewed overseas bases, its position has shifted in recent years. In 2017, the PLA opened a naval base in Djibouti, adjacent to military outposts operated by several other countries including the United States. The base is equipped with maintenance facilities for ships and helicopters, weapons stores, and a contingent of military guards.[94] "Setting up overseas military bases is not an idea we have to shun; on the contrary, it is our right. Bases established by other countries appear to be used to protect their overseas rights and interests," explained Fudan University professor Shen Dingli.[95]

### Arms Sales

During the Mao era, China provided weapons to revolutionary groups or communist partner states.[96] Today, China has reemerged as a sizable arms supplier—moving up from the world's sixth largest during 2004–2010 to the fourth position during 2011–2017.[97]

In addition to tanks, artillery, and small arms, China now sells corvettes, frigates, and fighter aircraft, along with a range of anti-ship and anti-aircraft missiles. Weapons sales include maintenance and training packages that facilitate continued security collaboration. Arms sales have been primarily to either nearby developing states, such as Bangladesh and Pakistan, or resource-rich but technologically weak countries, such as Iran or Nigeria. China has licensed production or agreed to joint weapons development with Pakistan, Thailand, and Indonesia. China and Pakistan, for instance, developed the JF-17 fighter-bomber for markets in the Middle East and South America. Although some buyers, like Turkey and Venezuela, may have purchased Chinese arms to send a political message to Washington, the weaponry's main attraction is its combination of cheap cost, high capability, and reasonable durability.

# Conclusion

China is conducting economic, political, and military engagement on an unprecedented scale throughout the developing world. To help create a world where it is safe from both internal and external threats, Beijing's policies are aimed at cultivating a like-minded, if loosely affiliated and sometimes fractious, coalition of developing states. To achieve this amid the "inevitable" emergence of multipolarity, China abjures political disputes, preaches non-intervention, actively engages governments of all political stripes, and works toward greater "democracy" in international affairs.

But Beijing's approach now faces real, new, and growing challenges. Even as Xi Jinping offers a "China Option" (中国方案), the sharp downturn in GDP growth and the CPC's ever harsher authoritarianism have damaged the country's image in many developing countries. Growing dissatisfaction with debt-for-infrastructure deals, empty MoUs, and Chinese firms disregard for local laws, environmental, and labor standards are all stimulating pushback against Beijing in many developing countries. Meanwhile, at home, critics of BRI are unlikely to remain quiet if unserviceable foreign debts continue to mount. Ultimately, the fate of Beijing's ambitions in the developing world will depend largely on whether it can resolve structural problems dogging the Chinese economy. But even if economic reforms succeed, Chinese wealth and power alone are unlikely to displace American global pre-eminence; to do that Beijing must put forward an attractive political alternative to the Western liberal order—a proposition that, at least to date, it has been unwilling or unable to make.

# Notes

1. Chen Xiangyang, "Xi Jinping Waijiao Sixiang Yinling Xinshidai Zhongguo Tese Daguo Waijiao" [Xi Jinping's Foreign Policy Thought Points the Way to a New Era of Major Power Foreign Policy with Chinese Characteristics], China Online, August 9, 2018, http://opinion.china.com.cn/opinion_79_190279.html.
2. "A Changing China and Its Diplomacy—Speech by Foreign Minister Wang Yi at the Center for Strategic and International Studies," February 26, 2016, https://www.fmprc.gov.cn/mfa_eng/wjb_663304/wjbz_663308/2461_663310/t1345211.shtml.
3. See, for example, Peter Van Ness, *Revolution and Chinese Foreign Policy: Peking's Support for Wars of National Liberation* (Berkeley: University of California Press, 1971).
4. Lin Limin, "Shibada Zhihou de Zhongguo Waijiao Xin Jumian" [China's New Foreign Policy after the 18th Party Congress], Sina News, January 9, 2014, http://news.sina.com.cn/c/2014-01-09/111129197073.shtml.
5. Zhang Hong, "Zhongguo Zouxiang 'Dawaijiao'" [China Moves Toward "Big Power Diplomacy"], *People's Daily Overseas Edition*, February 8, 2011, 6. See also "Dishici Zhuwai Shijie Huiyi Zai Jing Juxing" [The 10th Conference of Chinese Diplomatic Envoys Stationed Abroad Held in Beijing], *People's Daily*, August 30, 2004, 1.
6. "Xi Jinping Chuxi Zhongyang Waishi Gongzuo Huiyi bing Fabiao Zhongyao Jianghua," [Xi Jinping Chairs Central Conference on Work Relating to Foreign Affairs and Delivers an Important Speech], Xinhua News, November 29, 2014, http://www.xinhuanet.com/politics/2014-11/29/c_1113457723.htm.
7. In July 2008, Hu Jintao met with four leaders of "major developing states," including India, Brazil, South Africa, and Mexico. "China's Hu Proposes Priorities for Further Cooperation among Five Major Developing Countries," Embassy of the People's Republic of China in Australia, July 9, 2008, http://au.china-embassy.org/eng/xw/t472968.htm.
8. Chen, "Xi Jinping's Foreign Policy Thought Points the Way to a New Era of Major Power Foreign Policy with Chinese Characteristics."
9. Michael D. Swaine, "Chinese Views on Global Governance since 2008–2009: Not Much New," *China Leadership Monitor*, no. 49 (Winter 2016): 1–13.
10. The Chinese lexicon defines multipolarity as the autonomy or independence of states in the system and their ability to influence events at the regional level; that is, freedom from hegemony. In the American international relations literature, by contrast, "multipolarity" means there are several states with the independent capability to challenge the leading state. Brantly Womack, "Asymmetry Theory and China's Concept of Multipolarity," *Journal of Contemporary China* 13, no. 39 (May 2004): 351–366.
11. He Yafei, "China's Major-Country Diplomacy Progresses on All Fronts," March 23, 2016, http://www.china.org.cn/opinion/2016-03/23/content_38091993.htm.

12. Feng Zhongping and Huang Jing, "China's Strategic Partnership Diplomacy: Engaging with a Changing World," *European Strategic Partnership Observatory (ESPO) Working Paper*, no. 8, June 29, 2014.

13. Chen Xiangyang, "Zhongguo Tuijin 'Dazhoubian Zhanlue' Zhengdangshi" [The Right Time for China to Advance a "Greater Periphery" Strategy], January 16, 2015, http://comment.cfisnet.com/2015/0116/1300445.html.

14. These White Papers are available in Eisenman and Heginbotham eds., *China Steps Out: Beijing's Major Power Engagement with the Developing World* (New York: Routledge, 2018), 322–384.

15. Chen, "Zhongguo Tuijin" [The Right Time], http://comment.cfisnet.com/2015/0116/1300445.html.

16. As Xi Jinping said at Davos in 2017: "China has come this far because the Chinese people have, under the leadership of the Communist Party of China, blazed a development path that suits China's actual conditions." See Xi Jinping, "Xi Jinping Chuxi Shijie Jingji Luntan 2017 Nianhui Kaimushi bing Fabiao Zhuzhi Yanjing" [Xi Jinping Presented at the Opening Ceremony of World Economic Forum 2017 and Made Keynote Speech], Xinhua News, January 17, 2017, http://www.xinhuanet.com/world/2017-01/17/c_1120331492.htm.

17. Andreas Fuchs and Nils-Hendrik Klann, "Paying a Visit: The Dalai Lama Effect on International Trade," *Journal of International Economics* 91, no. 1 (September 2013): 164–177; Nick Macfie, "China Slaps New Fees on Mongolian Exporters amid Dalai Lama Row," Reuters, December 1, 2016, https://www.reuters.com/article/us-china-mongolia/china-slaps-new-fees-on-mongolian-exporters-amid-dalai-lama-row-idUSKBN13Q3I7; Robin Yapp, "Dalai Lama Snubbed in Brazil after Chinese Fury at Mexico Talks," *The Telegraph*, September 18, 2011, https://www.telegraph.co.uk/news/worldnews/southamerica/brazil/8772042/Dalai-Lama-snubbed-in-Brazil-after-Chinese-fury-at-Mexico-talks.html; "Thailand Rejects Chinese Pressure over Dalai Lama," United Press International, February 11, 1993, https://www.upi.com/Archives/1993/02/11/Thailand-rejects-Chinese-pressure-over-dalai-lama/6886729406800/.

18. Wang Wen and Chen Xiaochen, "Who Supports China in the South China Sea and Why," *The Diplomat*, July 27, 2016, https://thediplomat.com/2016/07/who-supports-china-in-the-south-china-sea-and-why/.

19. George Gilboy and Eric Heginbotham, *Chinese and Indian Strategic Behavior: Growing Power and Alarm* (Cambridge: Cambridge University Press, 2012), 72.

20. John Pomfret, "US Takes a Tougher Tone with China," *Washington Post*, July 30, 2010.

21. GDP estimates are from the IMF website. Accessed February 17, 2019.

22. Xi Jinping used the phrase in his 2018 and 2014 FAWC addresses.

23. Conclusion based on interviews conducted by Joshua Eisenman June 2018 with private Chinese businessmen in South Africa, Namibia, Ethiopia, and Ghana.

24. He Yafei, "China's Major-Country Diplomacy Progresses on All Fronts," March 23, 2016, http://www.china.org.cn/opinion/2016-03/23/content_38091993.htm.

25. He, "China's Major-Country Diplomacy"; Feng Zhongping and Huang Jing, "China's Strategic Partnership Diplomacy: Engaging with a Changing World," *European Strategic Partnership Observatory (ESPO) Working Paper*, no. 8, June 29, 2014.

26. Abdi Latif Dahir, "Twice as Many African Presidents Made It to China's Africa Summit Than to the UN General Assembly," *Quartz Africa*, October 5, 2018, https://qz.com/africa/1414004/more-african-presidents-went-to-chinas-africa-forum-than-un-general-assembly/.

27. Xu Xin, "Backgrounder: China-Arab States Cooperation Forum," *Xinhua*, May 12, 2016.

28. "Press Communique of the First Ministerial Meeting of the Strategic Dialogue Between the People's Republic of China and the Cooperation Council for the Arab States of the Gulf," PRC Ministry of Foreign Affairs, June 4, 2010, https://www.fmprc.gov.cn/mfa_eng/wjdt_665385/2649_665393/t707677.shtml.

29. "China-CELAC Trade to Hit $500 Billion: Chinese President," *China Daily*, January 8, 2015, http://www.chinadaily.com.cn/business/2015-01/08/content_19272865.htm.

30. Mwangi S. Kimenyi and Zenia A. Lewis, "New Approaches from Washington to Doing Business with Africa," *This Is Africa Online*, https://www.thisisafricaonline.com/News/New-approaches-from-Washington-to-doing-business-with-Africa?ct=true

31. Joong Shik Kang and Wei Liao, "Chinese Imports: What's Behind the Slowdown," *IMF Working Paper*, no. 16 (106), May 26, 2016.
32. "China's Trade Surplus Down 9.1 Percent in 2016," *China Daily*, January 13, 2017, http://www.chinadaily.com.cn/business/2017-01/13/content_27945655.htm.
33. IMF, Direction of Trade Statistics (DOTS). Southeast Asia figure does not include trade with Taiwan, but does include trade with Singapore. Afghanistan is included in South Asia number.
34. Foreign reserves continued to accumulate rapidly through June 2014, when they reached $3.993 trillion, before falling to about $3.051 trillion in November 2016. PRC State Administration of Foreign Exchange website, see http://www.safe.gov.cn/safe/2018/0612/9313.html, http://www.safe.gov.cn/safe/2016/1230/6183.html, January 12, 2018.
35. Jiang Zemin, "Genghao de Shishi 'Zouchuqu' Zhanlue" [To Better Enforce "Going Out" Strategy], the Central People's Government of the People's Republic of China website, http://www.gov.cn/node_11140/2006-03/15/content_227686.htm. Also see David Shambaugh, *China Goes Global: The Partial Power* (New York: Oxford University Press, 2013), chapter 5.
36. George Chen and Marius Bosch, "ICBC to Buy Standard Bank Stake for $5.6 billion," Reuters, October 25, 2007, https://www.reuters.com/article/us-standardbank-icbc-acquisition/icbc-to-buy-standard-bank-stake-for-5-6-billion-idUSSHA11075020071026; and "Standard Chartered Opens Its First Onshore Chinese Yuan (RMB) Account for South Africa's Portland Steel," Standard Chartered, May 23, 2011, https://www.sc.com/za/news-media/2011-opens-first-africa-onshore-renminbi-account.html
37. National Bureau of Statistics of China, "Zhongguo Tongji Nianjian" [China Statistical Yearbook], (Beijing: China Statistics Press, various years). Current-dollar figures converted to 2018 constant using GDP deflator.
38. Offshore financial centers include Hong Kong, Singapore, the Cayman Islands, the Virgin Islands, and Bermuda. The developed states of Asia are not included in the figures presented. PRC Ministry of Commerce, "2017 Niandu Zhongguo Duiwai Zhijie Touzi Tongji Gongbao" [2017 Statistical Bulletin of China's Outward Foreign Direct Investment], September 2018.
39. "Turning Tides: EY Attractiveness Program, Africa," October 2018, https://www.ey.com/Publication/vwLUAssets/ey-Africa-Attractiveness-2018/$FILE/ey-Africa-Attractiveness-2018.pdf.
40. Xiao Ren, "China as an Institution-Builder: The Case of the AIIB," *The Pacific Review* 29, no. 3 (March 4, 2016): 435–442.
41. "The Case for Reform at the World Bank," *Financial Times*, August 10, 2016, https://www.ft.com/content/b7da7178-5eec-11e6-bb77-a121aa8abd95.
42. Jordan Totten, "BRICS New Development Bank Threatens Hegemony of US Dollar," *Forbes*, December 22, 2014, https://www.forbes.com/sites/realspin/2014/12/22/brics-new-development-bank-threatens-hegemony-of-u-s-dollar/#7f85bbb57f89; "BRICS Cooperation Helps Build New International Framework," *Global Times*, July 13, 2015, http://www.globaltimes.cn/content/931748.shtml.
43. Jane Perlez, "China Creates a World Bank of Its Own, and the US Balks," *New York Times*, December 4, 2015, https://www.nytimes.com/2015/12/05/business/international/china-creates-an-asian-bank-as-the-us-stands-aloof.html; and Mike Callaghan, "The $100 Billion AIIB Opens for Business: Will China's Multilateral Ambitions Soar or Sour?" *The Interpreter*, January 19, 2016, http://lowyinstitute.org/the-interpreter/100-billion-aiib-opens-business-will-chinas-multilateral-ambitions-soar-or-sour.
44. "Why China Is Creating a New 'World Bank' for Asia," *The Economist*, November 11, 2014, https://www.economist.com/the-economist-explains/2014/11/11/why-china-is-creating-a-new-world-bank-for-asia.
45. Salvatore Babones, "China's AIIB Expected to Lend $10–15B a Year, but Has Only Managed $4.4B in 2 Years," *Forbes*, January 16, 2018, https://www.forbes.com/sites/salvatorebabones/2018/01/16/chinas-aiib-expected-to-lend-10-15b-a-year-but-has-only-managed-4-4b-in-2-years/#2e05a2e537f1.

46. "AIIB President Suggests Taking On More Chinese Projects to Improve Asset Quality," *China Knowledge*, February 1, 2019, https://www.chinaknowledge.com/News/DetailNews/85080/AIIB.

47. The third bank, the Agricultural Development Bank of China, has a domestic focus.

48. James Kynge, Jonathan Wheatley, Lucy Hornby, Christian Shepherd, and Andres Schipani, "China Rethinks Developing World Largesse as Deals Sour," *Financial Times*, October 13, 2016, https://www.ft.com/content/5bf4d6d8-9073-11e6-a72e-b428cb934b78.

49. This conclusion is based on interviews with businessmen in Beijing and Shanghai in May and June 2017. Total funding, which will primarily involve debt financing, remains uncertain but has been estimated at between $1 trillion and $4 trillion ("Our Bulldozers, Our Rules"); National Development and Reform Commission of the PRC, Ministry of Foreign Affairs, and Ministry of Commerce, "Tuidong Gongjian Sichouzhilu Jingjidai he 21 Shiji Haishang Sichouzhilu de Yuanjing yu Xindong" [Vision and Actions on Jointly Building Silk Road Economic Belt and 21st-Century Maritime Silk Road], Ministry of Commerce of the People's Republic of China, January 26, 2016, http://www.mofcom.gov.cn/article/i/dxfw/jlyd/201601/20160101243342.shtml.

50. National Development and Reform Commission of the PRC, Ministry of Foreign Affairs and Ministry of Commerce, "Tuidong Gongjian Sichouzhilu Jingjidai he 21 Shiji Haishang Sichouzhilu de Yuanjing yu Xingdong" [Vision and Actions on Jointly Building Silk Road Economic Belt and 21st-Century Maritime Silk Road], Ministry of Commerce of the People's Republic of China, January 26, 2016, http://www.mofcom.gov.cn/article/i/dxfw/jlyd/201601/20160101243342.shtml.

51. James Kynge, "How the Silk Road Plans Will Be Financed," *Financial Times*, May 9, 2016, https://www.ft.com/content/e83ced94-0bd8-11e6-9456-444ab5211a2f. The Export-Import Bank lent $80 billion for projects in forty-nine countries in 2015, compared to $27.1 billion for the Asian Development Bank (and less than $2 billion for the AIIB).

52. Yan Xuetong, "China Must Not Overplay Its Strategic Hand," *Global Times*, August 9, 2017, http://www.globaltimes.cn/content/1060491.shtml; and Yang Mu, Li Jingrui, and Qin Boya, "Shi Yinhong: Tuijin 'Yidai Yilu' Jianshe Yingyou Shenshen Xintai" [Shi Yinhong: We Should Be Cautious When Constructing 'One Belt One Road'], *People News*, July 5, 2015, http://world.people.com.cn/n/2015/0705/c1002-27256546.html.

53. Alex Dreher, Andreas Fuchs, Roland Hodler, Bradley C. Parks, Paul A. Raschky, and Michael J. Tierney, "Aid on Demand: African Leaders and the Geography of China's Foreign Assistance," *Aid Data Working Paper*, no. 3 (October 2016).

54. For the text of the 2014 Foreign Aid White Paper, see Eisenman and Heginbotham, eds., *China Steps Out*, 385–404.

55. James T. Areddy, "China Touts $14.4 Billion in Foreign Aid, Half of Which Went to Africa," *Wall Street Journal*, July 10, 2014, https://blogs.wsj.com/chinarealtime/2014/07/10/china-touts-14-4-billion-in-foreign-aid-half-of-which-went-to-africa/.

56. Information Office of the State Council of the People's Republic of China, *China's Foreign Aid*, July 10, 2014, http://english.gov.cn/archive/white_paper/2014/08/23/content_281474982986592.htm.

57. Ibid.

58. Xinhua, "China Unveils Cabinet Restructuring Plan," *China Daily*, March 14, 2018, http://www.chinadaily.com.cn/a/201803/14/WS5aa7ffd3a3106e7dcc141675.html.

59. Mateen Haider and Irfan Haider, "Economic Corridor in Focus as Pakistan, China Sign 51 MoUs," *Dawn*, April 20, 2015, https://www.dawn.com/news/1177109.

60. Winslow Robertson and Lina Benabdallah, "China Pledged to Invest $60 Billion in Africa. Here's What That Means," *Washington Post*, January 7, 2016; Yun Sun, "China's 2018 Financial Commitments to Africa: Adjustment and Recalibration," Brookings Institution, September 5, 2018, https://www.brookings.edu/blog/africa-in-focus/2018/09/05/chinas-2018-financial-commitments-to-africa-adjustment-and-recalibration/.

61. "Cooperation Plan (2015–2019)," China-CELAC Forum, January 23, 2015, http://www.chinacelacforum.org/eng/zywj_3/t1230944.htm.

62. Ren Mu, "China's Non-intervention Policy in UNSC Sanctions in the 21st Century: The Cases of Libya, North Korea, and Zimbabwe," *Ritsumeikan International Affairs*, no. 12 (2014): 101–134.

63. Cooper Inveen and Ruth Maclean, "China's Influence Looms as Sierra Leone Goes to the Polls," *The Guardian*, March 7, 2018, https://www.theguardian.com/world/2018/mar/07/chinas-influence-looms-as-sierra-leone-goes-to-the-polls.

64. See David Shambaugh, "China's External Propaganda Work: Missions, Messengers, Mediums," *Party Watch Annual Report 2018*, https://docs.wixstatic.com/ugd/183fcc_e21fe3b7d14447bfaba30d3b6d6e3ac0.pdf; Anne-Marie Brady, "Exploit Every Rift: United Front Goes Global," *Party Watch Annual Report 2018*, https://docs.wixstatic.com/ugd/183fcc_5dfb4a9b2dde492db4002f4aa90f4a25.pdf.

65. See David Shambaugh, "China's Soft Power Push: The Search for Respect," *Foreign Affairs* (July–August 2015).

66. Feng Wenya, ed., "Xi Jinping Tan Guojia Wenhua Ruan Shili: Zengqiang Zuo Zhongguoren de Guqi he Diqi" [Xi Jinping Talks About National Cultural Soft Power: Strengthening the Character and Integrity of Being a Chinese], Xinhua, June 25, 2015, http://www.xinhuanet.com//politics/2015-06/25/c_127949618.htm.

67. Yu Yunquan, "Zhongguo Wenhua Ruan Shili Jianshe Renzhongdaoyuan" [Shouldering the Heavy Responsibility of Building China's Soft Power], *International Communications*, no. 1 (January 10, 2007): 44–46; and Chen Xinguang, "Meiguo Ruan Shili Shuaitui yu Zhongguo Ruan shili Tisheng" [US Soft Power Weakening and Chinese Soft Power Rising], *China Daily*, June 23, 2015, http://column.chinadaily.com.cn/article.php?pid=8322.

68. Ministry of Education of the People's Republic of China, "Jiaoyuyubu fa Liuxue Dashuju: Zhongguo cheng Yazhou Zuida Liuxue Mudiguo" [Ministry of Education Sent Out Big Data on Chinese Students Studying Abroad and Foreign Students Studying in China: China Has Become the Largest Studying Destination in Asia], *Chinanews*, March 30, 2018, http://www.chinanews.com/gn/2018/03-30/8479732.shtml.

69. Ministry of Education, "2016 Niandu Woguo Laihua Liuxuesheng Qingkuang Tongji" [2016 Statistics Regarding Foreign Students in China], Ministry of Education of the People's Republic of China, March 1, 2017, http://www.moe.gov.cn/jyb_xwfb/xw_fbh/moe_2069/xwfbh_2017n/xwfb_170301/170301_sjtj/201703/t20170301_297677.html.

70. "About Confucius Institute/Classroom," Hanban, http://english.hanban.org.

71. Elizabeth Redden, "Closing Confucius Institutes," *Inside Higher Ed*, January 9, 2019, https://www.insidehighered.com/news/2019/01/09/colleges-move-close-chinese-government-funded-confucius-institutes-amid-increasing.

72. See David Shambaugh, "China's 'Quiet Diplomacy': The International Department of the Chinese Communist Party," *China: An International Journal* 5, no. 1 (March 2007).

73. Edith Mutethya, "CPC Holds Dialogue with African Political Leaders," *China Daily*, July 18, 2018, http://www.chinadaily.com.cn/a/201807/18/WS5b4e61a9a310796df4df70cb.html.

74. See Julia G. Bowie, "International Liaison Work for the New Era: Generating Global Consensus?," *Party Watch Annual Report 2018*, https://docs.wixstatic.com/ugd/183fcc_687cd757272e461885069b3e3365f46d.pdf.

75. For a description of African party cadre training programs see David Shinn and Joshua Eisenman, *China and Africa: A Century of Engagement* (Philadelphia: University of Pennsylvania Press, 2012), 75–79.

76. Yun Sun, "Political Party Training: China's Ideological Push into Africa," Brookings Institution, July 5, 2016, https://www.brookings.edu/blog/africa-in-focus/2016/07/05/political-party-training-chinas-ideological-push-in-africa/.

77. Stephanie Findlay, "South Africa's Ruling ANC Looks to Learn from Chinese Communist Party," *Time*, November 24, 2014, http://time.com/3601968/anc-south-africa-china-communist-party/; and "Beijing Will Increase Sway over African Policymaking," *Oxford Analytics Daily Brief*, August 8, 2016, https://dailybrief.oxan.com/Analysis/DB212857/Beijing-will-increase-sway-over-African-policymaking.

78. "Briefs from China—Learning from the Best for the Future: Notes from the ANC SG CDE Ace Magashule," *ANC Today*, June 2018, http://anctoday.org.za/briefs-china-learning-best-future/, accessed November 22, 2018.

79. "Groundbreaking Ceremony of Julius Nyerere Leadership Held," *The Herald* (Zimbabwe), July 17, 2018.

80. Shinn and Eisenman, *China and Africa*, 201–203; "Forum on China-Africa Media Cooperation," CCTV, 2012.

81. Iginio Gagliardone, "China and the Shaping of African Information Societies," in *Africa and China: How Africans and Their Governments Are Shaping Relations with China*, edited by A. W. Gadzala, 45–59 (Lanham, MD: Rowman and Littlefield, 2015); Iginio Gagliardone, "China as a Persuader: CCTV Africa's First Steps in the African Media Sphere," *Ecquid Novi: African Journalism Studies* 34, no. 3 (2013): 29; and Yu-shan Wu, "The Rise of China's State-Led Media Dynasty in Africa," *South African Institute of International Affairs Occasional Paper*, no. 117 (2012): 24.

82. Edmund Smith-Asante, "48 Journalists Begin Media Exchange Program in China," *Graphic Online*, March 3, 2017, https://www.graphic.com.gh/news/general-news/48-journalists-begin-media-exchange-programme-in-china.html.

83. See Ken W. Allen and Eric A. McVadon, *China's Foreign Military Relations* (Washington, DC: Henry L. Stimson Center, 1999).

84. For Chinese definitions of military diplomacy, see Jin Canrong and Wang Bo, "Youguan Zhongguo Tese Junshi Waijiao de Lilun Sikao" [On the Theories of China's Military Diplomacy], *Taipingyang Xuebao* 23, no. 5 (May 2015): 17–25.

85. Lina Benabdallah, "China-Africa Military Ties Have Deepened: Here Are Four Things to Know," *Washington Post*, July 6, 2018, https://www.washingtonpost.com/news/monkey-cage/wp/2018/07/06/china-africa-military-ties-have-deepened-here-are-4-things-to-know/?utm_term=.f6c39ce0f2d4.

86. United Nations, "Contributors to United Nations Peacekeeping Operations as of 3.01.19," https://peacekeeping.un.org/en/troop-and-police-contributors, accessed February 17, 2019.

87. Roy Kamphausen, "China's Military Operations Other Than War: The Military Legacy of Hu Jintao," paper presented at SIPRI Conference, Stockholm, April 2013.

88. *China's National Defense in 2008*, Information Office of the State Council of the People's Republic of China website, January 20, 2009, http://www.china.org.cn/government/white-paper/node_7060059.htm.

89. "The Diversified Employment of China's Armed Forces," Xinhua, April 16, 2013, https://www.nti.org/media/pdfs/China_Defense_White_Paper_2013.pdf

90. See Han Xudong, "Guofang Daxue Jiaoshou: Baohu Haiwai Zhongguoren Jidai Wozu Zhunjian Junshi Liliang Jieru" [Chinese National Defense University Professor: We Must Urgently Establish Military Forces for Intervention in Order to Protect Overseas Chinese Citizens], *Huanqiu Shibao*, February 2, 2012, http://opinion.huanqiu.com/1152/2012-02/2402155.html; Yue Gang, "Zhongguo Junli Ying Hanwei Haiwai Liyi Juebu Rongren Paihua Beiju Zaiyan" [The PLA Must Protect China's Overseas Interests and Never Tolerate Any Anti-Chinese Tragedy Again], *Sina News*, April 18, 2013, http://mil.news.sina.com.cn/2013-04-18/0824722110.html; and Andrea Ghiselli, "Diplomatic Opportunities and Rising Threats: The Expanding Role of Non-Traditional Security in Chinese Foreign and Security Policy," *Journal of Contemporary China* 27, no. 112 (February 15, 2018): 611–625.

91. "The Diversified Employment of China's Armed Forces."

92. Xue Chengqing and Cui Xiaoyang, "Haijun Di Sanshiyi Pi Huhang Biandui Chenggong Chuzhi Liusou Yisi Haidao Mubiao" [The 31st Navy Convoy Successfully Got Rid of Six Suspected Pirate Targets], PLA Navy Website, January 24, 2019, http://navy.81.cn/content/2019-01/24/content_9412725.htm.

93. "China to Help with SADC Regional Logistics Depot," *Defense Web* (South Africa), September 7, 2018, https://www.defenceweb.co.za/joint/logistics/china-to-help-with-sadc-regional-logistics-depot/.

94. "China Formally Opens First Overseas Military Base in Djibouti," Reuters, August 1, 2017, https://www.reuters.com/article/us-china-djibouti/china-formally-opens-first-overseas-military-base-in-djibouti-idUSKBN1AH3E3.

95. Shen Dingli, "Don't Shun the Idea of Setting Up Overseas Military Bases," China Online, January 28, 2010, http://www.china.org.cn/opinion/2010-01/28/content_19324522.htm.

96. Joshua Eisenman, "Comrades-in-Arms: The Chinese Communist Party's Relations with African Political Organizations in the Mao Era, 1949–1976," *Cold War History* 18, no. 4 (March 20, 2018): 429–445.

97. "SIPRI Arms Transfer Database," www.sipri.org/databases/armstransfers.

# 15

# Regional Multilateralism
# with Chinese Characteristics

SRIKANTH KONDAPALLI

In China's diplomatic practice, bilateralism—rather than multilateralism—has been predominant. There are a number of reasons for this: China was intentionally kept out of the international institutional order by the West during the Cold War; Mao was long suspicious of these organizations as instruments of imperialist domination of the world; and China has long been suspicious of the binding obligations that come with being a member of an organization (preferring the diplomatic flexibility of bilateral relationships and shifting alignments). However, Deng Xiaoping and subsequent Chinese leaders took a more positive view of international institutions after China was admitted to the United Nations in 1971. They came to realize that multilateral organizations could provide important financial and technical resources to help develop China. They thus came to understand that being part of these institutions was part and parcel of "reform and opening," but would also accrue to China's global standing as a rising power.[1] By the end of 2008, China had become a member of more than 130 intergovernmental organizations (IGOs), twenty-four UN specialized agencies, and was a signatory to more than 300 multilateral treaties.[2]

While it is notable that China has become a member of almost all international organizations (excepting the OECD, International Energy Agency, and Missile Technology Control Regime), much less noticeable has been China's steadily increasing involvement in *regional* multilateral organizations and groups of nations. As China has expanded its global footprint into literally every continent and part of the planet, as described well in the previous chapter by Joshua Eisenman and Eric Heginbotham, Beijing has sought to join existing institutions in those regions—but what is particularly noteworthy is that China has stimulated and created a wide range of *new* organizations and regional groupings all around the world. That is what this chapter is about—China's regional

Srikanth Kondapalli, *Regional Multilateralism with Chinese Characteristics* In: *China and the World*. Edited by: David Shambaugh, Oxford University Press (2020). © Oxford University Press
DOI: 10.1093/oso/9780190062316.003.0015

multilateralism (whereas Katherine Morton's contribution to this volume focuses on global issues and institutions).

Such Chinese initiatives most notably include: the Asian Infrastructure Investment Bank (AIIB), Shanghai Cooperation Organization (SCO), Association of Southeast Asian Nations Plus China (ASEAN + 10), Brazil-Russia-India-China-South Africa (BRICS), Forum for China-Africa Cooperation (FOCAC), China–Arab States Cooperation Forum (CACF), China–Central and Eastern Europe Countries (CEEC), and a series of group-ings in Latin America (China–Latin America Forum, China-Caribbean Economic and Trade Cooperation Forum, China–Latin America Common Market Dialogue, and China–Latin America Business Summit). China has been either the initiator of, or actively engaged in, the creation of all these groupings. In addition, while not being the initiator, China is also active in the regional groupings of APEC (Asia-Pacific Economic Cooperation), the East Asian Summit (EAS), the Asia-Europe Meeting (ASEM), ASEAN + 3, and a variety of bilateral "strategic partnership" dialogues around the world.

China's involvement in stimulating and participating in these regional group-ings has been motivated by several factors. First and foremost, they are tangi-ble manifestations of Beijing's long-term desire to create a "multipolar world." Second, China has long had a notable distaste for (and opposition to) Western-style security alliances, which it regularly labels as "Cold War relics." Instead of the principle of collective security which underpins these alliances, China instead promotes "comprehensive" and "cooperative" security. Third, Beijing prefers to promote commercial exchange through such organizations. Fourth, China has long critiqued the post–World War II international organizational (or liberal) structure as being biased in favor of the West and against the interests of countries in Asia, Africa, Latin America, and the Middle East. Beijing's critique is that this bias is both participatory and structural, that is, that these countries are not adequately represented and placed in a dependent relationship to the Western countries that set up and control these institutions.

For these main reasons, China has long been discontent with global *and* regional institutions and Beijing has despaired about attempts to reform them. Instead, since the mid-1990s, Beijing decided to take matters into its own hands and to set up new regional institutions and groupings—which would mainly be structured as "China + ." That is, most of the new institutions would have "China" in the name paired with the other countries or a geographical region, as noted above. These new institutions would operate according to the princi-ples of "comprehensiveness" and "cooperation," and would normally have some variation of the Five Principles of Peaceful Coexistence written into their char-ters. Thus, rather than being security-oriented alliances like most Western insti-tutions, the new China-initiated regional institutions would focus primarily on various dimensions of socioeconomic development. Beijing termed this "new type multilateralism" (新型多边主义).

## China's Perceptions of Multilateralism

As a large country and interacting extensively with the world, China has built up considerable experience with multilateralism. It has now interacted with international multilateral bodies in the political, economic, cultural, and security fields for decades. It has also been increasingly involved in addressing in global issues through multilateral institutions—such as nontraditional security challenges, energy security, environmental issues, terrorism, public health pandemics, climate change, and other global issues.[3] In many of these multilateral institutions, instead of seeking to undermine or overhaul these institutions, during the post-Mao era China has generally upheld the overall rules and norms that have evolved since 1945—although Beijing, as noted above, has also simultaneously shown occasional frustration and ambivalence with some of the ways in which these postwar institutions have operated.[4] Its primary complaint has been that they are not representative or inclusive of developing countries from the Global South, and are structurally biased against those countries.

In its actual practice of involvement in multilateral institutions and diplomatic processes, China's experience has been mixed and diversified, and its "comfort level" has grown gradually. It was during the late 1990s that China began to overcome its ambivalence and distrust, and began to observe, and then progressively join, a larger number of international organizations. This growing comfort level was reflected at the Sixteenth Party Congress in November 2002 when President Jiang Zemin stated: "We will continue to take an active part in multilateral diplomatic activities and play our role in the United Nations and other international or regional organizations. We will support other developing countries in their efforts to safeguard their legitimate rights and interests."[5] Subsequently, at the Seventeenth Party Congress in 2007, Jiang's successor Hu Jintao stated: "We will continue to take an active part in multilateral affairs, assume our due international obligations, play a constructive role, and work to make the international order fairer and more equitable."[6] Hu likewise stated at the Eighteenth Party Congress: China shall "play its due role of a major responsible country, and work jointly with other countries to meet global challenges. . . . We will actively participate in multilateral affairs, support the United Nations, G-20, the Shanghai Cooperation Organization, BRICS and other multilateral organizations in playing an active role in international affairs, and work to make the international order and system more just and equitable."[7] At the 19th Party Congress in October 2017 new leader Xi Jinping stated: "China will support multilateral trade regimes and work to facilitate the establishment of free trade areas and build an open world economy.... China will continue to play its part as a major and responsible country, take an active part in reforming and developing the global governance system."[8]

Foreign Minister Wang Yi also encapsulates the current priorities of China in this regard. In September 2018 speech at the UN, Wang Yi stated: "Today international rules and multilateral mechanisms are under attack, and the international landscape is filled with uncertainties and destabilizing factors.... China has upheld the international order and pursued multilateralism.... In the face of new developments and severe challenges, China will keep to its commitment and remain a champion of multilateralism.[9] At the 2019 Munich Security Conference, the Politburo member in charge of foreign affairs, Yang Jiechi, gave a strong defense of China's prioritization of, and contributions to, global and regional multilateralism.[10] Yang's speech echoed that of Xi Jinping at the 2017 World Economic Forum in Davos, Switzerland.[11] With Donald Trump's distrust of multilateralism and the United States' withdrawing from its seven-decade-long leadership role in international institutions, Beijing senses the vacuum and potential opportunity to expand its own influence.

## China's Regional Multilateralism in Practice

It is against this general backdrop and prioritization by Beijing that China's creation of, and engagement with, regional multilateral institutions must be viewed. What follows are brief studies of China's involvement in ASEAN-led institutions, the AIIB, SCO, CACF, FOCAC, CEEC, and the BRICS.

China's multilateral interactions with the Southeast Asian countries has paid rich dividends in terms of trade, investments, markets, and the recent community-building process, although it has also shown signs of tensions (mainly due to sovereignty disputes). Since the 1990s, this region became one of the major areas of multilateral interactions for China.

While the Association of Southeast Asian Nations (ASEAN) was established in 1967, China did not participate or interact with the group collectively until the early 1990s. In July 1991, China's foreign minister Qian Qichen attended the ASEAN Ministerial Meeting as a guest and later as a dialogue partner in 1996. A "strategic partnership" between the two was signed in 2003. China also signed the Treaty of Amity and Cooperation in 2003, the bedrock treaty of the organization, thus permitting it to become involved in various mechanisms such as ASEAN + 1,[12] the ASEAN Regional Forum (ARF),[13] Asian Defense Ministers Meeting Plus (ADMM + ),[14] and the East Asian Summit (EAS).[15] By acceding to ASEAN's Treaty of Amity and Cooperation (the first non-ASEAN member to do so), China adhered to the ASEAN "centrality" requirements of being the "leading" force and in the "driver's seat" of regional multilateralism.[16]

This facilitated the ASEAN-China FTA (CAFTA), which came into force in 2010. China and ASEAN are now engaged in CAFTA "upgrade" negotiations, which commenced in 2015,[17] and both sides have established a goal of $1 trillion in total trade by 2020. ASEAN has become China's third-largest trading partner (after the European Union and United States)—Malaysia is China's largest, followed by Singapore, Thailand, Indonesia, Vietnam, Philippines, Myanmar, Cambodia, Laos, and Brunei.[18] China's total trade with the ten-member ASEAN has grown to over $430 billion by 2017, with $11 billion in China's investments in the Southeast Asian countries by 2017, and twenty million Chinese tourists visiting ASEAN countries and ten million Southeast Asian visitors going to China.[19]

The ASEAN + 1 (China) dialogue came into being with foreign minister Qian Qichen's aforementioned visit to attend the ASEAN meeting at Kuala Lumpur in 1991. The "strategic partnership" between the two in 2003 elevated ties further. The ASEAN-China Center was established at Beijing in 2011 and China appointed an ambassador to the ASEAN the next year. Under this format, summit-level meetings are held annually (twenty-one meetings by 2018) to discuss political and security cooperation, facilitating trade, investments, and sociocultural cooperation between the two sides.[20]

Established in 1993 as a regional security cooperative mechanism based on a series of dialogues, in 1995 the ARF adopted many confidence-building measures (CBMs), making "preventive diplomacy" and approaches to conflict its centerpiece. The ARF now has twenty-seven members (ten dialogue partners and seven others). A vision statement for 2020 was adopted in 2009 and Hanoi Action Plan unveiled in 2010.

By October 2018, ADMM + had held five meetings since the 2010 Hanoi inaugural meeting. The organization of defense ministers now includes the ten ASEAN members plus eight defense partners such as Australia, New Zealand, China, South Korea, Japan, India, the United States, and Russia. They discuss traditional and nontraditional security challenges in the region, confidence-building measures, the Korean Peninsula, disaster relief and humanitarian assistance, direct communications lines, the Code for Unplanned Encounters at Sea (CUES) for naval ships, establishing a network of regional coordination centers, guidelines for air encounters for military aircraft, and others.

## The Asian Infrastructure Investment Bank

While many multilateral institutions that China supported, led, or joined are mainly in political, diplomatic, or security realms, the AIIB distinguishes itself as a multilateral lending and investment agency. The AIIB as a multilateral development bank was established in 2015. The Asian Development Bank estimated that Asia needed over $8 trillion in funding for infrastructure projects, which were hardly met by the existing lenders. The AIIB partly intends to fill this void. The initial ten members increased from twenty-one in 2014 to seventy-two members by 2019, with twenty-eight prospective members currently in the queue.

The AIIB aims to promote infrastructure projects, with an initial capital of $100 billion.[21] China has over 26 percent of voting power, followed by India at 7.51 percent and Russia 5.93 percent.[22] The AIIB is headed by Jin Liqun as its founding president for a five-year term (since 2016). Decisions are based on consensus rather than voting. Despite US opposition, several members of the European Union joined the AIIB.[23] The total lending of the AIIB by early 2019 was about $7.5 billion for thirty-five projects, although the lending and investment targets are increasing gradually.[24] The initial suspicion that the AIIB will be dominated by China's interests, or lacking professional or environmental standards, has been ameliorated by the lending criteria and projects, which have adhered to established international standards and practices. Further, an estimated two-thirds of such lending has the World Bank or Asian Development Bank as co-financers. The credit ratings of the AIIB are also high.[25]

## The Shanghai Cooperation Organization (SCO)

The first major multilateral institution that China initiated occurred in the mid-1990s with the establishment of the "Shanghai Five,"[26] which morphed into the Shanghai Cooperation Organization in 2001. Initiated in 1996 to resolve territorial disputes and erect military CBMs among the former Soviet republics, Russia, and China, it has evolved into a major institution with the addition of new members, observers, and dialogue partners. The original members of the SCO include China, Russia, Kazakhstan, Tajikistan, Kyrgyzstan (the "Shanghai Five" of 1996), and Uzbekistan (from an observer to member) in 2001. Later, India and Pakistan joined as members in 2017. SCO observer states include Mongolia in 2004, Iran in 2005, Belarus in 2010, and Afghanistan in 2012, while dialogue partners are Sri Lanka in 2009, Turkey in 2012, and Armenia, Azerbaijan, Cambodia, and Nepal in 2015. While Iran had applied for full membership, Armenia, Azerbaijan, Bangladesh, Egypt, Israel, Maldives, Nepal, Sri Lanka, and Syria have applied for observership status. Guests at the SCO meetings include the ASEAN, Commonwealth of Independent States, and Turkmenistan.

The SCO is known for its efforts to resolve territorial disputes and demilitarization, joint military exercises, counterterrorism, and counter drug trafficking efforts, and work related to regional stability and other issues.[27] It is working on improving economic and cultural connectivity, which will be enhanced by China's Belt and Road Initiative (BRI).

Table 15.1, which lists the announcements at the Shanghai Five-SCO's summit meetings, suggests an expanding discourse in the multilateral spheres.

Despite the efforts in promoting regional stability and energy cooperation, in many areas progress has been limited. Membership of India, Pakistan, Iran, and other countries into the SCO had been stalled for a long time, reflecting mainly geopolitical issues and suspicions in the region and thus affecting the "inclusivity" of this multilateral institution. There is also the reported reluctance of China to admit the United States or the European Union in some capacity.

Although the SCO withstood changes in the regional and global arenas, it remains underdeveloped and far from realizing its potential as a regional Eurasian institution. The economic dimension of the SCO is still particularly weak, despite growing bilateral economic ties between China and the SCO states.[28] China's trade with the SCO states is over $217 billion and its cumulative investments in these states was $83 billion by 2017. Four areas hamper trade in the SCO: customs procedures, harmonization of standards, business flows, and regulatory environment. Many SCO states are recent entrants to the WTO and the tariff structures are relatively high. A study conducted by China's Ministry of Commerce and International Trade and Economic Cooperation suggested that in order for the SCO states to enhance economic cooperation, they need to facilitate trade, liberalize market mechanisms, and discuss a Free Trade Area following WTO standards.[29]

Despite its shortcomings, the SCO has emerged as a major regional multilateral institution with internal cohesion—achieved by authoritarian states being in the majority. While Russia still has a significant influence in this organization, the recent collaboration between the Eurasian Economic Union and the BRI provides an economic opening for China. The SCO's relevance is expected to increase in the coming years. Fluctuations in global energy prices also could enhance the SCO's appeal in the coming years.

## China–Arab States Cooperation Forum

Of the twenty-two Arab states, China has established strategic partnerships or cooperative arrangements with ten. It has upgraded relations by organizing the China–Arab States Cooperation Forum (CACF) in 2004,[30] and participating in a sub-regional Gulf Coordination Council (GCC). By 2018, eight ministerial meetings of the CACF had taken place, fifteen high-level official meetings, and four strategic and political dialogues had been held (see Table 15.2).[31] China has become the second largest trading partner for the Arab states (approximately

*Table 15.1* **SCO Summit Meetings, 1996–2018**

| *Meeting/Locations* | *Declarations and Main Accomplishments* |
| --- | --- |
| 1st Shanghai Five Meeting, April 1996, Shanghai | Agreements on "deepening military trust" in border regions; progress on border discussions. |
| 2nd Meeting, April 1997, Moscow | Agreement on mutual reduction of military forces in border regions—for demobilization of troops from the border areas and for confidence-building measures (CBMs). |
| 3rd Meeting, July 1998, Almaty | Security and regional cooperation. |
| 4th Meeting, July 1999, Bishkek | Proposed "adopting joint actions" to combat three hostile forces: national separatism, religious extremism, and international terrorism; regional security, regional cooperation, and international situation reviewed. "Zero tolerance to engagements damaging the sovereignty, the security and the social order of any member states within their territory." |
| 5th Meeting, July 2000, Dushanbe | Uzbekistan admitted as an observer. |
| 1st SCO Summit, June 2001, Shanghai | Communique on crackdown on "Three Evils" (terrorism, separatism, and extremism) issued. |
| 2nd Summit, June 2002, St. Petersburg | Declaration on the Charter—member states to "pursue close, productive, and diversified cooperation in the 'Shanghai Spirit,' which includes mutual trust and benefit, equality, mutual consultation, respect for the cultural diversity, and a focus on joint development"; Regional Antiterrorist Organization; regarded economic development a "very important matter" in SCO operations; nuclear non-proliferation and strengthening of nuclear arms treaties proposed. |
| 3rd Summit, May 2003, Moscow | Institutionalization process of the SCO began. Agreement on the procedure of drafting and implementation of the budget of the SCO, the statutes of the Council of heads of state, the Council of heads of government, and the Council of foreign ministers. |
| 4th Summit, June 2004, Tashkent | Convention on privileges and immunities adopted; SCO Secretariat established; drug trafficking issue discussed; Mongolia became an observer; practical steps in economic development initiated; development fund and a business council set up; tie-up with other multilateral institutions in Asia recommended. |

*Table 15.1* **Continued**

| Meeting/Locations | Declarations and Main Accomplishments |
|---|---|
| 5th Summit, July2005, Astana | Timetable for US withdrawal from Afghanistan; Pakistan, India, and Iran admitted as observers on July 5; counter-terrorism agenda proposed. |
| 6th Summit, June 2006, Shanghai | Counter-terrorism, economic development, energy, information security issues discussed; SCO Business Council and the Forum on Industry and Commerce set up. |
| 7th Summit, August 2007, Bishkek | Treaty on Long-Term Good-Neighborly Relations, Friendship and Cooperation signed—for establishing "eternal peace" among member states; to enhance the role of SCO-Afghan liaison mechanism; support for nuclear weapon free zone in Central Asia; indirect comments on US unilateralism. |
| 8th Summit, August 2008, Dushanbe | Backdrop of Georgian events; Russian side suggested drug control; Dialogue Partnership Protocol signed. |
| 9th Summit, June 2009, Yekaterinburg | Emphasized multipolarity; enhancing the coordination role of UN in world affairs; Global Financial Crisis; China announced $10 billion in credit for the SCO partners; Sri Lanka and Belarus as dialogue partners; to establish anti-narcotic and financial security belts in the Afghanistan peripheries in Central Asia. |
| 10th Summit, June 2010, Tashkent | Cooperation in the fields of agriculture and combating crime; welcomed the holding of the first visiting meeting of the SCO Business Council in Ulan Bator; lifted the moratorium on new memberships. |
| 11th Summit, June 2011, Astana | Membership based on consensus; approved the Counter-narcotics Strategy of the SCO member states for 2011–2016; expressed "grave concern over the instability in Northern Africa and the Middle East." |
| 12th Summit, June 2012, Beijing | Critiqued ballistic missile defense; supported nuclear weapon free zone in Central Asia; "oppose the application of information and communications technologies in a way that endangers their political, economic and security"; "regional affairs should be resolved through consultation between relevant countries in the region and international organizations"; expressed "deep concern" on events in West Asia and North Africa. Afghanistan became an observer, while Turkey was added as a dialogue partner. |

(*continued*)

*Table 15.1* **Continued**

| Meeting/Locations | Declarations and Main Accomplishments |
| --- | --- |
| 13th Summit, September 2013, Bishkek | Counter-terrorism Action Plan for 2013–2017; science and technology cooperation enhanced; membership guidelines and obligations adopted; proposal to form SCO Development Bank. |
| 14th Summit, December 2014, Dushanbe | Agreement on the facilitation of international road transport among the SCO member states; resolution on the seventieth anniversary of the end of World War II. |
| 15th Summit, July 2015, Ufa | SCO Development Strategy adopted; three-year program of cooperation (2016–2018) on counter-terrorism; process begun to include India and Pakistan as members; upgrading Belarus from dialogue partner to observer and Azerbaijan, Armenia, Cambodia, and Nepal as new dialogue partners. |
| 16th Summit, June 2016, Tashkent | Member states reaffirm their determination for "turning of the borders with each into the borders of eternal peace and friendship. . . . All relevant disputes [in the maritime domain] should be resolved peacefully through friendly negotiations and agreements between the parties concerned without their internationalization and external interference." |
| 17th Summit, June 2017, Astana | Issued joint statement: "[The SCO] has established itself as an internationally recognized and authoritative multilateral association . . . the SCO member states note the importance of creating a more equitable polycentric world order . . . freedom from confrontation and conflicts, and equal and indivisible security, and will contribute to forging a human community sharing a common destiny." |
| 18th Summit, June 2018, Qingdao | Issued joint statement: "[The SCO is] one of the most influential participants in the modern system of international relations. . . . the SCO sets an example of close and fruitful cooperation in building a more equitable and balanced world order based on an equal, cooperative, indivisible, comprehensive and sustainable security, ensuring the interests of each and every state in accordance with the norms and principles of international law." |

*Source*: SCO Secretariat website (http://eng.sectsco.org).

*Table 15.2* **The China-Arab States Cooperation Forum, 2004–2018**

| Meetings | Declarations and Main Accomplishments |
|---|---|
| 1st Ministerial Conference, September 2004, Cairo | "Strengthen dialogue and cooperation and promote peace and development." |
| 2nd Ministerial Conference, June 2006, Beijing | President Hu Jintao suggested four measures: enhance political cooperation; intensify economic cooperation for mutual benefit and win-win outcome; promote cultural cooperation for peace and friendship; step up international cooperation for peace and stability. |
| 3rd Ministerial Conference, May 2008, Bahrain | Foreign Minister Yang Jiechi proposed to "promote prosperity and progress of mankind civilization and partners of coordination and cooperation to contribute to stability in the Middle East and to build a harmonious world." |
| 4th Ministerial Conference, May 2010, Tianjin | "Comprehensive Sino-Arab cooperation and common development of the strategic partnership." |
| 5th Ministerial Conference, May 2012, Tunisia | "Deepen the strategic cooperation and promote common development." |
| 6th Ministerial Conference, June 2014, Beijing | President Xi Jinping spoke on Belt and Road Initiative as a new structure of cooperation with Arab states. |
| 7th Ministerial Conference, May 2016, Doha | Foreign Minister Wang Yi: "We should . . . advance the joint construction of the Belt and Road between China and Arab states, improve the '1+2+3' cooperation pattern and give play to the '1+1>2' scale effect, so as to promote China-Arab collective cooperation to a new level." |
| 8th Ministerial Conference, July 2018, Beijing | "Future-oriented strategic partnership of comprehensive cooperation and common development." |

*Source*: China Ministry of Foreign Affairs, https://www.fmprc.gov.cn/mfa_eng/zxxx_662805/t1576621.shtml.

$200 billion in 2017) and invested $1.26 billion in the region.[32] In 2008, China and the League of Arab States released an action plan to further ties.[33] China also released a White Paper in January 2016, laying out a vision for broadening and deepening relations.[34]

On the eve of the first ministerial meeting at Cairo, Foreign Minister Li Zhaoxing said: "Shared interests of countries and common needs of the people are where diplomacy starts and ends."[35]

That the agenda of this Forum is fast-changing is visible in China's leaders' recent interventions, including the "non-binding" understandings on these states joining the Belt and Road Initiative. In his speech at the Arab League headquarters during his visit to Saudi Arabia and Egypt in January 2016, Xi Jinping offered a "China Plan" for the governance of the Middle East—to "jointly solve development problems in the Middle East, become a peace builder in the Middle East, a promoter, of development, a booster of industrialization, a supporter of stability, and a cooperative partner."[36] At the 2018 meeting, China pledged to provide Arab states with $20 billion in loans for industrial development and offered free trade deals.

As such, economic relations are improving. China's trade with Arab states increased from $37 billion in 2004 to $145 billion in 2010 and about $200 billion in 2017.[37] Further, to enhance communications between the two sides, in May 2017 it was decided to provide the Beidou navigational system to cover the region. However, an Egyptian diplomat, Mohammed Numan Jalal, who was involved in the Forum, argued that bilateral relations are crucial in the effectiveness of the Forum, even as certain "cautiousness" prevails in overall China-Arab relations.[38] Also, while economic relations are improving, people-to-people and cultural relations are lagging behind.[39]

## China–Central and Eastern Europe Countries (CEEC)

In April 2012, in Warsaw, Poland, China and the Central and East European Countries formed a group of "16+1"—with eleven European Union members plus five Balkan states. This became known as the "China–Central and East European Countries" (CEEC) mechanism.[40] At its inauguration, Premier Wen Jiabao stated: "The two sides should respect and equally treat each other, and address major concerns of the other side so as to deepen their political mutual trust."[41] Soon ministerial meetings were organized on energy, transport, and maritime issues.[42] After the Belt and Road Initiative was launched in 2013, increasingly many of these sixteen countries evinced interest in the Chinese-led BRI infrastructure projects. In 2017, the first summit-level meeting of 16 + 1 was held at Budapest, Hungary, where China announced $15 billion for the infrastructure projects (see Table 15.3).[43] Bilateral trade among the 16 + 1 has increased from $43.9 billion in 2010 to $58.7 billion in 2016. In 2014, China established an investment fund of $3 billion for investment in Central and Eastern Europe. In 2016 an additional $10 billion was allocated.

*Table 15.3*  **China-CEEC Summit Meetings, 2012–2018**

| Summit Meetings | Remarks and Main Accomplishments |
| --- | --- |
| 1st Meeting, April 2012, Warsaw | "Two sides should establish and perfect a working mechanism and an exchange platform as soon as possible, and specify the priorities for their cooperation," "to deepen practical cooperation in trade, investment, fiscal and financial areas." |
| 2nd Meeting, November, 2013, Bucharest | Hold a meeting of heads of government every year to review cooperation achievements and set the direction for future cooperation. |
| 3rd Meeting, December 2014, Belgrade | 16+ 1 has "built a new platform for mutually beneficial cooperation and served as a new engine for deepening." |
| 4th Meeting, November 2015, Suzhou | A medium-term agenda announced under the theme "New Beginning, New Domains, New Vision." |
| 5th Meeting, November 2016, Riga | Cooperation initiative involving the ports at the Adriatic, Baltic, and Black Sea and along the inland waterways "under the principle of drawing upon each other's strengths, win-win cooperation and common development." |
| 6th Meeting, November 2017, Budapest | Firmly oppose protectionism in all its forms and manifestations. |
| 7th Meeting, July 2018, Sofia | Reaffirmed "principles of mutual respect, mutually beneficial cooperation and building an open world economy, making economic globalization more dynamic, inclusive and sustainable." New initiatives taken on infrastructure and mutual investments, agriculture, tourism, and high-tech industry. |

*Source*: CEEC website, http://www.china-ceec.org/eng/.

Thus, China has created a corridor of ties from the Baltics in the north down to the Balkans in the south, and the sub-region of Central Europe is clearly a high priority for China. But Beijing's rather stealthy moves in this part of Europe have begun to attract much attention from the EU in Brussels as well as the United States. While primarily economic in nature, there are longer-term strategic and foreign policy implications of China's thrust into the region. The European Union in Brussels is keeping a close eye on CEEC developments as they potentially undermine EU unity—particularly Belt and Road projects that do not adhere to EU tendering and construction requirements.

To the north, China is concentrating its efforts on cultivating the three Baltic states (Estonia, Latvia, Lithuania), as well as Poland, the Czech Republic, and Slovakia—while Serbia and Romania seem to be the centerpieces of Beijing's thrust into the Balkan region.[44] President Xi Jinping paid a state visit to Belgrade in June 2016, the first ever by a Chinese head of state to the region, where he signed twenty-four agreements—covering industrial cooperation, finance, infrastructure, trade, energy, telecoms, science and technology, health care, culture, and tourism—and elevated China-Serbia ties to a "comprehensive strategic partnership."[45] Premier Li Keqiang also paid an official visit to Romania in 2013, the first by a Chinese leader in nineteen years. While in Bucharest, Li attended a meeting of CEEC and met all of his Balkan counterparts. No Chinese leader has yet to visit the other Balkan states, but a steady stream of Balkan officials below the rank of head of state regularly visit China.[46] An examination of these visits reveals that a broad range of functional ministries are involved. The Chinese Communist Party's International Department also maintains quiet but regular and extensive contacts with a range of political parties across the Balkans and Central Europe. Chinese commercial activities in the region are focused primarily on a range of infrastructure projects: bridges, rail lines, roads, airports, telecoms, electricity, and ports.[47]

Taken together, China is laying the groundwork for a long-term set of relationships and presence in Central Europe. Beijing sees this north-south corridor from the Baltics down to the Adriatic as "soft" and fertile ground for its initiatives. Many of these countries are not yet integrated into the EU, and thus are not susceptible to national security concerns that Brussels may have concerning Chinese presence on the continent. Many of these countries are quite underdeveloped, in the midst of long-term reconstruction, and they are in dire need of the infrastructure, energy, and other forms of development that China can offer. Many have high unemployment rates, and Chinese investment employs people. These countries have historical ties to China throughout the Cold War period, and many were former socialist states. Many of these countries still have autocratic leaders and political systems, much to Beijing's liking. These countries are geographically isolated, but Beijing is paying attention to them. These countries feel neglected by the European Union and the United States, while China is one major power that is supportive of their needs.

## Forum on China-Africa Cooperation (FOCAC)

FOCAC was formed in 2000 at Beijing and it has subsequently held seven ministerial meetings every alternate year and three summit meetings (see Table 15.4). The number of African states participating increased from forty-four in 2000 to

*Table 15.4* **FOCAC Meetings, 2000–2018**

| Meetings, Place, and Number of African States | Remarks and Accomplishments |
| --- | --- |
| 1st Ministerial Conference, October 2000, Beijing; 44 countries | Theme of "building a new international political and economic order and China-Africa economic and trade cooperation for the 21st century." "[T]he establishment of a joint and equitable new international political and economic order is indispensable for the democratization of international relations and for the effective participation of developing countries in the international process of decision making." |
| 2nd Ministerial Conference, December 2003, Addis Ababa; 44 countries | "Consolidate and develop China-Africa friendship, deepen mutually beneficial cooperation." |
| 3rd Ministerial Conference, November 2006, Beijing; 48 countries | 1st Summit-level meeting; "Friendship, Peace, Cooperation, and Development." |
| 4th Ministerial Conference, November 2009, Sharm El Sheik, Egypt; 49 countries | "Deepening the new type of China-Africa Strategic Partnership for sustainable development"; climate change, trade protectionism, developed countries should keep their commitments on "aid, debt relief, promoting and increasing investment, opening up and accessing market, and assisting developing countries to promote economic growth in order to achieve sustainable development." |
| 5th Ministerial Conference, July 2012, Beijing; 50 countries | "Open up new prospects for a 'new type' of China-Africa strategic partnership"; Initiative on China-Africa Cooperative Partnership for Peace and Security. |
| 6th Ministerial Conference, December 2015, Johannesburg; 52 countries | 2nd Summit-level meeting; co-chaired by China and South African leaders for the first time. |
| 7th Ministerial Conference, September 2018, Beijing; 53 countries | 3rd Summit-level meeting; ". . . to build a China-Africa community with a shared future that assumes joint responsibility, pursues win-win cooperation . . . ensures common security." |

*Source*: FOCAC official website, https://www.focac.org/eng/.

fifty-three in 2018.[48] Compared to other such international continental forums such as Europe-Africa Summit, France-Africa Summit, Tokyo International Conference on African Development, and India-Africa Summit, the FOCAC has steadily expanded in terms of influence and membership.

The issues that were raised at the inception of FOCAC include South-South developmental cooperation, elevating South-North dialogue, promoting the participation of developing countries in formulating international rules, and protection of both sides to reverse their global marginalization.[49] The Beijing Declaration of 2018 FOCAC summit meeting provided for the normative flavor of the grouping. It stated:

> We emphasize the importance of upholding the purposes and prin-ciples of the UN Charter and supporting the active role of the UN in international affairs. We advocate mutual respect and equal consulta-tion, firmly reject Cold-War mentality and power politics, and embrace the new approach to state-to-state relations that favors dialogue over confrontation, partnership over alliance. We follow the principle of achieving shared benefits through consultation and collaboration in global governance, advocate multilateralism and democracy in interna-tional relations, and believe that all countries are equal, irrespective of their size, strength or wealth. We oppose interference in others' internal affairs and arbitrary use or threat of force in international affairs, and we reaffirm the need to deepen mutual understanding and enhance coor-dination and collaboration with each other at the UN and other fora.[50]

Over a span of nearly two decades, FOCAC has emerged as a major multi-lateral process in terms of its membership. Normatively as well, there have been several aspirational statements. According to a Chinese assessment, "Since Africa is an important player in international politics, the natural alliance of China and Africa has boosted the multi-polarization and democratization of international order."[51]

Another major outcome of the FOCAC, apart from the coordination between the countries, is increased trade and investment and a moratorium on debts between China and Africa. China has also committed to providing enormous amounts of aid to Africa under FOCAC auspices. Bilateral trade increased from a mere $12 million in 1956 to a 2014 figure of $220 billion, although declining to $170 billion in 2017. In 2009 China became the biggest trading partner for Africa. Tangible benefits for Africa included canceled debts, market access, con-cessional loans, infrastructure projects, and personnel training.[52] At the Beijing summit, President Xi announced $60 billion in investments in Africa as a part of the Belt and Road Initiative.

Despite the increase in its influence, FOCAC has also exhibited several problems. While the declarations at the summit meetings mention about the reform and reorganization of the UN and its expansion to include African states, no such measures have been undertaken. China's contributions to UN peacekeeping missions has increased, but compared to Bangladesh, Pakistan, and India, the number of personnel deployed and financial contributions are still low, although these have led to increase in China's footprint in the continent, including the establishment of China's first naval base at Djibouti. China's stance on the Darfur crisis in Sudan or its military assistance has also been controversial.[53]

China also released two White Papers in 2006 and 2015 explaining the financial assistance it provided and the infrastructure projects it had undertaken in Africa. However, its grants, aid, and loans are still meager: China offered $5 billion at the 1st FOCAC in 2000, increased it to $10 billion in 2009 and $20 billion in 2012, and by 2014 to $10 billion. China's aid is invariably paid by African countries through commodities. Despite the political and security issues highlighted above, according to Osita Eze of the Nigerian Institute of International Affairs, China's interests in the FOCAC are mainly economic in nature.[54]

## China–Latin America Groupings

While the PRC was relatively new to the Latin American region until the 1990s, it has stepped up multilateral interactions over the last decade, mainly in the economic field initially (as with the other multilateral initiatives it had undertaken), but also increasingly in the political and security fields. China released two White Papers on Latin America and the Caribbean in 2008 and in 2016. It has become the region's second largest trading partner after the United States, displacing the European Union. It is the largest financier in the region. Total trade between China and the region expanded from $145 million in 1970 to $260 billion in 2017. A trade target of $500 billion by 2025 was announced in 2015. China is Latin America's second largest trading partner, although trade figures still lag significantly behind the United States (over $560 billion) and the European Union ($250 billion). A free trade agreement was signed with Chile and Peru. China has invested $150 billion in the South American region since 2005 and, as a part of the BRI, it is planning to invest more, specifically through state-owned banks like the China Development Bank and Ex-Im Bank. However, debts of South America are increasing as well.[55]

Growing economic influence provided depth to its interactions with the region. During his visit to Brazil in July 2014, President Xi Jinping proposed "1+3+6" cooperation framework (1 referring to China–Latin America and the Caribbean plan of 2015–2019; 3 relating to trade, investment, and finance; and 6 for cooperation in energy and resources; infrastructure construction;

agriculture; manufacturing; scientific and technological innovation; and information technology).[56]

In the political and diplomatic fields, Beijing has floated China-exclusive forums such as with the thirty-three-member Community of Latin America and the Caribbean States (China-CELAC) in 2011. Beijing adopted a "comprehensive cooperative partnership" with CELAC members in 2014.[57] Two ministerial meetings of this forum were held by 2018, with the first in Beijing. Under the theme "New Platform, New Starting Point, New Opportunity" it called for promoting "multilateralism and a multipolar world, and greater democracy in international relations."[58] At this first meeting, China passed a $35 billion package for the region. The second meeting convened in January 2018 in Chile with the theme "working for more development, innovation and cooperation for our peoples." China's proposal on the BRI was accepted.[59] The third meeting is slated for 2021.

Given the strategic significance of the region, China has multiple initiatives in the region—economic and trade cooperation, business forum, infrastructure forum, investors' forum, local government forum, and even in the security sector with a defense forum. Thus on February 2, 2005, the first meeting of the China–Caribbean Economic and Trade Cooperation Forum was held after the forum was established the previous year.[60] At the third meeting of this Forum in 2011, Beijing announced $1 billion in preferential loans to the region. Twelve meetings of China-Latin America Business Summit meetings were held by late 2018.[61] By 2018, four meetings of the China–Latin American and Caribbean Countries' Infrastructure Cooperation Forum had been held since its establishment in 2015, mainly focusing on connectivity issues.

Latin America today has become the second largest destination for China's overseas investment.[62] The Latin America China Investors Forum (LACIF) has held nine meetings by 2019. It brings together corporate leaders and policymakers from both sides for discussions and facilitating investments, mergers and acquisitions, etc. The China–Latin America Local Government Cooperation Forum came into being in 2016; a China–Latin America Think Tank Forum started 2010, and China–Latin America and the Caribbean (LAC) Media Forum meetings were held as a part of the mandate given by the Plan of 2015–2019. In addition, four meetings of the China–Latin America High-Level Defense Forum were held by 2018—which mainly includes exchanges and non-lethal cooperation between the security and defense establishments.[63] Day by day, these initiatives are enhancing integration between China and Latin America, despite distances, and are enhancing the profile of China.

China places enormous importance to the Latin American region and in the years to come it is expected to increase its footprint in the region to counter the

US influence, expand the multipolar club, and utilize the economic resources to reinforce its growth.

## The BRICS

Russia took the early lead in mobilizing the foreign ministers of China, India, and Brazil in 2006 for discussing the multipolar world order. The BRIC came into existence that year, with South Africa being added in 2010 and the acronym changing to BRICS (see Table 15.5 for a summary of BRICS summits). Since then it has established itself as a major intergovernmental, consultative, multilateral, transcontinental, and grouping of emerging economies. It resulted in the initiation of 2010 IMF quota reform to increase the voting share of the developing countries, establishment of the New Development Bank (NDB), and Contingency Reserve Agreement, and other initiatives.[64]

In this milieu, the BRICS provide a major platform for China to protect its interests in expanding on a global scale its trade and investments, as well as promoting its perspectives on regional security matters. Many perspectives are shared by China and the other BRICS members to varying degrees. For instance, after the Iraq, Afghanistan, Egypt, Syria, and Libya wars, China's position of observing the UN Charter, specifically the non-intervention principle, has been a constant theme in its foreign policy—as Beijing fears similar interventions in Xinjiang, Tibet, "color revolutions," and the like. By combining consumers and producers of energy resources, the BRICS provides a cushion for China, although the energy prices are based on an international market demand and supply equation. The BRICS also provides a chance for China to productively utilize its foreign exchange reserves through the New Development Bank and others, given the emerging economy status of the grouping and the demand for infrastructure projects in these countries.

However, differences persist within BRICS on the specifics of UN Security Council reform, membership expansion of the grouping, creating alternative credit rating agencies, the extent of internet freedom, free trade proposals, multiple entry visas, people-to-people contacts, and the like. The institutionalization process of the BRICS is still low without a fully functional secretariat.

In just over a decade the BRICS has captured the imagination of some in the global community—while others dismiss it as an acronym in search of an institution and an institution in search of a mission. While the BRICS has been dubbed as the club of emerging economies, three of the five economies in the BRICS (Russia, Brazil, and South Africa) are also facing economic problems, while China is entering into a "new normal" of "medium-high" growth levels. Politically, a majority of the BRICS countries are democracies and structural differences on rule of law, maritime commons, and others are emerging. In terms of

*Table 15.5* **BRICS Summit Meetings, 2009–2018**

| Meetings | Remarks and Main Accomplishments |
| --- | --- |
| 1st Meeting, June 2009, Yekaterinburg | Heads of states of four BRIC countries participated. Discussion on Global Financial Crisis, reform of the international financial institutions, major issues concerning the developing and less-developing countries, UN Charter, G-20, etc. |
| 2nd Meeting, April 2010, Brasilia | IMF reform proposed; multilateral diplomacy with the United Nations playing the central role; suggestions made for revising multilateral trading system, embodied in the World Trade Organization, climate change issues, Doha Round. |
| 3rd Meeting, April 2011, Sanya | "Broad Vision, Shared Prosperity"; South Africa joins to form BRICS. Information security, support to civilian nuclear energy. |
| 4th Meeting, March 2012, New Delhi | "BRICS Partnership for Global Stability, Security and Prosperity"; Rio 20; Green Economy; Security situation in Iraq, Syria, and Afghanistan discussed. |
| 5th Meeting, March 2013, Durban | "BRICS and Africa—Partnerships for Integration and Industrialization"; adoption of Counter Terrorism Convention; Non-BRICS observers. |
| 6th Meeting, July 2014, Fortaleza | New Development Bank and Contingency Reserve Agreement signed; Middle East Nuclear Weapon Free Zone mooted; Counter-piracy. |
| 7th Meeting, July 2015, Ufa | "BRICS Partnership—a Powerful Factor of Global Development"; Centrality of WTO, outer-space cooperation. |
| 8th Meeting, October 2016, Goa | "Building Responsive, Inclusive, and Collective Solutions"; draft on alternative credit rating agencies circulated. |
| 9th Meeting, September 2017, Xiamen | "BRICS: Stronger Partnership for a Brighter Future." |
| 10th Meeting, July 2018, Johannesburg | "BRICS in Africa: Collaboration for Inclusive Growth and Shared Prosperity in the 4th Industrial Revolution." |

*Source*: http://infobrics.org/news/summits/.

security, the Russian suggestion of converting the BRICS into a military alliance has hardly elicited enthusiasm among others.

# Conclusion

China's regional multilateral interactions have intensified since the 1990s and have impacted the political, security, and economic aspects of regional and global orders. China's role in these institutions illustrates six dimensions of Chinese diplomatic practice.

First, China's steadily increasing and active participation in regional, cross-regional, and global multilateral institutions is indicative of a broader move away from Deng Xiaoping's strategy of "keeping a low profile" (韬光养晦) to the more recent strategy of Xi Jinping of "striving for achievement" (奋发有为). Taking a cue from the party congresses on enhancing multilateral interactions, China has been expanding its role and footprint substantially. Increasingly, many of the multilateral declarations in which China has been participating include terms and concepts that China has been proposing for the domestic audiences previously. These include the "One China Principle,"[65] the "three evils,"[66] "harmonious world," "new type of international relations," "community of common destiny," Belt and Road Initiative, and others.

Second, China is adding its own flavor to regional multilateralism. This is related to membership (inclusiveness principle), equality and non-discrimination, reciprocity, peaceful resolution of conflicts, and other normative dimensions. Concerning non-exclusivity, there has been some debate on China's reluctance to admit other potential aspirants to the multilateral institutions. China itself had applied for these eagerly in the 1990s (such as in the ASEAN-led ones), although it had shown considerable resistance to the memberships of Australia, New Zealand, India, United States, and others in the East Asian Summit or India's membership in the SCO, even though it was eager to include South Africa at the Sanya meeting of the BRICS. While China had come under considerable pressure to adapt to the universal "one country, one vote" pattern at the Fortaleza meeting of the BRICS in the newly formed New Development Bank, the China-dominated AIIB is still to be tested on this count.

Third, while one of the principles in multilateralism is not to raise bilateral issues, specifically contentious sovereignty problems, China has been able to push its agenda and policies through many multilateral institutions, and it has successfully blocked verbiage or whole statements that it disagreed with. This is a kind of "veto diplomacy."

Fourth, the institutionalization process in multilateral institutions reveals a process that provided time for socialization between different ministries and other organizations among the member states, and the outcome of the summit meetings became much more predictable. It also provided scope for approving or disapproving potential aspirants to these multilateral institutions in terms of membership, as India encountered in the SCO membership issue. More significant, the institutionalization process provided China with a decisive role in shaping the aid or loan packages that it announced.

Fifth, China has benefited enormously economically from these organizations. Many of the multilateral initiatives of China resulted in China's becoming one of the largest trading partners in these institutions—CEEC, SCO, ASEAN, CACF, FOCAC, BRICS, etc. Much of the trade is in China's favor. While China's outbound investments are increasing, much of these investments are made by the state-owned banks or Chinese companies with little local economic input or financial transparency in their transactions, leading to controversies over "debt diplomacy." In the process, the European Union, Japan, India, and other multilateral partners' suggestions on rule of law, sound finances, environmental protection, and transparency have come under stress recently in the Belt and Road Initiative projects.

Sixth, through the multilateral institutions, China has proposed "multipolarity" as a way to shape the emerging world order and Beijing has suggested ways to counter and oppose American influence. In the process, China suggested a "revisionist" agenda of revamping the Bretton Woods institutions (specifically IMF voting rights), the UN system, and other long-standing multilateral institutions. While China suggests that global governance rules should be readjusted to better accommodate developing countries, in actual practice much of the actual work in the multilateral institutions is either to "bide time" or increase China's stakes and rights in these institutions. The IMF did increase the voting rights of China by nearly 6 percent (although the US Congress never affirmed the change, and this was one of the principal reasons China launched the AIIB). Except for releasing a White Paper and making statements, Beijing has not attempted any reform and reorganization of the UN Security Council so far—indeed, Beijing has blocked any consideration of adding Brazil, Germany, Indonesia, India, or Japan.

It thus appears that Beijing's regional multilateralism is an interim arrangement in China's drive to acquire regional and global dominance.[67] Multilateral diplomacy also provides an opportunity for establishing partnerships with targeted countries that could pave the way for supporting China's power transition with the United States in the coming years.

# Notes

1. For studies of China's progressive evolution into the international institutional order see: Alastair I. Johnston, *Social States: China and International Institutions, 1980–2000* (Princeton: Princeton University Press, 2008); Elizabeth Economy and Michel Oksenberg, eds., *China Joins the World: Progress and Prospects* (New York: Council on Foreign Relations, 1998); David Shambaugh, *China Goes Global* (New York and Oxford: Oxford University Press, 2016), chapter 4; David Shambaugh, "China and the Liberal World Order," in *The World Turned Upside Down: Maintaining American Leadership in a Dangerous Age*, edited by Nicholas Burns, Leah Bitounis, and Jonathon Price (Washington, DC: Aspen Institute, 2017); Wu Guoguang and Helen Lansdowne, eds., *China Turns to Multilateralism: Foreign Policy and Regional Security* (London: Routledge, 2008); Ann Kent, *Beyond Compliance: China, International Organizations, and Global Security* (Stanford, CA: Stanford University Press, 2007); Mark Lanteigne, *China and International Institutions: Alternative Paths to Global Power* (London: Routledge, 2005); and Gerald Chan, Pak Ki Lee, and Lai-ha Chan, *China Engages Global Governance: A New World Order in the Making?* (London: Routledge, 2015).

2. No author, "Guoji Diwei" [International Position], *Renmin Ribao* [People's Daily], September 23, 2009.

3. See Gerald Chan, Pak Ki Lee, and Lai-ha Chan, *China Engages Global Governance: A New World Order in the Making?* (London: Routledge, 2015); and David Arase, "Non-Traditional Security in China-ASEAN Cooperation: The Institutionalization of Regional Security Cooperation and the Evolution of East Asian Regionalism," *Asian Survey* 50, no. 4 (July/August 2010), 808–833.

4. See, for example, Suisheng Zhao, "A Revisionist Stakeholder: China and the Post–World War II World Order," *Journal of Contemporary China* 27, no. 113 (September 2018): 643–658.

5. Jiang Zemin, "Build a Well-off Society in an All-Round Way and Create a New Situation in Building Socialism with Chinese Characteristics," November 18, 2002, https://www.fmprc.gov.cn/mfa_eng/topics_665678/3698_665962/t18872.shtml.

6. Hu Jintao, "Hold High the Great Banner of Socialism with Chinese Characteristics and Strive for New Victories in Building a Moderately Prosperous Society in All," October 15, 2007, http://www.chinadaily.com.cn/china/2007-10/24/content_6204564.htm.

7. Hu Jintao, "Firmly March on the Path of Socialism with Chinese Characteristics and Strive to Complete the Building of a Moderately Prosperous Society in All Respects," November 8, 2012, http://www.china.org.cn/china/18th_cpc_congress/2012-11/16/content_27137540_11.htm.

8. Xi Jinping, "Secure a Decisive Victory in Building a Moderately Prosperous Society in All Respects and Strive for the Great Success of Socialism with Chinese Characteristics for a New Era," October 18, 2017, http://www.xinhuanet.com/english/download/Xi_Jinping's_report_at_19th_CPC_National_Congress.pdf. See also Chen Yan, "习近平多边外交思想研究" [Studies on Xi Jinping's Multilateral Diplomatic Thought] 渭南师范学院学报 [Weinan Normal University Journal] 32, no. 19 (2017).

9. Wang Yi, "Multilateralism, Shared Peace, and Development," September 28, 2018, https://www.fmprc.gov.cn/mfa_eng/wjdt_665385/zyjh_665391/t1600861.shtml.

10. Keynote Speech by H. E. Yang Jiechi, "Working for Community with a Shared Future for Mankind by Promoting International Cooperation and Multilateralism," Speech at the 55th Munich Security Conference, February 16, 2019, http://www.xinhuanet.com/english/2019-02/17/c_137827311.htm.

11. https://www.weforum.org/agenda/2017/01/full-text-of-xi-jinping-keynote-at-the-world-economic-forum/.

12. Twenty-one meetings of ASEAN+1 (China) had been held by 2018, expanding the subjects from trade and investments to traditional and nontraditional security aspects. For the latest see "Chairman's Statement of the 21st ASEAN-China Summit to Commemorate the 15th Anniversary of ASEAN-China Strategic Partnership," November 14, 2018, accessed at https://asean.org/storage/2018/11/ASEANChinaSummitChairmansStatementFinal1.pdf.

13. The ARF was formed in 1994 with the ten ASEAN members and eight others. The membership was expanded to twenty-seven by 2015. The security dialogue mechanism involved the participation of foreign ministers who discuss confidence-building mechanisms, preventive diplomacy, and constructive dialogue. Twenty-five meetings had taken place as of August 2018.

14. ASEAN Defense Ministers Meetings (ADMM) commenced in 2008 and in 2010 expanded to include the annual ADMM+ mechanism meetings with the eight dialogue partners.

15. Since its inception in 2005, the EAS held thirteen meetings through November 2018 with the participation of eighteen heads of state/government. It is intended to strengthen global norms, international law, rule of law, and international order.

16. Cheng-Chwee Kuik, "Multilateralism in China's ASEAN Policy: Its Evolution, Characteristics, and Aspirations," *Contemporary Southeast Asia* 27, no. 1 (April 2005): 102–122; and Zhao Suisheng, "China and East Asian Regional Cooperation: Institution-building Efforts, Strategic Calculations, and Preference for Informal Approach," in *China and East Asian Strategic Dynamics: The Shaping of a New Regional Order*, edited by Lee Dongmin and Mingjiang Li (Lanham, MD: Lexington Books, 2011).

17. See Wei Min, "Upgrading China–ASEAN FTA: Related Issues and Future Development," *China International Studies*, March/April 2015, 107–120.

18. US-China Economic and Security Review Commission, *China's Economic Ties with ASEAN: A Country-by-Country Analysis* (Washington, DC: US-China Economic and Security Review Commission, March 17, 2015).

19. "Overview of ASEAN-China Dialogue Relations" (August 2018), http://asean.org/wp-content/uploads/2012/05/Overview-of-ASEAN-China-Relations-August-2018_For-Website.pdf. Also see Zhao Hong, *China and ASEAN* (Singapore: ISEAS Yusof Ishak Institute, 2015).

20. ASEAN Secretariat Information Paper, "China," August 2018: https://asean.org/asean/external-relations/china/.

21. Natalie Lichtenstein, "Governance of the Asian Infrastructure Investment Bank in Comparative Context" (2018), https://www.aiib.org/en/about-aiib/who-we-are/yearbook/_download/governance-aiib-comparative.pdf.

22. Carry Huang and Andrea Chen, "China to Have 30 Percent Stake, Veto Power under AIIB Deal," *South China Morning Post*, June 14, 2018, https://www.scmp.com/news/china/diplomacy-defence/article/1829342/china-have-30-cent-stake-veto-power-under-aiib-deal.

23. Wang Yu, "The Political Economy of Joining the AIIB," *The Chinese Journal of International Politics* 11, no. 2 (June 1, 2018): 105–130.

24. See "AIIB," https://www.aiib.org/en/index.html; and Daniel Poon, "The AIIB's Creative Spirit: Experiments in Infrastructure Finance," *East Asia Forum*, April 19, 2018, http://www.eastasiaforum.org/2018/04/19/the-aiibs-creative-spirit-experiments-in-infrastructure-finance/.

25. Tamar Gutner, "AIIB: Is the Chinese-Led Development Bank a Role Model?," Council on Foreign Relations, June 25, 2018, https://www.cfr.org/blog/aiib-chinese-led-development-bank-role-model.

26. When the Shanghai Five was established in 1996, China's Foreign Ministry spokesperson stated three purposes for the new organization: "good neighborliness and mutual trust, fight against terrorism, and multipolarization." See "Spokesperson on the "Shanghai Five" mechanism," June 1, 2001, https://www.fmprc.gov.cn/mfa_eng/wjb_663304/zzjg_663340/gjs_665170/gjzzyhy_665174/2616_665220/2619_665226/t15379.shtml.

27. Pan Guang, "新形势下的上海合作组织:挑战、机遇和发展前景" [SCO under the New Situation: Challenges, Opportunities and Development Prospects], *International Studies* [国际问题研究], no. 5 (2002): 38–42.

28. Han Lu, "Deepening Economic Cooperation in the Shanghai Cooperation Organization: Opportunities, Barriers, and Approaches," *China International Studies*, no. 71 (July/August 2018): 39–56.

29. Ministry of Commerce and International Trade and Economic Cooperation, "上海合作组织区域经济合作研究" [SCO Regional Economic Cooperation Research], *Russia, Central Asia, East Europe Research*, no. 1 (2004): 2–13.

30. The "normalization, institutionalization" of this forum is seen in different communication mechanisms such as Ministerial Meetings, Senior Officials meetings, Entrepreneurs Conference and Investment Seminar, China-Arab Relations and Civilization Dialogue seminars, Sino-Arab Friendship Conference, Energy Cooperation Conference, News and Press Cooperation Forum, cultural festivals, Senior Officials Conferences in Health Policy, etc. See Yao Kuangyi, "China-Arab States Cooperation Forum in the Last Decade," *Journal of Middle Eastern and Islamic Studies* 8, no. 4 (2014); and Nicola P. Contessi, "Experiments in Soft Balancing: China-led Multilateralism in Africa and the Arab World," *Caucasian Review of International Affairs* 3, no. 4 (Autumn 2009): 404–434.

31. "关于论坛" [On the Forum], November 16, 2018, http://www.chinaarabcf.org/chn/gylt/t540745.htm.

32. "Fruitful Conference in Beijing Ushers In New Chapter of China-Arab Ties: Arab Experts," Xinhua, July 13, 2018, http://www.xinhuanet.com/english/2018-07/13/c_137320612.htm.

33. "Action Plan of the China-Arab Cooperation Forum (2008–2010)," May 22, 2010, https://www.fmprc.gov.cn/mfa_eng/wjb_663304/zzjg_663340/xybfs_663590/xwlb_663592/t466439.shtml.

34. "China's Arab Policy Paper," January 14, 2016, http://www.china.org.cn/world/2016-01/14/content_37573547.htm.

35. Li, cited at "Forum on Cooperation between China and Arab States about to Be Formally Launched," September 13, 2004, https://www.fmprc.gov.cn/mfa_eng/wjb_663304/zzjg_663340/gjs_665170/gjzzyhy_665174/2616_665220/2617_665222/t157698.shtml.

36. China-Arab States Cooperation Forum Research Center (Shanghai), "Joint Development of the 'Belt and Road,' a New Era of Promoting China-Arab Collective Cooperation—Achievements and Prospects of the China-Arab States Cooperation Forum," May 2018, http://mideast.shisu.edu.cn/_upload/article/files/95/d5/159cb85b4c218c71efee-7bb400c9/9b738dd6-d9d1-4217-b989-8c48cf8b12e4.pdf.

37. "China-Arab Forum to Broaden BRI," *Global Times*, July 9, 2018, http://www.globaltimes.cn/content/1110103.shtml.

38. Mohammed Numan Jalal, "The China-Arab States Cooperation Forum: Achievements, Challenges, and Prospects," *Journal of Middle Eastern and Islamic Studies* 8, no. 2, https://www.tandfonline.com/doi/pdf/10.1080/19370679.2014.12023244.

39. See Lina Benabdallah, "China's Relations with Africa and the Arab World: Shared Trends, Different Priorities," November 2018, https://saiia.org.za/wp-content/uploads/2019/02/saia_spi_67_-benabdallah_20181129.pdf.

40. See Weiqing Song, ed., *China's Relations with Central and Eastern Europe: From "Old Comrades" to New Partners* (London: Routledge, 2017).

41. "Wen Outlines Proposals on Building Closer China-Central and Eastern Europe Ties," April 26, 2004, http://www.china-ceec.org/eng/ldrhw_1/2012hs/hdxw/t1410542.htm.

42. Lucrazia Poggetti, "China's Charm Offensive in Eastern Europe Challenges EU Cohesion," MERICS, Berlin, November 27, 2017, https://www.merics.org/de/blog/chinas-charm-offensive-eastern-europe-challenges-eu-cohesion.

43. Jan Gaspers, "Divide and Rule," *Berlin Policy Journal*, March 2, 2018, https://berlinpolicyjournal.com/divide-and-rule/; and Gaspers, "China's '16+1' Equals Much Ado about Nothing?," December 5, 2017, https://reconnectingasia.csis.org/analysis/entries/chinas-161-equals-much-ado-about-nothing/. Gaspers notes that as a result of China's pressure on the countries concerned, the European Union's consensus process has been affected by Hungary's refusal in March 2017 to endorse violation of detained lawyers, and in June 2017 Greece also blocked an EU resolution on human rights issues in China.

44. See Matthew Karnitschnig, "Beijing's Balkans Backdoor," *Politico*, July 13, 2017, http://www.politico.eu/article/china-serbia-montenegro-europe-investment-trade-beijing-balkan-backdoor/.

45. http://www.balkaninsight.com/en/article/serbia-tightens-security-measures-ahead-of-chinese-president-arrival-06-16-2016; http://news.xinhuanet.com/english/2016-06/19/c_135449190.htm.

46. These visits are listed on the Chinese Foreign Ministry website: http://www.fmprc.gov.cn/mfa_eng/gjhdq_665435/3265_665445/.

47. Many of the following examples are drawn from Antonela Dhimolea, "Chinese Economic Cooperation in the Balkans: Challenges and Future Expectations," http://www.balkanalysis.com/blog/2017/05/11/chinese-economic-cooperation-in-the-balkans-challenges-and-future-expectations/. Also see Dragan Pavlicevic, "China's Railway Diplomacy in the Balkans," http://www.academia.edu/8933157/Chinas_Railway_Diplomacy_in_the_Balkans.

48. According to former foreign minister Tang Jiaxuan, the proposal for the forum came from the African countries (although this is doubtful). See his *Heavy Storm and Gentle Breeze* (World Affairs Press, 2009), 434–435, as cited by Zeng Aiping and Shu Zhan, "Origin, Achievements, and Prospects of the Forum on China-Africa Cooperation," *China International Studies* (September/October 2018), 88–108. See also Zeng Qiang, "FOCAC: A Powerful Engine for the Continued Development of Friendship between China and Africa," *Contemporary International Relations* 20, no. 6 (November/December 2010): 45–61

49. Osita Eza, "Africa's Perspectives on China-Africa Relations and Forum on China-Africa Cooperation (FOCAC)," *Global Review* 2, no. 2 (September/October 2009): 48–61.

50. "Toward an Even Stronger China-Africa Community with a Shared Future," September 12, 2018, https://www.focac.org/eng/zywx_1/zywj/t1594324.htm.

51. Zeng Aiping and Shu Zhan, "Origin, Achievements, and Prospects of the Forum on China-Africa Cooperation," *China International Studies* (September/October 2018): 88–108.

52. Tang Xiao, "非洲一体化与中非合作" [African Integration and China-Africa Cooperation] January 17, 2011, http://waas.cssn.cn/xscg/xslw/fz/201101/t20110117_1944109.shtml; and Zhang Zhongxiang, "A Win-Win Forum," *Beijing Review*, October 28, 2010, http://www.bjreview.com/print/txt/2010-10/25/content_305844.htm.

53. Nicola P. Contessi, "Multilateralism, Intervention, and Norm Contestation: China's Stance on Darfur in the UN Security Council," *Security Dialogue* 41, no. 3 (June 2010): 323–344.

54. Osita C. Eze argued here that more than half of Africa's exports to China are of energy resources; ores and metals about 17 percent and agricultural raw materials 7 percent. On the other hand, due to the cascading tariff structure in China, export of African processed products is at a disadvantage. Eze, "African Perspectives on China."

55. Margaret Myers, "JLAG Perspectives: China's Belt and Road Initiative: What Role for Latin America?," *Journal of Latin American Geography* 17, no. 2 (2018), https://digitalcommons.lsu.edu/cgi/viewcontent.cgi?article=1181&context=jlag.

56. Katherine Koleski and Alec Blivas, "China's Engagement with Latin America and the Caribbean," *US-China Economic and Security Review Commission*, October 17, 2018, https://www.uscc.gov/sites/default/files/Research/China%27s%20Engagement%20with%20Latin%20America%20and%20the%20Caribbean_.pdf.

57. "Ministerial meeting," March 6, 2018, http://www.chinacelacforum.org/eng/zyjz_1/bjzhy/t1539906.htm.

58. "Beijing Declaration," January 23, 2015, http://www.chinacelacforum.org/eng/zywj_3/t1230938.htm.

59. "Declaration of Santiago II Ministerial Meeting of the CELAC-China Forum," http://www.itamaraty.gov.br/images/2ForoCelacChina/Declaration-of-Santiago--II-CELAC-China-Forum-FV-22-01-2018.pdf.

60. "Zeng Qinghong Attends 'China-Caribbean Economic and Trade Cooperation Forum' and Delivers Speech," February 3, 2005, http://ee.china-embassy.org/eng/dtxw/t184238.htm.

61. "12th China-LAC Business Summit Opens with Shared Concern," *China Daily*, November 2, 2018, http://www.chinadaily.com.cn/regional/2018-11/02/content_37187400.htm.

62. "The 4th China-Latin American and Caribbean Countries' Infrastructure Cooperation Forum," June 8, 2018, http://english.mofcom.gov.cn/article/newsrelease/significantnews/201806/20180602756613.shtml.

63. "Fourth China-Latin America High-Level Defense Forum Launched," October 30, 2018, http://eng.chinamil.com.cn/view/2018-10/30/content_9326872.htm.

64. Abdenur argues that China's considerations in the NDB are primarily political in nature—in legitimizing its multilateral diplomacy, enhancing the image of a "responsible big country,"

and influencing norm setting in the field of development. See Adriana Erthal Abdenur, "China and the BRICS Development Bank: Legitimacy and Multilateralism in South-South Cooperation," *Institute of Development Studies Bulletin* 45, no. 4 (July 2014): 85–101.

65. While bilaterally, China insisted on abiding by the "One China" principle adopted by the other country, in the recent past it has also insisted on Anti-Secession Law adopted on March 14, 2005. For instance, twenty-one countries in Africa in FOCAC made statements to this effect.

66. The SCO requires all member states to oppose the "three evils"—separatism, extremism, and splittism—although these have specific Chinese national connotations. On the other hand there are also double standards that China had exhibited in abiding by the UN 1267 Committee on terrorism in relation to Pakistan-based terrorists.

67. Liu Qingjian of the People's University says it in as many words in his conclusion to a comprehensive review of China's multilateral diplomacy. See "挑 战, 应 对,构 建—中国多边外交探析" [Challenge, Response, and Construction: An Analysis of China's Multilateral Diplomacy] 思想理论教育导刊 [Leading Journal of Ideological and Theoretical Education] 9, Issue 81 (2005): 34–41. See also Barthélémy Courmont, "Promoting Multilateralism or Searching for a New Hegemony: A Chinese Vision of Multipolarity," *Pacific Focus* 28, no. 2 (August 2012): 184–204.

# SECTION VI

# PATTERNS AND PROSPECTS

# 16

# China and the World

## *Future Challenges*

DAVID SHAMBAUGH

The chapters in this volume are all testimony to the impressive breadth and depth of the People's Republic of China's ties to the world. This range of global engagement involves both state and non-state actors, spans a variety of functional domains (Section IV) and geographic regions (Section V), has followed a variety of twists and turns over the past seventy years (Section I), and is influenced by a variety of historical, contemporary, domestic, and external factors (Sections II and III). In this concluding chapter I wish to peer into the future by identifying seven challenges I anticipate China will face in the decade ahead.[1] Toward the end of this timeframe, I anticipate publishing a second edition of this volume, which will carry the analysis of China and its position in the world further forward. While my crystal ball gazing only looks out over the near-to-medium term and is *qualitative* in its approach, there are a few longer-term and *quantitative* indicators that can be extrapolated and will exist independently. Even allowing for variance in these projections, they nonetheless will be extant and impressive facts, and they will have an impact on the totality of China's external relations.

## Some Important Factors in China's Evolution of the Next Twenty Years

Let us consider several dimensions of China's likely growth over the next two decades: GDP, energy consumption, research and development spending, and military expenditure. These four areas will all have an independent and significant impact on China's global position.

David Shambaugh, *China and the World* In: *China and the World*. Edited by: David Shambaugh, Oxford University Press (2020). © Oxford University Press
DOI: 10.1093/oso/9780190062316.003.0016

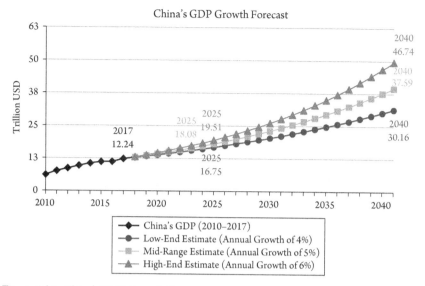

*Figure 16.1* China's GDP Growth Forecast

As Barry Naughton's chapter delineates in considerable detail, China's economy already has an outsized impact on the world. Even with a slowing growth
rate in recent years, in 2018 China's gross domestic product (GDP) accounted
for 18.7 percent of the global total, in purchasing power parity (PPP) terms.[2]
The PRC's percentage of global growth (as distinct from total GDP) in 2017
was 27.2 percent.[3] So, China is—and will remain—a major determining factor
in the evolution of the global economy. Figure 16.1 shows projections of the
size of China's GDP to 2040 based on three potential baselines (4, 5, and 6 percent growth). By 2025, China's GDP will thus likely be between $16.7 trillion
(low end) and $19.5 trillion (high end). By contrast, the US Congressional
Budget Office projects American GDP will be approximately $22 trillion (not
adjusted for PPP) in 2025.[4] So, while China already surpassed the United States
in purchasing power parity terms in 2014, its nominal GDP will remain less than
America's until the late 2020s. Given the size of China's economy and the continuing importance of exports and investment (inbound and outbound), it will
continue to be a major factor in global economic affairs. China was already the
primary trading partner of 124 countries in 2018,[5] and this is only likely to grow
over time. For the many nations that do not have a diversified export base, this
"trade dependency" on China is already a significant problem—as the cases of
Australia, New Zealand, Brazil, and most European countries already reveal.

Secondly, China's energy consumption will continue to steadily grow
(Figure 16.2), as will its importation of oil (Figure 16.3). This will certainly
have an impact on China's need to retain good relations with Persian Gulf states

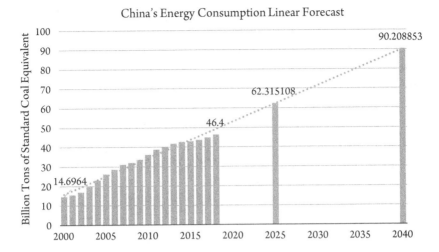

Figure 16.2  China's Energy Consumption Linear Forecast

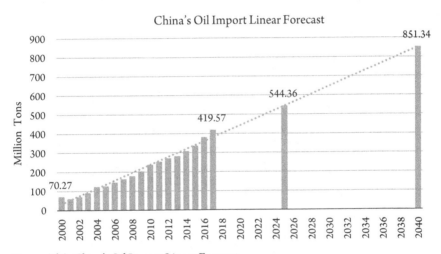

Figure 16.3  China's Oil Import Linear Forecast

(Saudi Arabia, Oman, UAE, Iraq, and Iran), African states (mainly Angola and Sudan), Central Asian states (mainly Kazakhstan), Russia, Libya, Venezuela, and Indonesia. All these countries are—and will remain—significant sources of oil supplies to China.

Another key factor in China's domestic economic development that will impact its relations with the world will be its innovation program. The PRC government has correctly identified innovation as a key—if not *the key*—to overcoming the "middle-income trap" and becoming a fully developed economy.[6] Its "Made in China 2025" program is a blueprint for achieving world-class status, if not dominance, of a dozen or more key technological sectors. This program in state-driven tech-industrial policy has already caused considerable controversy around the world (particularly the United States and EU)—which, as a result, has caused the Chinese government to stop referring to the program in public (although it no doubt continues).[7] China is already a global technological powerhouse, but is only likely to become more so over time—especially in areas it has prioritized: aerospace and aviation equipment, artificial intelligence, robotics, nano- and biotechnology, medical devices, electric and energy-saving vehicles, advanced rail equipment, new materials, information technologies, cloud computing, and semi-conductors. Whether or not China comes to *dominate* these sectors, its impact in global production will be major.

There are many methods to measure China's prioritization of innovation, but one common way is to examine a national government's research and development (R&D) spending. While sub-national governments (states, provinces, municipalities) and individual corporate companies also invest in R&D (so-called "in-firm" investment), and these are important additional sources, the normal measure is to gauge a central government's expenditure. At present, China currently spends about 2.3 percent of its GDP on R&D.[8] In aggregate percentage terms, this is significantly below the percentage spent by world leaders of South Korea (4.3 percent); Japan, Sweden, Denmark, and Finland (all 3.1 percent); Germany and Switzerland (2.9 percent); and the United States (2.7 percent). But given the gargantuan size of China's economy (currently $13.2 trillion), even 2.3 percent spending on R&D is an enormous amount ($442 billion in 2017). China surpassed Japan and already became the second leading investor in R&D around 2008. As Figure 16.4 illustrates, its expenditure has been steadily growing and will continue to do so.

Depending on the growth rate of China's economy in future years, and government decisions about how much to devote to R&D, Figure 16.5 illustrates four possible projections of China's total R&D spending out to 2040.

Even if China only maintains R&D spending at 2.5 percent, by 2025 Beijing would still spend approximately $452.2 *billion.* At the slightly higher level of expenditure of 3 percent, the average of those OECD economies cited above, this would amount to $542 billion. If China were to increase spending to 3.5 percent to be in the league of South Korea, this would amount to a staggering $632.8 billion in 2025 and $1.3 trillion per annum by 2040! Needless to say, this level of investment into innovation would be unprecedented in world history and, even at the lower levels, will produce a techo-superpower on a significant scale.

Of course, one dimension of this spending potential concerns China's future military modernization and capacities. Building a world-class military by mid-century is certainly China's goal, as explicitly indicated in Xi Jinping's address to the 19th Party Congress. To get there will involve more than investment,

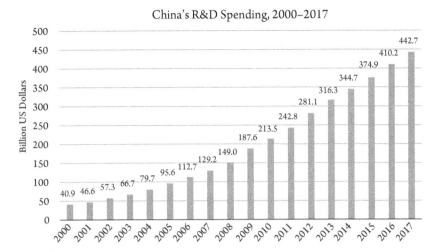

Figure 16.4 China's R&D Spending 2000–2017

Figure 16.5 China's R&D Spending Forecast, 2018–2040

to be sure, but money matters (a lot). China's current (2019) official defense budget stands at 1.19 trillion RMB ($177.61 billion in 2019 prices). This ranks China second in the world. Moreover, China has substantial defense expenditures that are *not* included in the official budget. The Stockholm International Peace Research Institute (SIPRI) estimates China's total military expenditure to be $228 billion in 2017.[9] At the 1.9 percent of GDP total expenditure that SIPRI calculates China's spends on defense, this would place China's total spending nearing $300 billion in 2020. SIPRI estimates aside, based on the announced official budget, Figure 16.6 posits three projections of China's military spending out to 2040, based on an estimate of 5 percent annual growth in GDP.

Whether at 2 percent, 2.5 percent, or 3 percent of GDP defense expenditure (assuming a realistic 5 percent GDP growth), it is clear that China will have substantial monies available for its military. By 2025 China would thus allocate between $390 billion and $585 billion for defense spending. And that is the *official* budget. As noted above in the SIPRI estimates, China likely spends between 15–20 percent more on its armed forces (which includes not only the PLA, but also the People's Armed Police, Coast Guard, and militia and civil defense forces) and military-related expenditure is buried in other budgets (such as the state science and technology budget). These monies can certainly buy a lot of hardware (weaponry) as well as a lot of "software" (human and technological capabilities). There is thus little doubt that China's military will grow over time to become the most significant and capable Asian military—and, as Phillip Saunders's chapter notes, will increasingly develop out-of-region capabilities as well. It will be second only to the United States, although its nuclear forces may grow to rival Russia's.

Given these empirical factors that can anticipated—GDP growth, energy consumption, R&D spending, and military expenditure—China's global footprint will only expand and exert a greater impact on world affairs. More specifically, though, I would identify seven specific challenges for China's foreign policy, external relations, and position in the world over the near-to-medium term.

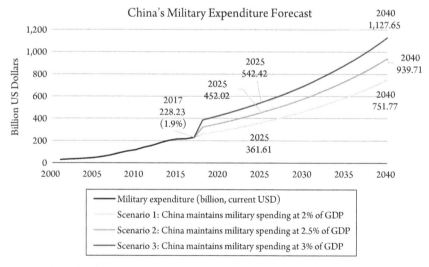

*Figure 16.6* China's Military Expenditure Forecast

# Challenge 1: The Impact of Domestic Affairs

All nations' external relations are profoundly conditioned by their internal affairs. But, in the case of China, I would argue that there is a considerable bifurcation between domestic and foreign policies. Part of this has to do with the fact that China is a highly authoritarian single party-state system, where external relations are managed by a number of dedicated bureaucracies (see Suisheng Zhao's chapter) and a handful of top leaders (mainly Xi Jinping at present). This said, as Peter Gries's chapter amply demonstrates, the role of nationalism and national identity are powerful social forces that influence and constrain those responsible for managing foreign affairs. Moreover, as discussed in chapter 1, there is a significant difference between foreign *policy* and foreign *relations*. That is, there are a number of Chinese actors—tourists, students, individual entrepreneurs, private companies, state-owned enterprises, municipalities, and provinces—that are all active abroad and are not (fully) under the control of the party-state. Zhao's chapter provides interesting examples of these sub-national actors. So, one challenge for the future will be the degree to which these actors undertake actions around the world that cause problems for the central government. Chinese corporations have established operations across the globe and in many volatile places. There have already been a number of kidnappings of Chinese workers, as well as terrorist attacks against Chinese entities abroad. As China's global footprint expands it will inevitably encounter resentment and frictions. How will the Chinese state handle these incidents?

But these are external manifestations of Chinese individuals and entities acting outside of China's borders. More directly, we must ask what impact domestic politics will have on China's external posture?

It is widely recognized that China's domestic politics under Xi Jinping have hardened significantly. China today is more politically repressive than at any time since the aftermath of the 1989 Tiananmen incident. The regime has cracked down—and hard—on intellectuals, journalists, dissidents, non-governmental organizations, religious practitioners, ethnic groups (particularly Uighurs and Tibetans), and other civil society actors. Surprisingly, the ramped-up repression has not produced a great deal of international condemnation from foreign governments, although a wide range of non-governmental organizations are outspoken. China seems to have effectively intimidated foreign governments into silence over these issues, lest a critical government be penalized economically by Beijing. The repression has produced a certain degree of the prized "stability" (稳定) inside China, as a result of the regime's feared "stability maintenance" (维稳) programs. But what would happen if mainland China were to erupt with some form of mass civil disobedience or revolt, as has occurred in Hong Kong?

What if there were a replay of 1989? China's international image would surely be damaged, but it would be interesting to see how other governments would react if there was a significant loss of life. The China of today is far different—and far stronger—than the China of 1989, and the fear of Beijing's retaliation may well cow others into silence.

Relatedly, the internal repression has multiple manifestations in how the Chinese party-state deals with foreign actors *inside* its borders. The space for foreign activities domestically in China has become increasingly restricted and circumscribed. Political campaigns against "foreign hostile forces" (境外敌对势力) have been unleashed. The passage in 2017 of the strict NGO Law forced all foreign NGOs to re-register, driving many out of China.[10] Similarly, the 2015 National Security Law has cast a further pall over foreign research and researchers in China. The 2016 Cyber Security Law has similarly tightened already draconian controls over the flow of electronic information. Many foreign embassies encounter great difficulties in carrying out public diplomacy programs inside China, public lectures by foreigners are not permitted, and foreign media operations are deeply circumscribed. Foreign governments, international institutions (such as the European Union), and non-governmental organizations (such as the Ford Foundation)—which used to carry out a wide range of capacity-building programs in China—have all had to drastically curtail their programs and they are subjected to greatly increased scrutiny by the Ministry of Public Security and other state oversight organs. The reason is simple: China's rulers fundamentally fear political subversion by outside actors. The collapse of the Soviet Union and East European communist party-states, Eurasian "color revolutions," the Arab Spring uprisings, and Islamic terrorism have collectively produced a profoundly paranoid Chinese party-state. This deep *insecurity* has, to some extent, impacted China's relations with Western nations that previously carried out such programs in China. So, the question going forward is whether these strict controls will be maintained and the impact they might have on China's interactions with the West.

Then there is the question of Chinese strongman leader Xi Jinping's future. While there is no current evidence of an end to Xi's rule over the near-to-medium term, it is still a question that must be considered. Indeed, at the 2018 National People's Congress the term limits on the state presidency (two consecutive five-year terms) were removed and thus Xi can literally rule for life (his positions of CCP General-Secretary and Central Military Commission Chairman have no term limits). But what if he were to fall ill or be removed from office? During his state visit to Italy and France in April 2019, Xi appeared to walk with a limp and had difficulty rising from chairs.[11] He has also been rumored to have Parkinson's disease (a progressive neurological disorder). For a man born in 1953, Xi's health is definitely a consideration in Chinese politics.

So too is potential opposition to him. It is no secret that there is a great deal of dissatisfaction domestically—in the party, state, military, and society. While Xi brooks no organized opposition, there is certainly considerable dissatisfaction in these quarters with the direction he has led China since coming to power in 2012. His anti-corruption campaign—which has gutted the upper echelons of the party, state, internal security services, and military—has made Xi a large number of enemies. As of 2018, an estimated 2.7 million party and state cadres have been investigated by Xi's anti-corruption campaign, with 58,000 trials held and 1.5 million being punished.[12] This includes seven national level leaders (four Politburo members), several thousand military officers, dozens of generals, and four Central Military Commission members. There have also been unverified rumors of assassination attempts against Xi.[13] While there is no other indication of a possible overthrow, and Xi has made sure to keep a tight grip on the Central Guards Unit,[14] one should never rule out the possibility of a coup d'état in authoritarian systems like China's. Indeed, when Politburo member and Chongqing Party chief Sun Zhengcai was abruptly purged and imprisoned for life in October 2017, in addition to financial corruption charges he was accused of conspiring to "usurp party and state power."[15] Were Xi to be removed from office, China's domestic politics—and thus its foreign affairs—could move in a radically different direction. The likelihood would be a return to a more liberal direction domestically—what I describe as "soft authoritarianism."[16] Externally, there would likely be greater continuity with the more assertive behavior that Xi Jinping has initiated, although a more liberal leader might well also take steps to ease tensions and strains that have arisen between China and its neighbors and with the EU and United States. This is all speculative, of course, but the point is that any China watcher should not simply assume that Xi Jinping's position is solid and that he will continue to rule China indefinitely. The political history of the CCP and PRC offers ample evidence that assuming continuity can be a fraught prediction.

## Challenge 2: Relations with America

For China, no single relationship is more important than that with the United States. The United States is fundamental to many elements vital to China's future: economic growth (two-way trade and investment); technological innovation; education of China's young people in American universities and secondary schools; China's relationship with Taiwan and, to a lesser degree, Hong Kong; national security around China's borders, especially in the western Pacific; and China's growing presence in Latin America and other regions. In these and other of Beijing's priorities, the "road runs through Washington." While there are certainly other actors in each case that will affect China, the United States has a unique ability to facilitate, block, or make difficult China's attainment of these and other national goals. While other nations in the world are certainly important to China, and China has a "diversified portfolio" of relationships, the United States has an overwhelming influence on China's place in the world and several dimensions of its domestic development. Thus, getting the relationship with the United States "right" is an imperative priority for Beijing.

Unfortunately for China, the relationship with the United States has grown considerably more strained in recent years. It is now a comprehensively competitive relationship. There are no shortages of friction points, divergences, and opposing positions between the United States and China. There are multiple reasons why the relationship has deteriorated so much in recent years, but there has been a gradual, fundamental, and qualitative change.[17] While the relationship has always been a combination of cooperation and competition (code word for friction, strains, and opposed positions), competition now substantially outweighs cooperation in the relationship. And it extends across *all* functional domains of the relationship: economic, diplomatic, military-security, technological, political, civil society, some aspects of education and research, regional (Indo-Pacific), and increasingly global. This comprehensively competitive nature of the relationship will continue to characterize US-China relations indefinitely. It is the "new normal."

Since the Trump administration took office, the United States has begun to "push back" much more assertively against China.[18] This has produced fresh frictions—as Beijing had grown accustomed to Washington's complaints without accompanying counter-actions (it had come to believe that the United States was a paper tiger). Washington counter-actions have produced counter-counter-actions from Beijing in several realms, and this escalating cycle has brought considerable new stresses to the relationship. The United States is thus now explicitly *competing* with China, not simply using the term "competition" to characterize frictions. This new reality will impact not only the United States and China, but most other nations in the world. It is global in character. Many other countries find themselves caught in a bind between the United States and China, most notably those in Asia. No nation wishes to have to "choose" in its relationships with the United States and China—as all seek to have the benefits of both.

Both sides bring different strengths and weaknesses to this global contest. It will be like a sports contest with no end—where there is constant ebb and flow in the game, with each side scoring tactical victories and suffering some setbacks, but with no final outcome to the contest. It can be argued that the United States enters the contest with a far stronger set of attributes, as well as the long experience of competing with the former Soviet Union in Cold War 1.0. China has no such experience, has never engaged in such a worldwide contest, and arguably possesses a considerably weaker set of instruments to deploy in the competition. At the same time, China certainly also has "agency" in the competition: a widespread economic presence and provision of goods and services that many countries need (particularly in regions where the United States is not commercially competitive); sound political and diplomatic relations and no enemies; a non-aggressive image and benign rhetoric; deep financial pockets and inexhaustible labor and personnel that can be deployed overseas. Both sides are capable of overplaying and underplaying their hands, but one thing is certain: it will likely be a *protracted contest*—unless a smaller trigger event (like an military air or sea accident) catalyzes an escalation into war between the two powers. This is certainly to be avoided, and being nuclear powers with bona fide second-strike capabilities, one assumes that rationality would prevail if the contest ever became kinetic (because of the uncertainties of escalation). But, unlike the case of the United States and Soviet Union during the Cold War, the United States and China do not have any strong crisis-management mechanisms in place to control potential escalation.

Simply learning to live with heightened frictions, and to co-manage a comprehensively competitive and stressed relationship, will thus be a central challenge for both sides.[19] Finding areas of tangible cooperation will be the opportunistic flip-side. Discussing differences in an attempt at better mutual understanding and perhaps narrowing disputes will also be important. But for multiple reasons, both sides are now locked into a comprehensively competitive relationship where their differences outweigh their commonalities, mutual distrust is high and growing, and the mechanisms for conflict management are few. Perhaps the best that can be hoped for is a relationship of "competitive coexistence."

## Challenge 3: Relations with Russia

China's third challenge will be to maintain its current high level of positive and productive relations with Russia. One must mention this as a challenge if, for no other reason, because of the long history of difficulties between the two countries. To be sure, when both Beijing and Moscow have in recent years pronounced their relations to be the "best ever," it is an accurate description—but it has not always been so. The world should not wish that these two powers and giant neighbors to be locked in antagonism. When this occurred during the 1960s–1980s it was highly dangerous and destabilizing. Beginning in the mid-1980s the former Soviet leader Mikhail Gorbachev and Deng Xiaoping orchestrated a series of mutual confidence-building steps to improve relations (which culminated in the renormalization of relations in 1989). Despite a brief hiatus following the collapse of the Soviet Union, the two sides continued their efforts to reduce sources of friction and rebuild their ties. A series of bilateral agreements were agreed to during the mid-to-late 1990s, with the capstone being the 2001 Treaty of Neighborliness and Friendly Cooperation. Then in 2005 and 2008 the final impediment to ties was removed with twin agreements to formally demarcate their long disputed 4,300-kilometer common border.

This set the stage for significant growth in the relationship over the past decade, as Alexei Voskressenski's chapter in the volume attests. Trade grew from a negligible $10 billion in 2003 to almost $100 billion in 2018. While still not in the league of China's trade with the European Union, United States, Japan, South Korea, or ASEAN, it is now reaching a respectable level. It will continue to grow steadily in the future as long as the Chinese economy and energy demand continue to grow. The two countries have essential economic complementarities—Russia has oil, gas, and raw materials, while China offers technology and consumer goods. But if Chinese demand for imported energy and raw materials declines in conjunction with a contracting industrial economy, so too will bilateral trade. The contraction of the Russian economy is also a factor. Russia also sells China weapons and transfers defense technology, although this defense trade has fallen considerably from a high of $3 billion annually during the 1990s–2000s to under $1 billion today. A master plan has also been concluded to develop 205 "major cooperation projects" in China's northeast (东北), which is contiguous to the Russian Far East (eastern Siberia), although this initiative has not progressed much.

The diplomatic relationship is better. The two leaders—Vladimir Putin and Xi Jinping—hold summits twice annually, and each was the other's honored guest for the military parades held in Moscow and Beijing in 2015 to commemorate the end of World War II. Prior to their 2019 summit, Xi Jinping proclaimed Putin to be his "best and bosom friend." The two autocratic leaders see eye-to-eye on a variety of international issues, their strategic interests align, and their governments consult and coordinate closely. The degree of considerable closeness between Moscow and Beijing has been, until recently, underappreciated in Washington and the West. But thanks to a recent series of studies undertaken by the National Bureau of Asian Research in the United States, there is now increased awareness—and rising concern—about this partnership.[20] It is now viewed not as a temporary tactical relationship—but increasingly as a long-term, coordinated, strategic alignment or axis. Indeed, the two sides themselves pronounced (in 2019) their relationship to be a "comprehensive strategic partnership of *coordination* [emphasis added] in the new era." The two find considerable common cause in their mutual opposition to the United States, although Moscow is both more outspoken and more assertiveness in making life difficult for the United States. The two regularly coordinate their positions in the UN Security Council and are not afraid to veto resolutions agreed to by the other

P-5 members (United States, UK, and France), particularly when it involves military intervention in third countries. The Russian and Chinese militaries also frequently partner in joint exercises, including unprecedented naval exercises recently in the Mediterranean Ocean and Sea of Japan.

Despite these commonalities and strategic coordination, there still remains an undercurrent of historical suspicion as well as contemporary irritants. A subterranean debate simmers in policy circles in Moscow about China's long-term intentions in Central Asia and whether China is manipulating Russia for its own strategic and development purposes.[21] Some observers of the relationship see it as entirely tactical and expedient, and they predict that the residue of historical distrust will again emerge to pit the two Eurasian powers against each other.[22] Just as US-China competition will be an indefinite feature in international relations over the coming decade(s), a China-Russia strategic partnership to counter the United States and the Western liberal order will similarly remain a core feature of global geopolitics. The "strategic triangle" may be returning, and it is tilted against the United States.

## Challenge 4: Relations with Neighbors in Asia

Another major challenge for China will be to continue to build its relationships with neighbors around its periphery in Asia—without alienating them and driving them into a countervailing coalition. This will not be an easy balancing act for Beijing.

Diplomatically, Beijing is proactively engaged throughout the Asian region—regularly convening bilateral and multilateral summits with regional leaders. No nation is too small or inconsequential for Beijing to pay attention to it. Beijing has been ramping up its diplomatic exchanges throughout Southeast Asia,[23] as well as the South Pacific.

When leaders meet, China's economic largesse follows. Money is the most important tool in China's foreign policy toolbox, and it is being utilized to an unprecedented extent. China is now the largest trading partner for every Asian nation except the Philippines, and the lion's share of its outbound investment remains in Asia. There is no doubt that China has become the center of economic activity and supply chains in Asia. This is not by accident, but very much by Beijing's design. The Chinese government calls this economic "connectivity." While it does benefit the region as a whole, it is also producing an increasing asymmetry and imbalance, and some of China's neighbors are beginning to chafe at the growing dependency on Beijing. Others, however, see the process as very natural and irreversible. Singapore's late leader and elder statesman Lee Kuan Yew, for example, observed in 2012: "China is sucking the Southeast Asian

countries into its economic system because of its vast market and growing purchasing power. Japan and South Korea will inevitably be sucked in as well. It just
absorbs countries without having to use force. . . . China's emphasis is on expanding their influence through the economy. China's growing economic sway will be
very difficult to fight."[24] Viewed more broadly, though, China's share of regional
trade and investment is far from being dominant. Beijing's investment in many
Southeast Asian countries ranks below that of Japan, the European Union, or
the United States, while its trade does not exceed 30 percent (usually 15–20 percent) of any individual Asian nation's total trade. All Asian countries maintain
diversified commercial portfolios.

Nonetheless, hardly a conversation in any Asian capital does not reveal a
growing sense of anxiety over China's economic heft and attempts to leverage it
for other purposes. Beijing also seems to mistakenly believe that economic relations trump issues of identity or other troubled aspects of its ties with neighbors.
Added to the economic concern is China's dramatic military modernization
and rapidly expanding naval presence throughout the Indo-Pacific region. The
"string of pearls" is becoming a reality, as China is establishing a series of port-
access arrangements all along the Indian Ocean littoral to East Africa. China and
its paramount leader Xi Jinping have made it very clear that it intends to become
a "strong maritime power" (海洋强国). In terms of surface ships, the People's
Liberation Army Navy (PLAN) is already the largest in the world (approximately 370 ships). By 2030 it is quite possible that China's navy could include
four or five aircraft carriers. In 2015 China published its first White Paper on
its military strategy, which explicitly identified the "strategic requirement of
offshore waters defense and open seas protection." The Chinese distinguish
between "near seas" (近海) and "far seas" (远海), the former being contiguous
to China's coastline and the latter being open-ocean "blue water" operations.
The White Paper indicated that the People's Liberation Army Navy (PLAN)
"will gradually shift its focus" from the former to the latter.[25] As the White Paper
starkly said, "The traditional mentality that land outweighs sea must be abandoned." China's island and military base building in the South China Sea has also
caused further wariness among China's southern neighbors, as its East China
Sea claims has done in Japan. Beijing's unilateralism and dismissiveness of these
concerns is further fueling regional anxieties. Polls of Asian nations conducted
by the Pew Global Attitudes Survey have revealed widespread concerns across
the region that China's territorial disputes could trigger conflict,[26] widespread
concern about China's military buildup, and China's rise generally.[27]

Thus, as Michael Yahuda's chapter illustrates, all around China's periphery its
relationships are a combination of sweet-and-sour, but are increasingly souring.
Many analysts view this as a secular trend that will continue over the next decade and beyond. What it may produce is one of the "iron laws" of international

relations: the law of counterbalancing. When a nation threatens to be a pre-ponderant hegemon, others naturally bond together to counterbalance it. The Obama administration's "pivot to Asia" (or rebalancing policy) was no accident when it was unveiled—it was a direct result of the nervousness that America's allies and many other nations in Asia felt about an increasingly assertive China during 2009 and 2010. This balancing behavior will likely continue indefinitely. The stronger China becomes, the greater the fears it provokes, and hence the greater the pushback and counter-measures it will trigger. If Beijing is trying to recreate a twenty-first-century version of the imperial "tribute system," it will inevitably fail, as other sovereign Asian nations do not desire to fall into such a patron-client relationship with China again. China's geographic location in the center of Asia is actually a great weakness as it enables such counterbalancing and encirclement responses.

On the other hand, there is another tendency in international relations under such conditions—so-called "bandwagoning." This is the tendency to align with the preponderant power for reasons of self-protection and security, but also to benefit from the economic and diplomatic largesse that the power can dispense to other states. This is normally a small-state strategy. While, to date, we only really see two countries in Asia adopting this strategy (Cambodia and Pakistan), several others are tilting toward China (Laos, Myanmar, and Brunei). Yet the majority of Asian countries (specifically Australia, New Zealand, the Philippines, Malaysia, Singapore, Thailand, and Indonesia) try to balance their relations with both the US and China and not fully tilt toward Beijing. Yet, pro-China advo-cates of this strategy exist in every one of these societies and foreign policy cir-cles, and this is a particularly pervasive narrative in Southeast Asian media—but they are not yet in the majority. There are countervailing voices who advocate maintaining close ties to the United States, and to diversify relations with as many "middle powers" as possible. Thus, in recent years and at the time of this writing (2019), the "China debate" continues across the region. Consequently, it is too early to conclude that China has turned Asia into its sphere of influence. Asia remains a multipolar and multidimensional region.[28]

In such a fluctuant and undetermined regional environment, Beijing has to be very careful about how it plays its hand—lest it drive countries away and into a countervailing coalition. We will have to watch carefully how this unfolds. China could well overstep and overreach through a combination of overcon-fidence and assertive actions. Beijing's greatest problems in this regard are its assumptions that Asia is its natural sphere of influence, that the United States is an extra-regional power that really does not have a legitimate role in region, and that other regional states should acquiesce to China's superiority and centrality. As noted above, this would simulate a twenty-first-century version of the impe-rial "tribute system."[29] While not an exact replica, there are indeed multiple signs that this is exactly what China is attempting to recreate. This is not a system built on either invasion or occupation. Rather it revolves around economic dependence, China's cultural centrality and other's obeisance, overwhelming military prowess, and a de facto "veto power" that Beijing wields over all other countries in the region (so that they would not dare to take an action that ran counter to Beijing's interests). This, it seems to this observer, is what China is trying to create in the regional order in Asia.[30] The question is, however, whether other countries can live in such an order? If not, what are they prepared to do about it? Some will resist, some will acquiesce, and some will try to hide and pretend it is not a problem.

## Challenge 5: The Belt and Road Initiative

A fifth challenge for China will be its handling of the Belt and Road Initiative. This gargantuan project is unprecedented in history. Although first signaled by Xi Jinping in twin speeches in Kazakhstan and Indonesia in September and October 2013 respectively, Xi formally launched BRI by inviting twenty-nine heads of state and other officials from 130 countries and seventy international organizations to Beijing for the inaugural Belt and Road Forum in May 2017. In April 2019, Xi presided over a second BRI Forum, bringing together thirty-six heads of state and a raft of other officials from a reported 150 countries.

The BRI plan envisions an expansive array of infrastructure projects that will connect Asia to Europe through an overland route across Eurasia (the "Silk Road Economic Belt"), and a second route spanning the South China Sea through the Indian Ocean and Red Sea to the Mediterranean (the "21st Century Maritime Silk Road"). Numerous commercial projects—including construction of ports, power plants, electricity grids, railroads, highways, industrial parks, commercial and financial centers, telecommunications facilities, and residential housing—are already under way, with many more on the drawing board. BRI also includes other elements of "cultural connectivity"—student and scholarly exchanges, think tank networks, tourism, cultural and sports exchanges, etc.

Given the pressing need for this kind of infrastructure in countries along these twin tracks, the BRI has been generally welcomed by most countries. At present, China claims that more than eighty countries are involved in the multi-trillion multiyear initiative.[31] Despite the grandiosity of the initiative, it will be at least five years, though, before analysts can assess the degree of success or failure of China's initiative. Beginning in 2017, a number of recipient countries began to encounter difficulties with the burdensome terms of financing made available by Beijing—leading to a prevalent narrative about "debt trap diplomacy." Others complained about the cost of certain projects. Yet others complained about the sometimes poor quality of the infrastructure construction. Others complained about the inappropriateness of some of Beijing's projects that were thrust on recipient countries, such as high-speed rail, when other more basic needs like electricity and water treatment systems were higher priorities. Others complained about the exclusive use of Chinese laborers for projects, with no or little employment of local workers. Others complained about the lack of ecological impact studies and wanton damage done to local environments. Still others viewed BRI as a barely disguised geostrategic power play to dominate the Eurasia continent and the Indian Ocean littoral.

Thus, a cacophony of complaints about BRI began to surface during 2017–2019. The question for the future, therefore, is how Beijing will respond to such complaints? In advance of the Second BRI Forum, China's foreign minister Wang Yi lashed out and threw down the gauntlet, by calling on countries to "cooperate or stop criticizing!"[32] Aware of the rising criticisms of China's financing practices, China's central bank governor, Yi Gang, told a pre-summit audience: "We need to objectively assess developing countries' debt problems."[33] For his part, in his speech to the forum President Xi Jinping ironically claimed that China had, in fact, inflicted heavy debt upon *itself* in financing many BRI projects—and he made a big plea for co-financing with other regional development banks and institutions. In another response to the rising criticisms, Xi also spoke of the need to "pursue open, green, and clean cooperation."[34] A separate study undertaken by the Rhodium Group, a respected private consultancy firm, found that China has renegotiated and refinanced $50 billion of Chinese loans over the past decade, with debt write-offs in fourteen cases.[35]

It remains to be seen whether China really recalibrates in these regards. If it does, then it will earn the respect of many other nations and international development institutions. If it does not, it will do considerable damage to China's reputation internationally and particularly among developing countries. As Joshua Eisenman and Eric Heginbotham's chapter amply demonstrates, Beijing has invested heavily in cultivating its reputation among developing countries in the "Global South" and, generally speaking, has a very positive reputation south of the equator. Belt & Road can either further consolidate this reputation—or undermine it. It will likely be another five years before the jury is in. My sense is that BRI infrastructure projects are, in fact, badly needed and are genuinely welcomed in many recipient countries (I have visited a number of BRI projects in Southeast Asia). But, at the same time, there is real resentment over the multiple complaints noted above. So, the outstanding question will be the degree to which China itself is able to reflect, recalibrate, renegotiate, and revise the problem projects. If it is able to do so, it will show the world that it is a caring superpower—if it does not, it will badly damage China's global reputation. China took the initiative to launch BRI—now it "owns it." This brings to mind former US secretary of state Colin Powell's "Pottery Barn rule" when referring to the invasion of Iraq: "You break it, you own it." BRI is such a significant and broad-gauged initiative of China's, as well as being one of Xi Jinping's signature policies, that its relative success or failure will have an outsized impact on China's global reputation as a major world power.

# Challenge 6: Global Governance

Another future challenge for China lies in the realm of global governance. Over time, the world has witnessed China gradually evolving from being a passive actor to a selective activist and now a fully engaged actor in global governance affairs. Many observers now see a shift in China's behavior as a more proactive shaper in international institutions, which reflects both its growing power and confidence. The uptick in China's participation and contributions has been particularly noticeable during Xi Jinping's tenure. Under Xi, there are thus encouraging reasons to believe that China is avoiding what Joseph Nye has described as the "Kindleberger Trap."[36]

While the overall trendline has been positive, this recent tendency should not be overstated though. As Katherine Morton's chapter discusses, China still exhibits ambivalence. Beijing remains very reluctant to become engaged on some issues and still displays a "selective multilateralist" posture. China also continues to display and practice a distinct "transactional" style of diplomacy—which carefully weighs national costs and benefits for any commitment of resources, rather than contributing to collective global "public goods" because it philosophically and selflessly believes in helping humankind. Until very recent years, China did not understand the concept of public goods and suspiciously viewed Western calls for China to become a "responsible stakeholder" and increase its contributions commensurate with its increasing capabilities. While assiduously and tenaciously guarding its own corner to protect its own national interests in the international institutional arena, China has also long articulated a foreign policy agenda that favors multipolarization, equality ("democratization") in international relations, and empowerment of developing nations. This has hardly been a hidden agenda. Now, with Beijing's own growing international influence, along with the reality of other rising powers and the general fluidity of the international system, the world is beginning to witness some modest steps by China that are attempting to redistribute power and influence in the system.

While China's ambivalence has been apparent throughout, it is also clear that China has become a better "global citizen" in almost all areas of global governance (in many cases halting its previously noncompliant behavior). China has become much more deeply involved in UN peacekeeping operations, international disaster relief, anti-piracy operations in the Gulf of Aden, global public health, counterterrorism, law enforcement, non-proliferation, climate change and environmental cooperation, global economic governance, overseas development assistance (ODA), financial contributions to the UN operating budget, and other areas.

Yet, China's ambivalence and discomfort with the liberal world order, constructed largely by the West over the past eight decades, remains apparent. While China definitely is a "status quo" power insofar as it seeks to *uphold* and even strengthen the core institutions and rules of this order, it is simultaneously a "dissatisfied" and (quasi) "revisionist" power insofar as it seeks to either selectively "opt out" of participating in certain aspects or spearhead new institutions (see Srikanth Kondapalli's chapter).

China will undoubtedly remain committed to its long-standing desire to "democratize" international institutions and more substantially empower other developing countries' voices and their international participation. This will become manifest both within existing institutions as well as by establishing new alternative institutions. Beijing has the financial wherewithal to fund many new institutions that will increasingly operate *in parallel* to the existing Western-constructed global governance system. In this regard, China *is a revisionist* power and it will present a challenge to the existing liberal order. But, to date, China's alteration to the existing order is coming "around the edges" and is not (at least yet) a frontal *illiberal* challenge as some had previously envisioned. It is not (yet) establishing exclusive blocs of states, separate spheres of influence, or mercantilist networks. The question remains, however, should Beijing begin to move in these directions, would others *follow* its lead? If others do not follow China's lead and if its promised resources for BRI do not materialize, or if China stumbles in trying to set up and make these institutions functional—then what impact will it have on China's credibility and image as a global power? Indeed, is the newfound proactiveness in global governance displayed under Xi Jinping irreversible? It is certainly to be welcomed, but is it indefinitely sustainable? These are questions and challenges for the future in the global governance domain.

## Challenge 7: Soft Power

The seventh challenge that I foresee in China's relations with the world is in the realm of soft power. To be a major world power, a nation like China needs to possess and project soft power. Soft power is not bought—it is earned. It is all about voluntary attraction. Harvard Professor Joseph Nye, the father of the concept, describes it as "co-optation" to "shape the preferences of others" by "getting others to want what you want."[37] And, Nye tells us, soft power emerges primarily and organically from society—and only partially from government. It is based primarily on culture, values, and norms—and only secondarily from policies or political systems (the latter reflect the former). Soft power should be thought of like a magnet—where others are attracted to you by what you stand for and the way you do things. It is the *power of attraction*.

As Shaun Breslin's chapter elucidates in considerable detail, the Chinese government has been investing heavily in various areas of soft power, public diplomacy, and cultural exchanges. Some of these date back to the 1950s—but many are new efforts since 2007, when then leader Hu Jintao first used the term 软实力 and called on the CCP and government to invest in and boost China's image— mainly its cultural image abroad. Xi Jinping has also prioritized this effort since coming to power in 2012.

Yet, despite the massive investment (in the range of $10–$20 billion per year), China's international image has not appreciably improved. In fact, it remains *mixed*—a combination of favorable and unfavorable views—across the globe, according to the Pew Global Attitudes Survey in 2018 (Figure 16.7).

As such, virtually all analysts of China's soft power judge, China possesses minimal soft power. So, what is the problem? One aspect is that the Chinese Communist Party and government seek to project its country's soft power abroad—when Nye tells us clearly that soft power must come organically from a country's society and culture. A government and a political system are only tertiary elements in Nye's analysis, and he argues that open democratic systems intrinsically possess soft power whereas authoritarian systems do not. Another problem is that Beijing fundamentally mistakes soft power for external propaganda (对外宣传) and influencing narratives abroad, because it conflates the latter with the former. This is public diplomacy and foreign propaganda, not soft power. The CCP believes that by controlling narratives and the way people think abroad, as inside of China, it can control others' behavior. The CCP thus attempts to be proactive in its united front and influence activities abroad[38]— when it should be more passive and simply let its society and behavior speak for themselves. If there is such a thing as a "China Model," others will surely find it and attempt to emulate it. This is another problem with China's soft power: it is sui generis (not universal). To really possess soft power, a country's culture and values have to "travel." They have to have universality and appeal beyond home borders. Not many of China's do (except among developing, authoritarian, and post-colonial countries). Thus, China and the CCP have multiple problems in their approach to soft power.

To be genuinely reassuring and persuasive with other countries, Beijing also needs to learn better how to listen and be genuinely responsive to other's concerns. The complaints about BRI practices noted above are illustrative. Unfortunately, there appears to be what I call "auto-pilot" and "echo chamber"

Global views of China split, though
pockets of favorability in some regions
*Views of China*

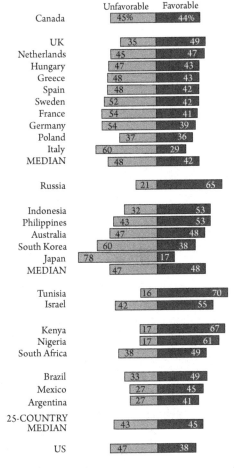

*Figure 16.7*  International Views of China. Source: Spring 2018 Global A_ritudes Survey.
Q17b. Pew Research Center.

effects in China's international narratives and policies. That is, Beijing has its
stock slogans and it just continues to present them to others in an unrelenting
fashion, and it allows for no alternative narratives to compete in people's minds.
Moreover, without any alternative sources of information this creates an "echo
chamber" effect among China's leaders, policymakers, and society. This is how
the CCP's internal propaganda system works: to bombard and numb the population with repetitive slogans (口号) and narratives (提法). In domestic politics, the recipients of these memes are supposed to literally repeat them back
verbatim, an act known to all Chinese as *biaotai* (表态), literally to "express an

attitude" or "declare one's position." This Leninist-Maoist propaganda method is meant to demonstrate political loyalty and is euphemistically intended to "unify thinking" (统一思想) by ensuring message discipline. This is what China does internally; the problem is that it expects foreigners to also *biaotai*. Yet, most foreigners do not understand the propaganda slogans, much less wish to mindlessly parrot them back (those who do are considered as "friends of China").

Why this is relevant to China's foreign relations and standing in the world is precisely because Beijing is seeking to export its internal propaganda methods. Instead of genuinely listening to the concerns of others, and *accepting criticism constructively*, Chinese officials tend to reflexively parrot whatever the slogan of the week or month is, and they regularly denounce foreign parties for "hurting the feelings of the Chinese people" and transgressing China's "core interests." Such practices ring hollow and do not have a reassuring quality. They do not reflect a mature, confident, and secure power. Chinese officialdom's zero tolerance for criticism and inability to apologize for—or even explicitly recognize— mistakes are major weaknesses in its foreign relations. What have the CCP or PRC apologized for in its seventy years of existence? The Cultural Revloution was denounced but no apology. The Great Leap, in which up to 40 million perished? No apology. Other mass campaigns that ruined or took the lives of millions of Chinese citizens? No apologies. Externally, no apologies to India or Vietnam for the wars that China launched against them. And so on. Big powers get criticized—it is part and parcel of being a power. But mature powers listen to, reflect on, accept criticisms, and adjust their policies and behavior accordingly. China's party-state still has a long way to go in this regard—unless and until Beijing begins to demonstrate such a capacity, it will find that others will treat its pronouncements and behavior with skepticism.

Recognizing all of these tendencies, China still possesses an enormous reservoir of *potential* soft power in its history, its culture, its arts, its traditions, its society, and its people. If the Chinese government would just get out of the way of its own creative society and stop attempting to package and control how it is presented to the world, China's soft power would have much more resonance abroad.

# Reflections

These are seven dimensions of China's foreign relations that I believe will be key challenges to its position and respect in the world and international community in the 5–10 years ahead. It will be interesting when we reach this period, and publish a second edition of this volume, to see how Beijing has handled these challenges. To be sure, there are other challenges—and the Chinese authorities would no doubt certainly frame their own future challenges differently—but these are the ones I see as most salient.

I close by hoping that—through these sixteen chapters—readers have gained a thorough and systematic, broad and deep, and stimulating exposure to China and the world today.

# Notes

1. Also see my book *China's Future* (Cambridge: Polity Press, 2016).
2. https://www.statista.com/statistics/270439/chinas-share-of-global-gross-domestic-product-gdp/.
3. "China to Remain Major Contributor to Global GDP Growth," *China Daily*, October 30, 2018, http://www.chinadaily.com.cn/a/201810/30/WS5bd7c3a7a310eff30328568e. html.
4. Congressional Budget Office, *The Budget and Economic Outlook, 2019–2029* (Washington, DC: Congressional Budget Office, January 2019), https://www.cbo.gov/system/files/2019-03/54918-Outlook-3.pdf.
5. See CSIS China Power Project, https://chinapower.csis.org/trade-partner/.
6. See the discussion in David Shambaugh, *China's Future*, chapter 2.
7. A great deal has been published about Made in China 2025, but among the best studies is European Chamber of Commerce in China, *China Manufacturing 2025: Putting Industrial Policy Ahead of Market Forces* (Beijing: European Chamber, 2017), available at https://static. europeanchamber.com.cn/upload/documents/documents/CM2025_EN_final_version_ 0301[473].pdf.
8. See China Power Project, "Is China a Global Leader in Research and Development?," https:// chinapower.csis.org/china-research-and-development-rnd/.
9. SIPRI Factsheet, "Trends in World Military Expenditure," available at https://www.sipri.org/ sites/default/files/2018-04/sipri_fs_1805_milex_2017.pdf.
10. According to the Ministry of Public Security, as of 2019 there are 469 foreign NGOs registered for operations on the mainland. See Chinafile, "The China NGO Project," http://www. chinafile.com/ngo/registered-foreign-ngo-offices-map-full-screen.
11. See Chun Han Wong, "Xi's Unsteady Steps Revive Worries over Lack of Succession Plan in China," *Wall Street Journal*, April 23, 2019.
12. Gerry Shih, "In China, Investigations and Purges Become the New Normal," *Washington Post*, October 22, 2018 (citing official Chinese anti-corruption statistics).
13. Aaron L. Friedberg, "Just How Secure Is Xi Jinping Really?" *The Diplomat*, September 12, 2014, https://thediplomat.com/2014/09/just-how-secure-is-xi-jinping-really/; and "Political Rivalry in China Part I: Plots to Overthrow Xi Jinping," *Chinascope*, March 22, 2016, http://chinascope.org/archives/7861.
14. Katsuji Nakazawa, "Power Struggle Has Xi Leery of Coup, Assassination Attempts," *Nikkei Asian Review*, May 23, 2015, https://asia.nikkei.com/Politics/ Power-struggle-has-Xi-leery-of-coup-assassination-attempts.
15. Wendy Wu and Choi Chi-yuk, "Coup Plotters Foiled: Xi Jinping Fended Off Threat to Save Communist Party," *South China Moring Post*, October 19, 2017; and Austin Ramzy, "Ousted Official Is Accused of Plotting against Communist Party," *New York Times*, October 20, 2017.
16. See David Shambaugh, *China's Future*, chapters 1 and 4.
17. In addition to Robert Sutter's chapter in this volume, there are multiple writings that detail and have tracked this changing nature of the US-China relationship. See, for example, Robert Sutter, *US-China Relations: Perilous Past, Uncertain Present* (Lanham, MD: Rowman & Littlefield, 2017); Aaron L. Friedberg, "Competing with China," *Survival* 60, no. 3 (2018): 7–64; Friedberg, *A Contest for Supremacy: China, America, and the Struggle for Mastery in Asia* (New York: W. W. Norton, 2012); David Shambaugh, ed., *Tangled Titans: The United States*

*and China* (Lanham, MD: Rowman & Littlefield, 2012); and Graham Allison, *Destined for War? Can American and China Escape Thucydides's Trap?* (New York: Scribe, 2018).

18. See Robert Sutter, "Washington's 'Whole-of-Government Pushback' against Chinese Challenges: Implications and Outlook," *Pacific Forum PACNET*, no. 26, April 23, 2019, available at https://www.pacforum.org/analysis/pacnet-26---washingtons-whole-government-pushback-against-chinese-challenges—implications.

19. See David Shambaugh, *US-China Relations at 40: Where Have We Been and Where Are We Going?* (College Station, TX: The Scowcroft Institute of International Affairs, The Bush School of Government and Public Service, Texas A&M University, Scowcroft Paper No. 15, February 2019), available at https://bush.tamu.edu/scowcroft/papers/Shambaugh/Shambaugh%20Scowcroft%20Paper%20No%2015.pdf.

20. See "Strategic Implications of China-Russia Relations," National Bureau of Asian Research, https://www.nbr.org/program/strategic-implications-of-russia-china-relations/; Robert Sutter, *China-Russia Relations: Strategic Implications and US Policy Options* (Seattle and Washington, DC: NBR Special Report No. 73, 2018); and Richard J. Ellings and Robert Sutter, eds., *Axis of Authoritarians: Implications of China-Russia Cooperation* (Seattle and Washington, DC: National Bureau of Asian Research, 2018).

21. For further details of this debate see my description in *China Goes Global: The Partial Power* (New York: Oxford University Press, 2013), 83–86.

22. See, for example, Bobo Lo, "A Partnership of Convenience," *International New York Times*, June 8, 2012, and his book *Axis of Convenience: Moscow, Beijing, and the New Geopolitics* (London and Washington, DC: Chatham House and the Brookings Institution Press, 2008); Jane Perlez and Neil MacFarquhar, "Rocky Economy Tests Friendship of Xi and Putin," *New York Times*, September 4, 2015.

23. See David Shambaugh, "US-China Rivalry in Southeast Asia: Power Shift or Competitive Coexistence?," *International Security* 42, no. 4 (Spring 2018): 85–127.

24. Graham Allison and Robert D. Blackwill, *Lee Kuan Yew: The Grand Master's Insights on China, the United States, and the World* (Cambridge, MA: MIT Press for the Belfer Center for Science and International Affairs, 2012), 6–7.

25. The State Council Information Office of the People's Republic of China, *China's Military Strategy* (May 2015), http://www.china.org.cn/china/2015-05/26/content 35661433.htm. Also see Peter A. Dutton and Ryan D. Martinson, eds., *Beyond the Wall: Chinese Far Seas Operations* (Newport, RI: US Naval War College China Maritime Studies Institute, May 2015).

26. See, for example, "Concern about Territorial Disputes with China," https://www.pewglobal.org/2015/09/02/how-asia-pacific-publics-see-each-other-and-their-national-leaders/asia-map/.

27. See Pew Global Attitudes Survey, "How People in the Asia-Pacific View China," October 2017, https://www.pewresearch.org/fact-tank/2017/10/16/how-people-in-asia-pacific-view-china/.

28. See David Shambaugh, "International Relations in Asia: A Multidimensional Analysis," in *International Relations of Asia*, edited by Shambaugh and Yahuda, 2nd ed., 3–32 (Lanham, MD: Rowman & Littlefield, 2014).

29. See Howard W. French, *Everything under the Heavens: How the Past Helps Shape China's Push for Global Power* (New York: Random House, 2017).

30. Also see Ashley J. Tellis, Alison Szalwinski, and Michael Wills, eds., *Strategic Asia 2019: China's Expanding Strategic Ambitions* (Seattle and Washington, DC: National Bureau of Asian Research).

31. See Nadege Rolland, "A Concise Guide to the Belt and Road Initiative," NBR *Backgrounder*, April 11, 2019, https://www.nbr.org/publication/a-guide-to-the-belt-and-road-initiative/.

32. Catherine Wong, "'Cooperate or Stop Criticizing,' China's Foreign Minister Wang Yi Says as Belt and Road Summit Nears," *South China Morning Post*, April 19, 2019.

33. Lucy Hornby, "China Pledges to Address Debt Worries over Belt and Road," *Financial Times*, April 24, 2019.

34. Chun Han Wong and James T. Areddy, "Beijing Seeks Partners in Global Program," *Wall Street Journal*, April 27–28, 2019.

35. Agatha Kratz, Allen Feng, and Logan Wright, *New Data on the "Debt Trap" Question* (New York: Rhodium Group, 2019), available at https://rhg.com/research/new-data-on-the-debt-trap-question/.

36. Joseph S. Nye, "The Kindleberger Trap," Project Syndicate, January 9, 2017.

37. Joseph S. Nye, Jr., *Soft Power: The Means to Success in World Politics* (New York: Public Affairs, 2005).

38. See Larry Diamond and Orville Schell, eds., *Chinese Influence and American Interests: Promoting Constructive Vigilance—Report of the Working Group on Chinese Influence Activities in the United States* (Palo Alto, CA: The Hoover Institution, 2018), https://www.hoover.org/sites/default/files/research/docs/00_diamond-schell-chinas-influence-and-american-interests.pdf.

# INDEX

All descriptive entries imply that China is the actor.
For the benefit of digital users, indexed terms that span two pages (e.g., 52–53) may, on occasion, appear on only one of those pages.